To Tom Mattox.

I've been looking for a new home for
this book for some time now. I do
hope that you'll get some little pleasure
during those long cold Texan nights! and
from time to time give a little
thought to those new friends you've
made in Woodhall Spa.
It was a pleasure to make your acquaintance

Neil & Gill Hayward.
August 2002

A GOLFER'S COMPANION

COMPANION

EDITED BY
CHRIS PLUMRIDGE & JOHN HOPKINS

SMALLMEAD
PRESS

Produced exclusively for Smallmead Press by
Lennard Books
Mackerye End
Harpenden
Herts AL5 5DR

A catalogue reference is available
from the British Library

ISBN 1 85291 111 5

First published in this edition 1992
© Lennard Associates Ltd

Jacket design by Pocknell & Co
Designed by Cooper Wilson
in association with Forest Publication Services

Printed and bound in Great Britain by
Butler & Tanner Ltd,
Frome and London

CONTENTS

INTRODUCTION

Chapter 4

LADIES' SECTION

Chapter 5

GREAT COURSES AND THEIR MAKING

SOURCES AND ACKNOWLEDGEMENTS

Chris Plumridge and John Hopkins

When we sat down to assemble the material for this anthology we discovered a number of things. We discovered, for example, that golf is rivalled only by cricket in the quality and prolific output of its writers. Down the years, some of the best writing in sport has emanated from golf writers who are perceptive, witty, literate and entertaining. Better still, most of them so obviously love the game that it shines through in their style. We were spoiled for choice with material from books and magazines dating back to the turn of the century. Thus our first problem was to distil all the pieces we wanted to include into proportions that would fit happily between hardback covers without making the book so heavy it would be impossible to pick up.

We established criteria. The material had to impart a sense of pleasure and history to the reader. Well-written stories, even if they had not been widely circulated, particularly if they had not been widely circulated, were not good enough to get in on their own. They had to record the historic moments of the game as well as being stories that were a pleasure to read. Writing about golf is a specialist art. Yet the aspects of the game are so diverse that it is possible to become a specialist in any part of the game or simply remain an excellent all-rounder. Subjects such as the development of equipment, course architecture or instruction do require extensive knowledge and we believe we have gathered the best in those particular fields.

The names of all the contributors take us on a trip through the ages. Bernard Darwin on the Great Triumvirate provides us with a perceptive view of the founding fathers of modern golf. Pat Ward-Thomas assesses the potential of a young Peter Thomson, O.B. Keeler, that Boswell to Bobby Jones's Johnson, reveals why Joyce Wethered was probably the finest women golfer to draw breath.

Selecting the most memorable moments in championship golf must always be a subjective task. There is such a cornucopia from which to choose. From Augusta to Carnoustie, from Pebble Beach to St Andrews the major championships have roamed freely, accompanied by those men and women whose sole purpose is to bring the drama to life through the printed word. We have been able to touch on only a few of them but they do capture the essential elements of how the game's greatest prizes are won and, sometimes, cruelly lost. We have acknowledged that golf is littered with absurdity and that much of the time the only way to cope with that is to laugh. Thus P.G. Wodehouse, Stephen Leacock and Patrick Campbell also grace these pages alongside that modern entertainer Peter Dobereiner.

We could not ignore Henry Longhurst because during his time he *was* golf writing. His lively mind ranged across all subjects but perhaps his greatest strength was that he had the uncanny knack of representing the views of the members at the golf club bar on a Sunday morning.

America is the continent on which golf has grown fastest and from where much of the game's drive is generated. It has more players, more money, more courses and more magazines and books to do with golf. Ergo, it has produced a considerable canon of golf literature that is in keeping with the size of the golf business in the USA. Therefore we could not ignore Herbert Warren Wind, Charlie Price, George Plimpton, Dan Jenkins and others even if we had wanted to, which we did not.

Much of golf writing is ephemeral. Yesterday's newspaper fits into today's damp golf shoes. This collection provides a small tribute to those men and women whose end-product often ends up being used to light fires, keep the kitchen floor clean when the dog comes home filthy or merely to carry home the fish and chips. A book commands and deserves a little more respect. This one is here to provide you with solace on long winter evenings, you can dip into it in your mellow moments and when you do we hope your enjoyment matches ours in its preparation.

Chapter 1

ALMOST STRAIGHT DOWN THE MIDDLE

P.G. Wodehouse

"After all," said the young man, "golf is only a game."

He spoke bitterly and with the air of one who has been following a train of thought. He had come into the smoking-room of the clubhouse in low spirits at the dusky close of a November evening, and for some minutes had been sitting, silent and moody, staring at the log fire.

"Merely a pastime," said the young man.

The Oldest Member, nodding in his armchair, stiffened with horror, and glanced quickly over his shoulder to make sure that none of the waiters had heard these terrible words.

"Can this be George William Pennefather speaking!" he said, reproachfully. "My boy, you are not yourself."

The young man flushed a little beneath his tan: for he had had a good upbringing and was not bad at heart.

"Perhaps I ought not to have gone quite so far as that," he admitted. "I was only thinking that a fellow's got no right, just because he happens to have come on a bit in his form lately, to treat a fellow as if a fellow was a leper or something."

The Oldest Member's face cleared, and he breathed a relieved sigh.

"Ah! I see," he said. "You spoke hastily and in a sudden fit of pique because something upset you out on the links today. Tell me all. Let me see, you were playing with Nathaniel Frisby this afternoon, were you not? I gather that he beat you."

"Yes, he did. Giving me a third. But it isn't being beaten that I mind. What I object to is having the blighter behave as if he were a sort of champion condescending to a mere mortal. Dash it, it seemed to bore him playing with me! Every time I sliced off the tee he looked at me as if I were a painful ordeal. Twice when I was having a bit of trouble in the bushes I caught him yawning. And after we had finished he started talking about what a good game croquet was, and he wondered more people didn't take it up. And it's only a month or so ago that I could play the man level!"

The Oldest Member shook his snowy head sadly.

"There is nothing to be done about it," he said. "We can only hope that the poison will in time work its way out of the man's system. Sudden success at golf is like the sudden acquisition of wealth. It is apt to unsettle and deteriorate the character. And, as it comes almost miraculously, so only a miracle can effect a cure. The best advice I can give you is to refrain from playing with Nathaniel Frisby till you can keep your tee-shots straight."

"Oh, but don't run away with the idea that I wasn't pretty good off the tee this afternoon!" said the young man. "I should like to describe to you the shot I did on the –"

"Meanwhile," proceeded the Oldest Member, "I will relate to you a little story which bears on what I have been saying."

"From the very moment I addressed the ball –"

"It is the story of two loving hearts temporarily estranged owing to the sudden and unforeseen proficiency of one of the couple –"

"I waggled quickly and strongly, like Duncan. Then, swinging smoothly back, rather in the Vardon manner –"

"But as I see," said the Oldest Member, "that you are all impatience for me to begin, I will do so without further preamble."

· · · · · · ·

To the philosophical student of golf like myself (said the Oldest Member) perhaps the most outstanding virtue of this noble pursuit is the fact that it is a medicine for the soul. Its great service to humanity is that it teaches human beings that, whatever petty triumphs they may have achieved in other walks of life, they are after all merely human. It acts as a corrective against sinful pride. I attribute the insane arrogance of the later Roman emperors almost entirely to the fact that, never having played golf, they never knew that strange chastening humility which is engendered by a topped chip-shot. If Cleopatra had been ousted in the first round of the Ladies' Singles, we should have heard a lot less of her proud imperiousness. And, coming down to modern times, it was undoubtedly his rotten golf that kept Wallace Chesney the nice unspoiled fellow he was. For in every other respect he had everything in the world calculated to make a man conceited and arrogant. He was the best-looking man for miles around; his health was perfect; and, in addition to this, he was rich; danced, rode, played bridge and polo with equal skill; and was engaged to be married to Charlotte Dix. And when you saw Charlotte Dix you realised that being engaged to her would by itself have been quite enough luck for any one man.

But Wallace, as I say, despite all his advantages, was a thoroughly nice, modest young fellow. And I attribute this to the fact that, while one of the keenest golfers in the club, he was also one of the worst players. Indeed, Charlotte Dix used to say to me in his presence that she could not understand why people paid money to go to the circus when by merely walking over the brow of a hill they could watch Wallace Chesney trying to get out of the bunker by the 11th green. And Wallace took the gibe with perfect good humour, for there was a delightful camaraderie between them which robbed it of any sting. Often at lunch in the clubhouse I used to hear him and Charlotte planning the handicapping details of a proposed match between Wallace and a non-existent cripple whom Charlotte claimed to have discovered in the village – it being agreed finally that he should accept seven bisques from the cripple, but that, if the latter ever recovered the use of his arms, Wallace should get a stroke a hole.

In short, a thoroughly happy and united young couple. Two hearts, if I may coin an expression, that beat as one.

I would not have you misjudge Wallace Chesney. I may have given you the impression that his attitude towards golf was light and frivolous, but such was not the case. As I have said, he was one of the keenest members of the club. Love made him receive the joshing of his *fiancée* in the kindly spirit in which it was meant, but at heart he was as earnest as you could wish. He practised early and late; he bought golf books; and the mere sight of a patent club of any description acted on him like catnip on a cat. I remember remonstrating with him on the occasion of his purchasing a wooden-faced driving-mashie which weighed about two pounds, and was, taking it for all in all, as foul an instrument as ever came out of the workshop of a clubmaker who had been dropped on the head by his nurse when a baby.

"I know, I know," he said, when I had finished indicating some of the weapon's more obvious defects. "But the point is, I believe in it. It gives me confidence. I don't believe you could slice with a thing like that if you tried."

Confidence! That was what Wallace Chesney lacked, and that, as he saw it, was the prime grand secret of golf. Like an alchemist on the track of the Philosopher's Stone, he was for ever seeking for something which would really give him confidence. I recollect that he even tried repeating to himself fifty times every morning the words, "Every day in every way I grow better and better." This, however, proved such a black lie that he gave it up. The fact is, the man was a visionary, and it is to auto-hypnosis of some kind that I attribute the extraordinary change that came over him at the beginning of his third season.

. . . • . . •

You may have noticed in your perambulations about the City a shop bearing above its door and upon its windows the legend:

COHEN BROS.
SECOND-HAND CLOTHIERS

a statement which is borne out by endless vistas seen through the door of every variety of what is technically known as Gents' Wear. But the Brothers Cohen, though their main stock-in-trade is garments which have been rejected by their owners for one reason or another, do not confine their dealings to Gents' Wear. The place is a museum of derelict goods of every description. You can get a second-hand revolver there, or a second-hand sword, or a second-hand umbrella. You can do a cheap deal in field-glasses, trunks, dog collars, canes, photograph frames, attaché cases, and bowls for goldfish. And on the bright spring morning when Wallace Chesney happened to pass by there was exhibited in the window a putter of such pre-eminently lunatic design that he stopped dead as if he had run into an invisible wall, and then, panting like an overwrought fish, charged in through the door.

The shop was full of the Cohen family, sombre-eyed, smileless men with purposeful expressions; and two of these, instantly descending upon Wallace Chesney like leopards, began in swift silence to thrust him into a suit of yellow tweed. Having worked the coat over his shoulders with a shoe-horn, they stood back to watch the effect.

"A beautiful fit," announced Isidore Cohen.

"A little snug under the arms," said his brother Irving. "But that'll give."

"The warmth of the body will make it give," said Isidore.

"Or maybe you'll lose weight in the summer," said Irving.

Wallace, when he had struggled out of the coat and was able to breathe, said that he had come in to buy a putter. Isidore therefore sold him the putter, a dog collar, and a set of studs, and Irving sold him a fireman's helmet: and he was about to leave when their elder brother Lou, who had just finished fitting out another customer, who had come in to buy a cap, with two pairs of trousers and a miniature aquarium for keeping newts in, saw that business was in progress and strolled up. His fathomless eye rested on Wallace, who was toying feebly with the putter.

"You play golf?" asked Lou. "Then looka here!"

He dived into an alleyway of dead clothing, dug for a moment, and emerged with something at the sight of which Wallace Chesney, hardened golfer that he was, blenched and threw up an arm defensively.

"No, no!" he cried.

The object which Lou Cohen was waving insinuatingly before his eyes was a pair of those golfing breeches which are technically known as Plus Fours – all the club cracks wore them – but he had never seen Plus Fours like these. What might be termed the main *motif* of the fabric was a curious vivid pink, and with this to work on the architect had let his imagination run free, and had produced so much variety in the way of chessboard squares of white, yellow, violet, and green that the eye swam as it looked upon them.

"These were made to measure for Sandy McHoots, the Open Champion," said Lou, stroking the left leg lovingly. "But he sent 'em back for some reason or other."

"Perhaps they frightened the children," said Wallace, recollecting having heard that Mr McHoots was a married man.

"They'll fit you nice," said Lou.

"Sure they'll fit him nice," said Isidore, warmly.

"Why, just take a look at yourself in the glass," said Irving, "and see if they don't fit you nice."

And, as one who wakes from a trance, Wallace discovered that his lower limbs were now encased in the prismatic garment. At what point in the proceedings the brethren had slipped them on him, he could not have said. But he was undeniably in.

Wallace looked in the glass. For a moment, as he eyed his reflection, sheer horror gripped him. Then suddenly, as he gazed, he became aware that his first feelings were changing. The initial shock over, he was becoming calmer. He waggled his right leg with a certain sang-froid.

There is a certain passage in the works of the poet Pope with which you may be familiar. It runs as follows:

> "Vice is a monster of so frightful mien
> As to be hated needs but to be seen:
> Yet seen too oft, familiar with her face,
> We first endure, then pity, then embrace."

Even so was it with Wallace Chesney and these Plus Fours. At first he had recoiled from them as any decent-minded man would have done. Then, after a while, almost abruptly he found himself in the grip of a new emotion. After an unsuccessful attempt to analyse this, he suddenly got it. Amazing as it may seem, it was pleasure that he felt. He caught his eye in the mirror, and it was smirking. Now that the things were actually on, by Hutchinson, they didn't look half bad. By Braid, they didn't. There was a sort of something about them. Take away that expanse of bare leg with its unsightly sock-suspender and substitute a woolly stocking, and you would have the lower section of a golfer. For the first time in his life, he thought, he looked like a man who could play golf.

There came to him an odd sensation of masterfulness. He was still holding the putter, and now he swung it up above his shoulder. A fine swing, all lissomeness and supple grace, quite different from any swing he had ever done before.

Wallace Chesney gasped. He knew that at last he had discovered that prime grand secret of golf for which he had searched so long. It was the costume that did it. All you had to do was wear Plus Fours. He had always hitherto played in grey flannel trousers. Naturally he had not been able to do himself justice. Golf required an easy dash, and how could you be easily dashing in concertina-shaped trousers with a patch on the knee? He saw now – what he had never seen before – that it was not because they were crack players that crack players wore Plus Fours: it was because they wore Plus Fours that they were crack players. And these Plus Fours had been the property of an Open Champion. Wallace Chesney's bosom swelled, and he was filled, as by some strange gas, with joy – with excitement – with confidence. Yes, for the first time in his golfing life, he felt really confident.

True, the things might have been a shade less gaudy: they might perhaps have hit the eye with a slightly less violent punch: but what of that? True, again, he could scarcely hope to avoid the censure of his clubmates when he appeared like this on the links: but what of *that*? His clubmates must set their teeth and learn to bear these Plus Fours like men. That was what Wallace Chesney thought about it. If they did not like his Plus Fours, let them go and play golf somewhere else.

"How much?" he muttered, thickly. And the brothers Cohen clustered grimly round with notebooks and pencils.

In predicting a stormy reception for his new apparel, Wallace Chesney had not been unduly pessimistic. The moment he entered the clubhouse Disaffection reared its ugly head. Friends of years' standing called loudly for the committee, and there was a small and vehement party of the left wing, headed by Raymond Gandle, who was an artist by profession, and consequently had a sensitive eye, which advocated the tearing off and public burial of the obnoxious garment. But, prepared as he had been for some such demonstration on the part of the coarser-minded, Wallace had hoped for better things when he should meet Charlotte Dix, the girl who loved him. Charlotte, he had supposed, would understand and sympathise.

Instead of which, she uttered a piercing cry and staggered to a bench, whence a moment later she delivered her ultimatum.

"Quick!" she said. "Before I have to look again."

"What do you mean?"

"Pop straight back into the changing-room while I've got my eyes shut, and remove the fancy-dress."

"What's wrong with them?"

"Darling," said Charlotte, "I think it's sweet and patriotic of you to be proud of your cycling-club colours or whatever they are, but you mustn't wear them on the links. It will unsettle the caddies."

"They are a trifle on the bright side," admitted Wallace. "But it helps my game, wearing them. I was trying a few practice-shots just now, and I couldn't go wrong. Slammed the ball on the meat every time. They inspire me, if you know what I mean. Come on, let's be starting."

Charlotte opened her eyes incredulously.

"You can't seriously mean that you're really going to *play* in those? It's against the rules. There must be a rule somewhere in the book against coming out looking like a sunset. Won't you go and burn them for my sake?"

"But I tell you they give me confidence. I sort of squint down at them when I'm addressing the ball, and I feel like a pro."

"Then the only thing to do is for me to play you for them. Come on, Wally, be a sportsman. 'I'll give you a half and play you for the whole outfit – the breeches, the red jacket, the little cap, and the belt with the snake's-head buckle. I'm sure all those things must have gone with the breeches. Is it a bargain?"

•   •   •   •   •   •

Strolling on the clubhouse terrace some two hours later, Raymond Gandle encountered Charlotte and Wallace coming up from the 18th green.

"Just the girl I wanted to see," said Raymond. "Miss Dix, I represent a select committee of my fellow-members, and I have come to ask you on their behalf to use the influence of a good woman to induce Wally to destroy those Plus Fours of his, which we all consider nothing short of Bolshevik propaganda and a menace to the public weal. May I rely on you?"

"You may not," retorted Charlotte. "They are the poor boy's mascot. You've no idea how they have improved his game. He has just beaten me hollow. I am going to try to learn to bear them, so you must. Really, you've no notion how he has come on. My cripple won't be able to give him more than a couple of bisques if he keeps up this form."

"It's something about the things," said Wallace. "They give me confidence."

"They give *me* a pain in the neck," say Raymond Gandle.

• • • • • • •

To the thinking man nothing is more remarkable in this life than the way in which Humanity adjusts itself to conditions which at their outset might well have appeared intolerable. Some great cataclysm occurs, some storm or earthquake, shaking the community to its foundations; and after the first pardonable consternation one finds the sufferers resuming their ordinary pursuits as if nothing had happened. There have been few more striking examples of this adaptability than the behaviour of the members of our golf club under the impact of Wallace Chesney's Plus Fours. For the first few days it is not too much to say that they were stunned. Nervous players sent their caddies on in front of them at blind holes, so that they might be warned in time of Wallace's presence ahead and not have him happening to them all of a sudden. And even the pro. was not unaffected. Brought up in Scotland in an atmosphere of tartan kilts, he nevertheless winced, and a startled "Hoots!" was forced from his lips when Wallace Chesney suddenly appeared in the valley as he was about to drive from the 5th tee.

But in about a week conditions were back to normal. Within ten days the Plus Fours became a familiar feature of the landscape, and were accepted as such without comment. They were pointed out to strangers together with the waterfall, the Lovers' Leap, and the view from the 8th green as things you ought not to miss when visiting the course; but apart from that one might almost say they were ignored. And meanwhile Wallace Chesney continued day by day to make the most extraordinary progress in his play.

As I have said before, and I think you will agree with me when I have told you what happened subsequently, it was probably a case of auto-hypnosis. There is no other sphere in which a belief in oneself has such immediate effects as it has in golf. And Wallace, having acquired self-confidence, went on from strength to strength. In under a week he had ploughed his way through the Unfortunate Incidents – of which class Peter Willard was the best example – and was challenging the fellows who kept three shots in five somewhere on the fairway. A month later he was holding his own with ten-handicap men. And by the middle of the summer he was so far advanced that his name occasionally cropped up in speculative talks on the subject of the July medal. One might have been excused for supposing that, as far as Wallace Chesney was concerned, all was for the best in the best of all possible worlds.

And yet –

The first inkling I received that anything was wrong came through a chance meeting with Raymond Gandle who happened to pass my gate on his way back from the links just as I drove up in my taxi; for I had been away from home for many weeks on a protracted business tour. I welcomed Gandle's advent and invited him in to smoke a pipe and put me abreast of local gossip. He came readily enough – and seemed, indeed, to have something on his mind and to be glad of the opportunity of revealing it to a sympathetic auditor.

"And how," I asked him, when we were comfortably settled, "did your game this afternoon come out?"

"Oh, he beat me," said Gandle, and it seemed to me that there was a note of bitterness in his voice.

"Then he, whoever he was, must have been an extremely competent performer," I replied, courteously, for Gandle was one of the finest players in the club. "Unless, of course, you were giving him some impossible handicap."

"No; we played level."

"Indeed! Who was your opponent?"

"Chesney."

"Wallace Chesney! And he beat you playing level! This is the most amazing thing I have ever heard."

"He's improved out of all knowledge."

"He must have done. Do you think he would ever beat you again?"

"No. Because he won't have the chance."

"You surely do not mean that you will not play him because you are afraid of being beaten?

"It isn't being beaten I mind –"

And if I omit to report the remainder of his speech it is not merely because it contained expressions with which I am reluctant to sully my lips, but because, omitting these expletives, what he said was almost word for word what you were saying to me just now about Nathaniel Frisby. It was, it seemed, Wallace Chesney's manner, his arrogance, his attitude of belonging to some superior order of being that had so wounded Raymond Gandle. Wallace Chesney had, it appeared, criticised Gandle's mashie-play in no friendly spirit; had hung up the game on the 14th tee in order to show him how to place his feet; and on the way back to the clubhouse had said that the beauty of golf was that the best player could enjoy a round even with a dud, because, though there might be no interest in the match, he could always amuse himself by playing for his medal score.

I was profoundly shaken.

"Wallace Chesney!" I exclaimed. "Was it really Wallace Chesney who behaved in the manner you describe?"

"Unless he's got a twin brother of the same name, it was."

"Wallace Chesney a victim to swelled head! I can hardly credit it."

"Well, you needn't take my word for it unless you want to. Ask anybody. It isn't often he can get anyone to play with him now."

"You horrify me!"

Raymond Gandle smoked a while in brooding silence.

"You've heard about his engagement?" he said at length.

"I have heard nothing, nothing. What about his engagement?"

"Charlotte Dix has broken it off."

"No!"

"Yes. Couldn't stand him any longer."

I got rid of Gandle as soon as I could. I made my way as quickly as possible to the house where Charlotte lived with her aunt. I was determined to sift this matter to the bottom and to do all that lay in my power to heal the breach between two young people for whom I had a great affection.

"I have just heard the news," I said, when the aunt had retired to some secret lair, as aunts do, and Charlotte and I were alone.

"What news?" said Charlotte, dully. I though she looked pale and ill, and she had certainly grown thinner.

"This dreadful news about your engagement to Wallace Chesney. Tell me, why did you do this thing? Is there no hope of a reconciliation?"

"Not unless Wally becomes his old self again."

"But I had always regarded you two as ideally suited to one another."

"Wally has completely changed in the last few weeks. Haven't you heard?"

"Only sketchily, from Raymond Gandle."

"I refuse," said Charlotte, proudly, all the woman in her leaping to her eyes, "to marry a man who treats me as if I were a kronen at the present rate of exchange, merely because I slice an occasional tee-shot. The afternoon I broke off the engagement" – her voice shook, and I could see that her indifference was but a mask – "the afternoon I broke off the en-gug-gug-gagement, he t-told me I ought to use an iron off the tee instead of a dud-dud-driver."

And the stricken girl burst into an uncontrollable fit of sobbing. And realising that, if matters had gone as far as that, there was little I could do, I pressed her hand silently and left her.

· · · · · ·

But though it seemed hopeless I decided to persevere. I turned my steps towards Wallace Chesney's bungalow, resolved to make one appeal to the man's better feelings. He was in his sitting-room when I arrived, polishing a putter; and it seemed significant to me, even in that tense moment, that the putter was quite an ordinary one, such as any capable player might use. In the brave old happy days of his dudhood, the only putters you ever found in the society of Wallace Chesney were patent self-adjusting things that looked like croquet mallets that had taken the wrong turning in childhood.

"Well, Wallace, my boy," I said.

"Hallo!" said Wallace Chesney. "So you're back?"

We fell into conversation, and I had not been in the room two minutes before I realised that what I had been told about the change in him was nothing more than the truth. The man's bearing and his every remark were insufferably bumptious. He spoke of his prospects in the July medal competition as if the issue were already settled. He scoffed at his rivals.

I had some little difficulty in bringing the talk round to the matter which I had come to discuss.

"My boy," I said at length, "I have just heard the sad news."

"What sad news?"

"I have been talking to Charlotte –"

"Oh, that!" said Wallace Chesney.

"She was telling me –"

"Perhaps it's all for the best."

"All for the best? What do you mean?"

"Well," said Wallace, "one doesn't wish, of course, to say anything un-gallant, but, after all, poor Charlotte's handicap *is* fourteen and wouldn't appear to have much chance of getting any lower. I mean, there's such a thing as a fellow throwing himself away."

Was I revolted at these callous words? For a moment, yes. Then it struck me that, though he had uttered them with a light laugh, that laugh had had in it more than a touch of bravado. I looked at him keenly. There was a bored, discontented expression in his eyes, a line of pain about his mouth.

"My boy," I said, gravely, "you are not happy."

For an instant I think he would have denied the imputation. But my visit had coincided with one of those twilight moods in which a man requires, above all else, sympathy. He uttered a weary sigh.

"I'm fed up," he admitted. "It's a funny thing. When I was a dud, I used to think how perfect it must be to be scratch. I used to watch the cracks buzzing round the course and envy them. It's all a fraud. The only time when you enjoy golf is when an occasional decent shot is enough to make you happy for the day. I'm plus two, and I'm bored to death. I'm too good. And what's the result? Everybody's jealous of me. Everybody's got it in for me. Nobody loves me."

His voice rose in a note of anguish, and at the sound his terrier, which had been sleeping on the rug, crept forward and licked his hand.

"The dog loves you," I said, gently, for I was touched.

"Yes, but I don't love the dog," said Wallace Chesney.

"Now come, Wallace," I said. "Be reasonable, my boy. It is only your unfortunate manner on the links which has made you perhaps a little unpopular at the moment. Why not pull yourself up? Why ruin your whole life with this arrogance? All that you need is a little tact, a little forbearance. Charlotte, I am sure, is just as fond of you as ever, but you have wounded her pride. Why must you be unkind about her tee-shots?"

Wallace Chesney shook his head despondently.

"I can't help it," he said. "It exasperates me to see anyone foozling, and I have to say so."

"Then there is nothing to be done," I said, sadly.

· · · • · · ·

All the medal competitions at our club are, as you know, important events; but, as you are also aware, none of them is looked forward to so keenly or contested so hotly as the one in July. At the beginning of the year of which I am speaking, Raymond Gandle had been considered the probable winner of the fixture; but as the season progressed and Wallace Chesney's skill developed to such a remarkable extent most of us were reluctantly inclined to put our money on the latter. Reluctantly, because Wallace's unpopularity was now so general that the thought of his winning was distasteful to all. It grieved me to see how cold his fellow-members were towards him. He drove off from the 1st tee without a solitary hand-clap; and, though the drive was of admirable quality and nearly carried the green, there was not a single cheer. I noticed Charlotte Dix among the spectators. The poor girl was looking sad and wan.

In the draw for partners Wallace had had Peter Willard allotted to him; and he muttered to me in a quite audible voice that it was as bad as handicapping him half a dozen strokes to make him play with such a hopeless performer. I do not think Peter heard, but it would not have made much difference to him if he had, for I doubt if anything could have had much effect for the worse on his game. Peter Willard always entered for the medal competition, because he said that competition-play was good for the nerves.

On this occasion he topped his ball badly, and Wallace lit his pipe with the exaggeratedly patient air of an irritated man. When Peter topped his second also, Wallace was moved to speech.

"For goodness' sake," he snapped, "what's the good of playing at all if you insist on lifting your head? Keep it down, man, keep it down. You don't need to watch to see where the ball is going. It isn't likely to go as far as all that. Make up your mind to count three before you look up."

"Thanks," said Peter, meekly. There was no pride in Peter to be wounded. He knew the sort of player he was.

The couples were now moving off with smooth rapidity, and the course was dotted with the figures of players and their accompanying spectators. A fair proportion of these latter had decided to follow the fortunes of Raymond Gandle, but by far the larger number were sticking to Wallace, who right from the start showed that Gandle or anyone else would have to return a very fine card to beat him. He was out in 37, two above bogey, and with the assistance of a superb second, which landed the ball within a foot of the pin, got a three on the 10th, where a four is considered good. I mention this to show that by the time he arrived at the short lake hole Wallace Chesney was at the top of his form. Not even the fact that he had been obliged to let the next couple through owing to Peter Willard losing his ball had been enough to upset him.

•   •   •   •   •   •   •

The course has been rearranged since, but at that time the lake hole, which is now the 2nd, was the 11th, and was generally looked on as the crucial hole in a medal round. Wallace no doubt realised this, but the knowledge did not seem to affect him. He lit his pipe with the utmost coolness: and, having replaced the match-box in his hip-pocket, stood smoking nonchalantly as he waited for the couple in front to get off the green.

They holed out eventually, and Wallace walked to the tee. As he did so, he was startled to receive a resounding smack.

"Sorry," said Peter Willard, apologetically. "Hope I didn't hurt you. A wasp."

And he pointed to the corpse, which was lying in a used-up attitude on the ground.

"Afraid it would sting you," said Peter.

"Oh, thanks," said Wallace.

He spoke a little stiffly, for Peter Willard had a large, hard, flat hand, the impact of which had shaken him up considerably. Also, there had been laughter in the crowd. He was fuming as he bent to address the ball, and his annoyance became acute when, just as he reached the top of his swing, Peter Willard suddenly spoke.

"Just a second, old man," said Peter. Wallace spun round, outraged.

"What *is* it? I do wish you would wait till I've made my shot."

"Just as you like," said Peter, humbly.

"There is no greater crime that a man can commit on the links than to speak to a fellow when he's making his stroke."

"Of course, of course," acquiesced Peter, crushed.

Wallace turned to his ball once more. He was vaguely conscious of a discomfort to which he could not at the moment give a name. At first he thought that he was having a spasm of lumbago, and this surprised him, for he had never in his life been subject to even a suspicion of that malady. A moment later he realised that this diagnosis that been wrong.

"Good heavens!" he cried, leaping nimbly some two feet into the air. "I'm on fire!"

"Yes," said Peter, delighted at his ready grasp of the situation. "That's what I wanted to mention just now."

Wallace slapped vigorously at the seat of his Plus Fours.

"It must have been when I killed that wasp," said Peter, beginning to see clearly into the matter. "You had a match-box in your pocket."

Wallace was in no mood to stop and discuss first causes. He was springing up and down on his pyre, beating at the flames.

"Do you know what I should do if I were you?" said Peter Willard. "I should jump into the lake."

One of the cardinal rules of golf if that a player shall accept no advice from anyone but his own caddie; but the warmth about his lower limbs had now become so generous that Wallace was prepared to stretch a point. He took three rapid strides and entered the water with a splash.

The lake, though muddy, is not deep, and presently Wallace was to be observed standing up to his waist some few feet from the shore.

"That ought to have put it out," said Peter Willard. "It was a bit of luck that it happened at this hole." He stretched out a hand to the bather. "Catch hold, old man, and I'll pull you out."

"No!" said Wallace Chesney.

"Why not?"

"Never mind!" said Wallace, austerely. He bent as near to Peter as he was able.

"Send a caddie up to the clubhouse to fetch my grey flannel trousers from my locker," he whispered, tensely.

"Oh, ah!" said Peter.

It was some little time before Wallace, encircled by a group of male spectators, was enabled to change his costume; and during the interval he continued to stand waist-deep in the water, to the chagrin of various couples who came to the tee in the course of their round and complained with not a little bitterness that his presence there added a mental hazard to an already difficult hole. Eventually, however, he found himself back ashore, his ball before him, his mashie in his hand.

"Carry on," said Peter Willard, as the couple in front left the green. "All clear now".

Wallace Chesney addressed his ball. And even, as he did so, he was suddenly aware that an odd psychological change had taken place in himself. He was aware of a strange weakness. The charred remains of the Plus Fours were lying under an adjacent bush; and, clad in the old grey flannels of his early golfing days, Wallace felt diffident, feeble, uncertain of himself. It was as though virtue had gone out of him, as if some indispensable adjunct to good play had been removed. His corrugated trouser-leg caught his eye as he waggled, and all at once he became acutely alive to the fact that many eyes were watching him. The audience seemed to press on him like a blanket. He felt as he had been wont to feel in the old days when he had had to drive off the first tee in front of a terrace-full of scoffing critics.

The next moment his ball had bounded weakly over the intervening patch of turf and was in the water.

"Hard luck!" said Peter Willard, ever a generous foe. And the words seemed to touch some almost atrophied chord in Wallace's breast. A sudden love for his species flooded over him. Dashed decent of Peter, he thought, to sympathise. Peter was a good chap. So were the spectators good chaps. So was everybody, even his caddie.

Peter Willard, as if resolved to make his sympathy practical, also rolled his ball into the lake.

"Hard luck!" said Wallace Chesney, and started as he said it; for many weeks had passed since he had commiserated with an opponent. He felt a changed man. A better, sweeter, kindlier man. It was as if a curse had fallen from him.

He teed up another ball, and swung.

"Hard luck!" said Peter.

"Hard luck!" said Wallace, a moment later.

"Hard luck!" said Peter, a moment after that.

Wallace Chesney stood on the tee watching the spot in the water where his third ball had fallen. The crowd was now openly amused, and, as he listened to their happy laughter, it was borne in upon Wallace that he, too, was amused and happy. A weird, almost effervescent exhilaration filled him. He turned and beamed upon the spectators. He waved his mashie cheerily at them. This, he felt, was something like golf. This was golf as it should be – not the dull, mechanical thing which had bored him during all these past weeks of his perfection, but a gay, rollicking adventure. That was the soul of golf, the thing that made it the wonderful pursuit it was – that speculativeness, that not knowing where the dickens your ball was going when you hit it, that eternal hoping for the best, that never-failing chanciness. It is better to travel hopefully than to arrive, and at last this great truth had come home to Wallace Chesney. He realised now why pros were all grave, silent men who seemed to struggle manfully against some secret sorrow. It was because they were too darned good. Golf had no surprises for them, no gallant spirit of adventure.

"I'm going to get a ball over if I stay here all night," cried Wallace Chesney, gaily, and the crowd echoed his mirth. On the face of Charlotte Dix was the look of a mother whose prodigal son had rolled into the old home once more. She caught Wallace's eye and gesticulated to him blithely.

"The cripple says he'll give you a stroke a hole, Wally!" she shouted.

"I'm ready for him!" bellowed Wallace.

"Hard *luck*!" said Peter Willard.

Under their bush the Plus Fours, charred and dripping, lurked unnoticed. But Wallace Chesney saw them. They caught his eye as he sliced his 11th into the marshes on the right. It seemed to him that they looked sullen. Disappointed. Baffled.

Wallace Chesney was himself again.

GOLF BLIGHT

Michael Parkinson

The scientist and the doom-watchers have got it wrong. The greatest problem facing the world today is not overpopulation, or nuclear proliferation or pollution, it is golf blight. This disease, which has reached epidemic proportions over the past decade, means that our natural habitat is rapidly becoming turned into one huge golf course.

One could, if one so desired, play golf from coast to coast across the United States. A man getting off a train in Newcastle could tear up the return ticket and golf all the way home to Torquay.

Recent research shows that in Britain an increasing number of people play golf more times each week than they have sex – and, in the main, get more enjoyment out of a hole in one. Moreover, it is calculated that more man-hours are lost through executives practising their golf swings in office hours than accrue during an outbreak of typhoid.

But, most significantly, there are now more golf clubs in the world than Gideon bibles, more golf balls than missionaries and, if every golfer in the world, male and female, were laid end to end, I for one would leave them there.

I am the president of the Anti-Golf Society, a position I have held for many years in the face of stiff opposition from friend and foe alike and in spite of the aforementioned spread of golf blight.

My Society would not ban golf, it would simply provide rehabilitation centres where people could be taught that there are more important handicaps than golfing ones, that practising swings in public places is anti-social and that the reason why golfers' wives soon lose their girlish enthusiasm for love and marriage is that they know better than most exactly what a golf bag is.

Unlike other human beings golfers do not live at home, they live at the golf club. They are happier in these establishments because they guarantee their peace of mind by barring outsiders and only giving shelter to people of similar pigmentation of skin, background and religious and political views.

Thus there are clubs exclusively for the Jews, and clubs where a Jew could only gain admittance if he arrived on the doorstep with Moshe Dayan at his side supported by a regiment of Israeli paratroopers.

This unhealthy state of affairs can only damage the move toward better international understanding and will undoubtedly lead to dire consequences. Indeed, it is my belief that the Third World War will start at a golf club – probably the deliciously titled Honourable Company of Edinburgh Golfers – when Sammy Davis Jnr arrives at Muirfield unannounced and uninvited with Arthur Scargill as his partner.

It is difficult to find any justification whatsoever for golf. The people who play it might disagree with the criticism that it is simply an elaborate device for ruining a good walk. But they would be hard-pressed to convince me of its claims as a sport, particularly one to be watched.

One of life's great mysteries is just what do golfers think they are playing at, but even more mysterious is what those spectators who traipse around golf courses are looking for? They, at least, can claim the exercise as an excuse, but what about those noddies who sit at the 18th hole all day long? All they see – and I know because I observed them on television – is an alleged athlete fretting over sinking a two-foot putt.

There is more excitement and spectacle in a competition to decide the world's largest parsnip.

It is during events like those of last week that some of us despair for the future of the human race. The golfers are taking over, vast regiments of people whose only justification can be that they provide employment for people who make sad and gaudy trousers.

At such times I feel isolated but not alone. There are a few of us left to fight the rearguard action. Not all of us have been brain-washed.

Watching the Open on television – actually I was fretfully waiting for them to go back to a real game, cricket – my wife came into the room as some golfer was practising his swing. "He missed the ball," she exclaimed. I felt a new, stirring love for her. She looked more closely at the box. "Also he's lost a glove," she said. At that precise moment I knew I had married the right person.

If there is hope it is in my wife's unsullied innocence plus the expert backing of people like the environmental correspondent of *The Observer*, who recently suggested that in the national interest, all golf courses should be ploughed up and made into allotments.

There can be no arguing with this outstanding piece of common sense. Vegetables are more important than golfers and, aesthetically speaking. I'd rather watch a cabbage grow than a man worrying his guts over a two-foot putt.

THE LUNATIC FRINGE

Alistair Cooke

Just after dawn on a brisk but brilliant December day a couple of years ago, I was about to ask Raquel Welch if she was all set for a droll caper I had in mind, when the telephone went off like a fire alarm, and an eager voice shouted, "All set?" It was, alas, not Raquel but my golf partner, a merry banker of indestructible cheerfulness who calls all stock-market recessions "healthy shake-outs." I climbed out of my promising dream and out of bed, and in no time I was washing the irons, downing the Bufferin, rubbing resin on the last three fingers of the left hand, inserting the plastic heel cup, searching for my Hogan cap – performing the whole early morning routine of the senior golfer. This was the great day we had promised ourselves ever since I had suffered the shock of hearing Herbert Warren Wind confess he had never played Century, the tough and beautiful rolling course in Purchase, New York, where Ben Hogan had his first job as a teaching pro. It seemed ridiculous that the man who had helped Hogan lay down "The Modern Fundamentals of Golf" should never have played the course on which Ben laid them down. Another telephone call alerted Wind to get the hell out of his own variation on the Welch fantasy. An hour later we were on our way, up the West Side Highway and the Saw Mill River Parkway, and on to Purchase.

Century is the private domain of some very well-heeled gents from Wall Street, but they are so busy watching those healthy shake-outs that none of them has much time for weekday golf. Furthermore, in December, the caviar and hamburgers are stacked in the deep freeze. But, since it is very difficult to close a golf course, the course is open. The caddie master had been briefed about the signal honour that Wind was going to confer on one of the 50 toughest courses in America and he had obligingly mobilised two of his veteran caddies.

As we swung around White Plains and began to thread up through the country lanes of Purchase, we were puzzled to see strips of white cement smearing the grassy banks of the highway. They got thicker as we turned into the club driveway, and as we came out on the hill that overlooks the undulating terrain, we saw that the whole course was overlaid not with cement but with snow. The caddies were already there and looking pretty glum. They greeted us by stomping their feet and slapping their ears and otherwise conveying that, though our original idea was a brave one, it had obviously been aborted by the weather. "You serious about this thing, Mr Manheim?" one of the caddies asked the banker. "Sure," said Manheim, who would play golf in a hammock if that's what the rules called for.

We started off with three reasonable drives, which scudded into the snow the way Hawaiian surfers skim under a tidal wave. The caddies went after them like ferrets and, after a lot of burrowing and signalling, retrieved them and stood there holding the balls and looking at us, as the song says, square down in the eye, as if to say, "What are you going to do with these damn things?" We had to find little slivers of exposed ground (no nearer the hole) and drop them and swipe off once more. The greens were either iced over or had sheets of ice floating in little lakes. After several five-putts on the first two greens, we decided that anybody who could hold a green deserved the concession of two putts.

This went on for eight holes, at the end of which, however, Wind allowed that Hogan sure loved to set himself problems. Plodding up the long 9th fairway, with Cooke beginning to turn blue and the banker humming happily to himself (it was the two-putt rule that did it), Wind turned and said, "Tell me, Manheim, do you do this because you're nuts or because your PR man says its good for your image?" We three-putted the 9th green, which "held" with the consistency of rice pudding, and that was it.

As I recall this Arctic expedition, there is a blustery wind bending the trees in Central Park and a steady rain, a combination of circumstances that fires many a Scotsman to rush out and play a round of golf in what one of them once told me are "the only propair condeetions". But, because this is America, they are conditions that immediately empty the golf courses from Maine to San Diego, forcing the sons of the pioneers to clean their clubs, putt on the bedroom carpet or sink into the torpor of watching a football game. We have it from the Mexican ambassador himself, His Excellency Lee Trevino, that there are Texans who will not play at all whenever the temperature toboggans below 80° Fahrenheit. And there are by now many generations of Dutchmen who gave up the game once it moved off ice onto grass.

It is a wonderful tribute to the game or to the dottiness of the people who play it that for some people somewhere there is no such thing as an insurmountable obstacle, an unplayable course, the wrong time of the day or the year. Last year I took Manheim – whose idea of a beautiful golf course was a beautiful park – to play his first links course. It is the home course of the English golf writer Pat Ward-Thomas (Ward-Thomas's idea of the most beautiful golf course in the world is his home course). It is up in the bleak stretch of south-eastern England known as Norfolk, a sort of miniature prairie exposed to the winds whistling out of Siberia. The course is called Brancaster, and you can drive up to the rude clubhouse, a kind of Charles Addams gabled shack, and start asking people where is the golf course. For ahead of you is nothing but flat marshland – which floods at the high tide – and beyond that the grey North Sea and a chorus of squawking gulls. The flags are about two feet high, so as to encourage the notion that man has not been known to tamper with a masterpiece of nature.

When we went into lunch it was spitting rain and when we came out it was raining stairrods. The wind gauge at the clubhouse entrance registered 43 knots. There was Ward-Thomas; a handsome and imperturbable Englishman named Tom Harvey; Manheim and I. There were also two caddies, aged about ten, already half-drowned and cowering in the whirling sand like two fugitives from Dotheboys Hall.

Nobody raised a question or lifted an eyebrow, so Manheim and I – remembering the good old White House slogan – soldiered on. By about the 7th, Manheim, who wears glasses, had to be guided to the proper tees. We were all so swollen with sweaters and raingear we looked like the man in the Michelin ads. Well, sir, they talked throughout in well-modulated tones about "sharp doglegs" and "a rather long carry" and "it's normally an easy five-iron, but maybe with this touch of wind you'd be safer with a four-iron, even a four-wood, I shouldn't wonder." We were now all water-logged, from the toenails to the scalp, and Manheim came squelching over to me and said, "Are these guys nuts?" I told him that on the contrary this was for them a regular outing: "You know what the Scotsman said – "If there's nae wind, it's nae gawf." Manheim shook his head like a drenched terrier and plodded on. The awful thing was that Harvey, a pretty formidable golfer, was drawing and fading the damn thing at will, thus proving the truth that if you hit it right, even a tornado is not much of a factor.

Outward bound, we'd been carried downwind. But as we were bouncing like tumbleweed down to the 9th green, Ward-Thomas came staggering over. I should tell you that he is a gaunt and a very engaging gent who looks like an impoverished Mexican landowner (a hundred acres in beans and not doing very well), and he has a vocabulary that would have qualified him for an absolutely top advisory post in the last Republican administration. He came at me with his spiky hair plastered against his forehead and water blobbing off his nose and chin. He screamed confidentially into the gale: "If you think this (expletive deleted) nine is a (expletive deleted) picnic, wait till we come to the (expletive deleted) turn!"

He was right. We could just about stand in the teeth of the gale, but the balls kept toppling off the tees. It was a time to make you yearn for the old sandbox. Manheim's glasses now looked like the flooded windshield of a gangster escaping through a hurricane in an old Warner Brothers movie. Moreover, his tweed hat kept swivelling around, making him stand to the ball like a guy who'd been taught about his master eye by a one-eyed pirate. At this point, Ward-Thomas offered up the supreme sacrifice. He is a long-time idolater of Arnold Palmer and he cried, "Hold it!" and plunged into his bag. He came up with a faded sunhat and tendered it to Manheim with the reverent remark: "It was given to me by Palmer. Try it." As everybody knows, Palmer's head is on the same scale as his forearms, and this one blotted out Manheim's forehead, nose, glasses, master eye and all. What we did from then on was to slop our way down the last nine, pity the trembling caddies and throw murderous glances at Harvey, who was firing beautiful woods into the hurricane.

Very little was said as we retired to Harvey's home, fed every strip of clothing into a basement stove and stewed in baths that would have scalded a Turk. At dinner it came out. All through the first nine, Harvey and Ward-Thomas had been muttering to each other just as Manheim and I had been doing: "They must be out of their minds, but if this is what they're used to . . ." Harvey said, "We decided that since you were our guests, the only thing to do was to stick it out."

．　．　．　●　．　．　．

If these are fair samples of maniacal golfers, how about crazy golf courses?

You would not think, looking at the stony rampart of the mountain face behind Monte Carlo, that anyone could plant a one-hole putting green between those slabs of granite. But when you get to the top, there the indomitable British have somehow contrived a course that lurches all around the Maritime Alps. There is rarely a straightaway drive. On the very first tee, you jump up in the air and see the flag fluttering in a depression way to the left. You ask the caddie for the line. He points with a Napoleonic gesture to a mountain far to the right. "La ligne!" he commands. And if you believe him and bang away at the mountain top, you then see the ball coming toppling about a hundred yards to the left and going out of sight. Which is the proper trajectory to the green.

The golf *clubu* at Istanbul is, if anything, more improbable still. The banks of the Bosporus are studded with more boulders than Vermont. But when the Scots took Constantinople at the end of the First World War and laid in an adequate supply of their *vin du pays*, what else was there to do but build a golf course? The original rude layout is still there in the *clubu* house, and on paper it looks like a golf course. In fact, it is simply a collection of flags stuck at random on a mountainside of boulders. Every ball comes to rest against a rock. The local rule is a free drop on every stroke. You drop it and drop it till it stops, and never mind the fussy business of "no nearer the hole".

In Bangkok, before the natives took to cement and the automobile, the canals looked like irrigation ditches slicing every fairway. Forecaddies, as nimble as grasshoppers, spent the day diving into the canals and surfacing with an ear-to-ear grin while they held aloft a ball drenched with cholera. Once they'd wiped it and dropped it, you were on your way again, and free to enjoy the great game in a dripping temperature of 110°.

A lion, you might guess, is not a normal item of wildlife on your course or mine. But in Nairobi once, a tawny monster strolled out of the woods, sniffed my ball and padded off again, while my partner, a British native of the place, tweaked his moustache and drawled: "You're away, I think." At about the 3rd hole I pushed my drive into the woods, and when I started after it, the host screamed at me to cease and desist. "Snakes, man, snakes!" he hissed; "leave it to the forecaddies." They plunged into shoulder-high underbrush, and I meekly muttered, "How about *them*?" "They?" the man said, "Good God, they're marvellous. Splendid chaps; lost only two this year." That round, I recall, was something of a nightmare, what with my pushed drives and the caddies (the ones who survived) chattering away in Swahili. The whole place was so exotic that I began to wonder if any of the normal rules of golf applied. One time, we came on a sign which read "GUR". I gave it the full Swahili treatment. "What," I said, "does GHOOOR mean?" He gave a slight start, as if some hippo were pounding in from the shade. Then he saw the sign. "That," he said firmly, "means Ground Under Repair." And he sighed and started to hum a Sousa march. After all, you must expect anything in golf. A stranger comes through; he's keen for a game; he seems affable enough, and on the 8th fairway he turns out to be an idiot. It's the rub of the green, isn't it?

Well, it takes more sorts than you and I have dreamed of to make up the world of golf. In Japan, they take a ski lift up to the tee of a famous par-three. In Cannes, the club members never bat an eyelid as they board a ferry from one green to the next tee.

But for sheer systematic nuttiness, nothing can compare with an annual ceremony put on by the Oxford and Cambridge Golfing Society, a collection of leather-elbowed oldsters and shaggy-haired youngsters who play for the President's Putter, no less, every year in the first week of January at Rye, on the coast of Sussex, another treeless links course fronting on a marsh which gives out into the English Channel. This tournament is intended to prove the English boast that "we can play golf every day of the year". If they can do it at Rye in January, they can do it at the South Pole, which in some sharp ways Rye resembles. At any rate, under the supervision of Gerald Micklem, a peppery stockbroker in his sixties who is the Genghis Kahn of British amateur golf, these maniacs go through with this tournament on the scheduled date no matter what. Snow, hail, wind, torrents – nothing can keep them from the swift completion of their Micklem-appointed rounds.

I was there four years ago. On the first morning, the small town and the course were completely obliterated in a fog denser than anything in Dickens. It seeped into the hotels so you needed a links boy to light your way to your plate of bacon, baps and bangers. I assumed the whole thing was off, till a telephone call warned a few dallying competitors that their tee-off time was about to strike. We crawled out to the course, and the first person I ran into, marching around the clubhouse, was Micklem. I asked him if anyone was out there, and if so, why. "Nonsense," he barked. "they're all out there. Haven't lost a ball yet." He motioned toward the great grey nothingness outside, not fog, not landscape, but what John Milton (13 handicap) once called "not light but darkness visible". I hopped off into what might very well have been the edge of the world, as it was conceived by those Portuguese mariners who would have liked very much to discover America but who were afraid to sail out into the Atlantic, beyond sight of land, for fear of falling off. The word, God knows how it got through, was that Donald Steel was doing nicely toward repeating his win of the previous year. He had just teed off on the second nine. I ran into a swirl of nothingness and, sure enough, there emerged, like a zombie on the heath in a horror film, a plumpish, confident figure recognisable at three yards as Steel. He took out an iron for his approach shot, though what he thought he was approaching I have no idea – San Salvador, no doubt. He hit it low and clean, and a sizable divot sailed away from him and vanished. He went off after it and vanished too. I kept following in the gloom, and from time to time a wraith swinging a golf club would loom up, take two steps and be gone.

It was true! They all finished, and nobody lost a ball. I felt my way back to the clubhouse, and at the end the last ghost was in. Within five minutes they were up against the bar, chests out, faces like lobsters, beer mugs high, slapping thighs, yokking it up. Queer fish, the Oxford and Cambridge Golfing Society. They behave just as if they'd been out for a round of golf. What they play every year on that barren fork of Sussex that reaches out to the Channel, and Holland, and eventually to the Bering Strait, is a wholly new game: Invisible Golf.

GOLF THROUGH TV EYES

Frank Hannigan

The USGA is grateful to the advertising firm of Tension, Nettled and Timorous for granting permission to print the result of its recent Golf TV Audience Survey.

This survey sheds light on that phenomenon of the 1960s, the New Golf Fan, whose knowledge of the game, gleaned from television reports, has transformed golf into a basic American industry.

TNT's trained investigators talked to thousands of viewers. The taped interviews were fed into an electronic computer which digested the material and then spewed out a Master Interview, which purports to represent accurately the average television viewer's thoughts on golf.

The Master Interview is now being weighed carefully by a *TNT* client who contemplates sponsorship of yet another Golf TV Extravaganza next fall. Tentative plans call for a first prize of $250,000, a seat on the New York Stock Exchange, and fifteen acres of real estate in New York's Murray Hill district.

The Master Interview follows:

Q: *When and how did golf begin?*

A: Arnold Palmer invented it about eight years ago in a little town outside Pittsburgh.

Q: And who was the first woman golfer?

A: I'm not sure, but it was either a tall blonde named Mickey Wright or a little French girl named Brigitte Bardot. Anyhow, they took it up in Portugal and the French girl lost.

Q: Then golf has become more popular recently?

A: Absolutely. Now it is even being played in England, where there is a British Open tournament.

Q: Has this British Open become an important event?

A: It sure has. The winner qualifies for the World Series every year in Ohio.

Q: To what do you attribute the growth of golf's popularity?

A: Are you kidding? It's the cash. Some of these guys make more money than Willie Shoemaker.

Q: What about the rules of golf? Where do they come from?

A: Palmer and a bunch of the other pros sat down and made them up.

Q: Suppose there's a dispute about the rules. How would such a dispute be settled?

A: That's a tough one. I suppose they'd have to go on to the sponsor of the program. If the sponsor didn't know what to do, maybe they could have a panel discussion with David Susskind.

Q: What is meant by a "golf handicap"?

A: That's something they made up so that Sam Snead can play Johnny Weissmuller and those other movie stars.

Q: Do you know the difference between stroke play and match play?

A: Match play is when they play two on a team on Saturday afternoons and the first prize is $50,000; stroke play is generally played on Sundays with one man against the other, but the money isn't so big.

Q: Who, in your opinion, is the greatest golfer to date?

A: Palmer – the founder.

Q: Has anyone come close to matching his skills?

A: Young Nicklaus, but he hasn't caught up to Palmer yet.

Q: How can you tell?

A: For one thing, there is no Jack Nicklaus building in New York.

Q: What about Bob Jones?

A: I hear it's a great movie, but it hasn't been on television yet.

Q: Does golf have a "czar", like baseball's Ford Frick?

A: Sure. I read that he's a young lawyer out of Cleveland who handles all the business for Palmer, Nicklaus and Player, the little guy with the funny accent who teams up with Palmer on weekends.

Q: Judging from what you've seen and heard, how far would you say the average professional drives a golf ball?

A: Between 325 and 350 yards.

Q: What happens when a tournament ends in a tie?

A: They go back to the 14th hole, where the cameras are first set up, and start over again from there.

Q: What role do amateurs play in golf?

A: They are like the minor leaguers in baseball or the college kids in football. The best ones get to turn pro and play the tour.

Q: Have you noticed much difference between the various courses you've seen on television?

A: Not much. All of them seem to have "one of the greatest finishing holes in golf".

Q: Who are your favorite golf announcers?

A: Frank Sinatra and Dean Martin. They go right out on the course in California and say funny things to the players between shots. Phil Harris is pretty good, too.

Q: Just one more question. More than one community lays claim to being "the golf capital of the United States". Which city do you think properly holds that distinction?

A: It must be Las Vegas. There were two tournaments televised live from there last year.

THE GOLFOMANIAC

Stephen Leacock

We ride in and out pretty often together, he and I, on a surburban train.

That's how I came to talk to him. "Fine morning," I said as I sat down beside him yesterday and opened a newspaper.

"Great!" he answered, "the grass is drying out fast now and the greens will soon be all right to play."

"Yes," I said, "the sun is getting higher and the days are decidedly lengthening."

"For the matter of that," said my friend, "a man could begin to play at six in the morning easily. In fact I've often wondered that there's so little golf played before breakfast. We happened to be talking about golf, a few of us last night – I don't know how it came up – and we were saying that it seems a pity that some of the best part of the day, say, from five o'clock to seven-thirty, is never used."

"That's true," I answered, and then, to shift the subject, I said, looking out of the window:

"It's a pretty bit of country just here, isn't it?"

"It is," he replied, "but it seems a shame they make no use of it – just a few market gardens and things like that. Why, I noticed along here acres and acres of just glass – some kind of houses for plants or something – and whole fields of lettuce and things like that. It's a pity they don't make something of it. I was remarking only the other day as I came along in the train with a friend of mine, that you could easily lay out an eighteen-hole course anywhere here."

"Could you?" I said.

"Oh, yes. This ground, you know, is an excellent light soil to shovel up into bunkers. You could drive some big ditches through it and make one or two deep holes – the kind they have on some of the French links. In fact, improve it to any extent."

I glanced at my morning paper. "I see," I said, "that it is again rumoured that Lloyd George is at last definitely to retire."

"Funny thing about Lloyd George," answered my friend. "He never played, you know; most extraordinary thing – don't you think? – for a man in his position. Balfour, of course, was very different: I remembered when I was over in Scotland last summer I had the honour of going around the course at Dumfries just after Lord Balfour. Pretty interesting experience, don't you think?"

"Were you over on business?" I asked.

"No, not exactly. I went to get a golf ball, a particular golf ball. Of course, I didn't go merely for that. I wanted to get a mashie as well. The only way, you know, to get just what you want is to go to Scotland for it."

"Did you see much of Scotland?"

"I saw it all. I was on the links at St Andrews and I visited the Loch Lomond course and the course at Inverness. In fact, I saw everything."

"It's an interesting country, isn't it, historically?"

"It certainly is. Do you know they have played there for over five hundred years! Think of it! They showed me at Loch Lomond the place where they said Robert the Bruce played the Red Douglas (I think that was the other party – at any rate, Bruce was one of them), and I saw where Bonnie Prince Charlie disguised himself as a caddie when the Duke of Cumberland's soldiers were looking for him. Oh, it's a wonderful country historically."

After that I let a silence intervene so as to get a new start. Then I looked up again from my newspaper.

"Look at this," I said, pointing to a headline, " 'United States Navy Ordered Again to Nicaragua.' Looks like more trouble doesn't it?"

"Did you see in the paper a while back," said my companion, "that the United States Navy Department is now making golf compulsory at the training school at Annapolis? That's progressive, isn't it? I suppose it will have to mean short cruises at sea; in fact, probably lessen the use of the navy for sea purposes. But it will raise the standard."

"I suppose so," I answered. "Did you read about this extraordinary murder case on Long Island?"

"No," he said. "I never read murder cases. They don't interest me. In fact, I think this whole continent is getting over-preoccupied with them –"

"Yes, but this case had such odd features –"

"Oh, they all have," he replied, with an air of weariness. "Each one is just boomed by the papers to make a sensation –"

"I know, but in this case it seems that the man was killed with a blow from a golf club."

"What's that? Eh, what's that? Killed him with a blow from a golf club!!"

"Yes, some kind of club –"

"I wonder if it was a iron – let me see the paper – though, for the matter of that, I imagine that a blow with even a wooden driver, let alone one of the steel-handled drivers – where does it say it? – pshaw, it only just says 'a blow with golf club'. It's a pity the papers don't write these things up with more detail, isn't it. But perhaps it will be better in the afternoon paper . . ."

"Have you played golf much?" I inquired. I saw it was no use to talk of anything else.

"No," answered my companion, "I am sorry to say I haven't. You see, I began late. I've only played 20 years, 21 if you count the year that's beginning in May. I don't know what I was doing. I wasted about half my life. In fact, it wasn't till I was well over 30 that I caught on to the game. I suppose a lot of us look over our lives that way and realise what we have lost.

"And even as it is," he continued, "I don't get much chance to play. At the best I can only manage about four afternoons a week, though of course I get most of Saturday and all Sunday. I get my holiday in the summer, but it's only a month, and that's nothing. In the winter I manage to take a run South for a game once or twice and perhaps a little swack at it around Easter, but only a week at a time. I'm too busy – that's the plain truth of it." He sighed. "It's hard to leave the office before two," he said. "Something always turns up."

And after that he went on to tell me something of the technique of the game, illustrate it with a golf ball on the seat of the car, and the peculiar mental poise needed for driving, and the neat, quick action of the wrist (he showed me how it worked) that is needed to undercut a ball so that it flies straight up in the air. He explained to me how you can do practically anything with a golf ball, provided that you keep your mind absolutely poised and your eye in shape, and your body a trained machine. It appears that even Bobby Jones of Atlanta and people like that fall short very often from the high standard set up by my golfing friend in the surburban car.

• • • • • •

So, later in the day, meeting someone in my club who was a person of authority on such things, I made inquiry about my friend. "I rode into town with Llewellyn Smith," I said. "I think he belongs to your golf club. He's a great player, isn't he?"

"A great player!" laughed the expert. "Llewellyn Smith? Why, he can hardly hit a ball! And anyway, he's only played about 20 years!"

SCENES FROM A MARRIAGE:
A GOLFER'S LAMENT

Peter Andrews

The most climactic moments in my marital life have all taken place on the golf course. I am not referring, of course, to those evanescent matters so briefly engaged in and so swiftly forgotten. But rather to those deeply felt watershed events that indelibly colour the relationship between a man and a woman. Joy and despair, elation and longueur. They have been the stuff of my marriage and all of them played out on the par-fours of life.

I met Marjorie some twenty years ago and was immediately taken with her. She comes from an extremely good family. Her father, who once saw Walter Travis play, still has a serviceable 18 handicap and uses the two-iron as if he really understands the purpose of that puzzling instrument. Her mother has a lovely compact backswing and plays a rock-steady game. She once hit into the rough in the spring of 1947, found it a bad place to be and has never been back. She is the kind of sweet, grey-haired old lady who lets you spot her seven shots a side and then putts your heart out.

Marjorie and I had courted during the winter and although we had not actually discussed playing golf together, I had, in view of her family, made certain assumptions. In my boyish enthusiasm, I had pictured the two of us teeing off down the fairway of our lives together, so to speak.

I was naturally delighted when Marjorie agreed to be mine, and immediately booked honeymoon lodgings at the Greenbrier in West Virginia. It was on those velvety confines that Sam Snead had once shot a 59, and I was certain that Marjorie, with her keen sense of the historical, would appreciate starting out our marriage on such a tradition-laden course. The morning after we were married, I got up to practise a few chip shots in the hallway and later, as I was shaving, I called out brightly, "Got to get up, darling. We have an eight o'clock tee time and we ought to hit a few to warm up first."

Marjorie, however, snaked out a piece of French toast from the room service tray, looked at me coolly and said, "There are a lot of dumb things in this world, Peter, but lashing away at a golf ball has got to be the dumbest of them all. You can go out and play if you want to. I'm going to stay here in bed."

Less than 24 hours after we had exchanged sacred vows, I learned that the woman I was to live with for the rest of my life didn't play golf. And didn't want to. When she was absolutely forced to go outside she much preferred – she told me as if it were a matter of no importance whatsoever – tennis. Tennis? My bride was engaged in a sport that people play in their underwear. I was appalled and left our first marital chamber with hot cheeks and stumbled to an erratic 94 in spite of unusually easy pin placements.

Our life had gotten off to an indifferent start but one of the best things about the marriage business is that you get to be an old hand at it very quickly. I soon discovered the joys of living with a non-golfing woman far exceeded those of living with one who does play. For several years, I had the best of both possible worlds; unbounded felicity in the home and blessed separateness away from it. When we journeyed to Washington DC for our annual spring visit, Marjorie would spend the day at the National Gallery looking at its exquisite collection of Vermeers while

I went about the Lord's work attacking the crown greens of the Chevy Chase Country Club. Chevy is a lovely course, especially in May when the ornamental trees are in bloom. But there were few sights more enchanting than the vision of my wife gaily waving to me as I came off the 18th green. We would have a cocktail on the patio and tell each other exciting stories of what we had done that day. Oh, I tell you, it was a perfect marriage. I wonder what ever happened to it.

I know what happened. Marjorie decided to take up golf and the captain's paradise I had lived in for a decade fell apart like Johnny Miller's long-iron game. At first it was a cloud on my horizon no larger than a wedge hurled angrily in the sky. Marjorie said she wanted to give up tennis for a while and learn to play golf so we could be together more. It seemed a reasonable enough desire at the time, but if I had known what was in store for me I would have gladly ponied up the dough to send her off for a weekend with Jimmy Connors so she could learn to talk dirty.

For a while it wasn't too bad. Marjorie thrashed around at golf raising her anger levels higher than her golfing expectations. We played the Big G course at Grossinger's in upstate New York a couple of times armed with a dozen extra balls and a thermos jug of Bloody Marys in my bag for emergencies. "This is a damned stupid game," Marjorie muttered after dropping three straight fairway woods into the water by the par-five 4th hole. "I don't see why people subject themselves to it."

"I never said golf was fun, darling."

Playing with a truly horrific lady golfer did offer some moments of high drama. For a season or so, Marjorie was an almost perversely consistent golfer. She could have played an entire round along a cart path, provided the path had been cut approximately 15 yards into the rough on the right. No matter what kind of shot she hit, slice, top, hook, fat or thin, she almost always wound up in the right rough. Every once in a while she would send a heroic pull into the left rough but then would slice back to where she was apparently more comfortable. After working her way up in the right rough a few yards at a time, Marjorie would at last emerge in the area of short grass near the green. Working as stealthily as an underwater demolition team, Marjorie snuck up on to the green and then after two or three extremely tentative putts she got to within three or four feet of the hole, which she referred to as her "range". Then Marjorie would suddenly turn into Wonder Woman in golf slacks and become the boldest, most ferocious short putter the game has ever known. Once she had a slightly uphill putt of not more than twenty inches. Marjorie took careful aim and rammed the ball – I am not making this up, I marked off the distance in front of witnesses – 38 feet past the hole. I sent the documentation of this to the *Guinness Book of Records* for inclusion as the longest leave from the shortest putt, but they wrote back saying if I was having marital difficulties I should try to solve them myself and not drag them into the situation.

Marjorie seemed to be fated to be the eternal lady duffer but she kept at it with a good will and we started to play together more on our vacations. It meant my having to give up a day or two to squire Marjorie through the woodlands, but it seemed a small enough sacrifice for a fine woman who had presented me with a beautiful daughter. Eventually, we settled into a pattern where we played together about nine or ten times a year. This seemed just about the right number of times to play with one's spouse on the golf course; enough to be a good sport but not so often your friends make fun of you when you beg off from your regular foursome to "play with the wife".

Marriage counsellors will tell you that the disintegration of a marriage is an intricate matter involving years of minor dislocations and small disappointments that eventually lead to a parting of the ways. It was not so with mine. I can pinpoint the collapse of our relationship with considerable exactitude. It came about at exactly 3:17 on the afternoon of 12 August 1976, on the 17th hole at Black Hall, a difficult course in Connecticut whose mountainous fairways were hacked out of a forest that would have scared off Hansel and Gretel.

Marjorie had been playing her usual game; a foozled wood here, a shanked iron there, and was finally laying a nervy seven about 165 yards from the green. Marjorie took her regular stance with a four-wood and then came back with a little loop at the top of the swing so reminiscent of a young Bobby Jones. Then she let fly. It was one of those glorious moments when every element of the golf swing falls into place; hips, shoulders and hands all in perfect synchronisation. The ball leapt off the club like a cannon shot and arced into the sky. It seemed to hang in the air for a moment as if it were lost – no golf ball struck by Marjorie had even before flown so far or so high – then it turned over with just a slight draw from right to left and dashed for the folds of the flag.

Now you must remember that Marjorie is an extremely gentle woman who has travelled through most of the civilised world, speaks three languages and always reads a few pages of Hazlitt before retiring. She stood transfixed as the ball bit into the green and then clawed its way toward the hole, finally coming to rest about four inches away.

"Jeeeezuz," she exclaimed. "Did you see that?"

I did. But it cannot be said that I have seen my wife in any significant sense of the word since then. With a single sweep of a fairway wood Marjorie became a total golf nut. Before, she was a regular earth mother who carefully tended the enormous amounts of greenery in our house, prepared gourmet meals and made her own linen from raw flax. Now, unless we hear her spikes clattering over the floor as she runs another of her innumerable golf outfits through the washer-drier, my daughter and I have no idea whether she is in the house or not. Except when it's raining, of course, and then she is in the living room putting.

Doing housework is something Marjorie will not even discuss anymore because it is well known that moving furniture to dust contributes to upper body tension. Cooking is out because it is not good to eat too much before a round. When last Christmas I suggested that a smallish cooked bird to commemorate the day would be not be considered excessive, Marjorie said no because earlier that morning she had seen a small patch of sun and the weather could break any minute. Nor will she help wash up after dinner because the heat from dishwater desensitises the fingers and makes for poor putting touch. And everyone knows, for heaven's sake, that putting is the most important part of the game.

The other day I came home to find a note wedged under the door knocker which said, "Have gone to have a mid-iron lesson with Vince. There's a TV dinner in the icebox. Keep the left side strong."

Marjorie maintains a drumfire correspondence with every golfing mail order house in America and the British Isles that has not been shuttered by the authorities for making fraudulent use of the postal service. There is not a nostrum, piece of special equipment, correctional device or instruction kit she has not purchased. As a result, our house, which was once a showplace, now resembled the pro shop of a particularly seedy public course in Guatemala. When we go away, which can't be too often to suit me, instead of the two of us pursuing our separate pleasures we now have, God save the mark, total togetherness. Marjorie never lets me out of her sight in case I might try to slip off and get in a round of men's golf without her. We played Spring Lake in New Jersey early this year. I have always liked Spring Lake with its broad, forgiving fairways, but this time the only peace I knew the whole day was when I had a Rum Collins with the naked men in the locker room and now she is starting to make ugly Friedanesque noises about that simple pleasure. Retreating to the male preserves of Pine Valley is something I can just forget about. Marjorie says she will be on the phone to her attorney while my car is still getting out of the driveway.

When she is not playing with me, Marjorie is usually off playing with those whom she describes as "the girls". A coarse, loutish group of women, they are in the main given to extravagant patterns of speech of a particularly startling nature. To a woman, they seem to have ingested the entire rule book of golf and call penalties on each other that have not been invoked since the death of Harry Vardon. Worst of all, Marjorie has begun to adopt the ghastly *patois* of the seasoned golfer. To hear a woman with whom you have lived for a score of years suddenly start saying things like, "Boy, I really hit that little sweetheart on the screws," is not a pleasant turn of events, I can assure you. All this from a lady with whom I was always able to exchange a pithy remark or two on the affairs of the day. Now, if it isn't advertised at the Food Fair or written up in Bob Toski's *The Touch System for Better Golf*, Marjorie hasn't got a clue.

Where it will all end, I have no idea. We are already planning a summer trip and Marjorie can't make up her mind between Pinehurst or the seaside links of the Irish coast. For myself, I suggested we go to the Hermitage. I have a sudden desire to spend an entire vacation indoors viewing the art treasures of ancient Russia. But Marjorie won't consider it. She says she's heard it is a terrible course.

A LADY OF QUALITY

Michael Williams

We first met, her ladyship and I, at Moor Park. In Ross Whitehead's shop to be exact. She caught my eye at once. It was not love at first sight, but there was an obvious purity about her, untouched by any other male.

I took her out on to the practice green. She was a nice weight with a good touch. She was, it soon became obvious, just what I had been looking for ever since my first love was spirited away some years before: stolen in fact.

I bought her ladyship, an Acushnet mallet-headed putter, for £6, I think it was, and we lived together happily for many years. We had our ups and we had our downs and, here and there, on less faithful occasions, I had other mistresses. But always we came back together, seeking the touch and understanding of the blissful days.

Like the time when together we reached the final of the club knock-out. I had been there once before but that was 11 years earlier when the game, certainly on the greens, was personally fraught with less difficulty. It was a 36-hole match and I will always remember the putts we sank together over the first six holes. We were as one, each confident in the other, three up at lunch.

Then the holes began to slip away. Back to two up, then one, all square, one down and now only nine to play. What I remember best were the last three holes, the match again level. At the 16th, the 34th, the enemy holed from a disheartening length for a four, but we followed him in from 12 feet for the half. The 17th, which plays longer than its yards, has never been my sort of hole, but somehow a three-iron second reached the green.

If ever there was a moment to get a birdie, this was it. We holed. One up. The last is a short hole and from the back of the green the two of us laid the ball dead for the three and the match.

That was our finest hour together. More painful ones followed and I don't think we ever quite got on when we went abroad. I never gave her ladyship a name like Bobby Jones and his "Calamity Jane", though calamitous moments there certainly were. Greens are not the same in foreign parts, and one or other of us would be upset by the weather or the watering, the grain or the deceptive undulations. We had our moments, but not many.

And then, for the first time, we went together to America for the 1977 Walker Cup. I could foresee some time on my hands in the week leading up to the match and it seemed a good idea to take clubs. Shinnecock Hills beckoned, and goodness knows where else, given a bit of luck and an invitation here and there.

The relationship between her ladyship and me had by this time become a trifle strained. We were missing more than we were holing, though I must say I think I was to blame. Other than a band of tape around the bottom of her grip, her ladyship had retained her figure – though her head did show some scratches, sustained on gravel and stones and the odd cuff about the ears as an iron club was thrust back in the bag.

We played together twice that September weekend and lost each time. Afterwards, while doodling round the professional's shop, I was startled to find what, for a moment, I took to be her ladyship's head lying on the counter, separated indeed from her body.

"Don't worry," I was told. "She's not yours. That's Steve Martin's. It broke while he was practising and it's not going to be easy to mend."

Now I am not always a selfish man and suddenly, in a blinding moment of intuition, I saw this as the chance for her ladyship to play in the Walker Cup, something we could never possibly do together.

Her ladyship, dozing quietly with the rest of my clubs in the caddie shed, knew nothing of her impending destiny. But through Sandy Saddler, the captain, I mentioned that I thought I had the twin of Martin's broken putter. Martin carried out an examination, said no, she was too heavy and her neck was not the same either. But when his reserve putter failed him in practice, he looked again. I renewed the offer of her ladyship's services and Martin said he would give her a trial.

It was Michael Bonallack who first predicted the news I half wanted to hear, half didn't. "I think you've lost your putter," he said. "I've just walked the first nine with Martin and he's holed everything."

When Martin came in at the end of the round, he confirmed her ladyship's willing compliance with his intentions and my one resolve now was to see her in action in the Walker Cup. It was quite a wait.

I stood behind the 1st green that first morning. Martin was playing with Allan Brodie. They were bunkered. Martin came out and Brodie holed. At the 2nd Brodie's tee shot ran through. Martin clipped dead and still her ladyship waited. At the 3rd Martin chipped in for a birdie. At the 4th the Americans drove into a bush, made a frightful mess of things and conceded the hole without asking the British to putt.

Finally, at the 5th, came the moment. Brodie putted a yard past, out came her ladyship and in went the ball. Satisfied, I moved off to leave Martin to the business of becoming one of the more successful members of an otherwise unsuccessful side. On the last afternoon her ladyship played top against Lindy Miller. There was a chance on the last green of an eight-foot putt for a halved match, but Miller holed his first for a winning three clean across the green.

Martin offered, without much enthusiasm, to return her ladyship, but I knew it was time to part. Anyway, I always have the happy days to remember.

DISPENSING JUSTICE
WITHOUT VENOM

Bob Sommers

The southwestern United States is a dry and arid place, unsuited for habitation except by reptiles who come to breathe the clean, pure air or perhaps simply warm themselves in the sun, and golfers, an unsettled lot driven by perverse nature to periodic fits of distemper.

On a bright and sunny morning, as the warming sun approached apogee, a resident rattlesnake poked his head above ground, sniffed the air to find if the morning mist had flown, and settled himself for a day of contemplation. Squirming to a comfortable state in a bed of soft and yielding sand, he wiggled his rattles to be sure they had retained their proper E-sharp tone overnight (he was blessed with perfect pitch), rested his head on his coils, and soon the soft sounds of sawn wood drifted across the desert. Ah, bliss.

Alas, it was not to be. Lost in a dream, he had barely entwined with his lady love when his peace was shattered by the thud of a foreign missile falling to the ground dangerously nearby. "What's this?" he cried. He jerked his head high and craned his neck in alarm. The thought of a meteor shower crossed his mind, but as he squinted his eyes against the glare he dismissed the possibility that a heavenly body had disturbed his slumber, for there, a yard or so away, lay the object – shiny, white, perfectly round and dented symmetrically.

"Good grief," he muttered, "another golfer. And a woman, at that."

Now he had nothing against women really: he was rather fond of a number of them, but they do have their place and he believed, like Tom Weiskopf, that their place was not on a golf course. If the miscreant who had interrupted his morning siesta thought he planned to lie docile while she blasted sand into his eyes in the act of extracting her ball, well she had another think coming.

He lowered his profile, so to speak, and hunkered down low while the culpritess walked sprightly into the sand pile. As she drew back her club, he thrust his head to a great height, wiggled his rattles and flicked his tongue menacingly.

A screech, followed by a shower of sand, and he was alone once more in his couch.

But not for long. Another female joined the first, and now they were in heated discussion, occasionally pointing towards him. He heard one say that she would stand by with a rake in the event that danger threatened. He hadn't counted on that. After all, he meant no bodily harm; just to frighten away the intruder so he could dream sweet dreams of *amour*.

After a few minutes of agitated discussion, he could see that the females were determined to carry on with their match, but at the same time he could see they were terribly troubled. Didn't want to go against the Rules of Golf, he supposed. Now the rattler hadn't survived these many years living on a golf course without learning a thing or two about the

Rules. He knew exactly what should be done, not only to preserve his own comfort, but also not to rouse the passions of the Rules of Golf Committee. But how to get his message across to those confounded females?

Then it struck him. It was as if a light bulb had suddenly been given the juice and blazed to life above his head. He'd listen to the possible solutions to the dispute and hiss – or shake or wiggle or do something nasty – if the players were wrong.

First one of the women decided he was a loose impediment, which he most certainly was not. Offended, he scowled, shook his tail and swayed back and forth like a cobra in the throes of an exotic trance cast by an Indian fakir. They shrieked and clung to one another in terror, as colour drained from their faces and blood sought safer regions of the anatomy. They stared spellbound, unable to move.

Suddenly the rattler changed his motion. No longer did he move menacingly: rather his head began to move gently from side to side, as if saying "No".

After a moment the ladies broke from their hypnotic state, their eyes focused, and their blood, sensing that all was safe after all, crept cautiously back to its accustomed reaches.

"Why, I believe that dear little thing is telling us he's not a loose impediment," one startled lovely said to the other.

"Do you think that's possible?" the other asked.

"Let's find out," the first said. Looking the rattler squarely in the eye, she posed the question. "Are you a loose impediment dear?"

Blushing modestly at the endearing term, the rattler shook his head.

"Amazing!" the second cupcake gasped. "A rattlesnake who knows the Rules."

The snake, his face awash with a smile of beatitude, nodded his head, and with a twitch of his brow suggested they continue the interrogation.

"If you're not a loose impediment," commented the owner of the ball that had caused all the ruckus, "then maybe you're an obstruction?"

Again the rattler shook his head negatorily at this unsettling suggestion. Unlike a loose impediment, an obstruction can be lifted with disdain and cast out of the bunker like an old beer can. He was apalled that he could be considered a candidate for such cavalier treatment. And he thought they were getting along so well.

"Well then, I suppose you must be an outside agency?" one said.

Grinning hugely, he agreed and made the proper notion to indicate that now they had the message.

"But," one said, frowning, "you're a dangerous outside agency, aren't you?"

Much as it pained him, he had to agree, and so he bared his fangs and, with the speed of light lunged towards them. Not very close, mind you; he wouldn't think of hurting anyone. He was just getting his message across.

It was understood, of course.

What then to do, they wondered?

From their deep frowns, he could see they were puzzled. Oh well, he thought, there's only one thing to do. Uncoiling himself slowly, lest he send them scampering back to the safety of the ladies' locker room, where he dare not enter, he slithered across the sand to a point well out of range of a fangy thrust, but still within the bunker, and tapped his nose into the sand three times, indicating that the ball should be dropped on that spot.

Then he crawled back to his original slumbering post, carefully smoothing his footprints, so to speak, wrapped himself in his coils, and settled down to watch the finish of the hole.

Catching on immediately, the woman whose waywardness had begun all this bother dropped her ball on the spot indicated and played a reasonably useful shot on to the green, but lost the hole when her opponent holed what the rattler heard them call a snake. And they moved on.

Alone again, the rattler settled down for some shuteye against the time when he would have to creep through the cactus and put food on the table. Little did he know, however, that his days of wistful bliss were coming to an end, for even now word of his remarkable powers was sweeping through the Sagebrush Country Club. His fate was sealed.

That is how Sagebrush came to have the world's most famous Rules Committee Chairman. From January through December, when first light creeps across the desert, the rattlesnake climbs on to a high rock that overlooks the 13th green, slips into his blue and red USGA armband, and waits for the day's business to begin. He sits in regal splendour and adjudicates disputes brought before him with all the aplomb and compassion and wisdom of P.J. Boatwright, Bobby Furber, and Judge Roy Bean. Only occasionally does he become provoked by a golfer who presses his case too strongly, and then he opens his jaws wide, curls back his upper lip and threatens to sink his fangs into one of the golfer's more sensitive parts.

But a few members know that this is a just a sham. Every fourth Monday, you see, he's seen creeping across the sand to the local dispensary and donates venom for what he assumes is a worthy cause.

A word of warning. If you're ever in the vicinity of the Sagebrush Country Club and feel the urge for a stimulant, watch out for the martinis. They pack quite a wallop.

LE STYLE,
C'EST LE SCRATCH HOMME

Patrick Campbell

The 1st tee on this chilly Sunday morning is in its usual state of tension.

The constituents of half a dozen fourballs stand about, swishing their drivers, waiting to get off.

They are all handicap players, and they look like it. That is, they wear clothing specifically designed for the game. Zippered jackets with gussets let into the back to provide an easy movement of the shoulder. Rubberised, waterproof shoes, felt caps and hairy jerseys. Some of them, looking like post-operative lobectomies, wear white woollen hats with bobbles. Others have gone so far as to tuck the ends of their trousers into their socks. Nearly all of them have trolleys.

They are joined by a common emotion. Acute anxiety.

This is caused by the fact that they don't know from Adam what's going to happen when their turn comes to strike off – when they have to step up onto the tee and balance the ball on a peg and, in death-like silence, have a rigid waggle or two and then, rather suddenly, a bash at it, with everyone watching.

The north-east wind is making their eyes water. They may not be able to see the ball at all, so that it will shoot off the toe of the club into the car park where they'll have to rootle about for it under a lot of Mini Minors with the match behind them growing more and more restive on the tee.

Alternatively, they may hook it, as usual, into the long and tangled grass behind the 3rd green and lose a brand-new ball first crack out of the box while the next two matches play through, getting the day off to a jagged start from which it will certainly not recover.

Some of the fourballs have not yet been fully organised. They toss for partners and get the very chap they didn't want so that an argument develops about tossing again, on the grounds that one of the coins came down sideways.

No sooner is this matter settled than two of the players refuse to play for ten bob a corner, because they thought it was only going to be a dollar, so they have to toss all over again to decide this, too.

Someone, feeling his muscles stiffening in the chill wind tries a practice swing and cracks someone else on the head with his driver. The apologies fatally interrupt a player driving off at that very moment.

Just as his partner is about to strike someone else finds his caddie is missing and starts roaring across to the caddie master, causing the man to top his drive.

In the midst of this nervous chaos the man who looks like a Scratchman appears on the steps of the clubhouse, and one sees at once how it ought to be done.

He is dressed, for a start, in a way which gives the onlooker no clue that he is going to play golf at all. Where the handicap men wear the muddy, shapeless slacks they keep specially for golf, he wears the trousers of what is obviously a very, very good tweed suit. They are narrow, immaculately pressed and carry, like as not, a beige overcheck on a darker, heather-mixture ground.

The beige motif is repeated in his V-necked, cashmere pullover, under which he wears a navy-blue shirt of fine wool, tieless but buttoned neatly at the neck. The sleeves of the pullover are pushed up not quite to the elbow, lending the suggestion of a workmanlike quality to his otherwise casual air.

He is hatless. Some of the handicap men are wearing green berets, pulled down over their ears.

He wears a thin, brown leather glove on his left hand. The few handicap men who wear them have chosen red, blue or even yellow.

The only real clue that the man who looks like a scratch golfer is about to play golf is to be found in his shoes. They are of grained, black leather, dubbined rather than polished. They have Norwegian toe-caps, with a raised seam, and are fiercely armoured with long pointed spikes, like running shoes.

Over his arm he carries a thin, buttoned cardigan, of the same beige wool as his pullover. He is in no hurry at all.

He is, in fact, in so little hurry that he pauses on the steps of the clubhouse to exchange the time of day with two pretty women whose husbands are already waiting for him on the tee. Laughter rings out. He leaves them, with gloved left hand raised in formal farewell.

The husbands urge him to hurry. They're off next. He gives them a reassuring wave – and walks thoughtfully across to examine the surface of the 18th green. It takes a little time. He presses his spikes into the turf, making – one would hazard a guess – a test for moisture content. As he is about to walk away he stops and looks across the green, head slightly on one side. Facts – we imagine – are probably being correlated about the length and texture of the grass which may be useful for one of those awkward 15-footers later on. He concludes his examination with a slight shrug of the shoulders, indicating – we can only presume – that conditions are not nearly as good as they are, say, at a real course like the Berkshire, but will have to be endured. He joins the other players on the tee, to be greeted with a barrage of complaint that it'll be dark if he doesn't hurry up and get on with it.

The Scratchman is entirely unperturbed. "There's ample time, gentlemen," he tells them calmly, "for all of us to notch our usual 93." He looks round. "Where's my lad?" he enquires. "Or perhaps he's still in bed –"

His caddie steps forward. The Scratchman's caddie is always there before him. No shouting at the caddie master is ever required. "Morning, Jigger," says the Scratchman. "I hope you spent a quiet night, Sir's just this side of the grave."

Sir, of course, always knows his caddie's name or, rather, the nickname by which the caddie is known from Troon to Sandwich by other caddies on the tournament circuit.

Jigger nods, without saying anything. He knows better than to try to get in on the act. He isn't, in fact, too stimulated by it, having seen it too often before. He only hopes that the news about Sir being just this side of the grave isn't true, or they'll be spending even more of the day than usual in the long grass.

The Scratchman ties the arms of his cardigan round Jigger's neck. "We'll keep that in reserve," he says. "The blood's liable to thin out just before lunch." Fastidiously, Jigger removes the cardigan and puts it in the bag.

"Well, now," says the Scratchman, "who's playing with what, and for how many?"

The other players, in an effort to get *some*thing moving, have already tossed for partners, so that Willy, the odd man out, gets the Scratchman.

Willy, in fact, owing to a habit of twitching his chip shots clean over every green, is absolutely useless off a handicap of 14. The Scratchman, however, appears overjoyed to have him as a partner. "The result," he announces, "is unclouded by doubt. We can only hope they save themselves a couple of shillings on the bye-bye. All right," he tells their opponents, "why don't you two top it first."

The opponents point out that it isn't their honour.

The Scratchman is surprised. He doesn't understand the complexities of handicaps, as he doesn't use one himself.

"Our honour?" he says. "Well, it's only the first of eighteen. Have a slash at it, Willy, while I have an attack of the shakes."

While Willy goes through the contortions that propel his tee-shot 125 yards into the rough on the right the Scratchman puts on a comedy impression of delirium tremens so acute that not even the experienced watchers can make an estimate of what he was doing the night before. The Scratchman fills it in for them.

"Pernod," he explains, "with tiny actresses. Never again, till tomorrow night."

Willy steps down off the tee. It's the Scratchman's turn to play, and all at once a remarkable change comes over him.

He becomes extremely serious. All trace of the earlier comic element is switched off. He throws his cigarette away – half smoked – and mounts the tee, his gaze fixed on a point 300 yards away, down the middle of the first fairway. Slowly, he peels the paper off a new ball, handing the paper to Jigger, who resignedly drops it in the tee box immediately beside them.

Still looking at the distant target, he goes over to Jigger and rests a hand on top of his woods, in their leather jackets.

"What d'you think, Jig?" he says.

This is the part that Jigger can't stand. The first hole is wide open, and mainly downhill. It's more than 400 yards in length and no human being on the face of the earth could conceivably take anything else except a driver. Jigger starts to take it out.

The Scratchman stops him. "I'm not sure –" he begins. He comes to the big decision. "Okay," he says. "You're probably right."

He occupies the whole of the next half minute with a clinical survey of the ground, looking for the exact position on which to tee his ball, eventually choosing a site far over on the left. He tees the ball and puts the clubhead behind it. Delicately, like Menuhin at work on a Stradivarius, he eases his fingers round the shaft of the club, into the Vardon Grip. At the moment when it might be presumed – and many of the handicap men are deceived – that he might be about to settle himself to hit the ball, the Scratchman suddenly loses all interest in it. He steps away, holding the club out almost horizontally, his eyes once again fixed on the target 300 yards away. "Keep her leftish, Jig?" he enquires, very seriously.

Jigger nods. He wishes to God he was carrying for one of the other cripples who, if they can't hit it out of their way, at least do it a lot quicker.

"Right," says the Scratchman. And at last he steps up to the ball. He looks really menacing. The jaw is set. He beds his ferocious spikes deep into the ground. He turns his head a fraction, to pin-point the target 300 yards away. Then he cocks his chin, so that it points an inch behind the ball.

It's the long-awaited signal – a gesture matched only in suspense by the officer in charge of the firing-squad raising his right arm. HE'S GOING TO DO IT NOW!

The Scratchman starts slowly back, clubhead low to the ground, left arm and left side all in one piece. He hasn't the faintest idea what the result of the shot will be. Probably the usual whistling hoot into nettles behind the 3rd where Jigger, as usual, will make hardly any effort to find it, so that's the end of a new ball. About halfway up the Scratchman takes a muscle-wrenching grip with his left hand, letting the right go slack. If he can only cut it, or push it, it'll finish up on the 13th fairway, where at least they'll be able to find it . . .

He starts down too quick. His head comes up. With a single split-second to spare the clubhead just catches the upper half of the ball, launching it straight down the middle, very low, but all of 240 yards.

"Great shot," murmurs the audience, who genuinely believe, in view of the ceremonial preceding it, that it was.

The Scratchman stops to pick up his tee, using the opportunity to take a quick sideways look down the course. He's no idea where the ball went to. He lost sight of it the moment he started his downswing, and never caught a glimpse of it again. If anything, it felt hooky, and is almost certainly in the nettles. The Scratchman suddenly sees it, a white dot on the verdant fairway, a surprising distance away.

"Well," he allows to the profoundly envious handicap men, "it's adequate." With apparent sincerity he commends the revolting strokes played by both his opponents, and then strides off, relaxed and easy, and already launched upon a controversial theme which has nothing whatever to do with golf.

The reputation he leaves behind is secure. It is, the handicap men agree among themselves, the concentration that does it. They could see, from the moment he stepped up on to the tee, that he knew what he was doing, that he had a clear mental picture of the shot he was going to play. And he played it. He *looked* as though he was on top of the game.

It is, perhaps, fortunate for the Scratchman that they don't see his second shot, a rather snatchy little jerk, so that he plays his third from under a tree and subsequently just manages to shovel in a curly four-footer for a half in five, but by this time they're too busy with troubles of their own. And in any case the Scratchman, if he's up to his work, greets the snatchy little jerk with a cry of such genuine amusement and surprise that even his partner Willy, who was confidently anticipating a three, is moved to look upon it in the same light – i.e. a laughable aberration, solely due to Pernod and tiny actresses, and one which will certainly not occur again. When it does occur, again and again, the Scratchman's pantomime of bewildered astonishment is so amusingly played that Willy almost comes to the conclusion that he was doing it on purpose, even after they've been beaten four and three – despite some extraordinarily gallant putting, with a lot of free-sweeping and line assessing by the Scratchman, none of which actually finished in the hole. Even their opponents feel they were pretty lucky to win and can't make out, indeed, exactly how they did, specially by such a large margin.

They have been dazzled by the Scratchman's Aura.

BWANA GOLF

Chris Plumridge

It was hot. He looked across the flat, baked African veldt and cursed the sun, the dust and flies. His hat, with "American Open Golf Championship" written across its front, was smeared with dirt and sweat.

"Christ!" he said, as he picked his teeth with a tee-peg, "why on earth didn't I stay on the nice easy American tournament circuit instead of coming out here?"

He leaned back in his mobile caddie-cart and reflected. He was 35 and at the zenith of his career. Leading money winner on the American tour, where he could drop a Sante Fe housewife in Bermuda shorts at 200 yards with a three-iron or a Nassau businessman at 280 yards with a driver, he had the world at his spike-shod feet. Then Grabber, his manager, had told him he would never be considered really great unless he went to Africa. So he had come.

That was two years ago and here he was on his fiftieth safari, still searching for M'buru, the great elephant the natives called He-whose-tusks-are-thicker-than-Arnold-Palmer's-forearms. M'buru was an obsession, he must have him for himself to complete his Grand Slam. The Grand Slam consisted of a lion, a leopard, a rhino, a water buffalo and an elephant – he had bagged four of them but the elephant eluded him. Getting M'buru would give him the Grandest Slam of all.

That night they had pitched camp on the edge of a small donga (gully). Earlier, he had called for his chief caddie.

"Kidoko, come here you lazy nugu [ape] and bring my matched set of Scottish-made irons with the whippy shafts. I spy dinner out there."

Kidoko came running towards him, the big leather golf bag across his shoulders.

"Bwana," he said, a huge grin spreading across his dusky face, "is the Bwana going to shoot us some dinner?"

He looked at Kidoko with affection, the affection born out of two years of much laughter, a few tears and too many golf shots.

"Yes, Kidoko, I am going to shoot us some dinner."

About 100 yards away were a flock of guinea-fowl, quietly pecking at the arid earth. He selected a four-iron, just right for a low trajectory and with enough power to do the job. He dropped half-a-dozen re-painted Dunlops on the dusty ground and took a couple of practice swings. The guinea-fowl were still unaware of his presence when the first ball took the head off the leading bird. The others stood stock still for about 20 seconds, during that time three more shots found their mark. The remainder of the flock shot off at high speed and he ceased firing. The native caddies rushed out to the dead birds and cut their throats with swift strokes of their pangas (knives).

"Not bad, eh?" he said to Kidoko, "Four out of four."

"The Bwana is truly a wonderful player," replied Kidoko, "we will eat well tonight."

And Kidoko loped off to help prepare the fires. He felt good, these four shots had reminded him of the four kilted Scotsmen he had downed on the 16th at St Andrews when he had won his third British Open. He ate and slept well that night as the stars of the African sky twinkled like dew on the first green at Wentworth. The messenger came at first light. He staggered into the camp, breathless and sweating.

"Bwana," he croaked, "I have seen him, not the length of Carnoustie from here, it is He-whose-tusks-are-thicker-than-Arnold-Palmers's-forearms as sure as God made little Gary Players."

A buzz of chatter rose from the natives and all eyes turned to Bwana.

"Kidoko," he said quietly, "fetch my deep-faced driver with the stiff shaft." Kidoko came forward bearing the beautifully balanced hand-made club, the best St Andrews could produce, and handed it to him. He felt the tacky leather grip in his hands and looked down the tempered steel shaft to the fine persimmon head – a feeling of almost sensual pleasure swept over him.

"This time," he thought, "this time I shall get you, M'buru." Then he walked over to the mobile caddie cart that Kidoko had already loaded with three dozen high-compression Dunlop 65s and a gross of extra-long tee-pegs.

"We are ready, Bwana," said Kidoko.

"Right," he replied, "let's go!"

They drove for about half an hour in the direction the messenger had pointed out. They drove in silence over the rough terrain and when they were 500 yards from a clump of mopani trees, they saw him. It was M'buru. The great pachyderm was resting in the shade of the trees, his tusks stretching out in front of him, a cloud of flies forming a black halo above his wrinkled head. Kidoko stopped the cart and they alighted, keeping downwind from the clump of trees that shaded M'buru. Kidoko silently handed him the deep-faced driver and a fresh dozen balls and they crept towards M'buru. They stopped 200 yards from their quarry and he set up the dozen balls on the tee-pegs.

He stepped back and checked his line, set himself up and with a preliminary waggle, swung the club in that lovely rhythmic motion that was known from Sunningdale to San Francisco and hit it. He hit it with a hint of draw to bring it homing in on M'buru's head at the soft point below the ear, but as soon as the ball had left the club he knew the shot was wrong. It struck M'buru just above the leg in the hardened muscle of the shoulder and with a trumpeted scream of pains, five tons of enraged elephant lumbered to its feet, trunk extended, questing for this threat to its existence. The great ears flapped and M'buru faced his tormentors. Another block-busting drive caught M'buru in the chest.

"Too low," he muttered. M'buru pinned his ears back, folded his trunk under to expose the menace of his tusks and charged. One, two, three successive shots thudded into M'buru's skull and he stopped, shook his head as if to clear his brain, then he crashed to the ground, rolled over and lay still. Kidoko exhaled through flared nostrils.

"Bwana," he said, "today you have slain M'buru, the one we call

He-whose-tusks-are-thicker-than-Arnold-Palmer's-forearms. You are indeed a mighty golfer and I salute you."

"I see you, Kidoko," he replied, "and I salute you also. Let us go and examine the spoils of triumph."

When they reached the grey bulk that was once M'buru, the vultures were gathered in the surrounding trees, their hooked beaks sunk into the white collars of their necks.

"They look like greedy cousins waiting round a rich relative's death-bed," he said, "only this relative is dead and everything has been left to them."

He pegged a ball up and sent a shot clattering through the vulture-infested branches. They rose in clouds and circled wildly, squawking as they flew.

"Bloody aasvolës [vultures]," he said.

They had returned to the camp and sent the natives back to collect M'buru's tusks and cut up the carcass for fresh meat. It was a happy camp that night with much singing and drinking among them. Tomorrow he would have to begin the long trek back to the city and inform Grabber of his completion of the Grand Slam. He was not looking forward to it. Two years was a long time to spend in one country and during that time he had grown to love Africa and its myriad faces. No doubt that greedy little swine Grabber would have another circuit lined up for him, probably something in the Amazon basin, hunting anacondas. He sifted the remains of his drink in his glass and threw them into the fire. It had been a long day.

Kidoko and the others watched him load up the caddie cart with his two sets of clubs. They watched him as he placed M'buru's tusks in the back and their hearts were heavy.

"We see you, Bwana," they chanted, "we see you are going and our hearts are heavy."

"I see you too," he replied, "and my heart is also heavy, but I must return to the city and catch the great silver bird that drops from the sky and seek the land of my forefathers. You must go to your kraals [huts] and service your wives and tend your cattle."

They watched him, Kidoko and the others, as he drove off and their chanting grew louder.

"Aieee!" they wailed. "Bwana Golf, we salute you."

"Bwana Golf," murmured Kidoko, "he was a man."

Soon, all they could see was a cloud of dust on the horizon and the rattle of his clubs was no more.

OF GAMES AND GOLF

Norman Mair

The tall and friendly stranger fell into step with me among the gallery following in the wake of Bernard Gallacher during the 1967 Youth's championship at Copt Heath. "How is that electric blanket of yours doing then?"

The Murrayfield blanket is, of course, one of the wonders of the sporting world; and, though none too pleased at thus having my attention diverted from the business in hand, I nodded enthusiastically: "It really is marvellous – it means we can get cracking no matter the weather and it is so much less bother than all that business with straw and braziers . . . ."

He looked at me, as I thought, very oddly. And did not reply. At lunch my wife – we had been married some six months – pointed him out to me as having been a guest at our wedding. I did not have to ask what he and his wife had given us by way of a present.

Such an occasional crossing of the wires is, I suppose, an inevitable hazard of being interested in, and associated with, more than one sport. Yet, for myself, I think a love of other games, if anything, sharpens a man's appreciation of golf. For instance, you recognise more readily that there is more than one form of courage.

I remember in my student days playing cricket for Edinburgh University against Durham University, who had a fast bowler – then almost wholly unknown – by the name of Frank Tyson. My fellow opening bat survived perilously, for an over or two, this totally unexpected and hair-raising experience, then was comprehensively castled, the air alive with spinning stumps and flying bails. Whereupon he turned and ran like the wind all the way back to the pavilion.

"What's the hurry?" his colleagues asked, as he clattered up the pavilion steps.

"I was afraid," he explained, peering fearfully back over his shoulder, "I might be given not out!"

Save that the cry of "Fore!" may not always come in time and that there are golfers whose rapturous practice-swing is always liable to catch the unsuspecting the mother and father of an uppercut, golfers are not obviously exposed to physical danger.

Bob Charles is indisputably a devil of a chap to tackle in his own New

Zealand, as the like of Arnold Palmer and Tony Jacklin have found to their cost. But it is still not quite the same as arriving to play rugby against the All Blacks.

"Is it true," the New Zealand press reputedly inquired of Bryan Thomas, the alleged hard man of Welsh rugby, "that you have come to New Zealand to sort out Colin Meads?"

"Not me!" exclaimed Thomas, "I want to die in Wales . . . ."

Yet, in a different way, as much or more is required in the way of guts to hole the kind of agonising short putts that Brian Huggett sank on the 17th and 18th greens in his match against Billy Casper on the last day of the 1969 Ryder Cup at Birkdale – believing as he did, alas erroneously, that he was putting for an overall and overdue British victory.

There is a close analogy between kicking goals in rugby and holing putts in golf. And when, like the writer, you have missed a penalty goal from almost straight in front to lose a comparatively important representative match, you are that much less likely to write, of a three-footer in the realm of golf, that the player in question "had only . . . ."

Jack Nicklaus – who, at Wentworth in the autumn of 1970, greatly surprised me by observing that even if it hadn't been golf, he would still probably have turned professional at some other sport – was a promising place-kicker in American football in his youth. However, when I think of Nicklaus in terms of courage, it is of the Old Course and the Road Hole in his Open Championship play-off with Doug Sanders.

Earlier in the round, that masterly American golf writer, Herb Warren Wind, and I had agreed that the winning of the Open that day could presage for Nicklaus – who had not won a major title since the 1967 American Open – a kind of second coming.

Four strokes ahead with five holes to play, Nicklaus was now only a shot in front. And Sanders's cunning five-iron had escaped by a whisker the veritable whirlpool of green and sand that is the Road Bunker to finish some eighteen feet past the flag. As Nicklaus settled to his approach, the world shrank to a man, a green and his ball. In my ear, Herb Warren Wind prophesied softly: "Jack's career has reached a turning point, a crisis . . . ."

Jack Nicklaus's answer was a seven-iron, sumptuously struck, inside Sanders. A stroke which, whenever now I play the Road Hole, seems still to linger in the air.

Jack Nicklaus himself tends to make light of that unflinching riposte. "My lead was slipping, but I was still playing well. And so long as I was still confident, it was not that difficult a shot."

He did something similar later in the season in that unforgettable final of the Piccadilly World Match-Play Championship at Wentworth. Having played the first 27 holes in 98 strokes – 33, 33, 32 – he was 12 under par and five up on Lee Trevino. Nevertheless, by the 33rd there was only one hole in it and Trevino, having greened a glorious three-iron, was home in two. Nicklaus – just when almost any other golfer would have been about to crack wide open, his lead evaporating, his opponent rampant – replied with as lovely a four-iron as a man may hit. And, for good measure, holed the putt for an eagle.

It is, for all the milling crowds of great championships, a lonely courage that golf demands. Though he carried a nation on his shoulders, was ever a mortal more alone than Tony Jacklin as, with a two-stroke lead over Bob Charles, he shaped to the drive from the 72nd tee of the 1969 Open, the terrain before him pitted with last hopes yet framed in the swelling optimism of a vast multitude?

Golfers of fibre come in so many different temperaments from the highly combustible Tommy Bolt – whose clubs, so swears Paul Hahn, have got in more flying time than the average Pan-Am pilot – to so engagingly resilient a character as Fred Daly, who has the Irishman's traditional ability to improvise whether it be on the links or in repartee.

Some time ago, a brother member of the Fourth Estate happened to come across Fred Daly in a golf outing. Afterwards, in the bar, Daly amiably questioned my friend: "With a grip like that, I don't imagine you're normally very straight?"

"As a matter of fact, in my own golfing circle, I am rated remarkably straight . . . ."

"I suppose," said Daly blandly, "you play an awful lot of golf?"

"In point of fact," came the reply, not without a certain smug satisfaction, "I hardly play at all . . . ."

"Well," exclaimed Fred triumphantly, "the more you play, the worse you'll b—— well get!"

It is often said, with much justification, that professional golfers are the new élite of the sporting firmament. Nonetheless, if the odd one does succumb to delusions of grandeur, many remain refreshingly down to earth.

None more so than Eric Brown, for all his deserved Ryder Cup fame and other exploits. Recently a chap I know chanced upon Eric Brown shortly after the Ryder Cup captain and his family had moved from Bearsden in Glasgow through to Edinburgh.

"This," indicated Eric, with a jerk of his thumb, "is my new house. Do you like it?"

The other was visibly impressed. "It looks terrific – and you know, Eric, this is a *very* select district."

"We will," promised Eric cheerfully, "damn soon change that!"

A great competitor in his heyday when in the mood – for all that he is so highly strung – Eric Brown has always been quick to anger. And seldom minded who knew it. But he has always had, too, the ability to laugh at himself.

Once when he was a professional in the South, a retired Colonel stumped into his shop and deliberated between the tray of tees priced at a penny each and those at a halfpenny. In the fullness of time, he selected one solitary halfpenny tee.

Eric Brown was genuinely outraged. "No Scot," he told that military gentleman indignantly, "would have had the brass effrontery to do that. No Sir! – no matter how long he had to scrub round on his knees to find one!"

One of the best of all rugby stories is that of the French referee whose control of a match involving a British team was sadly handicapped by the language barrier. Finally, after several warnings given with the aid of much Gallic gesticulation, he sent the worst offender off.

"Get stuffed!" advised the said transgressor warmly.

"Zee apologee," insisted the referee firmly, "eez too late . . . ."

Yet, though the game is spreading, rugby has not yet developed globally to anything like the same extent as golf, to which almost no frontier is closed. Consequently, for one who spends his winters reporting rugby, one of the great pleasures of the world of golf is the positively cosmopolitan conglomeration of a major championship.

The much-loved Roberto de Vincenzo's rendering of the tongue that Shakespeare spoke is essentially his own; but I have known him, more improbably for a South American, even have problems in making himself understood in Spain – most memorably when, in the 1965 World Cup in Madrid, he hooked out of bounds and an over-zealous official refused to let him back on the course without a ticket.

With the coming of the holiday package deal, you don't have to be either fabulously rich or a world-class golfer "to follow the sun". It is not so easy for those – for example, that wonderfully accomplished shot maker, Neil Coles – who have a rooted aversion to flying; but they can always emulate the famous boxer – the entertaining Terry Downes, if memory serves me aright – who always preferred to go by sea on the very logical grounds that "while I can swim a bit, I can't fly at all".

Golf spans the generations from that astonishing octogenarian Mrs Charlotte Beddows, who was still reporting for regular lessons when well past her 80th birthday from Gordon Durward, 1970's Club Professional of the Year, down to that fetching little sprite, the seven-year-old Bridget Gleeson, who has already been round her native Killarney off the LGU tees in a gross 100 and whose passion for the game is such that in 1969 she contrived 362 days golf out of a possible 365.

Not many games so readily as golf bridge the generation gap – though it is part of Scottish legend how Harry Haddock, the Clyde left-back, when congratulating Stanley Matthews at the end of an international in which the ageing maestro had given him the run-around, made the immortal sally: "Why don't you pick on someone your own age?"

Cricketers also, admittedly, have been known to enjoy careers of remarkable longevity – Jack Hobbs making, after all, a hundred centuries after his 40th birthday. But reminders of the fleeting years are apt to come earlier and rather more humiliatingly than in golf – though victims of the twitch might disagree.

For my own part, I recollect with painful clarity the afternoon that finally persuaded me that the time was nigh when, as a participant, I should be well advised to devote my summers exclusively to golf. Thrice a ball from a bowler, whose victims over the years had included batsmen of world renown, was cut narrowly past me in the gully.

"Would you," asked our wicket-keeper captain of the perspiring bowler, "like gully squarer?"

"Not squarer," retorted the bowler bitterly, "but younger!"

Mark you, cricket and golf have more than a little in common – sharing, to cite but one obvious example, a degree of euphemism worthy almost of angling. The sort of careful phraseology epitomised by Sir J.M. Barrie's classic observation: "In the first innings, I made nought not out, in the second I was not so successful."

The only other sex that as yet we have play golf. And the image of the golfers of the distaff side as grunting creatures, hirsute and only with the greatest reluctance not on all-fours, is certainly no longer valid, if it ever was.

Most of them, too, take commendable trouble with their golfing attire even if the widespread introduction of slacks and Bermuda shorts cannot be a uniformly good thing, since that is, so to speak, a sphere in which, undeniably, some have larger handicaps than others.

Again, they can be alarmingly temperamental. Indeed, my wife still tells of the occasion she was playing in an open stroke-play competition and holing putt after putt – to the growing disgust of the girl with whom she was paired, whose token congratulations had long since died in her throat.

At last there came a time when the girl could stand the sight no longer: "Hole just one more putt," she hissed through clenched teeth, "and I'll slap your face."

The awe inspired by officialdom in women's golf does not always derive from exceptional administrative ability, far less golfing prowess. Not so long ago a couple of our more gifted young fillies were playing with an embattled matriarch of markedly inferior skill.

To their mingled horror, amazement and glee, she succeeded in depositing her drive smartly between her legs into the tangled rough adjoining the tee. Mercifully, she had not the foggiest notion where the ball had gone; and, frightened to tell her, the girls solemnly joined in the search a flattering 150 yards from the tee.

Not only does golf belong to both sexes and all generations but its exponents come in all shapes and sizes. From Frank Sinatra – to whom, in the singer's younger and skinnier days, Bob Hope wished to attach a red flag preparatory to putting him on duty in the hole – to those like the writer those best irons are all too patently the knife and fork.

The curse of modern golf, it is often averred, is slow play; but, if it is getting worse, it is no new malaise. For was not the incomparable Bernard Darwin moved to observe tartly that "golf is not a funeral, though both can be very sad affairs". Of course, golfing galleries, even when irritated beyond belief by golfers whose activities on the green would be hard pressed to keep pace with coastal erosion, would seldom, if ever, dream of giving vent to their feelings, as did a gentleman one afternoon at Edgbaston when a cricketing companion of mine had taken root at the wicket.

"Whatever else you die of," opined the aforesaid frustrated spectator in a voice of thunder, "it won't be from a stroke!"

To practise a team game one so often needs either others or plenty of imagination. One afternoon, nearly a decade ago, I chanced, in the height of summer, to stroll across a famous rugby ground whose boundary wall fronts an asylum.

Although it was June, the 1st XV scrum-half was there, stripped to the waist and armed with a cluster of elderly rugby balls he periodically dipped in a bucket of water, to reproduce the all too prevalent conditions of a Scottish winter, before bouncing each ball against the wall and whipping it away to an imaginary stand-off.

Over the wall peered, with frank amazement, a long line of the inmates – obviously wondering just what on earth they had done to be put away. But no one looks askance at a golfer practising – not even, nowadays, in Britain.

It is sometimes said that only when he stands at the altar on his wedding day does a man experience quite the same sensation of impending doom as he feels each week on the 1st tee of a Sunday morning. In truth, others are much less interested in our golf than we incline to think they are . . .

Not that the matches fore and aft do not sometimes add to the store of memory. In fact, only recently, I happened across my own account of the day, immediately following the 1968 Curtis Cup at Royal County Down, that four itinerant golf writers sampled that majestic links. Among them, myself.

We had come to the short 7th, measuring somewhere around 130 yards. One of our number, burly and bespectacled, hit what he modestly deemed a perfect shot, which that mischievous green shrugged off with a light laugh.

"There is," he cried, wrathfully "no way to stay on that green!"

We left the tee arguing the pros and cons of links golf in general and the merits of that short 7th in particular.

The small gaggle of women playing immediately behind us included that marvellously repetitive technician, Mrs Jessie Valentine, six times Scottish champion, thrice British. Off the 8th tee, I let fly. "By Jove," yelped the bespectacled one, "a hole-in-one."

I must say I was surprised, for the eighth stretches some 425 yards and, despite a wider arc and a resolve to get a little more right hand into the shot, it seemed unlikely that I should have suddenly uncovered an additional 200 or so yards. Nonetheless, while it lasted, it was a pleasing thought, not sullied by the faintest knowledge of where the devil my ball had gone.

Wheeling round, I was, though too late to see the tee shot from the ladies behind cavorting merrily into the hole at the short 7th, in plenty of time to join in the spontaneous applause. "That," we pointed out to our disgruntled companion, "is one very good way of staying on the 7th green!"

He, though, was now smiling happily. "That is the first time I have seen a hole-in-one actually going into the hole. I did not," he added, making his point neatly, "see my own."

PLAYING THE NINETEENTH

Mike Britten

You will not find his name in any roll of championship winners. Like the majority of amateur golfers, he plays for fun in between the demands of earning a living and raising a family. Yet for some two dozen patrons of the men's bar at Moortown Golf Club, enjoying lunchtime refreshment on a May day in 1974, he provided one of those rare cameos that are cherished long after the champion of the moment is forgotten.

It was a typical early summer morning – a warm sun dispersing the shower clouds with just enough heat to persuade the Yorkshire club members that watching the opening round of the English Stroke Play Championship was thirsty work. Then Nigel Denham, or rather the ball he struck towards the 18th green, burst on the convivial scene.

It should be explained that at that time the Moortown clubhouse was not out of bounds, nor was the concrete path encircling it and running alongside the 18th fairway and green. In golfing parlance, the whole edifice, measuring some 60 by 30 yards, was an immovable obstruction. As such it was a place to be avoided by any golfer intent on returning an unblemished medal round. Denham, a Yorkshire county player, had every intention of so doing until he struck his mid-iron to the home flag from an uphill lie, and instantly realised he had applied a vicious hook to the ball. What followed would have made a classic script for W.C. Fields.

Denham's ball bounded off the concrete path, leapt up the clubhouse steps and after cannoning off the framework of the open french windows rolled gently to rest in the centre of the bar carpet. Denham approached base with that look of desperation common to all golfers who fear impending doom. Preliminary enquiries revealed that the ball was indeed closeted indoors, and he mounted the steps in pursuit.

First there were formalities of etiquette to observe. Like most clubs, Moortown does not permit spiked shoes to be worn within its inner precincts, nor allow caddies to enter carrying the tools of their trade. The bar steward was very much a custodian of the law and if Denham wished to pass through the portals he must remove his golf shoes. Nigel complied and padded into the bar in his socks, leaving his clubs and caddie parked on the doorstep.

An expectant gallery had encircled the errant missile. Nigel surveyed it with a mixture of relief and perplexity. It was his all right – and at least the lie was perfect – indeed the carpet had been freshly cleaned. The ball was not damaged, nor was it bearing any loose impediment. There was room to swing a club, and he was still only 30 yards from the flagstick.

Denham could have ended all speculation there and then by declaring the ball unplayable, accepting a penalty stroke, and following the appropriate procedure. But a Tyke is never one to give owt for nowt, and this one needed little encouragement from the drinking gallery to be intrigued by the alternatives.

"It's an Axminster lie, just perfect for a pitch shot," declared one jovial drinker. "That may be," declared another, "but are you allowed to play this watering hole before the 18th? There should be a two pint penalty!"

Denham consulted his scorecard. There was nothing in the local rules to prevent his playing his next shots from inside the clubhouse, but how and to where? He strode to the bay windows overlooking the green and peered out at a sea of grinning faces. There was only one real avenue of escape – pitch through the window and the ball with any luck would clear a bank and run down towards the hole.

The voice of officialdom sensed his thoughts: "Don't you dare smash that glass with your golf ball!" it bellowed as the occupants of the window seats moved hastily out of the firing lane. Denham did not argue, Instead he slipped the casement catch, leant out for a closer study of his likely landing area, and to the onlookers' astonishment politely requested they clear a path to the pin. Sustained applause greeted his announcement that he was going to wedge the ball through the open window.

Opinion inside the bar was sharply divided. The sober faction decided he was crazy – the rest had nothing but praise for his daring. This was the spirit that had put the Great into Britain and would that there were more like him. Denham collected his pitching wedge from his bemused caddie and zeroed in on the target. At a range of 25 feet the rectangle of open air measured four feet by two. Respectful silence greeted his first practice swing. Several more were required before the precise weight of shot and trajectory were established.

Denham took a last deep breath – and struck his third shot to the 18th. The ball described a gentle parabola, neatly bisected the uprights of the window frame, and rolled down the greenside bank to pull up 12 feet below the hole. A roar of appreciation greeted Nigel as he emerged triumphantly into the sunshine.

Sadly his putt for a fairy-tale par four lingered obstinately on the lip of the cup and the final score was an unremarkable 74. But for twenty-four hours Denham was a national hero as the first man to play Championship golf from the 19th to the 18th.

Immediately afterwards the Moortown committee met in solemn session and decided that as the game was meant to be played outdoors the clubhouse and its environs would in future be out of bounds. The Rules of Golf committee of the Royal and Ancient Club of St Andrews then decreed that Denham's bogey five at the 18th should not have been accepted. By opening the bar window Nigel had improved his line of play. The clubhouse was an immovable obstruction and no part of it should have been moved. It was perfectly permissible for him to have changed the position of a chair or a stray shoe (as loose impediments) but opening windows was a contravention of rule 17–1. He should have been penalised two strokes. No matter. Nigel's niche in the folklore of the game is secure, and the old adage that the best golf stories originate in the bar remains unchallenged.

DOING A DANECKI

Bob Rodney

Every golfing rabbit dreams of winning the Open Championship, but I never expected to see one try it, wide awake. It happened in the Hillside section of the 1965 Open, adjoining Royal Birkdale where the championship was to be played. Walter Danecki, a 43-year-old Milwaukee mail-sorter, who called himself a professional golfer – that was literally his position – took 108 shots to complete the course on the Friday, and added a further 113 on the Saturday for a two-round total of 221. This was the highest-ever qualifying two-round score in Open Championship history, and it missed the cut by exactly 70 shots.

Danecki's second-round figures were:

778	557	955 – 58
96 ten	465	546 – 55 (113)

That is, 43 over par.

Danecki, a tall, well-built, dark-eyed bachelor, turned out to be the perfect Walter Mitty. He told us that he had been playing for seven years on municipal courses, paying 1 dollar 50 cents for a round of 18 holes, that he had never had a lesson, and that he thought he might beat Arnold Palmer.

It came out that he had turned professional for the US Open. Danecki explained that he had been asked to state on the entry form whether he was an amateur or a professional.

"I wanted the crock of golf, so my conscience made me write down 'professional'," he said. "I don't charge if I give a lesson."

No, he continued, he had not joined the USPGA. He had found out that he would be required to serve a five-year apprenticeship, and as he has never been attached to a golf club or driving range, he decided that this was not a practical proposition for him.

"What I'll do is win one of the big ones," he declared. "Then they'll have to let me in."

Danecki had come to Britain on holiday. None of his workmates knew he was out of the country. He thought that if he won the Open, that would be just fine. If not it would be "my little secret".

He had not realised that his performance on the Lancashire coast that week was going to make him famous throughout the golfing world, and that his colleagues were going to find out all about it. Danecki's name was going to be written into all the record books. He could have added a new phrase to the English language – to do a Danecki.

Walter's only previous tournament was the US Open qualifying competition. He could not say what his best round had been.

"I was shooting good golf before I came over here," he said ruefully. "My partner and I felt a little bit discouraged after the first day. We thought we had to do two 75s to qualify."

(And Walter had shot 108, remember.)

"But, I don't like to quit," he went on. "I like to golf. That's what I came here to do."

Royal and Ancient officials did not expect Danecki to reappear for the second day's play. They underestimated the courage of this earnest American, and had arranged a substitute to play round with his partner, Bryan Hessay. Danecki astounded them, for the second time, by turning up.

He offered only one glimmer of excuse.

"I have a sore right hand," he explained. "Couple of years back, I dug a pivot and hit a tree root. My hand hasn't been right since. Once in a while it hurts, then I don't play so good.

"I want to say your smaller ball is right for this sort of course. If I had been playing our bigger ball I would have been all over the place."

Chapter 2

CHAMPIONS OF
A BYGONE AGE

Charles Price

By 1953, the year I went to work for and to live with Walter Hagen, the legend of him had become almost Greek in its proportions, half clubhouse myth and half real man, the myth part living everywhere golf was played and the man part living nowhere anybody was precisely sure about.

Although only 61, Hagen was so utterly removed from the golf scene there were probably not a dozen people intimate with the game who even know what part of the country he was living in, and probably not half of them knew his unlisted phone number. Even so, if you called, Hagen wouldn't identify himself until you gave him a name and a voice he could recognise instantly. Then, disarmingly, he'd ask where *you* had been. Even on the phone, Walter Hagen was the master match player.

Hagen had not played in a national championship even for old time's sake since the 1940 PGA, a title he had won five times, four in a row, all at match-play. It had been 22 years since he had played in a British Open, which had won four times, and 17 since his last National Open, which he had won twice. He had not won a mere tournament since the Gasparilla Open, back in 1935, the memory of which was hazy even to those who had played in it. But Hagen had brought it off big, scoring birdies on the last two holes. He had long since lost count of how many other tournaments he had won, but at least 60 of them had been against world-class players. In keeping with a man whose career had been so large he could not keep track of it, everyone, including his grown son, had been referring to him for years as "The Haig", for there was something undeniably royal about him. How else could you excuse the man for not being able to remember, as he sometimes couldn't, the years he won the British Open?

Still, there was something wonderfully human about him, something that crept through the newsprint in a way it had for no other golf pro before or since and which the electronic tube today seems incapable of transmitting, possibly because, through sitcoms and wildly inaccurate documentaries, it has made implausible figures, like The Haig, so commonplace. If you brought up The Haig's name among pros past 40 anywhere in 1953, their faces would light up, as though you had mentioned some comic uncle who had made boyhood unforgettable. This would lead immediately to some outrageously apocryphal anecdote, such as The Haig showing up an hour late half-drunk in a tuxedo for a national championship, and then winning it. Either that or a story of him doing something all too human, such as scoring a nine on a par-three hole, laughing all the way. Walter Hagen could do anything in golf – the more preposterous, it seems, the better. As big as the tour is today, what could professional golf give to see his likes again? They could try money. But it takes something beyond that to produce a Walter Hagen.

· · · **·** · · ·

When The Haig finally racked up his clubs, which was at some indeterminate date even The Haig couldn't remember, you almost had to drag him away from his hunting and fishing to be so much as a spectator. In retirement he lived in obscure villages where most of the neighbours, if they had heard of him at all, regarded him vaguely as some sort of athlete from a couple of wars ago. Here The Haig held court for those who took the trouble to find him. And there were hundreds who did, thousands more, it seemed, who would have liked to. Merely meeting the man had become a kind of golf tournament. Years later, in a hospital corridor the night before The Haig was to undergo surgery for cancer of the throat, I had to have a perfect stranger forcibly removed because he had ghoulishly persisted in taking what he thought was this final opportunity to shake the master's hand.

Typically for a man who might take three-quarters of an hour shaving, The Haig spent years trying to write his autobiography with the help of newspapermen who thought they had known him. Almost all of this time had been dissipated searching for just the right title, The Haig's theory being that nobody could possibly give birth to a book without having a proper name for it. All the newspapermen had long since left the scene with near-fatal hangovers. The Haig had then tried to induce the help of Ernest Hemingway, on the excuse they had once got drunk together in Paris, but Hemingway begged off on the not illogical grounds that he knew nothing about golf. Next, The Haig tried to persuade Gene Fowler, the popular biographer (*The Great Mouthpiece; Good Night, Sweet Prince*) with whom he'd partied in Hollywood. Fowler knew it was hopeless to argue, so he agreed and then quoted a fee that meant the finished book would have to be accepted by six book clubs before The

Haig would ever get a cent. The Haig told Fowler he would get back to him, and of course never did.

The Haig had now reached the bottom of the writing barrel, which is where he found me. I was 27 and had yet to write my first book. A number of my magazine articles on golfers, notably in *The Saturday Evening Post*, had been brought to his attention by his son, Walter Jnr. The Haig hadn't read them and never would, something he considered a mere oversight. But if Junior said so, then I was to be his man, or rather his boy, for I was not yet professional enough to tell immediately the difference between an autobiographical subject and a biographical one.

The Haig was definitely not autobiographical material. Not only was he incapable of writing objectively about himself, he was incapable of writing, period, a talent he considered strictly god-given, like carrying a tune, and not worth worrying about if you weren't born with it. As a matter of actual record, The Haig seems never to have so much as written a letter. At least his son had never received one. And as if this lack of literacy were not enough, he seems never to have read anything beyond *Outdoor Life*, and this only enough to make sense out of the pictures. While I did not know it at the time, The Haig and I together would be an experience I literally would never forget, but not one that anybody would remember literarily.

As I saw it, my job would be to separate the man from the myth, to find out where the man from East Rochester, New York, had left off and where The Haig, the romantic egoist, had begun. I had already had an inkling that there had been a vast difference between the two. The Haig, for example, had been internationally credited for having taken golf pros "into the clubhouse", meaning he had elevated their social status from servant to celebrity. But when, in preparation for the book, I interviewed the pro at the Country Club of Rochester, down the road from where Walter the boy had grown up and where he had learned to play, I was surprised to find that the pro and myself were obliged to have lunch in the kitchen.

I first met The Haig at a home he was renting at Lake Mohawk, New Jersey, a town that for its golfiness might just as well have been in the middle of Montana. That's the way The Haig liked to live – with golf at arm's length. The years had added ten inches to his waistline from his playing days, and his drinking had left his eyes baggy, his cheeks jowly, and his nose bulbous, giving him the look of a philosophical walrus. He was seated in an overstuffed armchair that had been angled into the centre of the living room, thronelike, and he was so thoroughly ensconced in it that getting out of it seemed beyond all human endeavour. But he tried, and failing, began to laugh at himself, far more than I thought the situation warranted. But, as I was to learn, The Haig was a man who could extract humour out of a nuclear accident.

In his day, The Haig had been considered the height of fashion. But now his dress had become a hodgepodge of golf-shop clichés and remnants from Savile Row that had gone out with Edward VIII. He was wearing alligator loafers with tassels, orange gym socks, cuffed flannel slacks that left him with a lapful of pleats, a silk shirt with French cuffs to which were attached links the size of champagne corks, and a florid ascot around his neck that the Duke of Windsor might have hesitated wearing on the Riviera, let alone in New Jersey.

Wrapped in a knitted coaster on the coffee table in front of him was a can of beer of some obscure brand that, I was to learn, nobody outside of Jersey City or Hoboken had ever heard of, either. It was a symbol in reverse. (Later, in the middle of Michigan, he would drink a local brand unheard of outside Grand Rapids.) The Haig's hands were very long and thin and surprisingly unmuscular, the way a pianist's are supposed to be but seldom are. For some reason, The Haig always held them upward, as though some poetic injustice had just taken something out of them, an analogy not too strained considering The Haig might have been the most divine putter the game has known. In them was always a cigarette, which he handled as though it were opium – and from which he could draw out more theatre than Franklin D. Roosevelt. To this day it is impossible for me to visualise The Haig without a Chesterfield between his fingers. In the 15 years I was to get to know him, I never saw him without one, not even after his larynx had been removed because of them.

With this imperial posture, I had somehow expected The Haig to have a stentorian voice. But it was not deep or loud, but high and raspy, like a falsetto that had grown rusty with age. Without his hands to help him, he couldn't have held the attention of a hotel clerk. To make matters worse, he was becoming absent-minded, constantly losing his train of thought and forever forgetting momentarily the names of people he had known half his life. The result was that his speech was constantly being interrupted by embarrassing pauses, theatrical coughs, stage laughs, and assorted heh-hehs and harrumphs. While he looked like His Royal Highness, ironically he sounded like Mr Magoo.

We never discussed money or the conditions under which I would work. I just seemed to have gone to work for him automatically. One word clinched the whole deal. The Haig had waved his arm grandly about the room, indicating the tools of our now mutual trade: a tape recorder every ten feet, blank legal pads every three feet, and a newly sharpened number two pencil seemingly on every vacant foot of tabletop. "You won't," said The Haig, pausing to take a "toot" of beer for emphasis. "You won't use any – heh-heh . . ." and now he paused to inhale his cigarette, blowing out enough smoke to inflate a water bed. "You won't use any of them big words, will ya? They don't sound like me."

"Walter," I said, realising he must have felt as though he were playing with an amateur. "The only five-syllable word I know is *Philadelphia.*"

He threw back his head and crackled. And I knew we were on our way, The Haig and I. That too was a title we never used, for the book never got written. But I like to think today it at least had the ring of a bestseller.

One day six months later, The Haig and I were driving south to Grand Rapids from Cadillac, where he had rented a couple of cottages for us by a lake for the summer. The Haig ostensibly had hired me to help him write his autobiography, but I was fast losing any semblance of a collaborator. An utter individualist, The Haig was constitutionally incapable of cooperating with anybody at doing anything, which may explain why he was a deplorable fourball player. (Paired with Byron Nelson late in his career in the old Inverness Fourball Tournament, The Haig would sometimes leave Nelson on his own for two or three holes while he repaired to the clubhouse for a quick drink or two.)

Instead of a co-writer, I was being turned into a glorified companion-stenographer, somebody to jot down the deathless details of his purple life during cocktails until he could get around to showing me how to write them properly, The Haig suddenly having materialised as a master of literary composition, this although he had never been known to write so much as a postcard. In six months, as a result, we hadn't been able to advance his life beyond his days in grade school, and he was now approaching the age of 62.

We were on our way to visit the plant where the clubs were made that bore his signature. The trip could not be called a business one in any sense, for The Haig had not stepped foot in the plant for so many years that he couldn't remember when the last time had been. The result would be that a lot of employees of The Walter Hagen Company would be seeing him for the first time, some of whom did not know he was still alive. We were just going there because The Haig thought he ought to, now that he had moved back to Michigan from northern New Jersey.

Once inside the plant, though, The Haig would soon be telling men who had been fashioning clubs for a generation how to go about it. While The Haig well knew what sort of clubs best suited him, he had actually never come closer to making one than he had as a boy serving as an apprentice to a mandolin-maker. However, that was qualification enough for a man like The Haig, who at a nightclub in New York once had taken it upon himself to tell Babe Ruth how to hit a baseball.

I was doing the driving. Although The Haig down through the years must have owned a hundred cars of some exotic make or another – Austins, Lotuses, Reos, and some even Detroit had never heard of – he preferred not to drive himself. As a result of this practice, he had made himself into a intolerable backseat driver, and he did not like the way I was handling his Buick convertible. "Slow down!" he'd say every 15 minutes. "We're not in any hurry." In The Haig's eyes, anybody who drove more than 40 miles per hour was a maniac.

As we crept down the US 131, I couldn't help thinking of the line that had been attributed to him for so long that he had begun to believe he had coined it. "Slow down!" the line went, "and take time to smell the flowers." It was alleged to be The Haig's personal philosophy. And it was. But the line was first used, in somewhat different wording, by Oscar Wilde, whom I doubt The Haig had ever read or even heard of. The last book he had read, if not the first, had been *The Rules of Golf*, his interpretations of which, all perfectly legal, had given the USGA and the R and A apoplexy.

In a play-off with Mike Brady for the 1919 National Open at Brae Burn, near Boston, The Haig had requested that he be allowed to identify his ball after if had become embedded in the bank of a bunker. Since he and Brady were the only two players on the course, and since hundreds of people in the gallery, including several USGA officials, had seen the ball socket itself, they thought his request senseless. But The Haig argued, not illogically, that it could have been a ball lost the day before, or the day before that, even.

The Haig squeezed the ball out of the bank between his thumb and his forefinger, and then began to examine it as though it were a rock somebody had sent him from the moon. After what seemed like an hour, The Haig declared the ball was his, after all. He carefully replaced it on the indentation that was no longer there, recovered for his par, and went on to win by one stroke.

The Haig was then the pro at the only club he would ever represent: brand-new Oakland Hills, near Detroit, which had not quite finished its golf course. At a dinner in his honour after defeating Brady, The Haig stood up to thunderous applause and then offhandedly announced he was resigning. Before the members could fully realise what he had said, The Haig announced he had already chosen his successor for them – Mike Brady.

Charisma was not a word used in the sports pages in The Haig's day. But he had it, in spades. It was just as kinetic in those days of the biplane and the Philco as that of any of the many pros who would follow him in jets and on Sonys and for whom The Haig broke a lot of ground they have taken for granted. Compared with the hat-in-hand professionals who had preceded him, his image was incandescent. The Haig literally lit up the sports pages with a game that not too long before him had been thought by some editors to belong in the financial section.

Great golfers have always come along in pairs, much of their greatness having been achieved by beating one another. Harry Vardon had his J.H. Taylor, Ben Hogan his Sam Snead, Jack Nicklaus his Arnold Palmer. Walter Hagen had Bobby Jones, no less.

From 1923 through 1930, Jones played in 21 major national championships, passing up 11 others. The Haig played in 32, passing up nothing. In that period, Jones played in only seven tournaments that were not national championships. The Haig played in at least three hundred. Jones played exhibitions only for an occasional charity, perhaps in those years no more than half a dozen. The Haig played more than one thousand, all of them for cash. When not competing, Jones played no more golf than the average dentist, probably not more than 80 rounds a year, and this in the comparative solitude of his home club near Atlanta. The Haig, who had no home club, played every day he wasn't on an ocean liner, often twice a day, usually on a course he had never seen before, and always in front of a stampeding gallery.

Because his appearances were only two, three, or four times a year, Jones was automatically awarded centre ring in the public arena of golf. He was the star they sounded the trumpets for, the daring young man on the flying trapeze. The Haig was a fixed star, an act that ran continuously. He was a professional strong man, the strongest in the world of golf, a professional so supremely confident that he could often afford to act more carefree than the amateurs who were watching him. And, in an age when highways were today's byways and aeroplanes flew only fast enough to stay airborne, he carried this act from Cape Cod to Catalina Island, from Quebec to Mexico City, and to places where Jones would only be read about: Singapore, Buenos Aires, Johannesburg,

Kuala Lumpur. While Jones, as it so happens, never played anywhere that wasn't near a major city, The Haig brought his circus-brand of golf to the backwoods of America and the hinterlands of the world.

Figuratively, the public had to crane its neck to see Bobby Jones. They could watch Walter Hagen at eye level. Spectators never thought of speaking to Jones when he was playing. They saw no reason not to speak to The Haig when he was playing. In 1914, during the last three holes of the National Open, which The Haig was winning for the first time, he smiled at a pretty girl on the 16th tee, struck up a conversation with her on the 17th fairway, and made a date with her as he walked off the 18th green. After The Haig, nobody would take golf *too* seriously.

I was to learn, though, that The Haig's career had not been altogether as cavalier as it seemed in retrospect. He had studiously built up a public persona, a façade of indifference in which every offhand gesture actually had been as studied as a matinee idol's. For an exhibition at ten o'clock in the morning, The Haig would get out of bed at his customary hour of 6.00 am, a habit he picked up as a country boy, and then lounge around for maybe three hours. When he was positive he couldn't be on time, he would have his tuxedo unpacked by his combination valet-chauffeur-caddie, a man from Los Angeles named Clark "Spec" Hammond, who would then roll it into a ball and throw it repeatedly against the wall to make it look as though The Haig had worn it all night. So dressed, The Haig would leap out of his Packard or Bentley, or whatever Spec happened to be driving for him that week, and trot to the first tee. Then he'd remove his coat, barrel into a tee shot, and walk down the fairway as though he had just bought the place. By the time his opponents got their minds back to golf, The Haig would order drinks for the house, at least a dozen of which would end up in his hands and most of which he would surreptitiously pour into a jardinière or a toilet. The heavy drinking came later, after the 11 major titles had been safely stashed away.

Technically, what made The Haig such a great player had always been a mystery. He was a terrible driver, neither long nor straight. His iron play was surpassed by at least a dozen of his contemporaries. He was an atrocious bunker player who admitted he was scared to death of sand. As a putter, he was superb, but not, from what I have heard, as great as Walter J. Travis or, from what I saw, as Bobby Locke. Every pro three-putts now and then, some have been known to four-putt, and a few have putted clear off a green. Incongruously for so renowned a putter, though, The Haig may have been the first and only pro of any kind to have jabbed a putt clear out-of-bounds.

What set The Haig apart from everybody before him, if not after him, was a unique knack for getting the ball in the hole some way, somehow, at sometime when you least expected it. You couldn't chalk it up to luck, because he invented and then perfected shots that had never occurred to the tradition-minded pros he played against. In those days before the wedge, every pro played the pitch-and-run shot now and then from, say, 30 yards out. At that distance, The Haig was known to cheat the wind by using his putter – a "Texas wedge" nobody from Texas has ever had the nerve to try. He once explained to me several ways of getting out of sand he had developed to take the place of that hairy blast with a niblick.

Between the First World War and the Second, The Haig was the best-known golfer in the world personally, not excluding Bobby Jones who seldom socialised with anybody other than his Atlanta cronies and who otherwise preferred the company of straight-arrow businessmen. The Haig hobnobbed with everybody: Babe Ruth, Al Johnson, Grantland Rice, A.D. Lasker, Oliver Hardy, Clarence Budington Kelland, Marshall Field, Jack Dempsey, Harold Lloyd, Ring Lardner, Charlie Chaplin, Warren Harding, Eugene Grace, the Prince of Wales. He didn't so much prefer their company as they did his, and as we drove in his car from Cadillac to Grand Rapids I began to wonder why.

Certainly, it wasn't for his sense of humour. Despite the slapstick life he led, The Haig was not verbally a funny man, his humour consisting mainly of embarrassing puns and practical jokes that never seemed to come off. At a dinner party in New York once, he was introduced to Ernestine Schumann-Heink, the famous contralto from the Metropolitan Opera. The Haig, who had never heard of her nor, surely, she of him, took one look at Mme Schumann-Heink's ample boson and pulled off what he thought was a jewel of a *bon mot*. "My dear," he said, "did you ever stop to think what a lovely bunker you would make?"

On the occasion of his son's twenty-first birthday, to give another example, The Haig sent him a cable from Rangoon made up of stock messages that was 21 pages long. Unfortunately, Junior had only turned twenty.

About half an hour outside of Grand Rapids, I asked The Haig who had known him best out of all the hundreds of people who considered themselves his friend. He thought for a while, and then thought some more, until I began to think he hadn't heard me. Finally, he spoke up. The names he gave me were of a retired milkman back in hometown Rochester, a car dealer in his adopted city of Detroit, and Spec Hammond. "Pretty soon," he added, "it might be you."

We eventually did become close enough to hug one another, although we mutually decided to drop the book project. (True to form, a woman got him to spill the beans in three months.) When The Haig died in 1969, Junior called me from Detroit to tell me there would be no funeral. Instead, a bunch of his cronies were going to throw a party at the Detroit Athletic Club. They thought The Haig would prefer that.

I didn't go. Like Hamlet, golf's sweet prince, I thought, deserved a grander exit than that. He was splendid. They should have carried him out on a shield.

STRENGTH OF MIND

Herbert Warren Wind

In the 1960s, when Bobby Jones was confined to a wheelchair, the word went round each winter that his condition had become worse, and everyone in golf speculated on whether he would be able to attend that year's Masters. He had suffered from heart trouble since 1952, and now that, too, became increasingly debilitating. Somehow he got to Augusta each April, though by then his body has so wasted away that he weighed scarcely 90 pounds. His arms were no bigger around than a broomstick, and he could no longer open his fingers to shake hands or grasp a pen. Yet this indomitable man kept going. For many years on the day before the start of the Masters, I called in on him in company with Ed Miles, of the Atlanta *Journal*, and Al Laney, of the New York *Herald Tribune*, who was one of his oldest and closest friends. We would walk over to Jones's cottage, near the 10th tee, torn by mixed feelings – the prospect of pleasure and the prospect of sorrow.

Mrs Jones or their son Bob or his wife, Frances, would be there to greet us. There would be a few cordially jumbled minutes during which personal news was exchanged and it was computed how many people wanted Coca-Cola and whether they wanted it in a glass or out of the bottle. But this time, Jones would have appeared and would be contriving a seating arrangement that enabled him to see everyone. He never looked as bad as you dreaded he might. While his body had withered to nothing, his handsome head and features remained relatively untouched, and his mind was as good as ever. We would ask him all sorts of questions we had stored up about new golfers and old tournaments, and he would answer them with amusement and flair. You could listen to him all day; he had the same feeling for words as Adlai Stevenson, and the same wonderful self-deprecatory sense of humour. Inevitably, as the session continued you became aware that you and your friends were doing all the talking – telling Jones what you had been up to and what you thought about this and that. Jones did not bring this about by any conscious technique; he simply was extremely interested in what his friends were doing, and you felt this interest. Leaving was always hard. When he put his twisted folded-up hand in yours as you said goodbye, you never knew whether you would be seeing him again. Each year when Miles and Laney and I left the cottage, we would walk 75 yards or so – nearly to the practice green – before we exchanged a word. My God, we felt good at that moment! We were so proud of Bob Jones! There was no need to feel sorry for a man like that. If *he* could rise above his misfortune *you* could jolly well rise above his misfortune. I think that everyone who called on him responded this way.

Jones did not like his friends to talk about his illness, and they honoured his wishes as best they could. However, in writing to him shortly after the 1968 Masters to ask a favour of him, I mentioned in closing how sorry I was that he had not been well enough to go out on the course in his golf-cart and watch some of the play, as he usually did, and to attend the presentation ceremony, at which he customarily presided. In his reply, which I received the following week, he wrote, after dealing with the main subject:

Really, I am not as far down the well physically as I appeared to be in Augusta. I picked up an intestinal virus a week or ten days before the Masters and could not shake the thing, even with a course of antibiotics. Even with that, I could perhaps have done a bit more than I did. Had I known in time that the scorecard episode was going to be present, I most certainly would have appeared at the presentation, both on television and on the putting green. This happened to be the one time that I felt I should have lent the weight of whatever authority I possess to these occasions.

From that paragraph, one would have assumed that, the virus past, Jones was now back in the pink of condition.

A few days later, I received another letter from Jones. The scorecard episode he had referred to in the first note was, of course, the one involving Roberto de Vicenzo and Bob Goalby in the Masters that year. Goalby and de Vicenzo had apparently finished the tournament in a tie with totals of 277. However, de Vicenzo's playing partner, Tommy Aaron, had written down a four, and not the three that de Vicenzo had made, as his score on the 17th; de Vicenzo had signed the card; and, under rule 38, paragraph 3, de Vicenzo had to be charged with the four. This gave him a total of 278, and Goalby was declared the winner. In my account of the tournament, I had attacked rule 38 as a bad rule. Jones had this to say:

> I find myself differing with you in your stand on the propriety of rule 38 under modern conditions. You make the point that in an event like the Masters, with hundreds of spectators at each hole and millions more watching on television, everybody knows the score.
>
> You may recall that on two occasions in Open Championship play, I ordered a stroke added to my score. In both instances, there were several hundred spectators around the green and, in each case, I had a scorer or marker, in addition to my playing companion. Both these men on both occasions were standing within 15 feet of me. Yet each time I had to call the marker's attention to the extra stroke; and on one occasion this gentleman went so far as to appeal to the committee after the round, affirming that my ball had not moved. There is scarcely any way the spectators around the green and no way the viewers on television could know that de Vicenzo had not inadvertently moved his ball and reported the fact to Aaron between the 17th green and the 18th tee . . .
>
> Believe me, I was thinking not only of de Vicenzo but of Goalby as well. Whereas de Vicenzo was the player penalised, both men were deprived of the opportunity to win the tournament to outright competition. This was as bad for one as for the other.
>
> The whole situation was tragic beyond expression. I like to think, though, that it serves one useful purpose in emphasising the respect which golfers must have for the rule book.

I find it pleasant to quote from these letters, because they so vividly evoke Jones's personality and his manner of expressing himself. He must have been one of the great letter writers of our time. Whenever one wrote to him – and my guess is that literally hundreds of people, from Sarazen, his exact contemporary, to youngsters just starting competitive golf, did so quite regularly – he answered very promptly and with obvious thought and care. It is an understatement to say that the arrival of a letter on the distinctive heavy bond stationery he used, with its familiar Poplar Street letterhead, could make your day.

While I gather from medical authorities that it would be wrong to credit Jones with living on for years after the average person would have picked up his ball and torn up his scorecard – how long anyone lives is not necessarily dictated by his will to live, they say – Jones deserves incalculable credit for how he lived out his life. Where he got the courage and energy to do all that he did there is no knowing. However, I think that Hogan put his finger on at least a part of the answer when he said, shortly after Jones's death, "The man was sick so long, and fought it so successfully, that I think we have finally discovered the secret of Jones's success. It was the strength of his mind."

About three days before Jones's death, when he knew he was dying, he said to the members of his family, "If this is all there is to it, it sure is peaceful." That is good to know. We were lucky we had Jones so long, for he had a rare gift for passing ideas and ideals on to other people. I think he probably enriched more lives than anyone else I have known. He enriched mine beyond measure.

BROADCAST ON THE DEATH OF VARDON

J.H. Taylor

By the death of Harry Vardon, the game of golf has lost one of its greatest friends and I, and many hundreds of others, a dear and valued friend. We had known each other for over 40 years. We both made our début in the Open Championship in the same year, 1893 at Prestwick. That is a long time ago and Vardon and I have been associated as servants of the game for nearly the whole of our lives.

Vardon, as is known, learned his golf in Jersey, a favoured spot for the development of skilful players. I am often asked whom I consider to be the best golfer I ever saw, and with a lifetime of experience behind me and having seen many of the great players in the last 50 years, I give it as my mature and considered judgement that Vardon was the greatest of them all.

His style was so apparently simple that it was apt to mislead. He got his effects with that delightful effortless ease that was tantalising. It is a legend of the game that Vardon was never off the centre of any fairway in two years of play. I can scarcely subscribe to this but I do say without fear of contradiction that Vardon played fewer shots out of the rough than anyone who has ever swung a golf club.

If the test of a player be that he makes fewer bad shots than the remainder then I give Vardon the palm. He hit the ball with the centre of every club with greater frequency than any other player. In this most difficult feat lay his strength.

In addition to his wonderful skills, Harry Vardon will be remembered as long as the game lasts as one of the most courteous and delightful opponents there could ever be. I have good reason to appreciate this because Vardon and I, in the pursuit of our calling, met some hundreds of times and although I was generally unsuccessful I give it to him that when I was fortunate enough to win he gave me the fullest possible credit.

Another tribute I should like to make to my old friend. Throughout the years I knew him, I never heard him utter one disparaging remark about another player. He was at all times most anxious with his help and advice. Allied to his magnificent show, Harry Vardon will be always remembered as one of the most kindly souls who ever existed and to know him was to love him.

THE TRIUMVIRATE

Bernard Darwin

There is a natural law in games by which, periodically, a genius arises and sets the standard of achievement perceptibly higher than ever before. He forces the pace; the rest have to follow as best they can, and end by squeezing out of themselves just a yard or two more then they would have believed possible.

During the last year or two we have seen this law at work in billiards. Lindrum has set up a new standard in scoring power and our players, in trying to live up to him, have excelled their old selves. The same thing has happened from time to time in golf, and those whom we call the Triumvirate undoubtedly played their part in the "speeding up" of the game.

Taylor, though by a few months the youngest of the three, was the first to take the stage, and it has always been asserted that he first made people realise what was possible in combined boldness and accuracy in playing the shots up to the pin. Anything in the nature of safety play in approaching became futile when there was a man who could play brassey shots to the flag in the manner of mashie shots. Mr Hilton has suggested that this raising of the standard really began earlier and was due to another great Englishman, Mr John Ball. It may well be so, for it is hard to imagine anything bolder or straighter than that great golfer's shots to the green, but Taylor, being the younger man and coming later, burst on a much larger golfing world than had Mr Ball. Moreover, he was a professional who played here, there and everywhere, and so was seen by a large number of golfers, whereas the great amateur, except at championship times, lay comparatively hidden at Hoylake. Time was just ripe when Taylor appeared: golf was "booming" and the hour and the man synchronised. Though in the end he failed in his first championship at Prestwick, he had done enough to show that he was going to lead golfers a dance to such a measure as they had not yet attempted. In the next year he won, and for two years after that the world struggled to keep up with him as best it could.

Then there arose somebody who could even improve on Taylor. This was Harry Vardon, who tied with him in the third year of his reign (1896) and beat him on playing off. There was an interval of one more year before the really epoch-making character of Vardon was appreciated. Then he won his second championship in 1898 and was neither to hold nor to bind. He devastated the country in a series of triumphal progresses and, as in the case of Lindrum, there was no doubt that a greater than all before him had come. To the perfect accuracy of Taylor he added a perceptible something more of power and put the standard higher by at least one peg.

And, it may be asked, did Braid have no effect? I hardly think he did in the same degree though he was such a tremendous player. He took longer to mature than did his two contemporaries. Of all men he seemed intended by nature to batter the unresponsive guttie to victory, and he won one championship with a guttie, but his greatest year, his real period of domination, came with the rubber core. He cannot be said to have brought in a new epoch except to this extent perhaps, that he taught people to realise that putting could be learned by hard toil. He disproved the aphorism that putting is an inspiration for, after having been not far short of an execrable putter, he made himself, during his conquering period, into as effective a putter as there was in the country. By doing so he brought new hope to many who had thought that a putter must be born, not made, and had given it up as a bad job.

Presumably everybody thinks that his own youth was spent in the golden age, and that the figures of that period were more romantic than those of any other. At any rate I can claim romance and to spare for my early years of grown-up golf, for I went up to Cambridge in 1894 and that was the year of Taylor's first win at Sandwich. Moreover, the Triumvirate were then, I am sure, far more towering figures in the public eye than are their successors of today. It was their good fortune to have no rivals from beyond the sea. They were indisputably the greatest in the world. Then, too, they had so few ups and downs. Today a professional is in the limelight one year and in almost the dreariest of shade the next, but these three, by virtue of an extraordinary consistency, always clustered round the top. Finally their zenith was the zenith of the exhibition match. They were constantly playing against one another and no matter on what mud-heap they met, the world really cared which of them won.

It is partly no doubt because I was in the most hero-worshipping stage of youth (I have never wholly emerged from it), but it is also largely due to the personalities of those great players that I can remember quite clearly the first occasion on which I saw each of them. It is a compliment my memory can pay to very few others. Taylor I first saw at Worlington (better, perhaps, known as Mildenhall) when he came almost in the first flush of his champion's honours, to play Jack White, who was then the professional there. I can see one or two shots that he played that day just as clearly as any that I have watched in the thirty-seven years since. I had seen several good Scottish professionals play before that, including my earliest hero, Willie Fernie, most graceful and dashing of golfers. I thought I knew just what a professional style was like, but here was something quite new to me. Here was a man who seemed to play his driver after the manner of a mashie. There was no tremendous swing, no glorious follow-through. Jack White, with his club, in those days, sunk well home into the palm of his right hand, was the traditional free Scottish slasher. He was driving the ball as I imagined driving. Taylor was altogether different and his style reminded me of a phrase in the *Badminton* book, which I knew by heart, about Jamie Anderson and his "careless little switch". One has grown used to J.H. long since, but the first view of him was intensely striking, and I am inclined to think that in his younger days he stood with his right foot more forward than he does now, so that the impression of his playing iron shots with his driver was the more marked. He was not appallingly long, but he was appallingly straight, and he won a very fine match at the 35th hole. Incidentally, the memory of that game makes me realise how much the rubber-cored ball has changed golf. The first hole at Worlington was much what it is today, except that the green was the old one on the right. Now the aspiring Cambridge undergraduate calls it a two-shot hole and is disappointed with a five there. On that day – to be sure it was against a breeze – Taylor and Jack White took three wooden club shots apiece to reach the outskirts of the green, and Taylor with a run up and a putt won it in five against six.

My first sight of Vardon came next. It was on his own course at Ganton, whither I went for the day from Whitby, and he had just won his first championship. He was playing an ordinary game and I only saw one or two shots, including his drive to the 1st hole. Two memories vividly remain. One was that he was wearing trousers and that from that day to this I have never seen him play except in knickerbockers, an attire which he first made fashionable amongst his brother professionals. The other is that his style seemed, as had Taylor's on a first view, entirely unique. The club appeared, contrary to all orthodox teaching, to be lifted up so very straight. Even now, when I have seen him play hundreds and hundreds of shots, I cannot quite get it out of my head that he did in those early days take up the club a little more abruptly than he did later. The ball flew away very high, with an astonishing ease, and he made the game look more magical and unattainable than anyone I had ever seen. For that matter, I think he does so still. In view of later events it is curious to recall that a good local amateur, Mr Broadwood, who was playing with him, talked then of his putting as the most heartbreaking part of his game, and said that he holed everything. I only saw one putt and that he missed.

It must have been a year later that there came the first vision of the third member of the Triumvirate, who had hardly then attained that position. This was at Penarth, where there was a Welsh championship meeting, and Taylor and Herd were to play an exhibition match. Taylor could not come; at the last moment Braid was sent for to take his place and arrived late the night before. I remember that he did in his youthful energy what I feel sure he has not done for a long time now; he went out early after breakfast to have a look at the course and play some practice shots. His enemy, by the way, had come a whole day early and played a couple of rounds. I have almost entirely forgotten the

Penarth course, and the shots I played on it myself; the only thing I can vaguely remember is the look of the 1st hole and of Braid hitting those shots towards it. Here was something much more in the manner that one had been brought up to believe orthodox, but with an added power; save for Mr Edward Blackwell, with whom I had once had the honour of playing, I had never seen anyone hit so malignantly hard at the ball before. Mr Hutchinson's phrase about his "divine fury" seemed perfectly apposite. One imagined that there was a greater chance of some error on an heroic scale than in the case of Taylor and Vardon, and so indeed there was, but I remember no noble hooks that day, nothing but a short putt or two missed when he had a winning lead so that Herd crept a little nearer to him.

From the time when I was at Cambridge till I sold my wig in 1908, my golfing education was neglected for, if I may so term it, my legal one. I played all the golf I could, which was a good deal, but watched hardly any. Therefore I never – sad to say – saw Vardon in his most dominating era, nor the great foursome match over four different courses in which he and Taylor crushed Braid and Herd, chiefly through one terrific landslide of holes at Troon. However, in the end I managed to see each of the three win two championships, Braid at Prestwick and St Andrews in 1908 and 1910, Taylor at Deal and Hoylake, 1909 and 1913, Vardon at Sandwich and Prestwick, 1911 and 1914. I suppose the most exciting was in 1914 when Vardon and Taylor, leading the field, were drawn together on the last day, and the whole of the West of Scotland was apparently moved with a desire to watch them. Braid, too, played his part on that occasion, for had he not designed the bunker almost in the middle of the fairway at the 4th hole? And was it not fear of that bunker that drove Taylor too much to the right into the other one by the Pow Burn, so that he took a seven? No wonder J.H. said that the man who made that bunker should be buried in it with a niblick through his heart. Yes, that was a tremendous occasion, and Braid's golf in 1908 – 291 with an eight in it at the Cardinal – was incredibly brilliant; and Vardon's driving when he beat Massy in playing off the tie at Sandwich was, I think, the most beautiful display of wooden club hitting I ever saw; but for sheer thrilling quality give me Taylor at Hoylake in 1913. There was no great excitement since, after qualifying by the skin of his teeth, he won by strokes and strokes; but I have seen nothing else in golf which so stirred me and made me want to cry. The wind and the rain were terrific, but not so terrific as Taylor, with his cap pulled down, buffeting his way through them. There are always one or two strokes which stick faster in the memory than any others, and I noticed the other day that my friend Mr Macfarlane recalled just the one that I should choose. It was the second shot played with a cleek to the Briars hole in the very teeth of the storm. I can still see Taylor standing on rocklike feet, glued flat on the turf, watching that ball as it whizzes over the two cross bunkers straight for the green. There never was such a cleek shot; there never will be such another as long as the world stands.

It is surely a curious fact that, though these three players dominated golf for so long, and the golfer is essentially an imitative animal, no one of them has been the founder of a school. They made people play better by having to live up to their standard, but they did not make people play like them. Here are three strongly marked and characteristic styles to choose from, and yet where are their imitators? Vardon had one, to be sure, in Mr A.C. Lincoln, an excellent player who belonged to Totteridge; he had at any rate many of the Vardonian mannerisms and a strong superficial likeness. There is George Duncan, too, with a natural talent for mimicry; he remodelled the swing he had learned in Scotland after he first saw the master. Imagine Duncan slowed down and there is much of Vardon. Beyond those two, I can think of no one in the least like him. It is the same with Taylor. His two sons, J.H., Jnr and Leslie, have something of the tricks of the backswing, but nobody has got the flat-footed hit and the little grunt that goes with it. Braid, with that strange combination of a portentous gravity and a sudden, furious lash, seems the most impossible model of all. I know no one who has even copied his waggle, with that little menacing shake of the clubhead in the middle of it. Each of the three was so unlike the other two that the world hesitated which model to take and ended by taking none. American players look as if they had all been cast in one admirable mould. Ours look as if they came out of innumerable different ones, and as if in nearly every mould there had been some flaw. It was part of the fascination of the Triumvirate that each was extraordinarily individual, but now it seems almost a pity for British golf. If only just one of them could have been easier to imitate! In other respects, of course, they did all three of them leave a model which could be imitated. By all the good golfing qualities of courage and sticking power and chivalry, by their modesty and dignity and self-respect, they helped to make the professional golfer a very different person from what he was when they first came on the scene. Their influence as human beings has been as remarkable as their achievements as golfers.

LORD NELSON AFTER
PEARL HARBOR

Al Barkow

During the Second World War, the British dug wide trenches across the fairways of many of their golf courses to keep German aircraft from using them as landing strips. And because German bombers would sometimes attack golfers at play, a set of war rules was drawn up. One allowed that "in competition during or while the bombs are falling, players may take cover without penalty for ceasing to play." Good show. Not all the rules were as lenient, though. "A player whose stroke is affected by the simultaneous explosion of a bomb or shell, or by machine-gun fire, may play another ball from the same place. *Penalty, one stroke.*" Gee, guys.

Golf in the United States, much farther from the harsh realities of the war, did not go to such extremes, but there were definite cutbacks. The USGA cancelled the official US Open from 1942 through 1945. However, if you ask Ben Hogan how many US Opens he won, his answer will be a curt, unequivocal "five". He won four official national opens, but in June 1942 the USGA, in conjunction with the Chicago District Golf Association and the PGA did mount a tournament to raise money for the war and called it the Hale America National Open. It was played in Chicago on the Ridgemoor Country Club course, which was not at all representative of US Open courses, but Hogan counts it a US Open. He won it.

Hogan had one round of 62 in the tournament, the next day the course-proud members had their greenskeeper cut the holes into any little knobs he could find on the greens. Hogan then shot 72. By the way, the Hale in Hale America is not an incorrect spelling. The tournament also promoted a national health programme backed by John Kelly, father of actress Grace and Olympic rowing champion Jack. So Hale America, the *double entendre* an appropriate accident. There was also an auction after the event, the money going to charity. Hogan's putter fetched something around $1500.

The USGA also suggested that, for the Duration, golf clubs turn portions of the rough on their courses into victory gardens. Could it be that from this such terms as *spinach, broccoli,* and *cabbage* became popular for off-fairway grass? Maybe not, since few clubs followed up on the idea.

As for the PGA and the tour, from 1943 through 1945 there was no count kept of total annual purse money, and the official record lists those years as "No Tour". But the people played golf, and there was a tour. . .of sorts. The government encouraged Ed Dudley, President of PGA at the time, to keep the professional game alive, as a diversion from the war effort for the workers, by getting pros to play exhibitions at military hospitals and by staging tournaments to spur war-bond drives. Purses were paid out in war bonds. In addition, the equipment manufacturers, under their blanket organisation (The Athletic Institute), put $20,000 into the tournament bureau in 1944 and 1945, $25,000 in 1946. The tour fire was kept flickering. Gas rationing kept the tournament schedule somewhat contained and limited, but it was something.

In one wartime event, the Knoxville Open, only 18 pros entered. The prize list called for 20 money places, so those who played were assured of getting some of the "cheese", as Tommy Bolt calls it. All they had to do was finish – a sure thing. But there is no such thing, right? Lefty Stackhouse had entered this Knoxville Open and played the last round after a sleepless night. By the 9th hole, he was wavering like a thin reed in a hurricane. Fred Corcoran had brought Sergeant Alvin York, the First World War hero, out to the course, and when York, who had never seen golf played before, saw Stackhouse, he said to Corcoran, "I had no idea golf was such a strenuous game." Anyway, Corcoran told Stack to go into the clubhouse and have a nap, then come out to finish his round so he could pick up his war bond. But Lefty never saw the light of that day again, and finished out of the money. Incredible!

Almost all the top US tournament pros went into military service, but there was no mass enlistment of pros in the cause of peace, as there had been in Britain during the First World War. Ed Oliver was the first well-known US pro to be drafted. Jimmy Thomson, the man who once hit a golf ball over 600 yards in two blows, entered the Coast Guard. The Navy got Demaret, Snead, Lew Worsham, and Herman Keiser. Lloyd Mangrum, Jim Turnesa, Vic Ghezzi, Dutch Harrison, Jim Ferrier, Clayton Heafner, Horton Smith and Ben Hogan were in the Army. Craig Wood was rejected because of a back injury sustained in an auto accident, Harold McSpaden because of sinusitis, and Byron Nelson because of a form of haemophilia.

As most name athletes generally do in the military, the majority of the pros stayed Stateside and were in Special Services, which is the military euphemism for playing golf with the generals. Jimmy Demaret was candid enough to say that he never got out of Sherman's, which was not a tank but a favourite bar in San Diego. Hogan and Smith were together in Army Air Force Officer Candidate School, in Miami Beach. They did drills on a golf course levelled for the purpose, but also found time to practise and play their golf. Lieutenant Hogan later served for a time as officer in charge of Army rehabilitation at the Miami-Biltmore hotel-golf-course complex. A bit of good luck in that assignment location. Hogan, Smith, Demaret, Snead, and others eventually got away to play in a few war-bond tournaments.

Five name pros went overseas: Keiser, Ghezzi, Heafner, Smith, and Mangrum. Mangrum was the only one to see real combat. He was wounded in the Battle of the Bulge and received the Purple Heart. No one will ever know how many potential Sneads and Hogans were lost in the war. The others undoubtedly missed some valuable time for their playing careers, but golf is a game that can be played at top efficiency for many more years than most games, and maturity often makes players even better performers. While Hogan was the tour's leading money winner from 1940 through '42, he did not win his first *official* US Open until after the war, in 1948. Over all, none of the top pros lost peak years as did Ted Williams, for example, and they could not really complain of severe deprivations as a result of their military stints.

During the war years, though, professional baseball, and even football, which was not yet the new national game, could weather the Duration with less talented athletes or retired greats on the rosters, since they had a broader, deeper base of public interest. The St Louis Browns had a one-armed outfielder, Peter Gray, and I recall seeing the fabled Bronko Nagurski play some football for the Chicago Bears and batter a goal post with one of his thunderous charges. Golf, however, was not that well fixed in the public mind, and even the periodic appearances of Hogan, Demaret, and Snead could not be enough to sustain interest in the game. The game and the tour needed, as they always seem to periodically, war or not, dramatic exposure to keep them from taking six steps backward. The drama would require an electric personality, or someone who could make 18 straight holes in one. And, as it also always seems to happen in and for golf, there came Byron Nelson to keep golf and the tour on display. Indeed, Nelson would twice be named Athlete of the Year, in 1944 and 1945.

Nelson was not an electric personality. He was tall, expressionless, usually wore a white tennis visor, and always wore plain clothes. Neither did he make 18 aces in a row. But he did accomplish something almost as unreal. In 1945 he won 11 straight professional tournaments. For the entire year he won 19 times. These records are not ever likely to be equalled, much less broken. That is always a dangerous prediction, but I'll bet it holds. The years of the Second World War, in any case, belonged to Lord Byron Nelson of Texasshire.

Competitive records in sport made when a game is going through a format change, such as an extended baseball season or the depletion of the quantity of talent and the quality of competition by the war, tend to get qualifying asterisks. The * is a favorite conceit among purists, who can be rather arbitrary. For example, when Roger Maris broke Babe Ruth's season home-run mark, his achievement was studded with a star – he played in more games. But has anyone seen Ruth's original record of 60 qualified by the fact that he was hitting the first "live" baseball? A ball, by the way, purposely goosed up so he could belt more round-trippers. So, records are often as much emotional as they are cold figures in a book, and Byron Nelson's skein of triumphs has invariably been qualified, if not with the ink-spot star, then with a diminishing pause in the minds of many.

The conditions placed on Nelson's run begin with the fact that he played against a grab bag of mediocre golfers. Then, too, he played those "dubs" on many short, fast-running roughless golf courses. Not only that; in a couple of instances Nelson played winter rules, which allowed him to move his ball onto a piece of good grass for fairway shots.

All is true, but the asterisks need exclamation points, nevertheless. His golf was just too good. Byron Nelson was one sweet and great golfer. Standing over six feet, Nelson took a swing that made maximum use of his height. It was straight up and down, his body not turning so much as moving laterally, an unusual action that has not often been seen. At impact he made a little dip of his knees, as most tall players do. Nelson once told me that a golfer cannot stand too close to the ball. . .before he hits it. I tried it for a season, getting up close to the ball at address, and hit my shots straighter than at any time in my checkered playing history.

The position forces an upright swing with the hands and arms remaining in close to the body, thus making them less apt to stray out of position. It is difficult to deviate from the swing plane. This position also produces a cramped feeling, however, one that brings a fear of, and sometimes a shockingly real, shank. Nelson himself occasionally slipped into this most discouraging of golf errors, known among those frightened by just the word as a lateral. Except for those rare lapses, Nelson was an incredibly straight hitter. He hit "frozen ropes", the ball seldom moving from right to left in flight or vice versa, unless he willed it so. He was not exceptionally long off the tee, but, like all great golfers, he had an extra fifteen yards on call when he needed it. He could also summon up the rest of his game when required. In an early round of a PGA Championship match against Mike Turnesa, Turnesa had Byron down by four holes with five to play. Mike played those last five holes in one under par, and lost the match one down. Nelson finished with four birdies and an eagle. He went on to win the Championship.

Through Nelson's entire 1945 record run of victories, and even including the times he didn't win (he was second seven times, never worse than ninth), Byron averaged 68.33 strokes for a single round of golf. When he was 33, Byron played 121 rounds in the year, usually the last 36 holes in one day, which gives him high grades for endurance alone. By contrast, in 1972 the 23-year-old Lee Trevino played 101 rounds of golf, 18 holes a day, and had a scoring average of 70.89. In one stretch of 19 rounds, Nelson was under 70 every time. Say what you will about courses, preferred lies, and all the rest, anyone who has ever made a serious attempt at the personal, inner-directed, inner-motivated game of golf will understand the magnitude of Nelson's performance.

The courses Nelson played were admittedly not up to the standards of difficulty of those played on the circuit now, but neither were they conditioned as today's velveteen carpets of grass are, and some allowance must be given Nelson for that. As for the winter rules, Charles Price, the keen-eyed American golf writer-historian, recalls that when Nelson did have the advantage of the preferred-lies rule he made the most minimal use of it, never moving the ball more than a turn or two from its original position to get it into playable turf, and then only with the clubhead, not with the hand. This in contrast to many who play field hockey with club and ball, not only improving the lie of the ball on the ground, but the angle of approach to the green as well. That's called Creative Rules Interpretation. Nelson didn't need it.

Byron's main competition in the first years of the war came from Harold "Jug" McSpaden, a prognathous Kansan who wore sunglasses, changed his clothes three times a day, and hit a powerful, controlled slide. He and Byron were longtime friends who travelled together and played as partners in four-ball tournaments. In a *Saturday Evening Post* article McSpaden by-lined in 1947, entitled "Nuts to Tournament Golf", the pro said that "the glittering cavalcade of tournaments made you famous but left you broke in spirit and poor in purse. . . . In 1944 I received $18,000 in war bonds. When I cashed them in I cleared $134.55."

McSpaden also had due cause to be broken in spirit. He once shot a couple of 64s in the closing rounds of a tournament and finished second . . . to Nelson. McSpaden's claim to fame, in fact, is being runner-up to Byron during the war years tournaments, which is always a demoralising situation. At the beginning, Jug gave Nelson solid challenge. When Byron didn't win, McSpaden did. Through one set of 10 tournaments, Nelson was 60 under par and Jug 69 below. McSpaden's touch waned after that, and over all he was never a real threat in championship competition, although he did win some 17 tournaments. He and Byron were called the Gold Dust Twins, but McSpaden saw more dust than gold.

Aside from McSpaden, when Nelson made his Electrifying Eleven and captured the sports pages, no less a player than Sam Snead was a regular on the tour. Snead had been discharged from the Navy with a slipped vertebra, but that did not hamper his golf. Sam won five times during the 1945 season, was 21 under par in winning the Pensacola Open, and beat Nelson in a play-off for the Gulfport Open. During a midsummer break in the tournament schedule, Snead and Nelson played a "World's Best Golfer" match – head to head at stroke-play, then match-play. Snead won the 36 holes of stroke-play by one shot, then the next day Nelson took Snead in the 36-hole match-play segment, winning 4 and 3. Snead broke his wrist playing baseball later that summer and did not compete in the last three of Nelson's streak of 11, or in the remainder of the year's tournaments.

But by the end of that summer Ben Hogan was discharged, and with a public expression of vengeance at having missed a couple of years of regular tournament golf, and some prideful jealousy of Nelson's having taken over as the king of pro golf, Ben got his game geared up quickly. In the 1945 Portland Open, Hogan set a new PGA scoring record of 261 with rounds of 65, 69, 63, and 64. You would have to say that Lieutenant Hogan was doing a bit more than returning salutes while in the Army. Nelson had been playing an exceptional amount of golf that year, which can be wearying and damaging to a man's game, and for all his physical size, he was never a robust man. Yet, two weeks after Portland, Byron found the energy to break Hogan's mark with rounds of 62, 68, 63 and 66, totalling 259, with Hogan in the field. This score was made on a par-70 course, while Hogan had scored on a par-72 layout, but it was nevertheless brilliant golf. In short, golf tournaments usually become contests between two, three, or four of the best players in the field, particularly when such as Hogan and Snead are in the group. And

Nelson won often with these two of the best players the game has had against him and playing quite well.

Finally, Nelson was not just a slightly-better-than-average golfer taking advantage of a situation. Byron was already an established champion before he went on his rampage. He won the Masters in 1937 and won it again in 1942, before most of the other golfers went into the military. In 1939 he won the US, Western, and North–South Opens plus some lesser tournaments. He won the PGA crown in 1940 and again in 1945. Almost all his major victories came before anyone was off to the other war.

John Byron Nelson, Jnr began in golf as a 10-year-old caddie in Fort Worth, Texas. Ben Hogan was a fellow bag packer, and the two once tied for the caddie championship at Glen Garden Country Club. Many years later, when asked to compare himself with Hogan, who had actually turned pro six months before him, Byron said that he was simply more fortunate than Ben: he did not have to work as hard to perfect his golf. By the grace of gods, or something, he had it sooner. Nelson turned pro in 1932, won $12.50 during his first ride on the tournament circuit, quit in something close to despair to seek another line of work, but came back to golf in 1934 to make some high finishes in winter-tour events. He took an assistant-pro post with George Jacobus, in New Jersey, and in 1936 won the Metropolitan Open, then a fairly big-time event.

Throughout most of his career, Nelson would be called by others and himself a club pro who played tournaments. Perhaps the chauvinistic influence of George Jacobus had a part in this, because Byron played an awful lot of tournaments. In any case, Nelson did become one of the most articulate "professors" of the golf swing, and has been credited with forming the considerable talent of Ken Venturi, a one-time US Open champion, and Frank Stranahan, the outstanding amateur who won against the pros.

Nelson's ability to transmit golf instruction has never come through on televised golf, which he came to announce, but it was no fault of his own. When given fifteen seconds to "analyse" a golf swing, which cannot be adequately broken down in a month of Sundays, Nelson has been reduced to reminding everyone to "clear the left side in the swing". One gets the impression that if a golfer does not clear his left side, he can't play on television.

In the end, Byron Nelson made history, important history, for the tour, which had the good fortune of a remarkable talent coming, as it were, to the tour's rescue. As the war wound down and concluded, the nation was prepared to go on a cathartic spending and recreation binge. Much of that would be channelled into golf, and while Byron Nelson alone cannot be credited with the boom that came to golf after 1945, he did keep the channel clear, the lighthouse beacon burning, and made the passage to bigger and better things for the pros to come more navigable.

COTTON: THE IMMORTAL

Peter Dobereiner

Yesterday's heroes soon fade from the public consciousness. Their fame degenerates like radio-activity and it takes the combination of a slack news day and an unimaginative sports editor, resulting in one of those "Where are they now?" articles, to produce a bleep of nostalgic recall on the national Geiger counter.

In rare cases sporting fame can be extended beyond its natural span. Henry Cooper is a good example of a sportsman who is as well known today as he was when he was at the height of his boxing career. He has to work at it and these days he is mostly famous for being famous, as a professional celebrity.

In even rarer cases the legend is powerful enough to endure and even grow without any special cultivation by the hero. W.G. Grace and Don Bradman are candidates for this category and in golf Thomas Henry Cotton in an obvious example, along with Young Tom Morris, Harry Vardon and Bobby Jones. Theirs is the nearest state to immortality that man can achieve.

The reasons for Cotton's success can be clearly seen in the events which caused him to take up golf as a profession. His father, George Cotton, was a modestly prosperous iron founder in Holmes Chapel, Cheshire, and when Henry was an infant the business was taken over to accommodate the expanding Crown wallpaper premises.

The family moved to Dulwich. Henry and his brother Leslie were enrolled at Alleyn's School where Henry's main sporting interest was cricket and his ambitions were centred on a career in civil engineering. He was thus embarked on the conventional middle-class track of public school, university, professional qualifications and a comfortable career with cricket and golf as recreational and strictly amateur pursuits.

Then came the incident which shattered that ordered destiny. At the end of an away match the prefects of the Alleyn's XI ordered the plebs of the team to return to the school with the cricket gear. Henry did not take kindly to the chore of humping the bags across London on trams and trains and posted a note that the prefects should do their share of the chores. For this mutinous act he was ordered a prefect's caning. Henry refused to be caned. The sports master decreed that Cotton could not play cricket until he submitted to his punishment and asked him: "What will you do now, Cotton minor?" Henry replied: "In that case I will play golf."

Thus was born Henry Cotton, the anti-hero. It was a role for which he was well fitted by his rebellious nature. He was arrogant, self-opinionated and ruthlessly committed to the proposition that he must be his own man and do things his own way. He was a kind of prototype Geoffrey Boycott (and what a professional golfer he would have made). The big difference was that Henry had charm, a quality which carried him through the hostilities of being a toff in an artisan's world and generated public affection along with the respect which his golf commanded.

He turned pro at 16 and obtained an appointment as junior assistant at Fulwell, a dogsbody job which gave him little chance to play. He moved on to Rye where he had much more scope for his own game and in 1926, aged 19, he was appointed full professional at Langley Park, Beckenham, thanks largely to the sponsorship of Cyril Tolley, the giant of amateur golf.

There were not many tournaments in those days and Cotton played at every possible opportunity. He was making good progress but he was always conscious that his success and his reputation were purely domestic; his ambition demanded that he must test himself against the dominant Americans.

He booked himself a first-class berth on the *Aquitania* (we can add style to charm as major strands in Cotton's character) and scraped together £300 for an onslaught on the United States. In strictly financial terms the tour was not a success. He merely broke even on the trip but in professional terms his visit was a vital element in his education as a golfer.

At this time he had a rather stilted, upright swing which produced a controlled fade. Using his hickory clubs he could not really compete against the power play of the best Americans with their new steel-shafted clubs. Cotton was an avaricious pupil, taking full advantage of the freely offered advice of the friendly American players such as

Tommy Armour and Sam Snead. It was in any case Cotton's practice to analyse the best parts of other people's games and to adapt them to his own use. He remodelled his swing, switching to a flatter arc which gave him a drawing shape to his drives and yards of extra distance. He returned home a better and wiser golfer, ready to command his place in the 1929 Ryder Cup team.

Cotton was constantly at loggerheads with his fellow professionals in the PGA, most of whom considered him to be conceited and standoffish. They had a point because Cotton, following the lead given by the American Walter Hagen, refused to be forced into the mould of the typical pro who was content to be excluded from the clubhouse and generally treated as a servant.

Between them Hagen and Cotton elevated professional golf from a trade to a profession but their ostentatious lifestyle earned them few friends at the time. In Cotton's case the antagonism meant that he was excluded from the next three Ryder Cup teams. Oddly enough, the old-timers such as J.H. Taylor, James Braid and Abe Mitchell approved of the brash young Cotton and encouraged him in his individual approach to golf.

It seemed to Cotton that since he was not becoming a prophet in his own country it would be an astute professional move to establish himself overseas. He took the pro's job at Royal Waterloo, near Brussels, and in 1930 he was invited to tour Argentina with Aubrey Boomer, a trip which was ultimately to add the final element to his apprenticeship for greatness. When he arrived at the Mar del Plata club he discovered that a wealthy young heiress had booked a course of 50 lessons with him. It was a case of antipathy at first sight. He told her brusquely that she would never make a golfer. Maria Isabel found him insufferable. Six years later they were married and their union founded a formidable sporting partnership.

In "Toots", as she was universally known, he found a personality in which ambition, determination and courage more than matched his own. In her case these forces were allied to a fiery Latin temperament which exploded at the slightest provocation. No wife was ever more loyal or more jealous of her husband's reputation. From officious dignitaries to churlish menials, all felt the sting of her lashing fists and rapier tongue. When Cotton publicly criticised his losing Ryder Cup team as captain at Wentworth the newspapers made a big thing of his remarks and Toots tore down the newspaper bills, belabouring the hapless newsagents with her umbrella.

Cotton himself was a frequent victim of her outrage. As the beneficiary of a lucrative contract with Saxones he once dutifully danced with the chairman's wife at Gleneagles. Toots thought he was overdoing the attention, marched on to the floor and punched him on the jaw.

At the Calcot Mixed Foursomes Toots warned Henry that if he drove their ball into the rough she would hit it back at him. Inevitably, Henry eventually hit a drive which rolled into the semi-rough. Toots took her spoon and, to the mystification of the crowd, belted it as hard as she could back towards the tee. Typically, Cotton then hit a brassey shot to within a yard of the flag and Toots holed for a birdie, but she was not mollified. "That's the only way to treat you, Cotton," she snapped.

Wildly extravagant, wildly generous, Toots was both the reason why Cotton had to be successful and the inspiration of his success. The tensions of tournament golf played hell with Cotton's sensitive nature, producing severe problems with the stomach ulcers which were eventually to cause him to be invalided out of the RAF. But with Toots following him every step of every important round he never flinched and never settled for the easy option. He did not dare. They enjoyed a turbulent, blissful marriage until she died on Christmas Day, 1982.

Their one serious conflict ended when Flight Lieutenant Cotton was detailed to march the Roman Catholic contingent to church. He was gently reprimanded at the church by Father Peter Blake SJ for being too regimental in marching his party into the House of God. That meeting began a lifelong friendship and Cotton's conversion to Catholicism.

After the war the Cottons settled in a grand house in Eaton Square and entertained royally. By now he had won three Open championships, had proved himself to be the best golfer in the world and had been honoured with the MBE for his services in raising £50,000 for the Red Cross with golf exhibitions. He had topped the bill at the Coliseum with his golfing act, relegating Nellie Wallace to second billing.

They gradually picked up their gracious pre-war lifestyle, wintering on the Riviera where Cotton commanded what most pros considered to be a king's ransom for teaching and playing with friends such as the Aga Khan. In 1951 he was engaged to suggest remedies for the ailing Mortonhampstead hotel and was even offered the chance to buy it for £21,000. It is a pity that he did not snap up that bargain, for what could have been better for British golf than to have Cotton as legend in residence at his own luxury hotel with its extensive sporting amenities, including a fine golf course.

It was not to be. Taxation drove the Cottons abroad, to another five-star hotel. Cotton designed three courses for Penina, on Portugal's Algarve coast, drawing on all his imagination and experience to convert a water-logged paddy field into one of Europe's most demanding and beautiful championship courses.

Friends and pilgrims arrived to play with the Master, or to have the acutest eye in golf diagnose their faults and exorcise them with his highly individual and effective teaching methods. While serving Beluga caviar and French champagne at £65 a bottle to his friends, Cotton complained that he was financially strapped. His villa and five servants had to go and the Cottons moved into a penthouse suite in the hotel. That way they were saved the embarrassment of having to serve Portuguese champagne.

The life gives him the leisure to write more books, which he does rather well and would do much better if he applied himself to the task with the concentration he once brought to his golf.

Above all he enjoys passing on his knowledge and wisdom to young professionals, exhorting them with such advice as "Never skimp on your meals; it is not an expense but an investment." Henry Cotton is quite a man, well worthy of his legend.

Chapter 3

RECENT

CHAMPIONS

Pat Ward-Thomas

A summer day in 1954 was drawing to its close, and there was a greyness in the evening light, as a great crowd concentrated its pursuit on the last few holes at Birkdale. Peter Thomson was moving towards his first victory in the Open Championship and, as he stood on the 16th tee high up amidst the dunes and willow scrub, he knew his position in relation to the rest of the field. In those days the leaders were not sent out last on the final day, and Scott and Rees had finished some time before with totals of 284. They were enduring that awful vigil, a compound of hope and fear, that comes to those who get their blow in first. For Rees there must have been remorse as well. After a superb attacking stroke to the last hole had run just through the green he had taken three more and so had only tied with Scott. Now Thomson needed to play the last three holes in level fours to beat them, and also to make the task of Locke, who was behind him, almost impossible.

Level fours was in effect par, for the 16th was barely in range of two strokes, the 17th was a short hole, and the 18th required about a medium iron for the second. This made no light task but it would be considerably easier if he could get a four at the 16th, and that is exactly what he did. A long drive, probably the finest he had hit all day, flew past the great guardian dunes far down the fairway. The green, like most of those at Birkdale, gives an impression of gathering the second shot, because it is cloistered in a little dell of its own, but in fact it does not gather. The shot, invariably with a wood, must be unerringly straight, if it is to find the green. Thomson pulled his and it came to rest in one of two bunkers on the left of the fairway, and moreover the one farthest from the hole. This meant that he had a blind pitch from sand of about 25 yards, a fearfully difficult stroke at any time, let alone at such a moment. He played it beautifully to within two feet of the hole, got his four, and one knew then with an absolute conviction that the championship was his.

It all seemed so disarmingly simple, as Thomson's golf normally is, but how easy it would have been to strike the shot a little heavy or a shade thin and then have to work for a five, or even take six. The slightest misjudgement might have cost the championship whereas he made it safe by producing a perfect stroke at the precise moment when it was necessary. Years afterwards I talked to him about that shot and his first comment, in so many words, was "I always remember that beautiful lie in that bunker. The ball couldn't have been placed in an easier position, slightly uphill on good sand – that's the kind of break you need to win." This remark was typical of an attitude he had revealed earlier that day at Birkdale. I had gone out to the 6th green to wait for him, and thought as I did so how even at an Open you can find solitude.

A soft breeze was stirring in the sand grass, and it was peaceful for a while in the morning sunshine. Then the distant island fairway was filled with people as Thomson prepared to play the long blind second shot with a brassey over the towering sandhills to the green. He played, the heads of the crowd turned upwards, but the ball did not appear, and then I saw him vanish behind the tallest dune, some hundred yards short of the green. It seemed ages before the long pitch floated high to the green and finished a few feet from the hole. After he had holed the putt, and was walking from the next tee, I complimented him on a remarkable four. His first remark was, "How lucky I was to find a good lie."

This might not seem extraordinary to those unused to listening to first-class golfers bemoaning their luck but to me it was most unusual. Self-excuse is an ever-ready companion of many golfers; to them a bad shot is caused by bad luck, but a good result is never good luck. I doubt whether many of the great players ever thought like this; it is an attitude of mind beset with danger. A refusal to accept misfortune or recognise good reveals a state of unpreparedness that eventually will betray. As a wise golfer of old once said, "The mark of a champion is the ability to make the most of good luck and the best of bad." Twice at least on that day at Birkdale Thomson achieved classic examples of how to make the most of fortune, and was wise enough to recognise the fact.

• • • • • • •

If a stranger should come upon him on an evening when he was leading in a championship, it could well be some time before the visitor realised who Thomson was. This is not because he is unduly self-depreciative or quiet, but simply because golf is not the be-all and end-all of life for him.

Neither is golf a complete expression of a personality that is more complex than at first it might appear to be. Thomson is no light-hearted boy, as some might think after watching him on the course, but a shrewd, most determined person capable of rational calculated thought who, even as a young man had a pretty clear idea of where he intended to go. And yet his outward manner is at once attractive and charming. He gives the impression of playing golf for fun, or as a sideline to other more worthwhile activities. His attitude when talking of it resembles that of a highly observant, intelligent amateur rather than that of a world-class professional. This impression of detachment is deceptive and fascinating, and unique within my experience of golfers. It could be contrived but I think not, for I believe that Thomson never has been, nor ever will be, dedicated to the game, or consumed by it as so many others are. He will never become a professional in the full meaning of the term, giving lessons, serving members, and so on, for these things are far removed from his scheme of life.

From the beginning he was blessed with great natural gifts for golf and a wonderful temperament, accepted them without question or fear, and turned them to rare capital advantage. His clearness of mind is exceptional. He had the facility of reducing things, such as the golf swing, to simple essentials. The Australian journalist responsible for transmitting articles that Thomson writes for a paper, has often told me what a pleasure it is to take copy from him, so fluently, concisely and accurately does he express himself. Few professional players of games have this talent. Although some of their expressions are undoubtedly concise, even crisply monosyllabic, they are rarely capable of lucid observant description. I often wonder how many readers of books ostensibly written by famous players, really believe that the man wrote it himself.

All these facets of Thomson's personality make for a remarkable balance in his approach to golf. If I had to choose one adjective to describe him as a person and a player it would be "balance" – for nothing that he does is in any sense exaggerated or unusual. When first he came to Britain in the early 1950s I was impressed by a philosophical outlook, rare in one so young, which permitted him to accept reverses of fortune without being distracted from the even tenor of his ways. So poised and assured was his manner at all times that some may have wondered whether it was assumed. It is now plain that this was not so because in all the years afterwards his serenity was disturbed but rarely and then not in moments of pressure on the golf course. That afternoon at Birkdale there was a final incident that revealed his remarkable composure. After missing the last green of all with his second shot he chipped to within five feet, and then had two for the championship. The first putt overran the hole by an inch or so, whereupon he leaned over and tapped the next one in back-handed. This seemed incredibly casual, and indeed foolish, but as he said later: "I had both hands on the putter." No matter, few men would have been so sure of themselves as to have done this.

Later that summer in the final of the matchplay championship at St Andrews Thomson met John Fallon. He had been expected to win comfortably but did not hole out as well as he might have done and Fallon, playing beautifully with, I understand, rather more at stake than Thomson, held on bravely until extra holes. Thomson was one-up going to the 34th; then Fallon holed clean across the green and the match was square; but Thomson only smiled, as if amused at what must have been, at the very least, an irritating and unexpected thrust. They reached the last green still even. Thomson putted first for his three and missed, and then came the one moment in the whole match when its destiny was out of Thomson's hands. There was nothing in the world he could do but stand and watch Fallon attempt his putt for victory. It was not long, eight to ten feet, and as he was preparing to putt, Thomson leaned on his putter and looked round at the crowd, hanging tense, eager and silent over the fences from the windows. Our eyes met for a second and he smiled cheerfully, although a title and a fair amount of money would disappear if Fallon holed. His putt trembled on the brink and away they went down towards the Swilcan for the third time in the day. I did not follow; there seemed to be no need for I knew then that Thomson would win.

BEN HOGAN TODAY

Nick Seitz

For millions of golf followers it will matter not a shred if Arnold Palmer wins the rest of the schedule, or Raquel Welch becomes a touring caddie, or the price of a hot dog on the course dives to a nickel. The year 1970 was made when 57-year-old William Benjamin Hogan, his swollen left knee squeezed into an elastic brace, limped intently out of retirement to finish ninth in the Houston Champions International and challenge briefly in the Colonial, which he has won five times.

Imagine Joe DiMaggio donning his old uniform and coming off the bench to rip a grand-slam home run before a capacity crowd in Yankee Stadium and you have some idea of the drama that drenched Hogan's performances on two of the most arduous courses in the sport.

The short return to professional golf of the man widely considered the greatest player ever, a winner of all four major championships, a national hero after he overcame the near-fatal effects of a 1949 car-bus crash, gives rise to fascinating questions. Why did he do it? What is his life like today? Has he, as some reports suggest, "mellowed"? What achievements mean the most to him? Hogan long has been the least understood of great athletes, often summarily characterised as "cold" and "aloof", and the years since he reached his playing zenith in the late 1940s and early 1950s have brought disappointingly little insight into his life style and outlooks.

Hogan permitted me to follow him for a week in Fort Worth, observing and questioning. I took up with him during the Colonial and spent two days with him afterward, as he reverted to his customary activities, which seldom include complete rounds of golf, let alone tour play. In that time, I think I came to know somewhat a Ben Hogan only remotely related to the single-dimensional, distant figure I had been led to expect.

The thing that surprised me most about Hogan was his sense of humour: droll, flavoured with an earthy Southwestern spice, often evident. I remember my unsuspecting introduction to it. I accompanied him to Shady Oaks C.C. for lunch – he is the Fort Worth club's most esteemed member – and he introduced me to the manager, who personally attends him. "This guy has 15 kids," Hogan said. Expressionless, he added, "*Bleeped* himself right out of a seat in the car." I had heard dozens of stories about Hogan's dourness, and in no way was prepared for this. I nodded innocuously. After a lengthy silence, I suddenly became aware of what he had said, and burst out laughing. Hogan, who had been watching me closely, joined in the laughter. He was amused not at his own line but at my delayed response. His probing blue-grey eyes suggested: "Didn't expect that from the austere Ben Hogan, eh?"

Of his friend, Jimmy Demaret, who does not have to be coaxed hard to sing, Hogan says, "I love Jimmy's voice . . . but I don't think I can stand 'Deep Purple' again."

Hogan is no raconteur, but he enjoys hearing a good story. Golf temper stories featuring Tommy Bolt and Lefty Stackhouse are his favourites. And he enjoys, even more, spontaneous humour. Paired with Bob Goalby in Houston, Hogan burned a long drive into the wind. "Who do you think you are?" Goalby asked, "Ben Hogan?" Hogan liked that.

During the Colonial, Hogan did his warming up at Shady Oaks, 15 minutes away. The practice area at Colonial Country Club is not large, and he always has preferred to practise by himself anyway ("You don't get in anybody's way, and nobody gets in yours, and you can have your own thoughts"). At Shady Oaks he hit balls from a spot between the 14th and 15th holes, across the 14th, 13th and 17th fairways. One morning, some writers covering the Colonial were playing at Shady Oaks, and "played through" Hogan's practice area. Hogan chatted with them and asked one, Kaye Kessler from Columbus, Ohio, about his swing. "It's kind of disjointed," Kessler said. "My boss told me I shouldn't take it out of town because if it broke down I couldn't get parts." Hogan chuckled delightedly. There is plenty of Irish in him.

Hogan spends several hours a day and an occasional evening at Shady Oaks, the club built by his close friend and early backer on the tour, Marvin Leonard. He is comfortable there. It is the poshest club in Fort Worth, but the members treat one another with a congenial irreverence, Hogan included. "Ben gets tired of people gettin' down on their knees when he walks into a room," Tommy Bolt says. "I've had some great name-callin' arguments with him and he loved it."

Early every afternoon, his leg and the weather permitting, he will empty an old shag bag and hit balls for 40 to 90 minutes, starting with a nine-iron and working through the set. With each club he will hit basic shots, then before putting it away will hit two different types of shot, moving the ball to the right or left, or hitting it low or high. "The basics of the swing remain the same," he says. "But I'm always experimenting, looking for better ways to hit finesse shots. I never hit a shot on the course I haven't practised." His clear voice, neutral at first, takes on more of the drawling intonations of Texas as he warms to talking. "I'm a curious person. *Experimenting is my enjoyment.* I won't accept anything until I've worked with it for a week or two, or longer. I bring out new clubs from the plant and try them out, and I get ahold of clubs that we've sold to check them. If something doesn't work, some part of my swing or a club, I throw it out."

The scientific method. Hogan is the Linus Pauling of his field, subjecting any hypothesis to rigorous, impartial testing. If it works, he keeps it, generalises from it. If it doesn't, into the garbage can it goes. Gardner Dickinson worked for Hogan when Hogan had a club job in Palm Springs in his younger years. Dickinson majored in clinical psychology in college, with a minor in psychometrics – mental testing. Intrigued by Hogan's personality, he would slip IQ test questions into conversations with him. "I knew I'd never get them all past him, so I'd give him only the toughest ones from each section, knowing if he could answer those he could get the others," Dickinson says. "I calculated that his IQ was in excess of 175. Genius level is about 160. Ben didn't go to college, he regrets that, but he's a brilliant person."

One reason Hogan practises where he does at Shady Oaks is to hit into the prevailing wind. When the wind moves, so does Hogan. "If the wind is at your back, it destroys your game. You tend to try to pull the ball, swinging from the outside in, which is bad. If the temperature is below 60 degrees, you lose me. You can wreck your swing playing in cold weather, bundling all up." Each shot is aimed at a target: a small nursery building near the 18th fairway. He uses no glove. "I never could feel anything wearing a glove." Traffic is light at Shady Oaks. Such is Hogan's eminence, when strangers playing the course interrupt his practice, they often apologise.

Shady Oaks, not as long or difficult as Colonial, where Hogan formerly belonged, is nonetheless challenging, and pretty, if that term may be applied to a golf course. Hogan designed most of the bunkers. They are numerous and imaginatively and variously shaped. They are not difficult to shoot from; they are not deep and do not have high lips. "Bunkers serve two purposes," Hogan says. "They are for framing a green – to give it definition and to give the player an idea of the distance he has in hitting the green. And for beauty. They are *not* for trapping *people*."

Hogan holds decided views on what a golf course should be, and no one knows more about shot values. It is his ambition to build The Perfect Golf Course, a project he has contemplated since his touring days. "I'm very close to buying the property now. The market research looks favourable. You have to know where you'll wind up before you start – otherwise you'll go broke. You have to have the right piece of land. I'm in hopes of getting a nice, rolling site with a lot of trees. That means it won't be in the Fort Worth area. I want a course that both the club member and the pro can play.

"Length isn't necessarily the key. Length has to do with climate. Where it's humid, you can't have too long a course. The greens have to be large to provide multiple pin placements and prevent their wearing out. You have to have heavy play or you're going to lose money. You give the greens character in the contouring. I like a clean course. You could grow rough for a tournament. Champions Golf Club in Houston is my idea of a tremendous course for the locale."

Hogan probably will build his course in or near sprawling, wealthy Houston. The course is sure to place a premium on driving, which Hogan deems the most important area of play. Expect the par-fours to bend slightly left or right (an equal number each way). The par-threes will call for iron shots, even short-iron shots, precisely placed. "I won't design it," Hogan says, inhaling hard on a cigarette. "I'm no architect. A person can have just so much knowledge, and there isn't enough time in a day to absorb very much and be proficient. I'll work with the architect, but not in detail. Everything takes a professional."

Hogan will build only one course.

It is common for a legendary athlete, no longer very active competitively, to sell his name – to let it be used for promotional purposes or to open doors, as the saying has it. Ben Hogan does not play the game of business that way. "I don't consider myself a businessman," he says crisply. "Once you consider yourself something, you fall flat on your face, you see." He is behind the wide wooden desk in his spacious office in front of two framed full-colour maps. Several neat foothills of mail have accumulated while he was playing the two tournaments.

A high-salaried executive in the employ of AMF, with stock options and the rest, he is in full command of the Ben Hogan Company, a firm which is doing so well it can't produce golf equipment fast enough to fill the orders. He does not play golf with customers. He plays company golf once a year at the principal sales meeting. He makes few speeches, although he is a captivating speaker. "Some people love that sort of thing. I don't like it. If I accept a speaking engagement, I do the best I can but I'm not comfortable."

The plant and offices are in a nondescript, outlying warehouse district. Fronted by a perfectly kept expanse of putting grass, they stand out. A visitor is asked to sign in with a receptionist, then is led to Hogan's office by Claribel Kelly, his trusted executive secretary. There are no slick public relations people around Hogan. He is not easy to see, but Claribel is his only visible shield. She went to grammar school with Hogan, and remembers him and his mother, who still lives in Fort Worth, attending a music recital she had a part in. She has worked for him for 18 years. She calls him "Mr Hogan" as often as "Ben".

She opens his mail, but does not screen it. He reads it all, scrawling terse notes across the tops of letters for her to amplify. Hogan is sterner in his office. Trying to reach a businessman on the phone, Claribel enters his office to report that he is in a meeting and will call back. "When?" Hogan asks. Gene Sheely, the man who puts together the models for

Hogan clubs, comes in with a wedge special-ordered by a tour star. Hogan puts on the glasses he wears for close work. "I found out playing in the Colonial I'm gonna need 'em to play golf, too. I couldn't see the pins. I had to ask the caddie." Hogan asks a couple of pointed questions, soles the club on the carpet. Sheeley wonders if the player should be charged for the club. "Well heck yes," Hogan answers softly but firmly. The player endorses the clubs of another company. "That's one reason we don't have playing pros on our staff," says Hogan. "Just me."

In the Hogan Company's early struggling years, Ben worked 14 and 16 hours a day to set up a system that was just as he wanted it. Walking through the plant, nodding at employees, occasionally stopping to inspect work at a particular station, he says, "I've done all these jobs myself. I like to work with my hands."

Dealing with his help, Hogan relies on a direct communication. He does not phone them or send them memoranda, he has them summoned to his office and talks to them. Directly.

Today, Hogan usually will work only in the morning, and is perhaps the only executive in the country who consistently can take off at noon for his golf club and not be second-guessed. He cannot understand modern golfers – or executives – who say they do not have time for golf. "I have other business interests that I find time for. I piddle around in the oil business. I fool around with the stock market quite a bit. I'm in the process of looking for a cattle ranch. I'll find what I want. I want it within 150 miles of Forth Worth. I keep hearing there's no money in it, but if that were true you couldn't buy a steak."

Each year Hogan is offered well-paying peripheral jobs, such as commenting on golf telecasts. Each year he declines. "Television is a different business entirely," he says. "It takes a professional to do a professional job. And I'm fed up with travelling."

He has been approached many times about involving himself in a tour event that would carry his name, but always has refused, in part because he is wary of lending his name to an undertaking if he does not have complete control over the quality, and in part, probably, because he has had it in mind to build his own course, the natural site for a "Ben Hogan Classic".

Hogan is considering writing an exhaustive instruction book. "It would be this thick," he says with thumb and forefinger as far apart as they will stretch. "It would confuse a lot of people, but I can't help that. I get so darn tired of these bromides that don't mean anything. Explain to me the expression 'coming off the ball'. What does that mean? What *caused* it, that's what I want to know. I never see that explained. Or 'stay behind the ball'. What does *that* mean?"

Gardner Dickinson says he has seen Hogan turn down $500 for a five-minute lesson. Why doesn't Hogan teach? "You can't find anybody who wants to learn." A silence. "I did teach at one time."

Hearing Hogan speak about the formative years of the tour is a remarkable experience. "I'll tell you how the tour got started, and I've never read this anywhere," he said one noon as we ate *chalupas*, a zestful Mexican dish that is perfect by Fort Worth criteria – hot enough to make your eyes water but not hot enough to make you choke. "The wives of a handful of club professionals in the East – Bob Cruickshank, Al Espinosa, Tommy Armour, I believe – took it on themselves to book a tour in the 1930s. Their husbands were off work in the winter. Before that you just had a smattering of tournaments across the country. The wives wrote to chambers of commerce, and so forth in California, and convinced several cities to have tournaments. Some of the purses were only a few hundred dollars, and we'd go to civic-club lunches to promote ourselves. The wives kept up all the correspondence and handled the books. Then the manufacturers saw what a great promotional vehicle the tour could be and hired Bob Harlow, Walter Hagen's manager, to conduct it. Later the PGA got in on it. That's how this $7 million business began.

"We'd play five exhibitions apiece to pay our Ryder Cup expenses. We got no money from the PGA. If somebody on the tour died or had troubles, we'd work out an exhibition schedule to help out. I never did make money playing the tour. It cost me more, total, than my purse winnings. I had to do other things.

"We travelled together and ate together and sat around hotel rooms and talked at night. We were a smaller group, and invariably more closely knit. It seems to me like we used to have a more *gracious* life playing tournaments in those days. In many places we dressed for dinner, in dinner jackets. I cringe when I see fellas today walking into nice restaurants in golf clothes."

I asked Hogan which of his 60-some victories, including nine of the modern major championships, an unequalled three in the same year (1953), means the most to him. The 1950 United States Open at Merion was his answer, because there he proved himself, in a tense, wearing, 36-hole final only a year after that horrendous car-bus accident, that he could be the best in spite of his injuries.

The past and the present were joined this spring when Hogan, away from tournament golf for nearly three years, his last victory 11 years ago, played back-to-back tournaments, and made them quite special. Each time he walked slowly onto a green with that rolling, purposeful stride, his younger playing partners often lagging respectfully behind, he was met with an ovation, an ovation very different from the usual. There was none of the raucous shouting that welcomes Arnold Palmer. This was loud, prolonged, sincere applause with an added depth. Bearing himself with customary dignity, Hogan nonetheless was moved. He frequently tipped the white cap he special-orders by the dozen. "I'm very grateful," he said in the locker room after one round. "These people are just wonderful, and I wish there was some way I could thank them."

He was, of course, thanking them merely by his presence. His huge galleries were heavily peopled with fathers in their forties and fifties who had brought youthful sons to see a man who was the best at his profession, who elevated it to the level of aesthetics. But there were, not entirely expectedly, thousands of teenagers on their own and young couples in their twenties. Yes, there were even a few dozen hippie types, protesting nothing except that it was damned difficult to get a look at Hogan.

Bob Goalby counted 31 of his fellow pros following Hogan on a hot afternoon in Houston, and said they were impressed. The deeply tanned Hogan's swing appeared superb. His putting stroke, once a shambles, was smoother. His yogic concentration, a striking amalgam of intensity and composure that suggests utter transcendence, seemed not to have been impaired by the long layoff; Herb Wind's description of Hogan competing "with the burning frigidity of dry ice" came to mind.

Hogan always has said he would not compete unless he believed he could win. Possibly he has softened that stance. Why did he play at Champions and Colonial? "I don't know what in the world he is trying to prove," Byron Nelson had said. Claude Harmon said he didn't know if Ben was trying to inspire business for the Ben Hogan Company, but that Winged Foot, where Harmon is the head professional, is selling a lot of Hogan balls to guys who never bought them before.

Hogan says he expects a business residual from his tournament appearances, but that isn't why he played. "I couldn't play until I got better," he says. "Plus I was overweight, and this is a good way to lose it. I used to run in place a lot and exercise. I like to hunt, but had to quit. I was up to 175. Now I'm about 165. In the 1940s I weighed 130 to 135, then after my accident it was 145 to 150. I was curious – I wanted to see if I could walk for four days. I wanted to see if I could play some kinda decent golf hitting off my back foot. The fact it was the 25th anniversary of the Colonial had something to do with it. I've played a lot, but I've missed a lot of years. I missed three years in the service. I missed a year after the wreck. I missed two years because of my shoulder and two years because of my knee. Time's runnin' pretty short if I don't play now. I *enjoy* practising and playing in tournaments. Besides, I haven't really done what I wanted to do."

"What is that?" someone asked.

"I haven't won enough tournaments."

BOBBY LOCKE

Michael McDonnell

The legacy of Bobby Locke is not simply the record of achievement he left for others to follow but rather the personal philosphy that made it all possible.

In truth, it was a doctrine that can be emulated by anyone who has ever swung a golf club and of all the legends, Locke offered evidence of qualities that are to be found in us all.

His perfection of those qualities, his utter reliance on them, is testimony to his greatness for they gave him global success. That is the lesson he passes on and why the South African has special relevance among the great players.

For us, it will never be possible to fashion strokes of Ballesteros artistry; to transport the ball with Palmer-like savagery; or grind on relentless with Hoganish efficiency. But we can all be Bobby Locke or rather adopt – albeit to a lesser extent – that attitude that took him to success.

He was not a great shot-maker. In fact the pardox is that he achieved so much from a game that lacked the completeness found in every other great golfer.

But Locke learned very early in his life that there is really only one important stroke in golf; one talent to possess above all the others no matter that it lacks the impressiveness of big-hitting or the dazzle of the spectacular shot.

The purpose of all skills between tee and green, he observed, was to place the ball safely in a position on the putting surface from which it could be struck into the hole. Thus all other talents were intermediate and supportive – big hitting, fairway technique, recovery work.

If the emphasis were reversed and the talent of putting raised above all others then those other shots became less onerous, less critical in their execution so long as they deposited the ball somewhere on the green where the real skill could take control.

Moreover such skill would work anywhere in the world. It was universal, needing adjustments for varying pace and texture of course, but unaffected by terrain, wind strength and direction and all the other factors that conspire to thwart the more general stroke-making skills.

In his time, during the Forties and the early Fifties, Locke was to apply this winning skill in the United States where his success was spectacular. That was specially important because it meant his later domination of the Open Championship could not be attributed to the absence of the Americans. He after all had beaten them in their own backyard.

He was golf's first globe-trotter. He won championships in France, Germany, Ireland, Mexico, United States, Canada, Holland, Switzerland, South Africa, Egypt and Britain. He won the Open Championship four times and transported his skills on a part-time basis to the United States to win a total of 13 tour events and was even banned for a time because of the closed-shop mentality of extremely jealous American rivals.

They had a point of course. On his first visit he never finished lower than seventh in 12 events and was second leading money-winner against professionals who had toiled all year round. The next year he finished fourth in the money list.

Even so, the hostile attitude of American professionals and his own preference for the golf and lifestyle in other parts of the world, particularly Britain, persuaded him to turn his back on the US Tour. He had, after all, proved a point as far as "Mecca" was concerned. He had been there and was not all that impressed and most certainly not overwhelmed by it.

There was in any case another dimension to Locke that made him see beyond golf to the world that existed outside. While other stars regard the Second World War as an outrageous interruption to their careers, he viewed it as another segment of life's journey. He could have found a safe military sinecure but instead chose to become a bomber pilot and logged 1,800 hours flying.

Those who saw him at his peak insist he was the best putter in the world. He had learned first-hand from Walter Hagen about the supreme importance of the putter and its great qualities of redemption and success.

He had also mastered Hagen's technique of drawing the club inside the line on the backswing so that the clubface seemed hooded then almost "topping" the ball with overspin so that it ran, hooking, into the hole.

He also hooked every shot anyway. The ball was aimed towards mid-off then brought back on an obedient parabola to the middle of the fairway. It was the only shot he knew or rather the one with which he felt safe and as its simple purpose was to get him to the green where he could demonstrate his true skills, its aesthetic merit mattered little.

He was therefore a most conservative player. He could afford to be because he knew his putter would not let him down. Even within range of a heavily-bunkered green, he would play up short and rely on his remarkable short game to see him through because inevitably his skill with the putter extended to the wedge itself so that he assumed the confidence of a man who knew he could always get out of trouble around the green.

Yet none of this is his true legacy. What Locke passes on to future generations at all levels is evidence that personal attitude matters just as much as personal skill; that temperament is the real difference between success and failure.

He acquired the serenity of a mystic, the acceptance to wipe the memory bank clean in an instant. It was not god-given but acquired through experience.

For him, the most important stroke was the one he now faced. How he got there – no matter how disastrous – was history and irrelevant. It was a remarkable attitude and there were many examples of its effectiveness.

In the 1939 Open at St Andrews he had a first-round 70 that contained an eight at the 14th and in his 1949 Open victory at Sandwich he opened with a 69 that included a seven at the 14th hole. In the 1950 Open, he fluffed a pitch shot into a bunker, took two more to get out and should have been finished. Yet the impassive mask never flickered and he marched on in his mayoral style for a 68 to retain his title.

He brought personal elegance and style to golf with his white cap and plus fours, though his measured pace often infuriated rivals who accused him of being deliberately slow. True enough, he could take 20 minutes to put on his golf shoes, five minutes to remove a golf ball from his bag and ten minutes over every shot on the practice ground.

It was deliberate on his part but not to upset his fellow professionals. In any case, he never took more than 3¼ hours for a round and the truth is that the unhurried pace was the result of earlier failure.

He remained convinced that he lost the first Open after the war because he became too excited at the prospect of winning and vowed thereafter he would never again get ahead of himself but would slow all his action to tranquil pace.

The record books show that it worked. It was perhaps his greatest victory. But then any success in golf is first a triumph over self and perceived imperfections. Thereafter, all else follows. That is the true legacy of Arthur D'Arcy Locke and one we can all share.

GOLDEN BEAR OF GOLF
FACES UP TO THE FIFTIES

Peter Dobereiner

Jack Nicklaus is 50 today. He thus achieves his seniority as a professional golfer and becomes eligible to ride on a golf cart playing pro-ams on shortened golf courses with easy pin positions and no rough for huge sums of money.

Unlike Lee Trevino, who could not wait for his fiftieth birthday to start making another fortune competing against the round-bellies, as he calls them, of the Senior Tour, Nicklaus is uncharacteristically indecisive about his future. He cannot decide whether he wants to settle for playing with, and perhaps being beaten by, the likes of Walter Zembriski and Butch Baird, not to mention better-known players he has been beating for 30 years.

He knows that he is still good enough to win on the regular Tour and that he could still add to his unprecedented tally of 20 major championships. The skills are still there; the putting nerve and touch are intact; although the years and a persistent back injury have clipped 40 yards from his legendary drives he is still rated as a long hitter, averaging 265 yards off the tee; and above all the desire and the strategic flair of the game's most potent competitor are undiminished. But to win at the highest level requires arduous and meticulous preparation. The questions which torment him are whether he can afford the time to prepare himself properly and whether his back would stand up to a punishing regime of practice.

This is not the classic mid-life crisis which confronts the fading athlete. Nicklaus went through all that in the early Eighties, when he won only two tournaments in five years. His playing career seemed to be in doubt in 1983 when he had to pull out of the Masters. He displayed his remarkable capacity for instant mastery of technical data by turning his press conference into an orthopaedic lecture, explaining that he had a herniated sixth lumbar vertebra. He may have thereby inadvertently revealed the secret of his golfing success, since we mere humans are equipped with only five lumbar vertebrae.

If that was a crisis he dispelled it in the most decisive and dramatic manner three years later when he won the Masters at the age of 46. His cavalier charge on the final day did more than prove that there was life in the old dog yet; it restored his Rottweiler confidence that he could make the others look like spaniels any time he cared to assert himself. That knowledge was as comforting as actually repeating his triumph, although it complicates his present dilemma.

He does not have to adjust to a new life because he already has several others running concurrently. As the head of the Golden Bear conglomerate of companies involved in golf course design, construction, management, publishing, promotion and sportswear, and turning over nearly $400 million a year, he has more than enough to keep him occupied.

The demand for his services as a golf course architect is so great that one man could not begin to handle the workload. He employs architects and technicians but he is constitutionally incapable of giving them a free hand and involves himself in every project down to the minutest detail. Many clients, who want the Nicklaus imprimatur only as a designer label to sell real estate, have been delighted with the completed course, only to have Nicklaus look it over and order extensive, and expensive, changes.

Throughout his golfing career he has gone to extraordinary lengths, and expense, to fulfil domestic obligations. He thought nothing of chartering a plane to fly a thousand miles home in the middle of a tournament to watch his son Stevie play an important school football match and then fly back through the night to make his tee time next day.

With three of his four children now married and his first grandchild on the way he is determined to devote even more time to his family. There is another aspect of his life which may well raise niggling doubts in his mind about becoming too involved with the Senior Tour. As the most prominent golfer of his era he automatically had thrust upon him the role which had been played most notably by his hero, Bobby Jones, that of Keeper and Grand Exemplar of the Golfing Ethic.

Recently the subject came up in conversation of his famous dispute with Colonel Tony Duncan, the referee during an early world match-play championship. Nicklaus commented fervently: "Bloody fool!" Someone remarked that it was curious Nicklaus should hold a grudge of such passion after a quarter of a century. Nicklaus quietly dispelled any ambiguity over his comment by replying: "Not him. Me!"

That incident barely weighs in the balance of a lifetime of the highest standards of sportsmanship, deportment and golfing diplomacy. Three generations of golfers have looked to Nicklaus as the very model of what a professional golfer should be and have tried to live up to his standards. Because of his example golfers such as Ronan Rafferty today set their ambitions at winning titles rather than grubbing for money.

Yet what is the Senior Tour but an unashamed exercise in acquiring money, as much a pension fund as a sporting circuit? It is not without honour but it is mainly an exploitation of honour won years ago.

Probably for the first time in his life Nicklaus is dithering about what to do. The question is whether a man who has conquered every mountain in golf worth climbing can devise a compelling ambition in the lowlands of senior golf. He probably could and would if he had nothing else to do, even though part of him would empathise with the dismay of his admirers at the sight of a fading Nicklaus competing at minigolf with a fading Trevino and a fading Player. Despite the pull of his competitive nature we may be sure that Nicklaus's involvement with senior golf will not endure if he feels he is not doing justice to his game.

He has always said that he will not play simply because people want to watch Jack Nicklaus. In his book it would be dishonest if he could not show them the real Jack Nicklaus golf. He may still be up to it but can he spare the time to produce real Jack Nicklaus golf?

That is the heart of his problem. For Nicklaus there are not enough hours in the day, not enough days in the week and not enough weeks in the year.

LATIN KING

Donald Steel

For some while before Roberto de Vicenzo's great and historic victory in the Open Championship at Hoylake in 1967, it seemed as though he would be denied the achievement which everyone wanted for him. For about as many years as he had given the assertion that each visit to Britain would be positively his last, he appeared slightly resigned about his chances, speaking humorously in his engaging broken English of "coming only to see his friends", or more colourfully and, in the last part inaccurately, "In England, always too much blahdy weend, too difficult for Roberto."

However accomplished a player may be, and Vicenzo has had few peers, repeated failure in an event can become a burden and confidence sabotaged by a growing awareness that people regard him as vulnerable. How else can one explain Snead's inability to win the US Open, the most bewildering failure in golf, unless fate decreed that even the most perfect swing should not win everything?

There have, of course, been precedents of great players and champions in other sports having their patience and perseverance tested. Gordon Richards had to wait until the year before he retired to ride his first Derby winner. Stanley Matthews won his coveted Cup-winners medal at his last opportunity, and Jaroslav Drobny was 32, a good age for a tennis player, before he won Wimbledon in 1954.

In the summer of 1967, Roberto de Vicenzo was in his 45th year and only Harry Vardon in 1914 was as old a champion. History was against him; but happily some benign force was at work and the climax that sunlit Saturday when the whole golfing world joined in salute as he strode majestically up the last fairway like a king returning from exile, was one of the most moving I have ever experienced.

Two years later at Lytham, Tony Jacklin received a similar hero's welcome; but, in his case, the sentiments were different. The cheers were those of relief and pride that a young British player had won our own championship again. It had been a long wait and the crowd were not going to stifle their delight, but Jacklin was a young man embarking on perhaps the first of many championship victories. For Vicenzo, time was slipping by.

Ever since 1948 when he finished equal third behind Henry Cotton in his first championship at Muirfield, the course he likes best in Britain, he has been wonderfully loyal to the Open. Up to and including 1970, he has played 13 times and nobody has a better record over a comparable period. Statistics can be dull but memories are short and, because so many young players today believe that golf begins and ends with Palmer, Nicklaus, Player, Casper and Jacklin, it is necessary to understand what victory meant when it eventually came.

His record in the British Open is: 1948 3rd, 1949 3rd, 1950 2nd, 1953 6th, 1956 3rd, 1960 3rd, 1964 3rd, 1965 4th, 1966 20th, 1967 1st, 1968 10th, 1969 3rd and 1970 17th.

My admiration of Vicenzo has never been concealed because I see in him the player I would most like to be. For the sheer joy of seeing the ball hit with effortless rhythm and power, I put him before anyone but, watching golf for around thirty weeks a year makes it possible to view players as more than just golfers.

In some it is not easy to respect much beyond a finely controlled swing or a magical short game, but there never lived a more loved or respected figure than Vicenzo; a man of dignity and kindness. In all the many countries in which he has played, no critical or unkind word has ever been spoken against him. He bears success and failure with equal grace and without a word of excuse, complaint or boast.

Like many huge men, he is a gentle soul. For a Latin, he is calm, the only sign of emotion being a shrug of resignation or a mild protest of "Stupid, stupid". He is quick to encourage and help young golfers and, as an example of his natural humour, I offer his explanation of why he was paired with Chang Chung Fa in a recent British tournament: "They do it to improve my English."

All these qualities will be quickly endorsed by those who know him well but very little has been written about his background, his boyhood and early beginnings in golf which form such a necessary part of his story.

He was born in Buenos Aires and started to play about the age of 10 as a result of one of his brothers being a caddie at the course near where they lived, and one day bringing home a golf club. His father was a working man with no relations or connections with golf and Vicenzo's interests were roused by caddying with his brothers, four of whom are now golf professionals. The other three, as he once said, with a gleam in his eye, "work".

At that time, golf was neither well known nor popular in the Argentine and Vicenzo began, as most caddies do, by relying on his instincts and muddling along on his own. He had no early lessons but later one of the professionals at a neighbouring club gave him some help and, though he had troubles for many years perfecting his grip, his game improved steadily.

Because of his grip, he was inclined to hook the ball but it was soon obvious that a great talent was emerging and in 1938, at the age of 16, he turned professional on the advice of Paul Runyan, the famous American. Runyan was visiting Buenos Aires to play and give exhibitions and he encouraged Vicenzo to play his first tournament; but it was another ten years or so before his name became known outside South America.

In 1947 he played for the first time in North America and the following summer came to Britain where he immediately won the North British tournament at Harrogate and later played in the Open. He started to travel because he felt he could make money and because he realised it was silly staying at home where there were so few opportunities and so few good professionals. He was, however, always conscious of the attempts on the British Open by a small band of distinguished Argentine golfers, notably Jose Jurado, and always anxious to crown their gallant performances.

Throughout the Fifties, he was busy compiling a high proprotion of his 140-odd tournament victories, a record matched only by Snead, but, like so many of his contemporaries, he missed out to a large degree on the rich rewards that would have been his, had he been born ten years later.

All the same, from about 1960 onwards, he sensed the game's new riches and his golf, while maintaining its old brilliance, acquired a consistency it had not previously possessed. This was partly due to a change of grip which made him less inclined to hook under pressure and I remember thinking that his second round of 66 in the 1966 Spanish Open at Sotogrande was one which only Jack Nicklaus, of all the other world-class players, could possibly have matched. Even with three putts from twelve feet on the last green, that round led to a handsome victory.

His thunderous hitting reduced a great, long course almost to the realms of pitch and putt and it remains one of the most outstanding rounds I have ever witnessed. It showed that, though now past forty, he was playing the best golf of his life, an impression that didn't have long to wait for unanswerable confirmation.

He approached the British Open the following year in a wonderfully relaxed mood and, looking back, this was a major factor. Perhaps as an influence of Hogan whom he regards as the best player he has seen, few have practised more than Vicenzo. He thinks nothing of hitting eight hundred balls a day and maybe playing a round as well on the course about five blocks from his home in Buenos Aires.

In the last four or five years, this ration has increased rather than decreased and he arrived at Hoylake in fighting trim. But while many went in search of their swings one windy practice day, Vicenzo spent most of the time on the superb putting green in front of the clubhouse. He had hit enough shots in his life to know that his long game would not betray him, and he also knew that, if he was to win at his age, he had to build a reliable putting stroke.

The other crucial factor was that, despite many disappointments and near-misses, he never lost faith in himself. One had often felt that he was a born pessimist, so resigned could he appear about not winning; but, in questioning him once on the subject, he firmly disagreed: "I say 'no good' all the time because, when I talk to my friends, I no want to say I am very good. Then, when I play bad, my friends are disappointed.

"The other way, when I say 'no good' and I play well, my friends feel happy. That is why so many people feel like I am pessimist but, inside, I am no pessimist. I fight like the optimist fellow. I fight every shot."

Anyway, what a triumph of virtue the week turned out to be. With enormous ease, his opening round of 70 and 71 put him right up among the leaders and then a magnificent third round of 67 took him clear of the field and face to face with the greatest test of nerve and skill he had ever encountered.

He must have known that Friday night that if he muffed this chance, he would never get another. His whole destiny as a golfer depended upon that final round. A number felt that the younger nerves of Player and Nicklaus, who both began the last day within three shots of him, would last the better, but, by the voice of the crowd, it was easy to tell that they wanted Vicenzo to win, and clearly this was the inspiration he sought.

He may have had fears that the pace might be too slow with Nicklaus ahead and the sometimes deliberate Player playing with him; but Nicklaus, all too often unfairly judged a slow player, moved well and there was no doubt that Player was far more anxious than Vicenzo.

Two masterly saving chips at the 3rd and 5th quickly put him at ease but the expected assault of Nicklaus was not long delayed. He had a two at the Dowie, not quite so fearsome without its out of bounds, and with another birdie at the long 8th, Nicklaus drew level with Player, two behind Vicenzo.

It was imperative that Vicenzo should maintain his lead and this he did with a gallant three from six feet at the 10th and a marvellous chip from a sandy lie at the Alps. The issue now lay between Nicklaus and Vicenzo.

Nicklaus, however, as part of a trend that has plagued him in many major championships these past few years, had holed nothing to speak of on the lovely, easy-paced greens and his inability to do so at this point allowed Vicenzo the peace of mind he so desperately wanted. It also put an end to Nicklaus's hopes of joining Jones, Sarazen and Hogan as the only men who have won the British and American championships in the same summer.

Although the finish at Hoylake is as demanding as any on our great seaside links, and Vicenzo dropped a stroke at the 15th where Nicklaus missed for a three, somehow one knew that the long shots would not worry him. All those thousands of practice shots had laid a solid foundation and at the 16th he hit probably the finest shot of his life.

Nicklaus, three behind, made a tremendous birdie, but Vicenzo followed by thundering a spoon across the corner of the out-of-bounds Cop. It finished in the heart of the green and he then knew that all his dreams were about to come true.

The sentimental undertones reached a crescendo as two prodigious drives left him only a nine-iron to the last two greens, and though Nicklaus typically made one last fling with a birdie at the 18th, Vicenzo, who averaged 32 putts a round was finally left with three putts to win the Championship.

All the way up the last fairway, the cheers echoed across to the Mersey and beyond; the huge, bronzed figure, cap held aloft, beamed in response and a few moments later the old Championship jug that had proved so elusive, was clasped in his mighty hands.

His place in history was assured and the celebrations were just that bit happier because the toast was "Roberto". Reaction, however, was inevitable, and the following week in the Esso he won only three of his 14 matches but how pleased the others would have been to have said, "I winna the big one last week."

The long-term effect of becoming champion was bound to be good for his confidence as he showed the following April in the ill-fated Masters at Augusta. If I hadn't experienced the joy of Hoylake, I don't think I could have endured the agony of Augusta when poor Tommy Aaron's pencil slip was made public and Vicenzo was deprived of the chance of the title in a playoff.

Perhaps a more ruthless man would have told those clamouring to interview him, to wait; perhaps a younger man would not have been quite so overcome with emotion and almost certainly Vicenzo was still mad with himself for taking five at the last hole.

Nearly all the British golf writers were on the phone to their offices, it being 11.30 pm in London, and they had to do an impromptu masterpiece of patching. Reading one or two of the reports later, one might have thought that they had a couple of hours to interview Goalby and Vicenzo and review the situation at their leisure; but the saddest part of the whole affair was that Vicenzo's truly great golf was eclipsed.

I am sure he could not have produced it without the pride he felt at being British champion for, having survived the pressures of one climax, he was that much better equipped to withstand and even relish another.

I fancy a great many of the crowd and the players hardly considered him a serious challenger when the day dawned, although he had played tournament golf in America long before most of them had taken three putts for the first time; and, indeed, loved playing on their courses which he regards as less penal and therefore easier than ours.

Altogether he has won eight tournaments in the States and one year came close to winning the US Open when he needed par for the last nine holes; but he never made long stays there because he never liked to be away from home for more than three or four weeks at a time; and, because of the distances involved, he couldn't have kept going to and fro in the days before air travel was as simple as it is today.

He once said, "If you start to follow the tournaments, you got a chance to lose your family," and, as you would expect, he always considered his family uppermost. He married when he was 23 and has two fine sons of 24 and 21. Neither plays golf, one of them, as his father says, being more interested in the girls, but a contented family life has contributed much to his golf.

On the final day at Augusta, everyone was delighted that Vicenzo was right there with a round to go and had played so well for three days but on his 45th birthday he silenced any doubters with as dramatic a start to his final round as any championship has seen.

His second with a nine-iron pitched crisply short of the 1st hole and rolled gently in for an eagle; and, after a birdie four at the second, he practically holed another second shot at the 3rd. The afternoon was alight. When he turned in 31, he must have had visions of taking the first green jacket back to the Argentine, and, as he advanced serenely along the back nine, a lot of other people thought so too, even though the leaders were tightly bunched.

There are few courses where a long, straight driver does not profit and Augusta is certainly not one of them. Vicenzo's controlled striking was seen at its best and further birdies at the 12th, 15th and 17th took him in sight of a 64.

Then, with a pulled second to the 18th and one careless moment when all was over, the birdie witnessed on the 17th by about nine million people, turned out not to be a birdie after all. If Cliff Roberts and Bobby

Jones cannot find a way round the rules, you can be sure there isn't one and it was in such circumstances that a nightmare was born.

At a stunned Press conference, I could have strangled those who tried to put words into Vicenzo's mouth and make him question the decision but, like a brave resistance worker facing torture from the Germans, he gave nothing away. If there had to be a reason for the awful calamity, I like to think that it was to show the model reaction to adversity.

His acceptance of what he had done was heroic but it was bound to have an effect on such a sensitive person and two or three years later, when one felt one could ask him about it, he confessed:

"When I sign the scorecard wrong, I lose interest. I don't want to practise; I go to the golf club, but I no work. In other words, I be too lazy.

"I think, you are professional, you no want to make this kind of mistake. When you make mistake on the golf course, you have chance to recover, but when you make mistake on the scorecard, you cannot say anything, you cannot blame anyone; you have to take the responsibility and inside you feel very bad, I felt very bad for months."

At the time, it seemed that one of the biggest tragedies was that Vicenzo would not be able to capitalise out of a possible victory in the way that he deserved but there were compensations. His conduct and play were recognised by the presentation of the Bobby Jones award for "distinguished sportmanship", and another from a group of American golf writers, both of which gave rise to amusing stories.

Asked by a Customs officer at Miami en route from Bogota whether he was going to New York for business, he said, "No, I go for dinner," and to the writers who, in making their award, had chided him in fun for his slip of the pencil, he replied, "You say that but you spell my name wrong three times, on the seating list, the menu and the trophy."

Owing to the fact that he was unable to stay in Britain after his triumph at Hoylake and that Buenos Aires is not commercially minded when it comes to golf, the British Open was not a great financial success for him, but after the Masters, he felt that the British Open began to be good for him. He estimated that a combination of both have made him in the region of $250–300,000 – "Very lucky because if I sign the scorecard right, I might not make anything."

Back home in Buenos Aires where he is treated like a king, he has consolidated his business interests, mainly in the shape of a city car park, and the future for him and his family seems assured. Happily, however, he shows no signs of retiring although he does think that his left hand is not in such a good position on the club and may need attention. It has a tendency to go over and that is why he says he misses more shots than he used to, but modesty is another of his engaging attributes and it did not stop him from heading the individual championship in the 1970 World Cup in Buenos Aires, a wonderful performance considering it is never easy to play well so near home.

It was an occasion I am sorry I missed; the jubilant scenes, the smiles and the homage paid to such a great golfer. It is as a champion in world-class company that he belongs, another reason which made his victory at Hoylake so important. His episode at Augusta, alas, is the only unwelcome part of his story, but it has not been merely as a winner that Vicenzo has commanded respect and given pleasure.

As a golfer he stands for all that is good but as a companion he is always fun and as a philosopher on that dreaded scorecard, he can still laugh. When told how much everyone admired the way he accepted his disappointment, he remarked, "There's no way to do otherwise; you have to accept and check better next time. You have to conform; and, anyway, worse be if you go across the street and you no see the car."

LAST LOOK AT TONY LEMA

Nick Seitz

It has been a year since Tony Lema died at the age of 32 in a fiery plane crash on, ironically enough, a golf course – a year in which to lament his passing, to remember the good times and the bad, to attempt to put him in perspective as a person.

Who was Tony Lema? He was a professional golfer, the winner of 14 tournaments including the British Open, a celebrity known to kings and Broadway columnists, but he also was a complex man never quite able to identify himself.

He was "Champagne Tony", a swinger to whom wine, women and song were a way of life. The stories of his wee-hours escapades were widely circulated. He once drove golf balls out of a hotel window, to the delight of a group of party-goers. To win his first professional championship he had to beat Paul Harney in a sudden-death playoff immediately after gulping down three Scotch-and-waters in the grill (Lema thought he had lost, and was ordering a fourth drink when he found out otherwise). On the Caribbean tour he had been known to set down a highball and demonstrate the fine art of blasting a golf ball out of the shallow end of a swimming pool while vacationing millionaires looked on in wonder.

The legend grew by bits and pieces, then by leaps and bounds. Unlike a good many legends, this one was grounded in fact. Until his marriage to the former Betty Cline in 1963, the handsome, debonair Lema fully lived up to his billing as a party boy extraordinary. "When he is playing well and getting his name in the newspapers, a touring pro can have his pick of the girls," he wrote later in a popular autobiographical book, *Golfer's Gold*. As a bachelor, Lema took his pick, and he showed his dates the town – whatever town he happened to be in. Las Vegas, Miami and San Francisco were his favourite spas.

"Tony was a man on vacation," says Ernie Vossler, who was playing the tour when Lema, a poor youngster from the cannery section of Oakland, California, turned pro in 1955. "In that respect, he never changed."

Doc Giffin, then press secretary for the Professional Golfer's Association tour, remembers how Lema acquired the nickname "Champagne Tony". It was in 1962, at the Orange County Open in Costa Mesa, California. Giffin had set up press headquarters in a small card room of the Mesa Verde Country Club. "The press corps was so small, the room wasn't even crowded," Giffin says. "We had a portable cooler of beer in there, and I can still visualise Tony holding up a near-empty can of beer after his interview following the third round and saying, 'Men, if I win tomorrow, we'll have champagne in here.' A West Coast freelance photographer, Lester Nehamkin, told the club manager to be sure to have champagne on ice. After he beat Bob Rosburg on the third hole of a sudden-death playoff the next day, Lema ordered the champagne. The late Charley Curtis of the *Los Angeles Times*, for one, and I believe at least one of the wire-service reporters used the 'Champagne Tony' tag in their stories. I told it many times in the next few months, and it caught on nationally."

It was one of the lesser ironies of Lema's short life that he preferred Scotch to champagne. The nickname resulted in a profitable endorsement for him, but he rarely drank the bubbly stuff except for publicity purposes after a victory.

His coup in that Orange County Open, his first official tour win, was the highlight of Lema's first really fruitful season. He earned more than $28,000 in 1962 after six years of frustration. His first full year, 1956, had seen him win only $385 to rank 147th on the money list, and the ensuing five years found him winning the unimposing total of $31,000.

"I wonder," he reflected later, "how I had the nerve to start out on the tour or stay with it as long as I did. Most of the players at least got in on the ground floor. I climbed in through a basement window."

If the youthful ex-Marine was struggling during those early days as a tournament professional, he concealed the fact nicely. "I don't think he had much money," says Vossler, "but you never would have guessed it. We'd be staying at the same hotel, and I'd always see him in the barber shop getting a manicure, or having his shoes shined in the lobby, or escorting a well-dressed woman into the cocktail lounge. He travelled first class."

Vossler adds that he believes Lema's fondness for liquor was exaggerated, a feeling I heard echoed many times while interviewing people who had been close to him. "He'd take a drink or two after he finished playing a round, like a lot of other players, but he never carried liquor with him."

Tommy Jacobs was Lema's best friend. The two rookies joined forces to save on expenses, and travelled and roomed together for 18 months, until Jacobs married. "If Tony was scoring well, he didn't party," says Jacobs. "But if he wasn't playing well, he would get real discouraged and start going out at night. Actually, he didn't party all that much – he just got a little more notoriety than some others. When he got in the mood, though, there was no stopping him."

It was not untypical of Lema that he was not speaking to Jacobs at the time of his death. Lema could change moods in a moment, and not even those who knew him best ever dared guess exactly what to expect from him. A writer for a national magazine, a man who engenders strong like or dislike among the tournament golfers, was preparing an article on Lema, and he wanted Jacobs to help him. Jacobs, who does not care for the writer, declined. The writer complained to Lema, and Lema turned a cold shoulder toward Jacobs at the PGA Championship, the last tournament in which Lema played. "That would've lasted about a week," Jacobs says.

Controlling and channelling his moodiness was Lema's foremost challenge. In his formative years in tournament golf he would shoot a bad round and, peeved at himself and the world, withdraw from the event and disappear for weeks. He was given to outbursts of temper that doubtless delayed his rise to stardom for a matter of years.

"Until 1961, he wasn't able to put together four solid rounds," says Vossler. "He often would win money because he would start fast. He led a lot of tournaments in the early rounds, but didn't win them. Later, when he learned what it takes to be a winner, he didn't get mad at himself on the course. At first he expected too much of himself. Nobody hits every shot exactly the way he wants to hit it, but Tony refused to accept that. His game was sound; he never had any bad habits."

The last four years of his life, Lema was a great putter. He would break into a delightful little jig that endeared him to the galleries when he sank a long putt. Accurate and long with his woods and a splendid scrambler around the greens, he was only mediocre – comparatively speaking – with the long and middle irons. It has been suggested that this was due to a lack of concentrated practice. "He must have worked hard when he was a kid to have that good a swing," says one veteran touring pro, "but I sure didn't see him on the practice range much. At the PGA the week he died, he didn't hit a bucket of balls all week. He played the front nine one day and the back nine the next, which is not how a Jack Nicklaus would prepare for a major championship. It looked to me as if he did naturally what the rest of us have to sweat and toil to do."

Tony Lema was not Jack Nicklaus, however, and there is another side to the manner in which he approached competition. His was the sort of swing that requires little work, and he was wise enough to realise his good fortune and leave well enough alone. The 6-foot 1-inch, 180-pounder would start the downward portion of his swing with a quick return of weight to his left side (he was right-handed), so that the club always was catching up with his weight – an ideal sequence. By shifting his weight so rapidly and smoothly, he kept swing errors to a minimum.

Also, his natural mental tendency was to take the game too seriously and beat himself. After his failures of 1956–61 he finally learned to relax.

"Tony had a formula, and it worked," says Tommy Jacobs. "He learned that he had to be loose to play well. He had come out on tour and practised and practised and practised and hadn't won, and then he changed his approach and he started winning. What would you do? Tony had to suit his game to his temperament, and vice versa. He quit letting little things bother him, stopped playing so conservatively and worrying so much, and became a successful charger, much like Arnold Palmer."

Lema charged to his high of five victories in 1964 and collected $74,000, fourth best on the tour. The next year he amassed official winnings of $101,800 to finish second to Jack Nicklaus in the money race. He had hit his stride. Before his death on 24 July 1966, the foremost instance of an athlete being killed in his prime, he had won $48,200 and was all but assured a spot among the top 10 money-winners for the fourth year in a row.

His last victory was at Oklahoma City in late May of 1966 where, all seriousness, he fired 65 on the final day, missing the course record by only a stroke and holding off intense bids by Nicklaus and Tom Weiskopf. Lema's total was 271, the lowest on the tour to that point. "If I never win again," he said in accepting the first-place trophy, "I won't be so disappointed it will kill me. Golf has been good to me."

The Oklahoma City triumph was particularly satisfying to him because he had been bothered by a sore elbow and had not won in eight months, and because it was accomplished in front of his wife's family and friends in her home town.

Everyone who knew them agrees that Betty was a steadying influence on her vagabond husband, whose brief, unsuccessful first marriage had produced a son. Betty frequently travelled with Tony from tournament to tournament, and converted to Catholicism, his faith. They had met and played cards in the back of a plane in 1961 while she was an airline hostess, and they were wed two years later.

"Marrying Betty helped Tony immensely," says Jacobs. "He changed a great deal in the last year he was alive. He was far closer to being content, whereas before he was liable to be sitting in somebody's living room talking to you and suddenly he would drift off into space. He seemed at times like that to lose touch with reality. Tony was aware of this distance between himself and others, and he definitely wanted to get in step. He wanted to do things for others, particularly for people who had helped him. He just wasn't sure how to go about it. Probably Tony lacked confidence more than anything else. He never had spent much time with the other golfers. They didn't really like him or dislike him – they didn't understand him."

To repay his fellows pros and the PGA the debt he considered he owed them, Lema shortly before his death made it known that he wanted to serve on the Tournament Committee, a thankless and financially unrewarding assignment. He began, too, taking part in the give-and-take on the practice tee and in the locker room, swapping theories and jokes with players he seldom had spoken to. Bob Goalby, who made the comeback of the year in 1966, gives a large part of the credit for his success to Lema. "I don't let a bad shot bother me now," Goalby says. "I can see the value of keeping calm, and as Tony told me, you have to live a little." Less than a week after Lema talked to Goalby, Lema, his beautiful wife and two other persons perished in the wreckage of a small private plane on the Lansing, Illinois, Sportsmen's Club golf course, trying to make a forced landing.

There were conflicting reports on the crash. The accepted version is that the plane had *not* landed and refuelled a few minutes before crashing, but that the pilot had put it into a stall and lost control.

The final irony is that Lema originally had committed himself to play in a posh pro-am sponsored by General Electric the next day, but reneged to attend the small pro-am for which he was headed when he died.

Newspaper stories reported that Lema's suitcase contained nearly $20,000 in uncashed checks, giving rise to some wild speculation that he must have been worth well over a million dollars. The truth is that he was worth about $250,000. Early in his career he had bought up his contract following a disagreement with a backer, and the transaction left him off-balance financially for several years. Also, he was investing money with an eye toward his long-range security.

He told friends he was looking forward to starting a family. "When Betty and I have children, I'll settle down," he said. "When the kids get to the age where a father should be around, I'll probably quit playing golf for a living. I don't think this life would do for children."

Tommy Jacobs mentions that Lema had a special fondness for children, perhaps because Tony himself grew up without a father. "He would urge kids to go to college," Jacobs says. "He hadn't gone himself, but he was sure he should have. If a caddie of his was in college, and did a good job for him, he would pay him more than the going rate. Tony was getting down to earth."

Who was Tony Lema? The tragedy is that Tony Lema was just beginning to find out himself.

FOR SAM THE PRICE IS ALWAYS RIGHT

John Underwood

Keep close count of your nickels and dimes, stay away from whiskey, and never concede a putt.
Samuel Jackson Snead, *The Education of a Golfer*, 1962

A club member in a red pinstriped blazer and grey-on-black patent leather shoes was coming out of the door of the Pine Tree Golf Club of Delray Beach, Florida, which is characterised by the membership as "selective" rather than "exclusive", when the Cadillac with the West Virginia licence plates pulled up. Sam Snead, the 62-year-old mountain of youth, the same Sam Snead once described by Lee Trevino as "the most outstanding athlete the world has ever seen", popped the trunk from a button in the glove compartment, got out on the driver's side and came around.

"Hey, Sambo," said the member. "What's this, no more Continentals?"

"Like the feller says, 'If the price is right,'" said Snead, and opened the trunk. From the hodgepodge of golf and fishing equipment he grubbed fresh balls and began stuffing the pockets of his golf bag. Then he unsheathed a new set of irons. "When I leave the air conditioning off, I get 14 miles to the gallon."

The man hefted one of the irons, giving it a 15-handicap half-swing. "Feels heavy, Sam," he said helpfully.

"Hell, they're for a man," said Sam Snead. "They're not for a damn child." He grinned, the right side of his mouth rising above the left.

An attendant took the bag, and the parking valet took the 14-miles-per-gallon Cadillac, and Snead went inside past the receptionist, who waved cheerfully, and into an elevator to the locker room, where he sat down before a stall marked Snead/Tutweiler and began changing to his golf shoes.

"They let me play in the club championship here three years ago," he said, lowering his voice. "I'd never played in one, and they let me in and, boy, you never heard such carrying on. I told Chuck Kelly, 'Listen, I'm playing, but if I win, I'm not taking anything.' I won by 10 strokes, but I couldn't get anybody to bet a damn nickel. Everybody was dying, but they weren't saying anything, and I wasn't, and finally at the banquet I got up and I said, 'I ain't your champion, Ed Tutweiler is. This is his trophy. I'm just grateful you let me play.'"

The right side of his mouth went up and his voice tightened with pleasure.

"Boy, I never had so many instant admirers."

Dressed in a yellow polo shirt that had a small tear at the seam near the waist, and blue pants and black shoes that needed polish, and wearing the familiar coconut-straw hat, Snead went down the hall and stood outside the pro shop where a burly black man had already attached his clubs to an electric cart. The man asked how he had done that weekend at the Quarter Century tournament at Disney World.

"Won by six," Snead said. "The feller says, 'It was worth the drive.'"

"How much you win?"

"Two thousand."

He got into the cart and whirred around the north side of the white stucco building, down a paved path to where a small group of early-in-the-weekers were slapping at balls on the practice tee. A pale man in aqua Bermuda shorts stopped and leaned closer to his wife, who had been chopping grounders. They stared at Snead with their heads together.

"Hey, hustler," said a tall man who was hitting practice shots. "Playing today?"

"One o'clock. I'm expecting you."

"I dunno, I may be stupid, but I . . . "

"We're going at one. Be ready. You can go." The man hit an iron shot high and far and Snead whistled admiringly. "Oh, looky there," he said. "You're swinging go-ood. Bring your purse."

"Wednesday," said the tall man. "I'll play Wednesday."

"Gotta go to the dentist Wednesday," said Snead.

"Good. Tell him to add four strokes to your game."

A second cart pulled up, driven by a stockily built man, fiftyish, with a square, tough-Irish face and greying hair.

"Chuckie baby!" Snead crooned.

"He can see my money through my pockets," said Chuck Kelly, winking at Snead's companion. Kelly is a coal-sales executive who winters in Florida. He has been playing golf for money with Sam Snead since they were both, as Kelly says, "much younger". With the help of a four handicap, Kelly holds his own. "Tut flashed a roll of bills in the lounge the other day, and Sam almost had a fit. 'Oh, my, look at that pretty colour,'" Kelly said, mimicking Snead. "'Oh, that's my favourite colour.' Tell you what, Sam, you go ahead and see if you can improve some, and I'll get a bite to eat and meet you on the tee."

"Don't get too far. I like to be near my money."

Snead scooped the new balls from his bag, speckling the grass around him, got out a nine-iron and began hitting rainbows to the left of the practice range. Along the tee line action stopped as the textbook came to life. The exquisite swing – time-locked, sealed in gelatin, smooth as a butternut – lifted the balls and rolled back the years. Slammin' Sammy. One after another the shots arched and landed, forming a cluster no more than five yards in diameter. Snead switched to another iron ("They're a little stiff," he complained), then another. Down the side of the range little floral arrangements of glistening white dots began to appear, each one deeper than the one before until, with a wood, Snead began hitting balls past the cut area into a plot of newly planted palms.

"Where'd you get that hook, Sam?" The tall man had come to watch.

"Hook? Hell, that's no hook. An Indian can't walk any straighter 'n that."

"Well, it looked a little low."

Snead swung again, and the ball got up and shrunk until it seemed to be suspended in the air. When it finally landed, it was deeper still in the young palms.

"High enough?" said Snead.

"Think you're ready for Johnny Miller?"

"I'd like to have that boy's nerves in this tired old body," Snead said. "But somebody's going to have to go get him, might as well be me." He winked, mounted his cart and headed upstream into the practice area.

"My accountant got to figuring one year," he said, bouncing along. "He figured I'd hit 1,640,000 balls, practice and tune-aments. For 13 years I never missed playing more 'n two or three weeks at a time. A reporter in England was interviewing me during the Benson-Hedges thing last year. He said, 'You a millionaire?' I said, 'Well, what do you call being a millionaire? One million? Two million? Four million?' He said, 'Gol-lee, what the hell are you doing out here, then?' I said, 'Cause I like to play.'

He stopped at the first cluster, bending from the cart to reclaim his property, twirling the handle and manipulating the machine like a vacuum cleaner and contorting his body. One ball was farther to the left than he would have liked and he leaned way out to get it.

"I don't have the control I used to have," he said. "No nerves in my hands and wrists. I lock everything in now. Used to be I could control every shot with my wrists, just flip it up there wherever I wanted. Can't do that anymore. When I was having trouble with my wrist last year they took X-rays, and the doctor said it looked like a damn rat had been in there, eating the metacarpal muscles. Just wear and tear."

He continued the harvest down-range, cleaning up the little patches of white, not missing a ball until he got into the palms, where he made a note out loud on which brand had gotten the best distance.

"I suppose I've lost 25 or 30 yards off the tee," he said as he turned back. "Every now and then, when I'm feeling really good, really oiled up, I put one out there, but most of the time you get to thinking about it, and you just tighten up and nothing happens. You gotta be loose to play this game. That's why Palmer and some of those boys have trouble. Especially the ones with short back swings. No elasticity. You gotta be loose. Looka here."

He guided the cart with his knee and with the forefinger and thumb of his left hand clasped the thumb of his right – a scarred, crullerlike appendage, thick as a cucumber – and bent it back so that the nail nearly touched his right wrist.

"Loose," he said.

He stopped at the bunker by the practice tee and deposited another bouquet of balls.

"I used to be the best sand player on the tour," he said matter-of-factly, moving into the trap. "Put it where I wanted, whichever side I wanted." His wedge flashed, and a ball popped through the cloud of sand and hit to the left of the flag; another hit right. The third skidded too far past. "At least *I* thought so," he said. "Here, I'll open the blade a little. See?" Another soft explosion, and the ball popped out, hit, ran gingerly and rimmed the cup."

"I've always had keys for myself like that. I don't understand it when I read, 'Nicklaus says he has to go see Jack Grout to check his game.' Shoot, I never took a lesson in my life except for shagging balls for my brother Homer. When I was a young pro at The Homestead I asked Fred Gleim to help me a couple of times. He said, 'Hell, *you're* a pro.'"

You gotta understand what Sam came from. Nothing. A barefoot hillbilly with a couple of shirts and a pair of wool pants, and it was a new world. The first exhibition I got for him he said, "Be sure to say I'm from The Greenbrier. They pay me $45 a month." Well, he learned early. The Greenbrier docked him $11.25 for being nine days late after he almost won the Masters that year. The thing about Sam is that he wants to win at everything he does. Golf, cards, pitching pennies. My eight-year-old daughter was in her room one time, and Sam went upstairs to visit her and play some gin rummy. My daughter said, "Uncle Sam cheats." I said, "Sam, did you fool around with that deck?" He said, "Sure. I was just having fun." I asked him once when he was at the top of his game if he'd play my brother John for $5 even. He said, "Well, how good can he play?"
Fred Corcoran, Vice-President, International Golf, Snead's Ex-Manager.

On his way to the first tee Snead stopped long enough at the Pine Tree snack bar to purchase a hot dog and diet cola. His companion ordered a chicken sandwich.

"Half or whole?" the waitress asked.

"Only place in the world you can buy half a sandwich," said Snead. He stuffed the hot dog in his mouth and put his foot down hard on the throttle.

Chuck Kelly was already on the 1st tee, waiting with a florid-faced man named Jim Raymond, who draws the comic strip *Blondie*, and the tall golfer from the practice tee. His name was Chuck MacCallum, a Florida real-estate man. He had been Pine Tree's club champion twice. At age 15, in Midland, Michigan, "When I was young and full of myself," MacCallum said, he got promoted into a driving contest with Snead. He said he hit three balls, the last one "about as far as anybody could hit it. Sam got up and hit his first one past me on the fly. With a four-wood." Snead said he did not remember the episode.

"How many shots you giving me?" MacCallum asked.

"The same," said Snead. "Four and three."

"The same? You beat me every damn time."

The smile lifted the right side of Snead's face.

"Well, you gonna have to *improve*."

The haggling went on until a full quota of bets were made, team (Snead pairing with Raymond) and individual. MacCallum improved his bet to four-and-four. Satisfied, Snead got up to hit, assuming the honour. "I'm gonna throw a little 32 at you today, Chuck, baby," he said. "A little old 32." And he hit his drive 20 yards farther than the others would.

"I shot a 63 here once," he said as he got in the cart, "and it'd been a 61 if I hadn't three-putted the last green. Ted Kroll wouldn't stop talking on my backswing."

He missed a 10-footer for a birdie, and three-putted the 2nd to fall behind. "I never play good after a tune-ament," he said, twisting the handle of the cart and stomping the accelerator. His passenger's head jerked back. "I always have a little letdown after a tune-ament."

He rolled in a 20-footer for a birdie on the 3rd. Driving again, he said he always preferred this kind of golf, man-to-man, "where you can look a feller in the eye." He said Dutch Harrison "used to make his expenses on the tour playing $2 Nassaus with the younger players. He'd say to one of 'em. 'Oh, my, you're playing so good,' then he'd beat 'em 2–2-and-2.'"

He said you had to have guidelines, though. "Never gamble with a stranger," he said, "and if you do and he stops arguing the handicap too soon, you know you got a hawk in the chicken yard. When I was at Boca there were three guys I didn't know asked me to play one day. I said, 'Well, you know my fee for a playing lesson is $100.' That didn't seem to shock 'em. And I said, 'And we'll play a $10 Nassau. What's your handicap?' It's a mistake not to know those things, especially since they sure as hell knew mine. They said, 'Five,' and I said, 'Fine, I'll give you six.' So we kinda played along without making a dent, and on the 4th or 5th hole I said, 'Listen, I'll dispense with the fee and play your best ball and cut you for $1,000.' They all said OK, and we wound up playing four courses over the next five days. I won $10,000."

He grinned and got out of the cart. They were on the 5th tee at Pine Tree.

"Hey," he said to the others, "I'll play your best ball from here in."

Jim Raymond said, "Well, I dunno, I'm not . . . "

"C'mon, Pidge, you're gonna get hot. You know you can play better."

"You're crazy if you do it," Chuck Kelly said. "I'll go along, but you're crazy if you do it."

"Hell, you boys are shooting par, and look at me? I ain't done nothing."

The mumbling continued until the bet was made. "Don't you like the way he did that?" Jim Raymond said, "'You three big bad guys against poor little me.' So why am I smiling?"

"What does he mean 'Pidge'?"

"Short for pigeon. He knows I hate it."

Snead plugged along, only moderately sensational, unable to stem the tide of his opponents' best-ball birdies and handicaps. But his putting began to come around on the back nine, and he gained ground; the irony was inescapable. On the tee his swing is the prettiest in golf; on the green his stroke is a curiosity. Sam faced the hole, crouching beside the ball as if he were about to slalom with a single ski. His right hand held the club down the shaft and his left, at the top, acted as a fulcrum. The pendulum action all but eliminated wrist movement, the root of most putting failures. Snead has called this invention the "sidesaddle".

He said he had started putting that way – except then he hit the ball between his legs, croquet style – "about nine years ago in the middle of the PGA when I got the yips so bad it was that or quit." When crossing the putting line was outlawed in 1968, he simply slid his right leg over to meet the left, enhancing the looks of the stroke, though not enough to satisfy the purists. ("Hogan would never have done it.")

"They used to laugh when I started putting like that," Snead said as he went for a cup of water on the 13th. "I'd see 'em snickering, and I'd always get those comments from the gallery. At the Masters one year Bobby Jones said, 'That's a helluva way to putt.' Well, I don't care what way it is, the object of the game is to get the ball in the hole and pick up the cheque. Putting is an entirely different game, anyway. You start out hitting the ball into the air, with a full swing, and you end up jabbing at it and rolling it. Hell, no, I wasn't embarrassed. Why should I be? I wanted to play.

"Funny thing is I go to these tune-aments now, and I see guys practising the sidesaddle. Two years ago at the PGA Seniors I was 20 under, and all those old geezers were out there trying it. Palmer tried it on a practice green once or twice. Freddie Corcoran says they're even teaching it in England."

He hit his next shot, then walked ahead to a bunker, checking the card and pacing off the distance. He had done this on almost every hole, though it mostly went unnoticed because he walks so fast and does not hold up play. Chuck Kelly watched him.

"We were playing in a pro-am one year at The Homestead in Hot Springs, and one of the guys had a flask of brandy he was sipping," Kelly said. "He just wasn't taking the game seriously enough, and Sam got sore. He said, 'Listen, I don't give a damn if it's a pro-am or the US Open, I play as good as I can every time I play, and I don't want to play with someone who doesn't do the same.' He laid it on him good. Sam's that way. He'll work as hard here in five days trying to win $65 as he would at an exhibition for $5,000. He turned one down at Hilton Head not long ago. He said, 'How much?' They said, '$5,000.' He said, 'I'll stay home and play.'"

The match and most of the bets were even at the 17th, a straight-on 430-yard par-four. Snead chose a seven-iron from a point near a trap at the left for his second shot. "Little baby," he said to the ball, "I'm gonna have to put a hit on you . . . just cut this little seven in there . . . just cut it . . . " Whap. "Oh, that'll play." The shot bedded down four feet from the pin, and his birdie closed out MacCallum and the best-ball portion of the bet.

"You'll have a tough time getting a match the rest of the winter," Jim Raymond said.

"Especially from me," said MacCallum.

"Well, how close do you want it?" said Snead. "You went to the 17th."

"I want to win one," said MacCallum. "Last time I won was when we played in that sixsome. And you were my partner."

Snead grinned. "Well, the feller says, 'You gotta give it a shot.'" They left the green and he launched into a story about "a feller who accepted a million-to-one bet that he couldn't jump across a lake. He ran and leaped and made a helluva splash, and the other feller says, 'Why'd you take such a stupid bet? There's no way you can jump across this lake.' And the feller says, 'For a million-to-one I had to try.'"

MacCallum laughed with the others.

On the 18th Chuck Kelly put a long mid-iron inside Snead's ball, which was already on the green, eight feet from the pin. Snead, standing on the fringe, threw his putter into the air. "Gee *whiz*," he shouted. "There's one in every crowd." The putter came down and stuck handle-first in the green.

Then Snead got down into his slalom and punched in the eight-footer, and Kelly missed the shorter putt and the match was over. Snead was delighted. "That was a $25 putt," he chortled, scribbling on the scorecard at his cart. "A $25 putt, Chuckie baby." He twirled the cart handle towards the clubhouse, where the attendant intercepted him outside the pro shop and began unleashing his clubs.

"You playing in the Seniors at Disney World next week, Mr Snead?" he asked.

"Yeah," said Snead. "I'm going up there to play with those old geezers. They're giving the winner another Continental this year, you know."

All I got from the first golf job I ever held was a free lunch and a spare-time chance to hustle a few guests into taking lessons.
Sam Snead, *The Education of a Golfer.*

I spend as much time now on Snead's activities as I do on Johnny Miller's. That's how popular he is. He could make money all the time if he wanted to.
Ed Barner, President, Uni-Managers International.

"I'd rather play with friends like that than play in a tune-ament any time," said Snead, turning the Cadillac out the long drive from Pine Tree and accelerating south toward Boca Raton. The windows were down, the air conditioning off.

Then why go to tournaments at all?

"The competition. Quit competing, and you dry up like a peach seed. But a lot of times I get out there, and I wish I was someplace else. Fishing or hunting. Then I say, 'What the hell, I'm here now, I might as well play.'"

He turned the car east on Spanish River Road, heading for the ocean and picking up speed. He passed cars, slipping in and out of the lane. He said his "tourning pro" relationship with The Greenbrier had been severed after 38 years. He indicated that the parting had not been amicable, much the same as his split with the Boca Raton club six years before. He had been the pro at Boca, his winter base, 14 years. In both cases, he said, a new management had decided to cut corners. Snead was the biggest corner. First they took over his carts, a major part of his revenue, then the pro shop.

"The new manager at The Greenbrier offered me a straight salary. I said, 'How much?' He told me, and I said, 'The hell with it.'"

Shortly after that, he said, Tom Lennon, an old friend and the president of The Homestead in Hot Springs, called and offered him that job. The Homestead is 45 miles from The Greenbrier across the West Virginia line and is the course Snead grew up on as a caddie, where he turned pro in 1933. "We made a cash deal, and if I want to give lessons I can charge whatever I want." He grinned. "Feller says, 'If you want some lessons, I'll come get you.'"

He passed another car, getting back inside the middle lane just ahead of a fuel truck.

"I can't complain," he said. "The Wilson clubs I endorse are still the biggest sellers they got, and I get about a penny apiece. That's $100,000 to $160,000 a year, for the last 10 years. That's not so bad, is it?" He said he has the house near Boca Raton and one in Hot Springs and a farm he works outside Hot Springs, and a 600-acre cattle ranch nearby and a couple little beer joints in Florida. Three years ago, he said, he had turned his finances over to Ed Barner's group in California. He now gets $7,500 for a one-day exhibition appearance and a minimum $15,000 for a four-day tournament overseas. In that time he has been to Japan four times, to Hong Kong, Brazil, Morocco and numerous European countries. He gets cheques as "spokesman" for a chain of banks and a manufacturer of component parts, and for endorsing Niko whiskey and a line of clothing in Japan. He has a new instruction book coming out in December. Barner estimates his outside income is four times what he makes playing in tournaments.

"I played in 14 last year, which is a couple more than I'll average," Snead said, "and made more money [$55,562] than I ever did. If we'd been playing in 1949 and '50 for what they're playing for now at the same tune-aments I'da won $400,000 both years. [Miller earned a record $353,021 last year.] You can figure it up. Hell, a guy can be a millionaire in five years playing the tour today. Resent it? Why should I resent that? What other field can you do that in?"

At Route A1A, Ocean Boulevard, he turned the Cadillac north and, shortly after passing a sign marked Highland Beach, turned toward the sea, up a private drive lined with lush tropical plants and trees and curving past a garage over which were guests' quarters, to the front of a two-story white-brick house. He said the house was now worth $300,000, three times what he had paid for it in 1965.

"Just painted the doors on that garage," he said. "My hands were so stiff the next day I couldn't grip a club."

He took his companion around back to see the ocean. A stand of sea grape with leaves like giant olive-green pancakes bunched along the property down a slope to the beach. "I cut 'em back myself," he said, "but I see nobody else does, so the hell with it." He said the gardener had doubled his prices, so he was taking care of those things himself. He had been making repairs – painting, fixing sprinklers – anticipating the annual move north in the spring.

"The house next door burned down three or four years ago," he said, "and the rats were running around and the damn hippies were camping in the ruins. I finally had to go down to city hall to get 'em to clean it out." He said his house had been broken into four times in the 10 years since it was built, usually when he was away, but he now had a direct hookup with the police. He passed a rusting air conditioner. "Third one we've had," he said. "The salt air does it."

He said he had sold his boat, but from his bedroom window he could watch the fishermen hauling in kingfish and dolphin. In a huge recreation room downstairs he indicated the evidence of his prowess as an outdoorsman – a onetime world record 15-pound bonefish, mounts of other game fish and heads of animals he had shot in Africa. The two elephant tusks, he said, "are too skinny to be worth much – only 40 or 50 pounds." In one corner of the room was a set of drums his son Jack used to play; across the way was a bar with eight stools covered in simulated leopard skin. He said he never saw a private bar as big as his own. Above the bar his wife Audrey had Scotch-taped a series of black-and-white pictures showing the definitive Sam Snead swing in a 40-sequence. "Audrey is a good housekeeper," he said.

"I made reservations at the Riverview for 7.30," said Audrey Snead, a blonde, buxom woman dressed smartly in a white pants suit. "Their seafood is delicious. But if we eat any later Sam's liable to go to sleep.

He never stops going all day, and then he goes to bed with the chickens, you know."

"Well, I'm 62, I need my rest," said Sam. "Audrey's two years older'n me."

"That's not true," said Audrey, taking the hook. "Sam was two years ahead of me in school, but he was so full of mischief, I mean just full of mischief, always running off chasing raccoons and things, that I wound up two years ahead of him. My daddy wouldn't let me date him. We were teenagers, but he thought I was too young."

Did Sam's obsession for golf have anything to do with her father's reticence?

"Oh, no. Sam was a wonder-ful teacher, everybody knew that from the start. I mean, he could teach any-body. He can get me out there now and tell me one little thing, and it just straightens me right out."

"I wouldn't be a teaching pro," Sam said.

"Well, why not?" said Audrey. "Nothing wrong with it."

"Too much aggravation. Too many experts screwing people up. You listen to all that talk about this muscle over-powering that muscle and this pressure and that pressure, and a feller doesn't even know how to hold the damn club. He's liable to wrap it around his neck and kill himself before he learns anything."

"Everybody has to learn from somebody," said Audrey. "Who would *you* go to?"

"Nobody. Nobody knows more'n me about golf. I go to somebody about my insurance and about my teeth. But I don't go to anybody about golf."

They got ready to leave. Audrey said the big house had gotten a little lonely for her, but that their Miniature Pinscher JoJo was good company. "We got a Doberman at the farm," Sam said. "He wouldn't harm a fly."

"Yes he would," said Audrey. "He'd bite."

"No, he wouldn't, Audrey. He's a cream puff."

Their son Jack had lived there until he was married, commuting to Miami to finish college, Audrey said. She still kept his room the way it was, with his yearbooks and pictures. There was a photograph of Jack with Sam in Africa. The picture showed a handsome young man with slightly crossed eyes. Audrey Snead said both boys, Jack, now 30, and Terry, 22, were born cross-eyed, and they couldn't understand it because neither she nor Sam had eye trouble or even wore glasses.

Jack was married and had two kids now, she said, and worked for his daddy in Hot Springs.

What about Terry?

"Terry's retarded," Snead said without hesitation. He said there had been a high fever at an early age. Terry had been in a home since he was five.

"He's a strong, fine-looking kid," said Snead. "You look at him and you'd think he was perfectly normal. He recognises me when he sees me, but that's about all."

"He loves his daddy," said Audrey.

"Yeah," said Snead. His eyes were red around the edges. "But I'll tell you, if they keep hiking those fees, I'm bringing him home. All they do is give him room and board, anyway. C'mon, let's go eat."

I've always said Sam Snead could balance the US budget, as smart as he is about money. I always said, "He made a million and saved three." One year I hand carried six dozen golf balls to Australia for the World Cup. A boy wanted Sam to autograph one, and I gave it to him, and when Sam got it he said, "Where'd you get this?" The boy said Corcoran gave it to him. Sam said, "I don't autograph new ones. Get an old one. It's the same autograph." But if you asked him for $50,000 to make a business deal, and he trusted you, he'd sign right now. He did that with Ted Williams on that tackle business they had. Ted used to rib him all the time about baseball being the harder sport to play, having to hit a moving target and all. Sam said, "Yeah, but you don't have to play your foul balls."
Fred Corcoran

"Trouble with living here," said Snead as he turned the Cadillac south on Ocean Boulevard, "is it's too far to the golf course. Twenty-five minutes to Pine Tree. And there's so many women there taking up times. What I'd like is a club where there's nothing but men."

"What about me?" said Audrey. "I play, too, you know."

"Well, you could join a club where there's nothing but women."

"There isn't any such thing, and you know it."

"Yeah, but it's a good idea," Sam said.

He turned the air conditioner on and pushed buttons to raise the windows. His dinner guest asked if he ever thought of quitting tournament golf.

"Never," said Audrey. "They'll have to carry him off. He plays too much now. He needs more rest. But he'll never quit."

"Not as long as I enjoy it," said Sam. "I'd like to win one more tune-ament [he has won 150, more than anyone]. You know, it's an amazing thing. I've won at least one every year since 1936."

"You didn't win one *last* year," said Audrey.

"Yeah, I did. I won that par-three before the Masters. No big deal, but all the good players were in it."

"I don't remember that."

"Well, I won it, Audrey. Just let me tell it, please. If I'd averaged 30 putts a round, I'da won five tune-aments. Up to the Kemper I'd broken par in every one. I woulda won the Masters if I'd averaged 30 putts. Johnny Miller averaged maybe 25 or 27."

"Oh, I like Miller, he's a darling boy," said Audrey.

"Yeah, he's a good one," said Sam.

"What was it you said to him at the LA Open last year?"

"Nothing, really. He got upset because he was playing poorly, and he started backhanding his putts, flipping the ball around, and I got him aside and I said, 'Johnny, you're the US Open champion. You should play as good as you can, whenever you play.' Later on he thanked me."

What about the Open, he was asked. Does it still bother him that he never won it?

"I coulda won it last year at Winged Foot. It was possible. I don't say it was probable, but it was possible. I had practice rounds of 70–71–70, and was even 36 after nine holes. Then I had to withdraw. I could hardly breathe. When they X-rayed, they found two broken ribs."

"Probably broke 'em when you had to jump off that tractor at the farm," Audrey said. "He'da killed himself if he hadn't jumped."

"Maybe. I heard something snap. But a 287 won the Open, and Winged Foot was my kind of course."

What about the other years? The other Opens.

Snead's eyes got round.

"I have to think there were people who didn't want me to win. One year they outlawed my caddie. Another time they paired me with the final threesome of the day, though I was still in contention. I can't blame anybody but me for blowing two or three, but I have to think there were some people who were just as glad to see it happen.

"The best golf I ever played, though, was right after the war when I came out of the service. I won five out of six tune-aments and lost the sixth in a double playoff with Mangrum. Nobody coulda beat me then. Hogan, Nicklaus, Palmer. Nobody. But '49 and '50 were the best years for winning. I retired after that."

"You *never* retired."

"Audrey, I retired. I'd won more money than anybody that year, I'd won the Vardon Trophy for best average. I'd won more tune-aments. But Hogan got Player of the Year because he won the Open. I said, 'Well, shoot, if I do all that and they make somebody else Player of the Year, what's the use?' So I quit."

"You didn't quit long."

"No."

The Riverview was crowded, but the waitress hailed them warmly and escorted the Sneads to a preferred table. Sam ordered the broiled snapper and Audrey the yellowtail. They were finished before nine. When the check came Sam grabbed it out of the hands of his guest.

I don't get excited about athletes. We manager Miller, Heard, Casper and Hill and Don Sutton of the Dodgers, and I have them in my house, but I don't get excited about it. But Sam, he's different. When I'm with that old man, I feel like I'm with a piece of history.
Ed Barner

Sam Snead crushed the box of cornflakes in his hands, opened it and spilled the crumbled contents into the bowl, then layered the top with bananas.

"I don't eat much lunch," he said. "I like to keep my weight about 190. I'm about 195 now." His thick fingers worked the spoon into the cereal. He was in the dining room of the golf club at Disney World, an hour from tee-off in the PGA Seniors tournament, which he had won six times. He complained that he had to pay the greens fee for the practice rounds he had taken the two previous days.

Tommy Bolt, heavier and greyer than remembered, came by and the two men exchanged greetings.

"I talked him out of this thing one year," Snead said, grinning. "He stuck his head over my locker and said, 'Hey, Nudie, what the hell you doing?' I said, 'Hey, what's the matter with you, Thunder?' He said, 'Whaddaya mean?' I said, 'You look awful. You look green around the gills. I never saw you look so bad.' 'Well, hell, I don't *feel* good, Sam.' 'Gee whiz, Thunder, you don't *look* good.' He went right out and withdrew, and he was the only guy in the tune-ament who could beat me."

The tour, he said, had changed a lot since the days he and Bolt were big numbers. "Motels made a difference," Snead said. "Everybody used to stay in the same place, sat around, got to know one another. I travelled with Johnny Bulla for about four years, splitting expenses. Now you never see the same guy twice in one year unless you play with him. And the young guys are more conscientious. Used to be they'd shoot a 65 and blow up. Now they do it four days in a row. They're more fit. They're in their rooms doing push-ups and eating Wheaties. Trouble is, you get so that's all you think about, and somebody asks you your name, and you can't tell 'em.

"I was always a loner. I liked to get away from it, to fish or hunt or watch a shoot-'em-up. I didn't hang around with anybody much, except Bulla. Hogan? You'd play a round with Hogan, and then only thing he'd say was, 'You're away.' But if you'd walk alongside him, you would hear him grunt, 'Unh, unh,' like he was talking to himself. I offered him a drink of water once at the Masters and he looked at me like I was crazy."

His companion noted that Snead had always seemed able to reduce golf to the most elemental level, to turn what was essentially a game of detachment (man against the beguiling irregularities of nature as produced by golf-course architects) into an emotional contest of individuals. At one time Snead won 13 consecutive man-to-man match-play events on television and, with one exception, had always beaten Hogan in match-play events and playoffs.

"There are some guys, you know, you just figure if you go out there and look 'em in the eye, you're gonna beat 'em," said Snead. "Valerie [Hogan] told me one time, 'We never relax until you're in the clubhouse.' Hogan never said anything like that, of course. But that's why I like to play with the guy I have to beat. Then I can watch him. See what he's doing. You watch a guy long enough, you pick up a pattern. Does he play fast? Does he talk a lot? Does he waggle his club before he hits? Then if he changes – a little hesitation, a little extra waggle – you know you got him. Hogan did that over a putt when we were in a playoff at the Masters one year. Hesitated over a putt on the 16th. I knew I had him then.

"C'mon," Snead said, "let's go see if I can put something together."

He went out into the Florida sun. He was wearing red-check pants, yellow shirt, blue sweater and black shoes. From the back he looked remarkably trim – his hips still slim, his torso broad and tapering with the familiar sloping shoulders and Alley Oop forearms. Only the paunch up front would give him away, and it was only a minor revelation. There are younger, rounder stomachs on the tour.

Another one of the seniors hailed him. Sam said he was in his late 50s. "That old so-and-so. He hasn't changed in 20 years. The feller says, 'He uses well.'" The man looks 10 years Snead's senior.

Hell, yes, he could still win one. If he's on he still plays as good as 99 per cent of them on the tour. The thing is, he's always stayed with it. And he has the desire. At our age there's also the matter of confidence. It's a little like sex, one bad performance and you begin to wonder. The thing about Sam is he's always correcting and experimenting, and he thinks he can do it. In the Seniors a couple of years ago he had a 268, and after every round he'd complain, "If I coulda putted, I'da had a 59." Hell, so could I.
Julius Boros, age 55, golf pro

In the first round at Disney World, playing in a foursome with Ted Kroll, Chandler Harper and Doug Ford, Snead shot a 74. He would finish sixth. It was, he said, the first time in three weeks he was over par. He took nine putts on the first four holes and had two three-putt greens. He complained that the greens were rough. After the 6th hole, where he rolled in a 20-footer for a birdie, he said, "I'm hitting 'em dead centre, but they're rolling up and bouncing away."

He strode down the fairway as fast as some people trot, pacing off his shots, checking distances. When others putted he stood off to the side, his legs crossed, his ball in his hand, examining it as if he had never seen one. It was, of course, vintage Snead.

As the round became irretrievable, he began talking to his shots. "That's enough, that's enough," he said as his drive faded on the 11th. The ball hit on the fairway and bounded into the rough. "Thank you, Lord," he said. On one hole he flipped a club; on another he kicked one into the air. In his book, Snead said, "Show me the feller who walks along calmly after missing a kick-in putt, showing the world he's under perfect control, yet burning inside, and I'll show you a feller who's going to lose."

Late in the day Snead and a friend went upstairs into the clubhouse lounge to have a beer. The lounge was packed, but Snead was recognised and quickly surrounded. Two beers were delivered to him simultaneously. He told a story about a mounted policeman and a parking ticket, and then one of his friends, an Italian with a blonde girlfriend in short shorts, joined the group and bought him another beer.

Snead asked the Italian if he'd heard the story about the guy, "who wanted to be a Polack".

The Italian grinned, and Snead continued.

"This old boy tells his doctor he's tired of all the Polack jokes, that he had sympathy for 'em, and he wants to be one. The doc says, 'It's all right, but we'll have to cut out half your brain to do it.' The feller says, 'OK, go ahead.' But when he comes out of the anaesthetic, the doctor is standing over him looking real worried. The doc says, 'I got something awful to tell you. Instead of half your brain, we took out three-fourths.' And the feller slaps himself on the forehead and says, 'Mama, mia!'"

The Italian's laughter mixed with the others, and Snead raised the side of his mouth with a grin and made his exit, depositing an empty beer glass on a table near the door.

"A damn 74," he said as he walked through the restaurant side of the lounge. "Well, tomorrow I'll just have to shoot a 66."

With that he swung his leg into the air in a perfect *battement* and kicked a metal sign that was hanging by chains from the ceiling at the entrance to the restaurant. The sign said "TROPHY ROOM, PLAYER'S GALLERY" . It was seven feet off the floor.

LIKE SOME DEMENTED HAMLET

Ian Wooldridge

There are many anecdotes about the legendary parsimoniousness of Severiano Ballesteros. Some are probably apocryphal. This one is not.

One fine spring morning, a business agent flew down from London to northern Spain with yet another commercial contract that would enhance the great man's income by many thousands of dollars for doing next to nothing. By arrangement, Ballesteros met him at Bilbao airport. They proceeded to the parking area where Severiano had left the family car. The businessman was shocked. The car appeared to have seen service in the Spanish Civil War. When it spluttered into life, it shed particles of rust like metal dandruff.

"Seve," said the agent as they jerked along the coast road to Santander, "what is a great international sports star doing driving a heap of junk like this? Would you like a Range Rover? I can arrange for you to have one on permanent free loan."

The Range Rover is Britian's most fashionable vehicle. The Queen drives one to pheasant shoots. Her son-in-law, Captain Mark Phillips, promotes their sale. His wife, Princess Anne, is photographed weekly at the wheel of one. Anyone in Britain with a bank account to match their social aspirations drives a Range Rover. "Okay," said Ballesteros, "fix it." And fixed it was.

Some months later the business agent returned to Bilbao for another meeting. Again Ballesteros met him at the airport and led him to the car park. To his surprise his transport was the same jalopy of Spanish Civil War vintage. "Seve," demanded the agent, "what happened to the Range Rover?"

"It's at home," replied the great golfer. "It uses too much petrol."

At around this period Ballesteros's income was conservatively $4 million a year, probably much more. But the spectre of imminent poverty still haunted him, and to begin to understand this gloomy, brooding man's genius you must know something of the inviolable structure of the society from which he springs. Spain, for all the democratising efforts of its motor-cycling monarch, Juan Carlos, remains something less than the egalitarian society portrayed on its florid tourist brochures.

Blue blood is still thicker than the ink on liberalising government decrees. If you were born on the wrong side of the donkey tracks you are liable, peasant as well as land-owner, to be thus categorised until the last rites make all men equal before their maker. Ballesteros was born on the wrong side.

You must understand his frustration. He can win the Masters and the British Open half a dozen times and remain the profit-motivated professional sportsman without honour in his own country. Golf, like dove-shooting, is socially acceptable in Spain. Professional golf is on a par with mending bicycles.

Last November Ballesteros made a stealthier attempt to infiltrate the rigid Spanish social bastion. He married Carmen Botin, a lovely 24-year-old eight years his junior. Cynics were swift to point out that she is heiress to a banking fortune and aristocratic tradition. Those of us who have seen them together would also say it is an idyllic love match. But the point is that the poor guy can't win. He is cast in the same mould as the handsome matadors who have tried to make the same transition. Iberian social mores are a darkly mysterious business to outsiders.

This may begin to explain to American golf galleries why Ballesteros, shoulders hunched, eyes blazing, seemingly frequently at war with his own caddie, strides the fairways like some demented Hamlet. It may explain to reporters who come into frequent contact with him why, with a black mood upon him, he can be graceless or devastatingly rude. It forgives nothing, but may make it easier to understand.

I have suffered his moody rebuffs, too, when he is contemplating whether to stare you down or give you both barrels of loaded sarcasm in his fractured but fluent English. Equally I have enjoyed his company when he is at his most charming.

We played golf together one morning at Wentworth, England, venue of the annual World Match Play Championship. The first hole is an extremely demanding par-four and in my nervousness, off a shaky 18 handicap, I took a four-iron off the tee to hit the ball straight.

"Why you take four-iron?" demanded Ballesteros. I explained with honesty that I was more concerned with keeping the ball in play than risking driving it 100 yards behind his. I swear he deliberately struck his next shot left into the woods to make me feel more relaxed. I won the hole with a five to his six. It was the first, last and only hole I won but I shall not forget the contradictory incident. Ballesteros is a man who beats up his child bride 21–0 at table tennis if he possibly can.

The only golfer I can compare him with is Arnold Palmer, whose similar blitzkrieg attitude to an immobile golf ball in the rough is to take about half a ton of flora and fauna with it in restoring it to where it should be. Ballesteros, however, does not share Palmer's social confidence, for he does not come from a nation in which accomplishment is the ultimate credential.

His spur to success is perpetual insecurity. It is a demon to live with and does not make him instantly likeable. It merely makes him a devastating opponent.

THE OLD TRANSVAAL

Gary Player

I suppose the two most critical factors in the creation of my personality have been the death of my mother when I was eight years old, and the fact that I am small.

I was born in 1935 in Lyndhurst, which was really a small village a dozen miles outside Johannesburg, but which is now in danger of being engulfed in the spread of Greater Johannesburg. The accident of birth made me a South African, living in the Transvaal, and the physical fact of place and environment and climate, and the society in which I grew up, would certainly also have had its effect on me, in making me what I am today. In that respect it might be useful to go back a little way into history to take a look at the Players that were. I have certainly not made a study of my family tree, but from what I know it seems clear that my great-grandmother was a remarkable woman. She had large brown eyes, and these have come down over the generations in a notable way. My father and his brothers have them, I have them, my brother Ian and his children have them, my own children have these large brown eyes. My great-grandmother was a of French Huguenot stock. Her family came out to the Cape in the early 18th century, and she was in the Great Trek of 1836–38, when the Boers were under pressure from the English in the Cape, moved north and went up into what is now the Orange Free State and the Transvaal. It appears that she was in an exodus, a large group of wagons led by Piet Retief and they came out of the eastern part of the Free State, and down into Natal. They laagered along the Tugela and Bloukrans Rivers below the Drakensberg, near Weenen, while Retief and sixty men went on to parley with Dingaan, King of the Zulus, over safe passage down towards the coastal plains. Dingaan murdered Retief and his men, then fell on all the wagons, massacring women and children. My great-grandmother was stabbed in the side by a Zulu spear, but somehow dragged herself off into the bush and survived.

In time she married James Power, from England, and they had seven children, and these children really were brought up in wild country, pioneering country, so that they thought with the spirit of pioneers. There are direct similarities between the South African history of the period and that of the opening up of the American West. I am sure the spirit of the people was the same. This was a time when a man lived with his rifle, his wagon and his horses, and when he had to be a man of the land, a good landsman, and apparently James Power was outstanding in this respect. In an era of great marksmen, he was an outstanding rifle shot, and was said to have great knowledge of country, of the kind of country that would be safe for wagons to go through, about grass and water and the lie of the land. All South Africans have a powerful feeling for land, and this has come down through the generations, too. My father had a keen eye. He was very good with a rifle, very good with golf clubs, and had this feeling for the lie of the land, for the shape and sweep of the country. And I do believe that I have some of it, in relation to golf, in the overall panorama of a course, in the shape and structure of a golf hole, and I feel in many ways that I can relate myself to it, that I can accommodate myself to the topography; I certainly have a feeling for the general drainage of a golf hole, the sheltering effect of trees, the feel of the surface soil under my spikes and so on. Again, in marksmanship, I was exceptionally good with a catapult as a young lad. I could knock over a bird once in three shots, at distances up to 50, 60 and 70 yards, and I don't suppose one person in 50,000 can do that. I don't boast about it – it was a fact of life. We had an old Zulu kitchen boy in the house who used to call me "Hasynioorni", which means "the man who killed the birds" and I'll try hard not to say anything about killing birdies today, on the golf course.

I was also fairly good with the air rifle which my father gave me. Ian taught me to shoot with both rifle and catapult, and I really was world champion with that catapult. My early life in the Transvaal was an outdoor life, an outgoing life. In a golden climate, sport played a prominent part in social life, in tennis clubs, bowling clubs, golf clubs for the adults, and with the schools setting great store on team games for young people. And the land lent itself, the open country beyond the city, to all the adventures which the fantasy minds of children build in their daily games. It was a very good country in which to grow up. My brother Ian, eight years old, had a positive influence on me. Because of my father's promotion to the Robinson Deep Mine, where he became mine captain, we moved back into town. He was provided with a company house, and we went to live in Booysens, in Beaumont Street, where my father had lived a few doors away earlier, before moving to the country, and where in fact Ian had been born. There was an old pear tree at the back of the house, and we hung a rope on it. About five hundred yards away was a golf course, the Turfontein course. We would climb up and down this rope, and if Ian did it once I would do it twice; if he did it twice, I would do it four times. If he jumped five feet, I would try to jump ten. Of course, he allowed me to do these things, and encouraged me to do them, but even then, I was trying to go one better with Ian and with other boys.

Rope climbing is an arduous business. It develops arm, shoulder, back and stomach muscles, but it also develops determination. If you do it once, you don't feel inclined to do it again, and you really have to force yourself a second time with a positive act of will. But I was determined to conquer that rope. There was an odd sequel. We left that house around 1947, and I suppose it was fifteen years later when I made a sentimental pilgrimage back to the house, to remind myself what it looked like. I found that same rope hanging in exactly the same place. I cut it down and took it away with me. The house in Beaumont Street in the early days for me was fine. Looking back on my life I can see that it was not the happiest of places for the family. For one thing, you would have to say it was the other side of the tracks in comparison to suburbs like Killarney or Lower Houghton, where rich South Africans live, and where, such are the quirks of life, I now live myself. The mine and the vast mountains of sand-coloured earth it spewed up in reefs dominated Booysens as it still does, and it seemed to be a place of bustle and noise and dust and constant movement and activity. I went to a school where many of my chums were wealthy and lived in large and palatial houses, and while I must say that I do not remember ever having a conscious feeling about this at the time, it may well have entered my subconscious. I know that Ian, for example, who went to a school even more swank than mine, has told me that he was always aware of this, and never quite happy about it.

Many things happened at this house, most important of all the death of my mother, from cancer. She had been ill for a long time. She was a small woman, which no doubt emerges in me, while my father is a big man, which emerges in Ian and Wilma, both quite tall. But she was highly intelligent, without having had the advantages of much formal education, a great reader, a loving and devoted and industrious mother to whom I have always felt very close. Wilma has told me how in the closing months of her life she was in great pain, but how when people asked her how she was, she would say, "Just fine" or "A little better today" or something of that kind. Wilma, who knew this was simply not true, would often chide her for this, and ask her why she said it, and smiled at everyone. She would always answer "People don't want to hear anyone complain. They have their own troubles. And they feel better if someone else says she feels better." My mother had so loved life in the country, at Lyndhurst, that she just hated to go back to Johannesburg. She was horrified at the thought, she disliked the particular suburb and the particular house, and she had a very powerful premonition that she was going to die in that house. She said this to Ian, not to me, but again it is something that may have reached into my subconscious, because the strongest recollection I have of my mother is her bravery in illness. Ian, by the way, had an incredible premonition about my mother. When she died, he was in Italy with the South African Armoured Brigade, yet long before he received the telegram with the news of my mother's death in it, he knew that she was dead. To this day he cannot explain how or why he knew, but he knew beyond doubt.

Ian's joining the Army is an extraordinary aspect of his life and character. He is a very strong and positive personality. When he was 12 years old, mountain climbing, a big rock came down and injured his right knee, which was badly smashed. He was left with a very puffy knee and a right leg slightly shorter than the left. Then when he was still in school, 16 years old, he went to my mother and father and told them that he wanted to "go North", which meant join the Army and go up to Europe and be in the fighting, be in the war. They were appalled and said how he couldn't possibly join the Army at his age, and with his bad knee. It seems incredible now, but he tried to enlist and was rejected because of his knee. He simply kept on trying until they accepted him, and eventually he did "go North" and fought in a tank in Italy with the South Africans. When he came back after the war, he tried a dozen jobs and failed to settle in any of them, not surprising when you think of the experiences he must have undergone in the war as a young boy. Then he applied for a post as a game warden, and is now Chief Game Conservator in Zululand, in the Hluhluwe (pronounce that Shloo-shloo-way!) and Umfolozi game reserves. He believes passionately in retaining and maintaining not only the wild life of our country, but the whole ecology of the thing, and over the years he has become a highly talented naturalist. His job is clearly the preservation of species, all kinds of species in his own domain, and much of his time is taken up chasing poachers. He had done a brilliant job in preserving the white rhino, which some years back was reduced to about fifty animals. Ian and his colleagues have now built up a herd of around six hundred, and they are regularly exported to zoos all over the world.

Ian lives a life which is wonderfully simple and natural in the literal sense of these words. He and his wife and children have a nice house in the little township of Hluhluwe, with plenty of space around, but the nearest hospital is something like ninety miles away, and there is no school for young children, so Ian's wife and the other wives teach the children, at least until they are old enough to go off to boarding school. His children speak African languages even better than they speak English, which is a little hard to appreciate. Ian of course will take off into the bush for days on end, in a Land Rover, often alone; and so his wife, like the other game wardens' wives, has to be very self-sufficient. A few years back, the MGM people came out to film a movie called *Rhino* and Ian gave them a good deal of technical help. In return they invited him to the States on a lecture tour, and he was quite terrified of New York City. He thought he was a good deal safer in the bush than he was there.

Perhaps his climbing accident turned him away slightly from sport at school, where he had been a fine games player, and towards a more academic attitude to things, but he still does a fantastic amount of reading. He says he just can't get to sleep without reading something. If he doesn't have a book, if there isn't a Bible in his bedroom, he will find anything that is printed, a bus ticket for example, and pick out a word from it, and build words round that, or a letter or a number and build permutations around it before he goes to sleep.

My sister Wilma, four years older than I, married when she was 17, and she too left the house in Beaumont Street. She must have played a formative part in my life after Mother died. She has had a hard life in the sense that she kept working for many years after she was married, to help her own household along, but fortunately she now spends a few hours each day helping with my affairs, in the office of my house in Johannesburg, and the warm, close relationship that I have always had with her is maintained.

Before my mother died, I used to have regular pocket money. After she died, it became irregular, and I became very careful with money. I hope I stopped a good way short of being a miser, but I became – well, careful with it. I had a money box. Ian and Wilma used to spend their money more carelessly than I did, and often they would borrow from me. I would dole out a shilling or two shillings or whatever it was, from the money box, and they would have to pay me double at the end of each month. I was a better businessman then than I am now – my accountants regularly have to call me and tell me to stop spending money. I feel the money box was quite significant in my early life. I'm not sure it I have ever been able to decide why, or in what way, but it lingers stubbornly in my mind, the memory of it.

In sport, Ian was the dominant influence on me, constantly encouraging me, constantly challenging me to run faster, jump higher, because there is no doubt I had a complex about being small. Ian knew this quite well, after one particular sports day at school. Someone said something to me, about being a shorty, just before I was to run the 100 yards. I ran it, and won. I ran the 220 yards, and won. Then I did the same in the 440 yards and the half mile, and when I was almost on the point of exhaustion, I went over to Ian and said, "Well, how's that for being a shorty?" When we did push-ups, and I would get to around 30, I would flop down and say to him, "I've had it." Ian would say, "All right, if you do another 15, I'll give you a bicycle for Christmas." Now I don't believe it is often a good thing to bribe children in this way, but he would say that, and I would do the extra 15. Then he would say, "Just a moment ago, you told me you couldn't do it." So he would be planting in my mind a challenge and also showing me at the same time the human body has hidden and surprising reserves that we can call on if only we apply the human will to the problem.

At school, if I was not a genius at work, I won honours in rugby, cricket, athletics, swimming and diving. I captained the first team at soccer and won the trophy for the best all-round athlete in the school and that included the big fellows of 18, everybody. So perhaps there I proved my point that being "small" doesn't necessarily matter. And perhaps since then, on the championship courses of the world, I have proved again that it doesn't necessarily matter, even in the world of adults. It doesn't bother me any more – that is one complex that has long gone.

Chapter 4

LADIES' SECTION

Enid Wilson

Mildred Ella Didrickson, subsequently Mrs George Zaharias (pronounced Zar-harris) and "The Babe", was a legendary figure in athletics before she occupied a similar position in the world of golf which she quit prematurely by dying of cancer at the early age of 42. Since then there has been some controversy as to her status in the hierarchy of the great women golfers, but none can dispute that, when she passed away in the autumn of 1956, after a prolonged and valiant battle with the dread disease, she had established herself as the outstanding competitor of her time.

The dynamic personality of "The Babe" was largely responsible for the success and development of the Ladies' Professional Golf Association in America. Her phenomenal power proved a great draw for spectators, and one of her delights was to wisecrack with the galleries, her freedom from inhibitions enabling her to be happy in any company. She attracted the limelight and adored it, and an example of her outlook may be gathered from her remark one morning to the starter on the East Course at Wentworth just as she was about to drive off in a tournament. "Babe" spotted his gesture of admonition towards an overzealous photographer who wished to get an action shot. "I would be the one to worry it they didn't want my photograph," she remarked, and the picture was duly taken.

With the passing years there has grown up a generation who never saw "The Babe", and to them she is a mythical figure, the first American to win the British Women's Championship. Of her early days and background they are completely ignorant, apart from knowing that before she turned her attention to golf, Mildred Didrickson broke world records and made history in the Olympic Games at Los Angeles in 1932. There she won gold medals for the javelin and hurdles, she also broke the record for the high jump, by several inches, but the judges would not allow this to stand because she used the then controversial style known as the Western Roll.

To appreciate "The Babe" and her achievements in their proper perspective it is necessary to know something of the background from which she came. As her maiden name of Didrickson would indicate, she came of Scandinavian stock. Her parents were Norwegians who began their married life in Oslo. Ole Didrickson was for a time a seafaring man, and during one of his voyages he was attracted by, and made up his mind that he wanted to settle at, Port Arthur in the Gulf of Mexico. His wife, Hannah Marie, approved of the idea of emigrating, and their family had grown to three by the time they had saved enough money to go to America.

When the Didricksons made their home in Port Arthur, Ole went to work in a furniture factory. The family increased, there were twins, then in June 1914 "Babe" was born, and she was followed by another child, so altogether there were seven young Didricksons, five girls and two boys.

Before "Babe's" fourth birthday they had moved to Beaumont, and it was there ten years later that she began to make a name for herself as an athlete in the Beaumont High School basketball team.

Her one big stroke of luck was being born in a land where there were plenty of opportunities for those with outstanding abilities, and although her early days were fraught with poverty she came of a happy family. On leaving school she went to work for an insurance company in Dallas, where she paid five dollars a month for a room, and sent more than half her salary home.

The story goes that it was on a driving range in Dallas that she made her début as a golfer, and in keeping with the many fabulous legends of her athletic prowess, she is reputed to have swatted the ball 250 yards at her first attempt, and during the follow through broken the shaft of the club by striking a stanchion.

During the 1932 Olympics at Los Angeles, "Babe" was the darling of the sportswriters, and they it was who took her out on a golf course, where she proceeded to astonish them by hitting several drives of well over 200 yards.

After the Olympics "The Babe" had several tempting offers from various firms interested in publicity promotions. Acceptance meant the loss of her amateur status as an athlete, but the bait proved too tempting, and amongst other things she did a variety turn on the stage in Chicago, and was lined up for a tour of the big cities. Although her act went down well, she began to pine for fresh air and an out-of-doors occupation, so she soon quit the theatre and returned to basketball for a while.

By then the golfing germ had taken root, and she made up her mind to learn to play and win the women's amateur title within three years. When she made this decision she thought she had enough cash put by, but it soon dwindled and she returned to her old job with the insurance company in Dallas. To augment her income she tried her hand at baseball and tennis, then after watching Bobby Jones in an exhibition match her desire to excel at golf was rekindled, and her firm co-operated handsomely by having her made a member of the Dallas Country Club, and footing the bill for her to be coached there by the professional, George Aulbach.

In the autumn of 1934 "The Babe" entered for her first tournament, the Fort Worth Invitational, and made the headlines by winning the medal with a score of 77, but she was soon eliminated from the match-play stages.

She then set siege on the Texas State title the following spring, and during the weekends practised up to 16 hours a day. The venue of the tournament was the River Oaks Country Club, Houston, and "Babe" achieved her ambition by defeating Mrs Dan Chandler two-up in the final over 36 holes. Naturally her feat received countrywide publicity, which was perhaps unfortunate for her, because three weeks later, before she could play in any further competitions the United States Golf Association stepped in and ruled that she was a professional, and declared her ineligible to participate in amateur events.

So, in the spring of 1935, "Babe" signed up with a sporting goods company and was booked to go on a tour of exhibition matches with Gene Sarazen. In this she was supremely luck for she could not have had a more understanding and sympathetic partner, and Gene spent a great deal of time helping her to improve her game.

During that tour with Sarazen, "Babe" twice played in matches against Miss Joyce Wethered. At Oak Park, Chicago, Britain's greatest woman golfer was paired with Horton Smith, and the scores of the quartet were Sarazen and Horton Smith both 71, Miss Wethered 78, and "Babe" 88. Meadowbrook was the course of their other encounter, and on that occasion Miss Wethered was paired with George Nagell, and the scores were Sarazen 72, Nagell 73, Miss Wethered 77, and "Babe" 81.

Two more contrasting characters than those of Miss Wethered and "The Babe" could not be imagined, and their methods were also totally dissimilar. The perfection of Miss Wethered's timing and her effortless swing, control, and artistry, were lost on "The Babe", who was then immature as a golfer, and more concerned with getting distance than anything else.

Miss Wethered's impression of the young American was that she had not had sufficient time in which to polish up her short game. "The Babe" was then too inexperienced to appreciate the Englishwoman's skill, and her recollection of those exhibition matches was that she could hit as far with a number two iron as Miss Wethered did with a driver.

There was nothing in the rules to prevent a woman from entering for the Los Angeles Open Tournament, a 72-holes medal event, for which there was no qualifying test, so in January 1938 the idea of playing in it appealed to "The Babe", and the officials put her down to play with the Reverend C.P. Erdman, a Presbyterian minister, and George Zaharias, a professional wrestler. They proved a considerable attraction to the gate. It was also the beginning of the romance between Mildred Didrickson and George Zaharias. They announced their engagement in the summer and were married the following December.

Because of her renown as an athlete, and the many occasions and different sports in which she had been matched against men, the majority of people were apt to gain a wrong impression of Mildred Zaharias. Most tended to imagine her as a big-boned, over-muscled, strident-voiced Amazon, whereas in fact anyone meeting her for the first time had no cause to suspect that she was endowed with an abnormal physique. Above average height, with slender build, straight-backed and graceful in her deportment, "The Babe" moved like a panther. Although she was generally photographed in sports clothes, which were not always becoming, she took a great interest in dress, and had done so from childhood when she often made her own clothes.

Soon after they were married, George and Mildred Zaharias went to Australia, and stayed there several months. There was no financial necessity for her to exploit her golf, for George was in the top income class in his profession, but it was not her habit to be idle or to miss any opportunity and she played in a series of exhibition matches.

On their return to America, in the autumn of 1939, "The Babe" was anxious to improve her golf with further competition, but then only two tournaments were open to her, the Western, and the Texas.

With George earning enough to give her all the golf she wanted, they came to the decision that the best thing she could do would be for her to send in an application to the United States Golf Association requesting reinstatement as an amateur. This course remained open to her as she had not been a professional for five years, but time was running out and her application had to go forward before May 1940. It was dispatched, and "The Babe" had then to wait for a period of three years before she became eligible to compete in amateur events.

Before this probationary time expired the war had put an end to tournament golf. "The Babe" resumed exhibition matches, but they were charity affairs from which the proceeds provided comforts for the fighting services.

So it was not until 1946 that "The Babe" went to her first women's National Amateur championship, which was held at the Southern Hills Country Club, Tulsa, Oklahoma, and attracted an entry of 60, 58 of them being starters. The match-play stages followed a 36-holes medal qualifying test which reduced the field to 32. Miss Dorothy Kirby headed the qualifiers with 152, Miss Louise Suggs came second with 154, and her score of 156 put "Babe" in third position. With a series of easy victories she progressed to the final, and there annihilated Mrs Clara Sherman by 11 up with 9 to play.

At her first attempt she had succeeded in winning the National, and with it the realisation of an ambition that had germinated 14 years previously.

Before going to the National, "The Babe" had captured the Trans-Mississippi, Broadmoor Invitational, and the All American tournaments, and she concluded the season with the Texas Open to make a run of five major events in succession.

In the spring of 1947 she mopped up the Florida championships, the Titleholders, and the North–South, and when she had notched up 10 more victories, to make 15 in succession, she looked abroad for further worlds to conquer, and the obvious plum was the British which had never fallen to an American.

The idea of taking this championship impelled her to make a lone voyage across the Atlantic.

When "The Babe" arrived at Gullane early in June, there were still evidences of the exceptionally severe winter. The frost had not worked out of the ground, so the top surface was unusually soft and heavy. These conditions suited her admirably, and the tremendous carry of her drives was utterly disconcerting to her opponents, for she often out-hit them by 100 yards from the tee. An instance of her power came in her match with Miss Frances Stephens, where on the 540-yard 15th hole, "Babe's" second shot with a No.4 iron pitched over the back of the green.

When she did this, the day was still and overcast, and after she had finished the hole I enquired of her caddie what club she had taken for her second.

Previously, in conversation "Babe" had mentioned that she had played round Muirfield, and needed nothing above a number eight to reach the greens on the longest holes. Another instance of her tremendous power was her method of dealing with the 5th at Gullane, some 460 yards uphill, which she treated disdainfully by driving over to the corner of the dog-leg, and flipping her second with a wedge up on to the green.

Although we did not know it at the time "Babe" was the first of the atomic and jet-age women strikers of the ball. She stood straight up and with squared stance delivered all the might she could muster. Her only mannerism was the curious one of licking the thumb of the glove on her left hand, which she then wiped on the slate-blue corduroy slacks which she wore throughout the championship. Her swing was too forceful to be pretty, and many of her strokes finished way off line. When they did so, it mattered not, for she had the strength to get home with her seconds from almost any position. After the grounding she had received in her early days from Sarazen, bunkers held no terrors for her, and although she frequently missed the greens at the short holes, she rarely missed getting threes, the excellence of her recoveries being equalled by her ability to hole out.

The Home Internationals were held at Gullane in the week prior to the Championship, and "Babe" was an interested spectator, they gave her a chance of seeing and measuring the calibre of her future opponents. She followed a match in which one of the players holed out with a full No. 7 iron, and the small gallery expressed their appreciation of that approach with silent awe. "The Babe" was amazed by their behaviour, and in tones of bewilderment addressed a bystander, "Don't people here applaud a good stroke?" she said, and it was then explained to her that the absence of outward emotion was a sign of respect.

Some days later, after "The Babe" had inflicted a severe defeat on her antagonist and they were faced with a long walk back to the clubhouse, she suggested that they might play in, and this they proceeded to do, followed by their gallery. To entertain them "Babe" started playing trick shots, but their effect was not what she had anticipated and the crowd melted away. They had come to see golf not showmanship, but that was something she could not understand.

The main road from Edingburgh to North Berwick runs through Gullane, and the first tee of Gullane's Number One Course is close to where the road bends at the beginning of the village street. The tee is surrounded by a fence of white posts with a top rail on which the natives like to lean and watch the players driving off. "Babe's" custom was to walk down to the course from her hotel at the far end of the village, and to vault lightly over the top rail on to the teeing ground. She did this without any perceptible effort, and to the considerable amazement of whoever happened to be standing there at the time.

Having spent so much of her life travelling "Babe" was in no way disconcerted by having to play on a type of course that she had not seen before. She was supremely confident of winning and buoyed by her unbroken run of successes over the past year. Moreover, she told the reporters that she had played and beaten without the aid of strokes, every member of the American Walker Cup team.

She came to Britain at a time when the austerities of the war were still prevailing, and when the older players were past their zenith, and the up and coming generation seeking to find their feet. Miss Pam Barton was one who would have stood up to "The Babe" without flinching but, alas, she had been killed in a flying accident whilst serving with the WAAF at Manston.

Miss Helen Nimmo, a member of Gullane, was the American's opponent in the first round of the championship, and "Babe" beat her by 6 and 5. She then met Mrs Sheppard, a sturdy Midlander and English international, with a good record in match events, but Mrs Sheppard's courage and fine short game were of no avail against "The Babe" who beat her by 4 and 2. In the third round, an ex-Irish champion, Mrs Val Reddan, who had represented Britain in the Curtis Cup match at the Essex Country Club, Massachusetts, in 1938, and came away with two points, was hammered by the American 6 and 4. Another Scot, one who had represented her country, and also Britain against France, Mrs Cosmo Falconer, fared slightly worse, losing by 6 and 5. Thus "The Babe" had accounted for four highly experienced golfers in the early stage of the championship, and fortune then decreed that her remaining opponents should be young ones.

In the fifth round she had her hardest match of the week, and that was with Miss Frances Stephens, whose seeming frailty then made people wonder if she would have the stamina to stay in big golf. The slender Lancashire girl stuck doggedly with "The Babe" for 12 holes, and then might prevailed by 3 and 2.

"Babe" was through to the semi-finals, and confronted with the Scottish champion, Miss Jean Donald, daughter of a local doctor. All Edinburgh and the East of Scotland had been anticipating and waiting for this meeting of champions, but, although "Babe" revelled in the size of the crowd, and was inspired by it, the effect on Miss Donald was not so good, and she began by taking three putts. Then the American had birdies on the 2nd, 3rd and 4th, and romped away to win by 7 up and 5 to play, her score that afternoon being five under fours.

Meanwhile, a strong, determined player from Middlesex, Miss

Jacqueline Gordon, had been making her way through the other half of the draw, and thereby vindicating her selection in the English team the previous week.

On the morning of the final, "The Babe" set off on her accustomed walk down the village street to the 1st tee, wearing a pair of pink and white check Bermuda shorts. Before she got to the course she was intercepted by the Captain of the Ladies' Section of the Gullane Club, and persuaded to return to her hotel and change into the blue corduroys which she had worn previously all that week.

Miss Gordon was not in the least intimidated by her foe that day, and started well by playing the first nine in 36 – one under par – and a birdie on the 11th enabled her to lead "The Babe" by two holes, but by the end of the morning round they were all-square, both players having gone round in 75. When they resumed Miss Gordon faltered on the 1st hole, "Babe" grasped the initiative and delivered a mortal thrust with an eagle three at the 2nd, and when the English girl slipped again on the 3rd, it was apparent that the championship was going to America. Miss Gordon did her best, but the situation was hopeless, and "Babe" ultimately triumphed by 5 up and 4 to play.

On her return to the United States "The Babe" received such tempting offers she was prevailed upon to turn professional again.

Maybe the sands had started to run out, for not long afterwards she was troubled by a pain in her left side. The greatest of her victories was the American Women's Open Championship, when at Peabody, Massachusetts, in 1954 she won that event for the third time. The previous summer she had endured a colostomy, and so commenced the fight against an enemy to which all human flesh is defenceless in the end.

YOU'VE COME A LONG WAY, BABY

Michael McDonnell

Just the sort of chap we're looking for, agreed the selection committee, when they looked at the letter of application for the job as golf professional. This chap Saunders was not only extremely intelligent, well-educated with a degree in psychology, but was also an accomplished golfer and fully-trained in the craft of club-making and repair. Get him along for an interview.

Saunders didn't get the job. The committee were staggered to find that Saunders was a *woman*. Good Lord! How could she possibly cope with men who might squabble over starting times on the 1st tee? How would men respond to her? Anyway wasn't it an unglamorous job for a woman?

Miss Vivien Saunders hit right back. Had they asked the same sort of questions of the *male* candidates? Of course they hadn't. It was a blatant case of sex discrimination, and yet another sad skirmish in the Battle of the Sexes.

The experience was nothing new for Vivien, one of the most articulate figures in golf, because she had been turned down for 17 previous jobs as club professional, once the committee realised she was not a man. This time she sued under the Sex Discrimination Act and while she received the support of the Equal Opportunities Commission, she lost a claim for financial compensation. The happy sequel was that Vivien went on to qualify as a lawyer, wrote a definitive work on the psychology of golf and, in the meantime, coached several outstanding golfers to the top. Even so, her experience was but part of a heritage of a struggle that strong-minded and ambitious women like herself have faced in order to do their own thing . . . despite male opposition.

From the moment young Gladys Ravenscroft shocked Edwardian society by rolling up her sleeves on a hot afternoon to expose bare arms as she played in the 1909 British Championship at Royal Birkdale, the battle for equal rights on the fairway was engaged. The restraints had been ludicrous. Long ankle-length skirts had to be worn on the fairways, which meant that on a windy day ladies had difficulty not only seeing but even hitting the ball. They wore a huge elastic band which, before each stroke, had to be rolled down to their knees to keep the skirt in place.

Even fairway fashion needed emancipation and – By Crikey! – a woman actually turned up on the first tee in *trousers*. You could actually see the contour of her – well – body. They called her The Woman in Black and she stunned her rivals and grabbed the front pages when she appeared at Westward Ho! in 1933. Her name was Gloria Minoprio, a woman of mystery. Tall, elegant and beautiful, she arrived, played her match and then left. She used only one club – but employed a caddie to carry it. She remained silent throughout, as if mockingly amused by the consternation she was causing. But this, in truth, was the reason for male opposition in clubs: the fear that women, if allowed to join, really would begin to wear the trousers. It is the reason why opposition still lingers, Ask, for example, why there are no women members of the Royal and

Ancient Club of St Andrews, the game's governing body, whose rules are observed by more than three million women throughout the world. You will be told it is because there are no plumbing arrangements for their convenience. Then ask why – in almost 300 years – nobody has thought to install such a facility. You will be told because there are no women members to warrant it.

There are many clubs throughout the world from which women are not only barred as members but which they dare not enter. Most ordinary clubs still cling to the tradition of men's bars where chaps can gather and use rough and ready words away from feminine ears. But in Britain, several historians acknowledge the crucial part that golf played in the success of the "Votes for Women" movement at the start of this century – and not simply because it was on a fairway that a group of irate suffragettes tried to take off the prime minister's trousers.

It was two key factors which brought golf into the fight for women's rights. First, the sport was played by a privileged class from which the movement sprang. At a country house party at the beginning of the century, an unnamed cabinet minister arranged a match against a lady in the group called Mabel Stringer and said: "I suppose if you beat me I shall have to support Women's Suffrage". She did and he kept his word. That incident gives a clue to the second factor. Golf was – and still is – an activity which demands total independence of spirit and character; the ultimate in self-reliance. Thus it was the epitome of Women's Liberation as perceived by the Edwardians.

Blanche Hulton, a distinguished writer of the period, spotted this aspect of the sport and wrote: "It marks an epoch in the history of the sex and, without unduly straining a point, it may be said that golf has been a factor of no small importance in the mental and physical development of the modern girl." She felt it offered an example of liberation from drudgery and routine that dulled and perhaps even shortened life. More than this, its heroines stirred an excitement beyond the sport itself. These were the free spirits for whom life was one long adventure; they were active and they were fearless. But, above all, they were in control of their destiny and independent.

The most charismatic of them all was Cecil Leitch, who in 1909 attracted thousands, who just wanted to see her play. She personified the new zest that had emerged in modern womanhood. They called her "the flapper from Silloth" because she strode gleefully down the fairways, her long hair tied in a bow and she gave the ball a fearful whack as though it was her worst enemy. There was nothing genteel about the way she played and that aggression, too, captured the imagination of a wider public.

Could she survive in a man's world? The idea was put to the test when she faced Harold Hilton, one of the best players of the time, in a two-day match over Walton Heath and Sunningdale. More than 3,000 people – not just golf enthusiasts – turned up to watch this Battle of the Sexes. Miss Leitch beat him by 2 and 1 and the suffragette leaders made a great issue of it because Miss Leitch had played from the men's tees, although they omitted to say that Hilton had conceded a total of 36 strokes in the 72-hole encounter. This was an important point because a definite and measurable difference in playing strengths between the very best men and women has existed down the generations, even though the top women professionals now hit the ball an average 240 yards from the tee.

By common consent of men such as Henry Cotton and Bobby Jones, one of the best golfers – regardless of sex – in their time was Joyce Wethered, who later became Lady Heathcoat-Amory. She had a textbook swing that others tried to copy and her technique, using legs and body to compensate for lack of arm strength, became the basis for the modern golf swing. Cotton was unstinting in his praise. In his book *This Game of Golf* he wrote a chapter entitled "The Best Player Ever?" which began: "Whenever golfers gather and begin talking about one of the game's most popular topics – 'Who is the best player ever?' – it is certain that before many minutes have passed the name of Joyce Wethered will be mentioned."

Joyce Wethered could hit the ball as far and as straight as most professionals and once halved a match at St Andrews with Bobby Jones. Yet even she admitted she was, on average, between two and seven shots worse than her illustrious brother, Roger, depending on the length of the course they played and the carries required (i.e. the distance through the air to the fairway). She cut a boyish and athletic figure which accounted for her flawless technique. Not for her the common feminine problem of whether to swing "under" or "over" an ample chest.

(In fact, there is no need to do either because well-endowed women have found the best swing technique is to stand close to the ball, stick the backside out so that the spine is straight, then turn the shoulders away from the ball for an unencumbered downswing.)

But Lady Heathcoat-Amory found herself at a disadvantage to her male opponents when trying to force the ball from a bad lie. She did not have the strength. She was as good as anybody – so long as she never strayed from the fairway. Indeed, all the evidence suggests that even though golf itself demands no physical clash of skills – as does tennis, football and other sports where the object is directly to prevent an opponent playing well – women remain the weaker sex. Accordingly, every course that acknowledges the existence of women provides forward tees (red markers), invariable many yards ahead of the men's tees for what is, in fact, a shortened course with a par valuation that differs from the men's version. For men, a par three can measure up to 250 yards, while women restrict their par threes to 225 yards. A men's par four can extend to 475 yards while women restrict theirs to 430 yards. In both cases, longer distances are regarded as par fives. So women's golf is less demanding and operates to different, more benign, values. Yet the popularity of women's professional golf tournaments on both sides of the Atlantic is because they play a "normal game". Even men golfers can relate to it in a way they cannot when watching the great men players.

Perhaps when men turn up to watch women play, there is the suspicion of sexual voyeurism as attractive, leggy beauties besport themselves in scanty shorts – Gladys Ravenscroft and your rolled-up sleeves, where art thou? – but there is also considerable golf knowledge to be gained. Some time ago, I played 18 holes with Tony Jacklin. It brought to mind something Bobby Jones said of Jack Nicklaus: "He plays a game with which I am not familiar." We hit our tee shots from the same place – his to the far horizon and mine just over 200 yards. We met later on the green to exchange scores and so it progressed. I learned nothing from the encounter.

I gained much more when I partnered Mickey Walker, one of Britain's best women professionals, in a tournament. We hit the ball a similar distance, which meant I could rely on her club selection for second shots and could study her strategy and variation of stroke-making to certain greens. I watched how she played to her strengths and protected her weaknesses and because we played a similar style I could follow and benefit. Simple things, like favouring an under-hit wood to make the distance from fairway to green rather than hit an iron full out, particularly from a bad lie. Jacklin? With his supreme strength, an iron club was no problem.

There is a widely-held notion that golf requires a mannish quality to withstand the demands of competition and critics point to the broad-beamed, tweed-skirted caricatures of women's golf to emphasise their point. Catherine Lacoste, daughter of the great French tennis champion, was perhaps the last outstanding amateur. She actually beat the professionals at their own game when she won the US Open in 1967.

But she quit, partly because the competitive demands were making her too tough – or so she thought. She explained: "I felt that the effort involved whenever I won somehow cost me another piece of my sensitivity. I was becoming too hard as a person, unable to switch off once the game was over." She had no regrets at leaving to marry and raise a family. Nor was she even hinting at the broader allegation that the sport attracts or promotes lesbianism within its ranks. Such sexual attraction does exist and there are well-known and devoted partners in the American tour – even talk of a "marriage ceremony" between one couple. Yet this has less to do with the nature of the sport itself as the day-to-day existence of players, living continually in a rather enclosed community with very little time to develop friendships outside it.

I once met an author doing research for a book on "community women" – i.e. those thrown together and confined by a common way of life – and the survey covered not only the golf and tennis circuits but also convents and schools where, the author claimed, mutual attraction and affection developed because of constant proximinity.

Such relationships are not inevitable. The modern golf heroine *can* break free from the narrow confines of the sport. Jan Stephenson's life story, for example, has been so adventure-packed that Hollywood considered it to be worth a feature film. She started as a reporter on a local paper in Australia and endured a series of escapades and marriages to emerge as one of the most talked-about women of her generation in the United States, the owner of a private jet, several homes, with a huge personal staff, her own TV chat show and in constant demand to pose for pin-up pictures. but most important of all, she could play outstanding golf and became US Open champion. She saw no treachery to the cause of women in demonstrating her femininity as well as her athleticism. It was a tremendous success story and fitted neatly into the campaigning tradition of golfing heroines who have overcome opposition on and off the fairways to succeed.

But while those early activists were debagging a man of state on the golf course and chaining themselves to railings in the cause of feminine equality, a more significant revolution – and more discreet – was taking place. There exists today in Britain three women's golf clubs – Wirral Ladies, Formby Ladies and Sunningdale Ladies – founded around the turn of the century to escape male discrimination. Indeed, the Sunningdale Club was founded by an irate father whose daughter was not allowed to play on the main course. However, these ladies' clubs have shown more tolerance to the opposite sex, permitting them membership but in some cases insisting that men can play at restricted times when women do not need the course. How the wheel has turned.

But don't ask for the gentlemen's toilets in Formby Ladies' clubhouse, There aren't any. As the Royal and Ancient club pointed out in a different context, there is no need for such plumbing arrangements. For male visitors, Formby Ladies' clubhouse is a water hazard with a difference – and a monument to a war in which peace has not yet been declared.

THE SOUND OF NANCY

Peter Dobereiner

The best way to watch women's golf is to keep your eyes closed. Perhaps I had better come up with a swift clarification of that statement before we get our wires completely crossed. Absolutely, item No.1 on the agenda of explanatory footnotes is that I do not, repeat *not*, mean that women golfers are not worth looking at.

Far from it. When it comes to bird-watching I count myself a connoisseur. The effects some of those lissom girls achieve when they swing a golf club really ought to be forbidden by law. I still break out in a hot sweat when I recall playing a pro-am with Jan Stephenson on a hot day in Spain when she was dressed for comfort. As for Laura Baugh, I am almost persuaded that it does not matter whether she can break 90.

And when Renee Powell is playing in a northerly direction, and I am observing from the south, if any member of the constabulary in the vicinity happened to be a mind-reader I could go to gaol for my thoughts. No, I have no complaints about the appearance of women golfers. For the moment my mind is strictly on the quality of the golf they play.

With the benefit of hindsight – or hindsound I had better call it, although the word frankly troubles me – I first became aware of the value of closing one's eyes at golf tournament when I went to watch the late and great Babe Zaharias.

Tramping cross-country through the woods to catch up with her I knew I was on track when I heard that characteristic sound of a golf ball being struck. Something troubled me about the noise, but I pressed forward and was soon engrossed by the sight of that magnificent athlete, combining grace and power in a way that seemed more appropriate to a member of the cat family than a human being.

After a few more holes I was still faintly disturbed because, with all her highly developed skills, there was an element which was not right. The clue hit me when she walked back to a tee and, because of the press of the crowd, I could not see her hit the drive. I fixed my gaze down the fairway to pick up the flight of the ball and listened for the shot. That was it. The sound was not that of a woman hitting a golf ball; it was the noise made at impact when the club is wielded by a good man player.

After that, I repeated the experiment, deliberately closing my eyes so that I could concentrate on the sound without distraction. There was no doubt about it. When a woman swings the club it sounds "whooooooosh, plop!" A good man player sounds "whizz, tok!" If you take a hard-boiled egg, remove the shell and hurl it against a wall, you approximate the sound of a women golfer's shot. A man's impact is harsher, crisper – more like a .22-calibre pistol being discharged in the next room

That crispness of impact, caused by the clubhead accelerating (and descending) into the ball, brings immense benefits to the shot in addition to extra length. This is where refinements of control originate – through backspin.

Women sweep the ball away. They may hit it long enough. The good ones hit it straighter than their male counterparts. And they undoubtedly make good scores like this. But what they do not achieve is that virtuoso shot-making ability, moving the ball this way and that and checking it sharply on landing, which is the essence of a genius such as Hale Irwin.

Many years later, having formed the habit of watching women's golf with my eyes shut, I heard that Zaharias sound again. It came from the clubs of Catherine Lacoste, of France, who, when barely out of her teens and an amateur, went to America and stood the world of women's golf on its ear by beating the professionals to win the US Women's Open.

Incidentally, Mlle Lacoste was given the full treatment by some of the girl professionals and cried herself to sleep every night over their bitchy hostility. All these years later, as the mother of a growing family and therefore an infrequent, although still formidable player, she does not care to recall some of the unpleasantness of the greatest weeks of her sporting life.

Anyway, my point is that I do wish that women golfers would give some attention to the quality of their striking and seek to reproduce the characteristic snapping-twig note at impact. I am not saying, of course, that the noise is a benefit in itself. It is simply an audible proof that the strike is a good one.

The women pros are eminently capable of working out their other problems, such as swing planes and directional control, for themselves.

But until they get that snap into the shot, everything else will be in a minor key and that, let me assure them, is not going to be good enough in the future. Women's golf is moving into a new era and if the professionals are to survive they must work and analyse and copy.

For I have heard that sound again. There is absolutely no mistaking it. It comes from the clubs of Nancy Lopez.

CATHERINE LACOSTE: CHAMPIONNE DU MONDE

Peter Ryde

Golf demands humility of its followers. Some of us never cease to pay our tribute. Others may seem to escape; the game leads them up to exaggerated pinnacles of fame and wealth; it may – it almost certainly does – grant them moments of infinite pleasure and satisfaction; but before the end, by some means or another, even the mightiest are humbled by it.

Every great player could furnish examples. In the past when a man's skill was measured by match-play, what shame those two giants of the game, Allan Robertson and Old Tom Morris, must have felt when they were beaten 12 and 11 over 36 holes by the Dunn brothers. To be sure they were playing on their opponents' home course, Musselburgh; but if that excuses the severity of their defeat, it cannot have made it any easier to bear. The Dunn supporters were a tough crowd who left no doubts where their sympathies lay.

Any one of us could make his own list of such occasions in the lives of his favourite hero and in these days when the glare of publicity is brighter than ever, examples are if anything more numerous. Even that most ruthless of golfers, Ben Hogan, paid the full price. In 1946 he was left on the final green of the US Masters and the Open with two putts to force a tie and a play-off; in each case he took three putts. Nine years later when he stood poised to realise his great ambition of winning a fifth Open, which not even Bobby Jones had achieved, he lost a play-off to one of the least considered champions of all time, Jack Fleck.

Arnold Palmer's career is a chequer of tragedy and triumph, but his throwing away of a seven-stroke lead in the last nine holes of the 1966 US Open, and then losing the play-off the following day, was as painful a humiliation as could be devised. Jack Nicklaus, detached though he is, cannot have relished the 10 he took at the 11th in the 1962 British Open at Troon; but even worse must be the memory of the way he let the 1963 Open slip from his grasp, by missing a short putt at the 15th, overshooting the 17th green, and bunkering his drive to the 18th.

The full drama of these occasions is only felt when the champion is at the height of his powers, and the débâcle is in full view of the public. Not every famous calamity may satisfy those conditions, but there is one champion for whom the moment of tragedy was all too completely staged. In the autumn of 1969 Catherine Lacoste let it be known that she was retiring from international competition. It was not to be a clean break. She was to marry a Spaniard, but since she would be living in that country she could hardly turn her back on the women's world team championship which was to be held there the following autumn. But her decision to pull out kept nearer to the truth than most announcements of that nature. It looked, then, as though she might escape unscathed, as though she might be one champion whom the game would allow to remain unhumbled. Her successes had been so numerous in her five-year career that she had hardly had time to throw a championship or quit on a tournament. Her whole story was one of dazzling success, proudly borne.

She had, of course, known defeat, as any great golfer must. Quickly as she rose to supremacy, she had first to establish herself against three of the finest golfers in Europe at that time. The Vicomtesse de Saint-Sauveur was coming to the end of a long and distinguished career; Brigitte Varangot and Claudine Cros were approaching the summit of theirs. All of them were French, and taking the long view her rivalry with them was the making of her as a champion; without such a tough initiation into the competitive world she might never have prevailed in America.

Although she had at the age of 19 contributed most to the victory of France in the first world team championship, she needed time to prove her superiority. It was not until two years later, in 1966, that she won the championship of France for the first time, overcoming an inhibition about beating Brigitte Varangot that was threatening to turn into a mental block. The following year she suffered what I have always supposed to be her most vexing defeat. At Harlech she led the qualifiers for the second year running in the British championship, only to find herself beaten in the first round by Martine Cochet, a compatriot who had scraped into the championship 16 strokes behind Catherine over the two qualifying rounds.

Vexing, yes, but that defeat hardly entered into the realm of grand drama. In the ultimate test of stroke-play Miss Lacoste had already made her mark; the hazards of match-play were another matter and had always frustrated the best. Bobby Jones, we hastened to point out, had won two British and three American Opens before he succeeded in winning the British Amateur. Moreover her main triumphs lay ahead; against the background of that historic Welsh city, she was not yet ready to play the leading part of tragedian.

From her childhood she had been cast in a heroic role, having champion's blood in her veins from both sides of the family. The ability to win does not of course depend necessarily on inherited talent in that particular field. Sheer adversity may force the genius out of a performer, and sometimes the parents of a champion may excel in another field. But with a father who had been singles champion at Forest Hills, and with a mother who, as Mademoiselle Thion de la Chaume, won a British championship in Catherine's favourite sport, it was not long before Catherine felt at home in the competitive atmosphere which some excellent performers never get used to at all. Her father, René Lacoste, confined himself to shrewd observations about her technique. A great theorist of this and other games, he perhaps had the good sense to realise that his daughter needed, not instruction for she was too good a natural ball player for that, but an outside eye that could supply what most players need, a diagnosis when things go wrong. Many a good golfer who can detect faults in others and correct them, can remain curiously blind to the fault that has crept into his own game.

Catherine's string of successes has its roots in the children's tournaments her mother used to organise during the summer holidays at their home course of Chantaco, down the road from St Jean de Luz. Madame Lacoste did her best to see to it that her daughter did not collar the first prize all the time, but it was hard work. They had given birth to a winner. She was young, she was powerful, she was scornful of opposition to the point of giving offence. Add to this some blunt remarks, remarkable more for their honesty than for their tact, and it is hardly surprising that, over and above her maddening habit of winning, she roused occasional animosity. She once admitted to being perhaps *"un peu cabochard"*. We must make what we can of that, but *caboche* is a hob-nail, and riding-roughshod over people's feelings might not be wide of the mark.

But how exciting a trait that was when translated into action on the course! She came to the first world team championship for women at the age of 19, junior champion of France and that was about all. The team event, the only one of its kind in which a player represents his country in stroke-play, is the most exacting of all. Yet Catherine played the last decisive round as though it were the height of enjoyment to her. We said that it was the innocence of youth, but even in full maturity she never lost that quality. Patty Berg, the famous American professional, was quick to observe it. She wrote: "She enjoys playing golf and anyone can see that sport is far from being the most important thing in her life . . ." This completely amateur approach helps to explain her victory later in the US Open where so much was at stake for the others, and it also helps to explain her ability to play her best when it mattered most. "I need a high stake to bring out the best scores in me," she once said. Such a remark may sound like tempting providence, but almost until the end of her career she made it look as though it were the right way to treat providence, and as though an assurance so complete had enabled her to earn exemption from the golden rule of humiliation.

In 1967 came the first thunderbolt, completely unexpected and almost unwitnessed and unreported from this side of the Atlantic. I was in Portugal watching the European women's team championship in which Catherine, to the irritation of her colleagues, declined to take part. They were standing in a huddle in the hotel lobby, and when I said in reply to their question that I had not heard the news, they told me that I must first be seated or the shock would be too great. Catherine had won the United States Women's Open championship. The surprise has worn off for all of us by now because we are familiar with the brilliance of her game. We accept that she can hit the ball harder and straighter than any other living woman, that she has more confidence in playing the one-iron than do most men. We know, or thought we knew until that last act in Madrid, that she will always knock the putts that matter in.

What lingers in my mind of that victory is the courage she showed in going over there and maintaining her game to the end. I sometimes pass the time thinking of the great occasions I have missed and would like again to have the chance of seeing. Catherine's triumph at the Cascades Club in Virginia is high on the list. She herself is not easily drawn on the subject but a French journalist, Renaud de Laborderie, in *Les Reines du Sport*, has reconstructed the ordeal with sensitivity. For days at the motel and at the course Catherine was completely alone. The championship journal, the press, the players ignored her existence. The only exception were two young girls seated at the next table to her. They got talking as Catherine sat munching her lonely corn flakes, and they persuaded their parents to stay on until their new friend had won. Her 70 in the second round hoisted her five strokes clear of the field and established her on the road to victory. It was one of the great rounds of her life, comparable to the fabulous 66 which she had scored at Prince's the year before in winning the Astor Trophy. Before the final round on a day of clouds and humidity she went to mass, praying no more fervently than usual for golf is not essential to life. It was this air of detachment that carried her through the final round, that enabled her to keep hold of a slipping lead, to drive across trees at the 17th, hole a three-yard putt, and make sure of the title.

Her victory was as complete as was to be that of the next foreigner to win an American championship Tony Jacklin. She was the first amateur to do so and the youngest player. It was the championship she most wanted to win, *ça va de soi*. But it was not the one she found hardest to win; that was the American Amateur; nor was it the one that gave her the greatest pleasure in winning; that was the British Amateur. She had to wait three more years for these two and one depended on the other. The British had been the stumbling block in her career, for here her predominance in stroke-play could not assert itself. But in 1970 she went early to the green shores of Northern Ireland to prepare for the championship that still eluded her. Already that year she had won the French championship and also, for what it was worth, the Spanish by 10 and 9. She allowed her mother to accompany her; in America she had wanted to make her own way to fame, apart from her parents. Now she wanted her mother with her, because it was down the coast from Royal Portrush at Royal County Down that she had won the same championship 42 years before. Only Ann Irvin looked capable of stopping Catherine that week on a giant course worthy of a true champion. Ann was three up on her after seven holes, and luck went against her when Catherine's approach to the 9th was deflected by a spectator's handbag from the rough to the edge of the green. But luck comes to all, and it is the ability to take advantage of it that marks the champion. Catherine holed that putt and banged her tee shot to the next hole 10 feet from the pin.

Coming back to London in the plane afterwards she was uncertain what to do next. She was contemplating marriage, but reluctance to return to America, where, to put it mildly, her triumph had been received with mixed feelings by players and press, was losing ground to the vision of her completing the grand slam of winning the American Amateur. This time she would land in that country not an unknown at the start of a great adventure, as had been the case in 1967, but as someone who was expected to win and whom every American would take delight in beating. "When you are a champion, if you win *c'est normal*; once you lose everybody says you are over the hill." Moreover, the championship was being held in Texas at the hottest time of the year. From the relaxed country-house atmosphere of the Côte Basque she would have to go forth into the furnace, summoning up for a final effort her great competitive spirit. In a temperature of more than one hundred degrees in which the iron clubs under the sun became too hot to handle, she clung like a leach to par. As had happened in the British she found herself three down in the final; as in the British she extricated herself, this time against Anne Welts, a golfer in the highest class, but one whom she had beaten when their Curtis Cup team visited Paris, and one who was beginning to show signs of having been so long at the top.

The grand slam was complete; that year she had won the French, British and American in succession. She was now ready to withdraw from top competition, with the finest record of all time and also the proudest. But by one of those quirks of fate the world women's team championship was the following year to be held in Madrid, the city where she was going to live and on the course of which she had recently become a member. Complete as her achievement was this was one last international championship on which she could not turn her back. In the six years of history her individual record of tied first, third and first was second to none; and of all the leading countries France alone had kept her team intact from the start.

She might joke that, being now married to someone who was half-Spanish, half-Chilean, she had a choice of three countries to represent; and it was certain that since the championship would take place a few weeks after her marriage she would not be in full competitive trim. Still, no matter; half a Lacoste was better than no champion. Slowly and inexorably the situation built up. In that type of championship, where the best two rounds of three count for four days, the climax sometimes passes unseen out on the course, and the result becomes a matter of statistics. In this case there was never any doubt where the climax lay, and the insignificant crowd that found its way out from Madrid, reinforced by members of other teams who had finished, watched the long drawn-out agony of those last nine holes. Catherine Lacoste blew up. She would not, I feel sure, with her own tremendously high standards, want to hide behind words. There were all kinds of extenuating circumstances and she finished with a plucky par at the 72nd hole which even in ordinary circumstances is not an easy four, but she blew it. I am concerned only to make that the point that at the eleventh hour the champion who looked to have got away without being humbled by the game she loved, was made to pay the tribute demanded of all other great players.

We can gloss over the details. The three strokes' lead Catherine held with nine to play vanished and the United States retained the title of world champions by one stroke out of 598. By ordinary standards the French girl did not collapse, but she would not forgive herself the shortness of the putt she missed on the 11th green or for having been short with her pitches at two relatively easy holes. Her opponent, Martha Wilkinson, was a lovely swinger of the club – one of these juvenile suntanned products of the American conveyor belt, who had played in 72-hole tournaments week after week through the summer. She did not have, as her opponent, packing cases full of unopened wedding presents in a still unfurnished home, and when she does I have no doubt she will not be playing for the United States. Sometimes as a spectator it is possible almost to hate the game one loves when one sees the full burden of a team event proving too heavy for one person. There had been an example of that the day when Catherine first burst upon the world and won the team championship for France six years previously. Then Barbara MacIntyre's failure to retain America's lead sent a chill through the hearts of the spectators. Today the boot was on the other foot as Catherine, waiting for Martha to take two putts and get her four, sat on the bank, at the back of the green, her head in her arms.

When the pain has worn off, comes the realisation that this is part of the greatness of the game; one comes to admire its cold impartiality. Catherine, whatever that day may have cost her feelings, is not diminished by it as a golfer. She remains nonetheless the greatest women champion of our times; and it would not be surprising if the experience had not left her a more complete person.

NEVER PLAY A WOMAN LEVEL

Henry Longhurst

One day in the summer of 1951, when the American women professionals were paying their first visit to England, General Critchley arranged a match for them at Wentworth against a team of London amateurs. These included Leonard Crawley, perhaps the second best player in the country at that time; Gerald Micklem, a Walker Cup player; John Beck, the only man to captain a successful British Walker Cup team, now in his fifties; an English international or two, and, at the very, very bottom your humble servant. However, at the last moment I had to go to France and so, unwittingly, escaped the slaughter. The match was to be played on level terms – an early psychological blunder: one should *never* play a woman level! – and the men, regardless of their doom, assembled with the pleasing prospect of a gallant day's golf in the sunshine, a substantial lunch, and refreshment in congenial company to round off the occasion. They won two of the foursomes and there was a certain amount of chaff at the expense of the other pair who only halved. A few hours later all were laughing on the other side of their faces. In the singles every one of them had been beaten, level, by a woman.

They took it in various ways. One to this day is hardly approachable on the subject. Another was heard to growl that it was "ridiculous to encourage these people". Crawley, defeated by Mrs Zaharias, after a good deal of technical stuff about fast-running fairways and not being able to take his driver from the tee, declared that next year on a course of his own choosing, he would raise a team to give them five strokes a round and beat them. . . .

Anyway, at a convivial pre-Ryder Cup gathering at the home of the Earl and Countess of Carrick, Harlow brought up the topic and I blithely, and as I thought safely, declared that, had I not had to go to France, I should without doubt have defeated my opponent-to-be, Mrs Betty Bush, and thus achieved world celebrity. I ought to have known better. The light of the publicist gleamed suddenly in Harlow's eye. Muttering "Boy, this is a natural!" he sprang to our host's telephone, located the lady in Chicago, fixed the match as a sort of comedy curtain-raiser to the Ryder Cup, and planted the story in all the New York papers and even, I believe, in London.

This, of course, condemned the reluctant and embarrassed correspondent, playing at that time excruciating badly, to long sessions on the practice ground, a tiddler among the big fish, with spectators who had assembled to watch Snead, Mangrum, Faulkner, Rees and the rest asking themselves, had the British really descended to *this*? I borrowed a fine flashy set of clubs – the very worst American club player habitually has four magnificent wooden clubs with leather "hats", 10 gleaming irons, and a cabin-trunk bag for someone else to carry them in. I also acquired a huge bag of practice balls belonging to the president of the Metropolitan Golf Association, Earl Ross, to say nothing of a faintly condescending negro assistant at a pound an hour.

Jack Hargreaves, of the British team, offered sympathetic advice about non-existent wrist action. Fred Daly, in the course of a kindly half-hour, detected a pronounced hook on the face of the driver and adjusted me till a few flew straight, if not far. "There you are, sorr," he said. "What's the matter with that, sorr?" Even the great Hogan, eyeing from afar, not only offered hints but later on gave the pupil a practical demonstration, not unlike the "unarmed combat" instruction in the war, of his theory of the straight-right-arm-after-impact. This provided the other occupants of the bar with much innocent amusement and the patient with severe cramp between the third and fourth ribs on the left side.

"Depend upon it, sir," said Dr Johnson, "when a man is to be hanged in a fortnight, it sharpens his mind considerably." To which I echo to any despondent golfer, "Depend upon it, sir, when you are due to play a diminutive woman professional, level, in circumstances exposing you to extreme ridicule, it sharpens your golf wonderfully." With two days to go I was hitting as many as three running plumb in the centre of the club.

Seeking to weigh up the opposition, I consulted the Pinehurst assistant professional. Did he know Mrs Bush? Sure he did. And what would she-er be likely to do on the No.1 course (par 71)? "Waal," he said, leaning his arm on the counter and contemplating for some time, "I guess she won't do no better than 72."

At this point there arrived a message from Mrs Bush. As she had said over the telephone, she had recently had an operation. Now her doctor had said she would not be fit to get round the course. She was sorry indeed to let me down like this.

Some other time. . . .

"Lucky miss," said some.

"Certainly not," said I. "Lucky Mrs."

THE THIN END

Stephen Potter

Not far from the ancient town of Rye there is a sea coast course famous for its mixture of rough beauty and of golf problems – problems so difficult that few men have been able to persuade themselves that women should be allowed even to set foot on it.

Nevertheless women have played this course and round about 1950 Mrs Basset, a wife well known in gamesmanship circles, was actually made a life member of the Club by her father, a former chairman of committee. She was entitled to play over the course and, though entry to the clubhouse was not allowed, she was permitted, owing to the distinguished record of her parent, to be handed drinks through a small window in a corner of the windward side.

In spite of that, this woman, Mrs Bassett, although there was a *sheltered* outdoor seat for her, used to complain openly, in January and February, and again and again older members asked themselves: how was she elected?

On one occasion she knocked on the window "because she wanted another", and although I knew I would be criticised, I myself handed her one.

Was I wrong? Twelve years later a woman's room was built. It had a dainty little shelf and a sort of cupboard door which, when opened, led to the back of the bar. But long before that happened I myself took Mrs Bassett to the Woking Club. I was not disappointed. There was a small women's changing room, complete with wash-basin and a coathanger which (she told me with shining eyes) "although it had the name Mrs Wilson on it was regarded as being free for use when Mrs Wilson was not present". But what she did not at first realise was that provided she stuck to a pre-arranged route, clearly recognised and agreed upon, she could walk, partly *through the club premises*, to a dining room *where men and women ate together*. I remember her coming in now, hiding so perfectly her excitement.

THE GREATEST?

O. B. Keeler

Bobby Jones and his party met Miss Wethered and Miss Shaw at the airport – it was the English girls' first journey by plane, and they liked it so well they would have said they were crazy about it, had they been American girls – and at dinner that evening Miss Wethered and Bobby talked golf incessantly and she told him how Bobby Cruickshank had suggested a change in her putting grip for the American greens – the reverse-overlap; it appeared to me almost identical with that suggested to Bobby so long ago by the late Walter Travis; and Tuesday was fair, and a fine gallery turned out to see the match at old East Lake.

From the start it was easy to see that the two principal figures were "putting out" – to employ the vernacular. I have watched many exhibition matches, but none like this one. Miraculously, Bobby's putting touch, deplorably off-colour these later years, had returned, as he laid a long one dead over the tricky Bermuda at the 1st green and holed a 30-footer for a deuce at the 2nd, to put his side two up.

And Miss Wethered, hitting 240 yards into a light headwind, laid her pitch four feet from the flag at the 3rd and holed the putt for a three, while at the 565-yard 5th, down the wind, she was level with Bobby in two great wood shots, just in front of the green, and squared with another fine wee pitch and a seven-footer, for a birdie four. Then it was Bobby again, who holed a 15-footer for a birdie three at the 7th, and pitched dead for another birdie three at the 8th; and then Miss Wethered, just short of the green with two wood shots at the 506-yard 9th, gained back a hole with an exquisite little approach that left her no putt at all.

Bobby was out in 34. Miss Wethered was out in par 36. And in the popeyed gallery people hammered each other on the back, and called attention to the fact that Bobby Jones with a 34 was just one up on the English girl. Between them they had a bestball of 31, and while Dorothy Kirby and Charlie Yates were playing admirable golf – the 15-year-old Atlanta girl did a 41 from the back tees – the combat was between the two greatest golfers, and that was what all the gallery had come out to see, though never expecting anything so utterly dazzling as this.

And Miss Wethered, driving level with Bobby across the lake and up the long hill of the 10th fairway, squared the match for her side, and with Bobby, at the 10th. And she was square also with par of the East Lake course from the back tees, through the 13th, where the little Dorothy, with an exquisitely placed wood second, catching the run of the narrow apron to the bunker-surrounded green missed a four-foot putt for a birdie three that would have been a hole won all by herself, in that company!

Miss Wethered's driving was simply tremendous. The wind was coming up, and when facing it she was hitting a low, raking drive of great carry and astonishing run. And at the 14th, a hole of 448 yards, there was, for the moment, a half-gale coming out of the west, straight in her face. And there – well, Bobby and Charlie Yates struck off two of their best, and Miss Wethered's ball was well in front.

Against the sweeping wind Miss Wethered was flag-high with her second shot, the ball curling off to the left into a bunker. And here ensued the most whimsical play of all the afternoon.

Miss Wethered, of course, was unfamiliar with East Lake bunkers in summer, or at any other time. This was her first recovery off what looked to her as if it might be sand. She essayed a good, substantial half-blast with the niblick, and the blade, ricocheting from the sun-baked surface under a thin layer of sand, clipped the ball fairly in the back and sent it flying 50 yards over the green and the gallery, to the frank amazement of the latter and no less of Miss Wethered herself.

But she trotted down into a little valley, found the ball in a difficult place, pitched back beautifully, almost hitting the flag – and holed a 20-foot putt for a five, to be a stroke above par, while Bobby won the hole with a four.

Charlie mopped his brow. "This is the first time," he said, puzzled, "I ever played 14 holes as a lady's partner before I ever figured in one." He reflected further, and added: "Well, as long as she's carrying me around on her back, I'll just try not to let my feet drag!"

They halved the 413-yard 16th with four all around, Miss Wethered nearly holing a five-yard putt for a three, and Charlie, in pursuance of his announced policy, squared at the 17th, when Bobby's long drive was hooked to a ditch by the roadway, and Miss Wethered, for the second time on the strange Bermuda greens, took three putts.

And then came the climax of a great match. The 18th hole at East Lake is two hundred yards, across the lake, from a hillside tee to a hilltop green. "I know a one-shot finishing hole is not usually well regarded," Big Bob Jones, Bobby's father, once said to me. "But when a player stands on that tee at East Lake, with the match square, or dormie – that drive calls for all there is, in the delicatessen department."

Miss Wethered drove first, a spoon into the wind, and her ball was dead on the line, stopping 20 feet in front of the flag. Yates's shot was the same distance from the pin. Dorothy's was short and to the right. Bobby's was shoved a bit, and his wee pitch from the side of the hill caught the slope and trickled down five yards below the hole. Dorothy came on for a four. Miss Wethered putted, and just missed a two. Charlie likewise. And the gallery pressed closer, for it was up to Bobby.

Odd, how the film spins back on the reel of memory to a certain scene, at a certain time. As I stood there watching Bobby line up that putt, I saw him again on the same green, and in the same spot, at the close of a round in the famous Southern Open, eight years before – the tournament he won from a great field, with eight strokes to spare, on his home course. And I saw him sink that putt, eight years ago, and then – well, then the roar of that faraway gallery went out under the roar of the gallery that stood all about me. For Bobby sank this putt, too. And the match was square.

Nothing devised in a scenarist's shop at Hollywood could have helped that climax. Bobby had done a par 71, on his home course. Miss Wethered, a 74. The little Dorothy, in the most distinguished company in which she will ever play, an 84. And Charlie Yates, at last travelling on his own feet in the pinch, a 76.

Miss Wethered's play was beyond praise. On Bermuda greens – more than a score of years ago characterised by one of her countrymen, Ted Ray, as "not grawss but grapevines" – which she then saw for the first time, she had needed three putts twice, and she had been a trifle off-line with two drives. And that was all that stood between Joyce Wethered and a level 70, the first afternoon she had seen the 6,600-yard East Lake course.

• • • • • • •

Going down the fairway toward the 16th green, I was walking momentarily with Miss Wethered, and, naturally, I was complimenting her on her brilliant play. She smiled and then became suddenly grave. "I had to play well here," she said, simply, "Bobby arranged the match, you know. And he's said and written so many kind things about my game. And then he was ill, and then he insisted on playing . . . I wish I were sure he *should* be playing, now . . . It's – it's the most sporting thing I've ever known. I had to play well, at East Lake. I couldn't let Bobby down, you know."

Yes – I knew. And I know, too, that I saw something that afternoon at East Lake that will stand out as the prettiest picture of a lifetime in sport – the two greatest golfers, playing all they knew in every shot, in generous and gallant complement to one another, in the greatest match I ever witnessed.

Chapter 5

GREAT COURSES AND THEIR MAKING

GOLDEN LINKS ON AN

ENDLESS CHAIN

Sam McKinlay

One of the most agreeable golfing exercises I ever put my mind to was set by an American friend who is wise in the ways of golf and of our great courses in Britain. He wrote from a snowbound New York saying he was coming to Scotland on a reporting assignment in May, asked me if I could take a week off for a golfing tour when his work was done, and concluded with the intriguing question – Where will we go?

He knew our championship links as well as I did. He had made the inevitable pilgrimage to Gleneagles, had been to the equally picturesque Rosemount at Blairgowrie, half an hour's drive north of Perth, and was no stranger to the more famous of the seaside links such as North Berwick and Western Gailes.

It was quite a problem and when I aired it in the columns of the *Glasgow Herald* I had invitations from golfers in the length and breadth of the land eager to display the glories of their own course to my friend and me. I fear that, in the end, I disappointed hosts of enthusiasts and in some clubhouses there is still lingering chagrin at being passed by on the other side.

But in making my choice I was lucky beyond all expectations. We picked a week of perfect weather, we chose only three courses in one relatively small corner of Scotland, my friend played beyond his most extravagant hopes, and we finished our week with the comforting thought that Scotland is so rich in golfing treasure that if we undertook the same enterprise every year until we were too old to swing a club, we would not exhaust the infinite riches.

Lest there be some reading these pages who would follow in our stud-marks I have to report that the three courses we visited were Nairn, on the Moray Firth; Royal Dornoch, by road 80 miles north of Nairn and at the mouth of the Dornoch Firth, and Golspie, a few miles further north still. Golspie is the least of these in length and quality and is, I suppose, in the main a holiday links rather than an examination of the player seeking to match his skill against the terrain. But it is wonderfully pleasant to play, it runs hard by the sea, and if the golfing birdies are scarce there is an abundance of bird-life to offer an excuse for mediocre play.

Dornoch is, of course, one of the great links, rich in history, foster-parent of famous players such as the Wethereds and Sir Ernest Holderness, who honed their games to a fine sharpness there when on annual holiday. In good weather such as we enjoyed in mid-summer it is an exacting but scrupulously fair test of both power and finesse, for some of the greens have kittle slopes that make for wary putting. When the wind blows out of the North Sea as it can blow, it is the devil of a course, demanding strong accurate hitting and control of the long approach shot that is not given to every golfer.

Dornoch is easily the best course I know that is not on the championship rota, where it assuredly would be if it were not tucked away in a remote corner of Scotland 600 miles from London (but only 60 miles from Wick, it is worth remembering, and Wick has a daily air service from Glasgow).

Of Nairn, the third course on our safari, I find it difficult to speak temperately – and not only because I am a country member and therefore have an interest to declare. It, too, lies hard beside the sea, which is never out of sight or sound of the player – or out of his mind, either, for even a modest slicer can find the beach off four of the first five tees, and at the short fourth even a small hook will hit the shore.

Nairn has enough quality to have housed many Scottish women's and men's championships, but it has something more than golfing difficulty – it has charm and beauty of surroundings and one or two holes that are just absurd enough to be memorable. It's a course, too, like Barrie's island – it likes to be visited. I could cheerfully play there for the rest of my life.

Scotland's courses are not all charming like Nairn or difficult like Dornoch, Some are quaint, some are very fierce, some are wonderfully comfortable. For example, there is a delightful corner just about as remote from Dornoch as geography will allow where the fierce and the quaint lie within a few miles of each other. Machrihanish, which is one of the truly beautiful golf course names, is in the south of Kintyre, and it can be a very fierce links indeed when the wind comes in from the Atlantic for there is nothing but ocean between the 1st tee and Long Island. It is one of the great natural links of Scotland, owing almost everything to the ancient action of wind and sun and shower, and always worth a visit. But only a few miles away, at Southend, is the quaint Dunaverty course that is best described as being a sporting, holiday links.

Wherever you go in Scotland the great and the quaint lie almost side by side. There are four main areas where golf at its best can be tasted or devoured, according to one's appetite. As a West of Scotland man I must, from a sense of local patriotism, put Ayrshire first. Here, as was said of another matter, is God's plenty, or, as a versifier of rare taste once put it –

> Troon and Prestwick – Old and "classy"
> Bogside, Dundonald, Gailes, Barassie.
> Prestwick St Nicholas, Western Gailes,
> St Cuthbert, Portland – memory fails –
> Troon Municipal (three links there)
> Prestwick Municipal, Irvine, Ayr.
> They faced the list with delighted smiles –
> Sixteen courses within ten miles.

And it is still substantially true, though Dundonald has gone and so has Prestwick Municipal. On at least 10 of the list even the most demanding golfer will find himself tested to the limit, and if he still thinks he is master of the scene he will come to earth if he motors south from Ayr for half an hour and takes the tee at Turnberry.

The Ailsa course there is probably now the best golf course in Scotland. It may lack something of the subtlety of St Andrews and Prestwick, something, too, of Carnoustie's forbidding bleakness. But it is a great course, again hard by the sea, beautifully designed, perfectly groomed, and although a terrifying test from the tiger tees, not too daunting for the ordinary golfer having a recreation round from the normal markers. It is, I think, a must for any golfer of call seeking to measure his talents against Scottish turf.

On the other side of Scotland there are three areas of high golfing distinction – East Lothian, Fife and Angus. The jewel of East Lothian is Muirfield, the home of the ancient Honourable Company of Edinburgh Golfers. Access to this exclusive course is hard to come by and most golfers see it only when the championships and international matches are played there, as they often and rightly are because it is a links of superb quality and character.

Muirfield is a model of design, with the first nine holes forming a loop running clockwise from clubhouse back to clubhouse, and the second nine forming another loop running anti-clockwise inside the first. In the result any wind is a good wind because the player has to master it coming at him from every which way.

Of Muirfield a wise and able golfer once said that, if he were at the peak of his form and had to play a match to save his life, he would choose Muirfield for the duelling ground. It is freer than most courses, certainly most seaside courses, of kinks and extravagances of terrain; the good shot is almost invariably rewarded and, what is more important, the bad shot is punished. It is a wonderful test and almost always produces a great champion.

On the east side of Muirfield lie the two fine courses at North Berwick and the Dunbar links; on the west side, and only a mile or so distant, lie the three Gullane courses, grouped on and around Gullane Hill, a modest eminence from which superb views unfold to the golfer who can lift his head once in a while. Cheek-by-jowl with Gullane is Luffness, of the immaculate putting greens, and then comes Kilspindie and later Longniddry, all charming courses of quality where a man could cheerfully spend day after blissful day.

Across the Firth of Forth to the north lies the Kingdom of Fife and the jewel in that crown is, of course, St Andrews. But there are other sparkling gems such as Lundin Links and Elie, Leven and Crail, to say nothing of Aberdour, Burntisland and Kirkcaldy that are worth examining. Still, the dutiful pilgrim will on to St Andrew and he should, at least for his first visit, go there by rail.

It is a subtle joy to change trains at Leuchars Junction and hear the porters turning up their words at the end with a true Fifeshire lilt, and then to putter alone in the diesel for six miles through the most famous golfing country in all the world till, of a sudden, you touch the hem of the Old Lady's garment and you are no sooner aware of the fact than you are in the station and bustling to get down to the 1st tee.

The approach to the Old Course is, I suppose, unbelievable. One minute you are in a pleasant grey town next you are turning a corner, walking 50 yards, and, behold, the Tom Morris Green lies at your feet, the old, squat Royal and Ancient clubhouse is only a wedge shot distant, and beyond it is the fairest prospect in all golf – St Andrews Bay with the rollers creaming white on the sand and you wonder what the wind bringing in those rollers is going to do to your swing.

St Andrews is beyond description, and I can do no better than misquote Alphonse Daudet on medieval Avignon – "The golfer who has not seen St Andrews has seen nothing". There are, as all the world knows, four courses – the Old, the New, the Eden, and the Jubilee, but although the three last-named are good, exciting, and interesting places to play golf there is only one Old Course. It will infuriate you, it will thrill you, it will tantalise you, it will even flatter you. You will either love it or hate it or develop what it is the fashion to call a love-hate relationship; but you can never be indifferent to it.

From St Andrews can be seen the coast of Angus, across the Firth of Tay, another notable golfing district with fine courses such as Monifieth, Barry, and Montrose to supplement the two championship links at Carnoustie. You could linger there for a week and leave much to learn behind you, but it is worth pressing on to the north to see and play two exceptionally fine courses at Aberdeen – Balgownie and Cruden Bay, both of the highest quality which is enhanced because the club members are among the kindest and most hospitable in a hospitable land.

Their courses, like Dornoch, are thought by ignorant southerners to be too remote from the heart of golfing civilisation, but they are only a few hours from the Central Scotland belt and are, again, true seaside links, with crisp turf, spiny bents, and sand dunes, the best of golfing ground.

It is worth while completing the northern circuit, taking in Peterhead before turning west along the Moray Firth coast by Banff to Lossiemouth, another first-class seaside course of which the only unkind thing one may say is that it suffers from a plague of jet fighters operating from the Royal Naval air station nearby. And, unless we step aside for a game at the charming Forres course, good enough to house the Scottish Professional Championship, that brings us back to Nairn to complete a rough sweep of the main seaside courses.

There are two other famous courses by the sea of which I have heard great things but which I have not yet visited – Machrie in Islay and Southerness on the Solway. Both have their zealous and jealous supporters though Machrie, I am told, has more blind holes than any other course of distinction.

But Scotland is not mainly a country of seaside links. It has many fine parkland courses, such as Killermont and Pollok on the fringe of Glasgow; Barnton, Bruntsfield and Dalmahoy in the Edinburgh conurbation. Perth has its famous island course of the King James VI Club and the mountainous Craigie Hill where Mrs Valentine perfected her game. Near Larbert is Glenbervie, a fine parkland course where John Panton, that model professional, presides, and there are many others in and around the main centres of population.

There are, too, a host of attractive courses in the country towns, such as Edzell, Pitlochry, Grantown, Boat of Garten, Newtonmore, and Kingussie, and there is a further list of courses that are outstanding less for their intrinsic quality – though that is high enough in all conscience – than for their situation on the Firth of Clyde.

The Firth is, it will be conceded, one of the great estuaries of the world, and I can think of no better way to appreciate its beauties than to survey these from any one of half a dozen courses. Helensburgh, Cowal, and Largs, on the mainland, are challenged for the pre-eminence of their views by Gourock and Greenock, both high above the nearly landlocked seaway.

Rothesay, on the Island of Bute, has its loyal supporters, but my own preference is for the Millport course, on the Great Cumbrae (less than a dozen miles in circumference) from which wonderful views are obtained to north, west, and south. He would be a dullard of a golfer whose heart did not beat faster for standing on the topmost tee, with the great river and the mountains or Argyll, Jura, and Arran under his every gaze.

Happy, then, the golfer who has never been to Scotland, be he tyro or tiger. If he is a man of sensibility at all he cannot fail to savour the sweetness of the game in the home of the game, with every kind of course no more than a few hours' motoring from almost any point in the country. I have mentioned some, but only some – there are almost as many more to beguile the passionate pilgrim.

PINE VALLEY

Robert Green

While it's certainly not true that all great golf courses are located in grotesque surroundings, the thesis is not without foundation. Ballybunion is besides a caravan camp in an unsalubrious seaside resort, Augusta National is opposite a Piggly Wiggly store and a succession of filling stations along Washington Road, and Pine Valley is to be found in Clementon, New Jersey, a billboard-strewn and burger-bar infested town some 45 minutes across the Delaware River from Philadelphia.

Finding a jewel like Pine Valley in such a neighbourhood is as incongruous as it would be to see the Taj Mahal in the middle of Spaghetti Junction. Its name is apt – the 6,765-yard course is lined with pines (as well as oaks, firs and birches) and most holes run through a valley of trees and the fairways run a terrifying gauntlet of sand. There's more sand than on Copacabana Beach. One disheartened professional called it "a 184-acre bunker".

At Pine Valley there are tees, fairways and greens. There is almost no rough. Instead, there is perdition. The course is theoretically fair – the fairways are generous and the greens large where appropriate – but the penalty for missing either target is so severe that one is intimidated into doing just that. Many holes demand a long carry from the tee and the punishment for being short, left or right is frightening. Miss a green and your score can move into double figures well before you start to negotiate its fierce contours with your putter.

But though the course is so unremittingly tough and remorselessly unforgiving that even the Light Brigade might have been inclined to retreat, this is no Valley of Death. Pine Valley is beautiful. The trees and the magnificent terrain, the splendid isolation of each hole, the quietness without contrasted to the turmoil within as one seeks to conquer the mental and physical examination set by each shot – all these facets and more produce an awesome combination, a mixture of thrill and fear. Confronted by the stupendous 2nd hole, one English visitor asked: "Do you play this hole or do you photograph it?"

It is also a privilege to play to play there. Not only does the course have a worldwide reputation unmatched by any other unexposed to regular public scruntiny via television, it is as exclusive a golf club as exists. Perhaps those with the best deal in this respect are the overseas members, who pay a nominal sum having been selected for membership because of their material contributions to the good of the game. Among them are professional Gary Player, actor Sean Connery, R & A secretary Michael Bonallack, journalist Donald Steel and Gerald Micklem. But the name of Pine Valley is not primarily known because it may be the hardest course in the world to get on. It's because it is the hardest to get round.

The Machiavelli who designed the course was George Crump, a Philadelphia hotelier and fine amateur golfer who proved himself the world's greatest amateur golf architect. He vanished into the wilderness of the pineclad New Jersey sandhills in 1913 and by the time of his death in 1918 he had produced a masterpiece.

The criteria he laid down were followed religiously, although he received assistance from the renowned British architect, Harry Colt, and after Crump's death in 1918 Hugh Wilson, the creator of Merion, and the British firm of Colt, Mackenzie and Alison completed holes 12 to 15 on the principles Crump had enunciated.

One of Crump's original stipulations was simple and precise. He wanted "two three-shot holes, nicely separated, and never to be reached in two". The 7th (585 yards) has never witnessed a man putting for an eagle, while until the former US tour player Gary Groh accomplished the feat last April, neither had the 603-yard 15th.

The 7th features Hell's Half Acre, an unraked Sahara which begins 285 yards from the tee and stretches for over a hundred more. There is no way round it, only over or through it. The green is set on an island, surrounded by what is effectively one huge bunker. There is less sand on the 15th, but a lengthy carry over water with the drive is followed by a gradually rising and narrowing fairway to an elusive green. Miss it to the right and you may need crampons to finish the hole.

There is said to be a standing bet at Pine Valley – in fact, two. The first is that nobody can break a hundred first time out. (Personally, I believe this is harder to achieve on the second visit because one has been made well aware of where *all* the trouble is.) The second is that nobody can complete a round 18 up on par despite a handicap of five shots a hole. A study of Pine Valley's four par-threes will tell you why.

The 3rd measures 185 yards. One distinguished member, British businessman and golf writer Sir Peter Allen, once topped his tee shot with awful consequences. "I took 11 on the hole without hitting another bad shot." The 5th is 226 yards, but maybe its length is compensated for by the realisation that this is the only short hole where one can miss the target and still find grass. On the other hand, it is wiser to heed the old members' saying: "Only God can make three on the 5th."

At 145 yards, the 10th appears a pushover on paper. However, just short of the green is a satanic pot-bunker, appropriately named something like the Devil's Armpit. The latter word is actually lower down the anatomy, although it does begin with the same letter. Whatever one calls it, the solids doubtless hit the fan on the day an eight-handicap guest came to the 10th having played the front nine in a commendable 38. He found the sand bunker with his tee shot and recorded 38 strokes on that hole alone, a victim of an evil, optional local rule which forbids relief for an unplayable lie. One fourball once totalled 88 for the 10th, an astonishing statistic which can only be trumped by the hapless member who carded 44 shots on the wonderful but wicked 185-yard 14th, where the water laps against what appears to be a greenside bunker but is in fact a little beach.

Don't imagine that the par-fours are pushovers. The 8th measures a gentle 327 yards. That great writer, Bernard Darwin, once played the first seven holes in even par but picked up after nine shots on the 8th had not got him near the cup. "It is all very well to punish a bad stroke," he later remarked, "but the right of eternal punishment should be reserved for a higher tribunal than a green committee."

There are alternative greens on the 9th; overshoot the left-hand one and experience on Everest is a prerequisite to retrieving the ball. A British Ryder Cup player once notched up 17 on the 11th, another hole of under 400 yards. A member has returned an 85 with an 11 on the 15th and a 12 on the 16th, where the drive has to clear a small desert. Sadists are fond of recalling the man who needed a bogey five at the last for an 84 and thereby to win a substantial bet that he couldn't break 90. His final tally was 97. If that is not sufficient, I should add that the 446-yard 13th is often heralded as the toughest par-four in America.

Though Pine Valley is so testing that the 36-hole club championship has been won with 173, it will succumb, if not to brilliance then at least to magic. A leading amateur, "Woody" Platt, began one round by making a birdie at the 1st, holing his approach for an eagle at the 2nd, aceing the 3rd and sinking a putt for another birdie at the next. Six under par after four holes, Platt retired to the clubhouse bar, close beside the 5th tee. Though he'd been playing like God, he obviously felt a three there was beyond him. Some years later, Arnold Palmer played his first game at Pine Valley under the pressure of a bet which would earn him $200 for every stroke he was below 72. Palmer shot 68 and collected $800 towards an engagement ring for his wife, Winnie. Such is the lure of the course that in 1960 an amateur called Jack Nicklaus interrupted his honeymoon for the privilege of a round.

The course record is 64, six under par, achieved by the top American amateur, Bob Lewis, in September 1981. A month previously Lewis had been a member of the victorious American Walker Cup team at Cypress Point. This August, that same competition returns to Pine Valley, 49 years after the club hosted its one and only major international competition. The British did not win a single match in the 1936 Walker Cup. We should improve on that this time, even if victory in unlikely, but whatever else happens the amateur golfers of Great Britain and Ireland will relish the challenge of playing a course which is unequalled in its demands on every shot and where the reward for excellence is all the greater for knowing the consequences of failure. As I have indicated, Pine Valley can be distressingly penal in strokeplay. It is, however, perhaps the ultimate match-play examination. The 18 holes at Pine Valley may well be the best, all told, anywhere. None is weak or even mediocre; all range from great to greater.

George Crump ploughed an estimated $250,000 of his own money into the creation of Pine Valley; a significant sum today, a vast fortune 70 years ago. Doubters called the project "Crump's Folly". That Crump never saw the completed work may lend some credence to the theory but not a lot. He bequeathed a genuine masterpiece, a *Mona Lisa*, to the sport.

The building of Pine Valley was demonstrably not a waste of time, even granted that Crump spent the last six painstaking years of a full and successful life on the scheme. Time is not of the essence when one is dealing with genius. After all, Michelangelo spent eight years with brush in hand, painting *The Last Judgement* on the altar wall of the Sistine Chapel, but nobody has ever seriously suggested he should have used a roller.

GOLF'S ARTFUL DODGER

Raymond Jacobs

Some say God made the Old Course as a kind of practice shot before he addressed the real business of Creation. Others insist that instead of resting on the seventh day He built the Old Course simply to keep his hand in. Yet others maintain that He devised this unique stretch of coastline in nothing more than a fit of absent-mindedness. But the fanciful explanation must eventually give way to the real. The Old Course just emerged as the sea withdrew leaving, in the words of Sir Guy Campbell the golf historian, "a perfect example of an original layout of nature, interpreted and completed by beast and man".

This triumph of evolution over the mechanical grab, this exercise in judgement over the yardage chart is to golfers what Florence is to artists and what Paris is to lovers. A museum piece, yet it has consistently influenced course architecture and, curiously shapeless and deceptively flat, it remains still a searching examination not only of the skills of the contemporary masters of the game but also of their temperament.

The specific terrors of the 17th, the Road Hole, are dealt with elsewhere. Sufficient to say here that before this championship is out the customary noises of exasperation about the course's unique and most durable features – the crumpled fairways, the hidden hazards, the gigantic greens – shall be heard.

Not every horror story at the Open Championship last year derived from the welter of the disasters at the 17th. The Old Course, like any aged retainer worthy of respect and consideration, must be coaxed rather than bullied into serving a good score. That conclusion is the more readily drawn after consulting the cumulative statistics from last July when, for example, at the first and last holes which together provide probably the two widest driving areas in Christendom, 15 players had scores of two over par or more.

To be sure, the Old Course lacks that element most sought after in a modern golf course – fairness. The absence of clear definition of targets, inconsiderable kicks, the unlevel stances, the concealed bunkers, the vast and sometimes steeply sloping greens see to that. But a degree of patience often yields some solace.

Watch for indecision criss-crossing the faces of world-class professionals, in full possession of their faculties, as they assess the club they need for their approach over the Swilcan Burn to the 1st hole. A similar optical illusion complicates the second to the 9th green, a mown extension of a dead flat fairway that persistently confuses judgement.

For the spectator then, if not necessarily for the player, the Old Course's strongest appeal is that nothing expected regularly happens here. The outcome of the last two Open Championships and the 1971 Walker Cup match are only two illustrations, and it will be the least surprising happening this season if in this championship the course does not apply the proverbial sackful of wet sand to the base of some unsuspecting skull or other.

I have listened to players with as diverse views on life, love, liberty, and the pursuit of the golf ball as Bernard Gallacher and Peter Thomson select, without having had an arm twisted half-way up their back, the Old Course as their favourite in Scotland. Agnostics, even those who are not true believers, might be converted by their views.

Gallacher has said: "It's one of the easiest courses, on paper, but when you try to make birdies, even pars sometimes, it's a different story. It has a special magic." Thomson, who won the second of his five Open titles at St Andrews, has said: "It's the great original; it's positive, rewarding, inspiring and exciting."

Bernard Darwin wrote once suggesting that the course that was totally honest and above board might justifiably be described as rather dull. When one sees some of the modern manifestations of design one is disposed to agree with him. If the Old Course could be dressed in the clothing of a human character that of the Artful Dodger might fit it the best. Unless conditions overhead and underfoot are exceptionally docile the price of a low score is always the kind of respectful wariness needed to cross a room crowded with pickpockets. Otherwise a scorecard as bulging with birdies as a wallet with banknotes is liable to be pilfered by some sleight of hand masquerading as a bogey or worse. And the loss is not less painful for having been predictable.

So whatever else may be said of the Old Course – and much has been said of a less than complimentary nature – it is never boring. And if it was good enough for Bobby Jones to nominate it as the course where he would play for the rest of his days, if he could choose only one, it should be good enough for the rest of us.

THE HOLE IN THE ROAD

Chris Plumridge

There is a vague recollection lurking in the back of my mind concerning an enterprising American newspaper publisher who, sick of war, strikes, floods, rape, pestilence, famine and other myriad horrors that filled his daily columns, decided he would publish a paper which contained nothing but good news. Within the week the paper had folded for the very simple reason that nobody bought it thereby leaving the anguished publisher, who really should have known better, to reflect on the perversity of human nature. While the story is probably apocryphal, it nonetheless serves to illustrate the age-old principle that bad news attracts, a message that is revealed to us not only via the media but also in our everyday lives.

I remember standing behind the 13th green at Wentworth watching the final of last year's Colgate World Match-Play when, the players having holed out, the crowd dispersed and a large man wearing spiked golf shoes jumped down from one of those infernal ladders that spectators carry and landed with no small effect upon my left ankle. That story is thoroughly authenticated by the dull ache that even now pervades my left foot, but the point of telling it is that within seconds of my being pole-axed a reasonable crowd had gathered, some solicitous as to whether any of my regulation eight pints were staining the grass.

The incident was not without humour for a few months earlier I had been summoned by a totally misguided captain to open the innings for the Association of Golf Writers in their annual cricket match against the touring golf professionals. The venue for this contest was no less a shrine than The Oval and again, it pains me to recall, I was felled by a sharp outswinger which struck me on, you've guessed it, the left ankle.

Back to Wentworth and as I lay writhing on the ground I spat out through clenched teeth, "It's the same bloody ankle I was struck on at The Oval" – a remark that my colleague Norman Mair later reported as causing a by now respectful crowd to draw back, fearing perhaps that one of England's mainstays in the coming defence of the Ashes would not be able to make the trip to Australia.

The bad news theme is well-strummed in sport. Spectators gather at tortuous corners on Grand Prix racing circuits not to study the drivers' technique in negotiating the bend but in the hope that they will witness a multiple crash. In cricket, the sight of a bowler inflicting grievous bodily harm on a batsman rouses the crowd's blood lust to shout for more. Has not the popularity of the Grand National been founded on the well-orchestrated crunch of bone on gristle? The so-called noble art of boxing has its roots in the jungle and virtually every sporting contest is a throw-back to the days of the gladiators when the combatants fought for the ultimate prize.

"Ah," I can hear you saying, "that may well be so but we golf spectators are a civilised bunch, our game is free of physical contact, we are purists come to study at the university of immortals, such base behaviour is beneath us." Well, dear golf spectator, I am sorry to disillusion you. While it is true there is no real blood spilt during actual play, you too exhibit the perfectly natural human desire to be present at the scene of an accident.

There are many potential black spots on the world's golf courses and when the world's leading players set foot on such holes, the noise of the galleries can be likened to the squabbling of vultures awaiting their turn at the carcass. Among such holes could be listed the 12th at Augusta National with its swirling winds waiting to push the ball back into Rae's Creek; the 17th at Carnoustie with the insidious Barry Burn snaking across the fairway; the 18th at Pebble Beach where the Pacific Ocean washes away any stroke which has the hint of a hook. All of these examples have the ingredient of water in their sometimes indigestible recipe and there is nothing surer to gather the crowds than the presence of that particular element. The finality of a stroke which sends the ball plunging into unknown depths is a spectacle no self-respecting disaster watcher can resist. But there is one hole in the world which although without a water hazard, is truly the Becher's Brook of golf. It is probably the most famous hole in the world, located on certainly the most famous course.

The 461-yard, par-four 17th at St Andrews, known universally as the Road Hole, has been drawing the metaphoric blood of golfers from the era of Tom Morris to the era of Tom Watson. Some of its teeth have been pulled, the removal of the old railway sheds and the resurfacing of the road itself may have caused some spinning in the more notable graves up in the local churchyard, but even in this age of atomic golf balls and wonder-flex shafts, the Road Hole can still exact savage retribution.

The hole is a marvellous example of the use of angles to confuse and frustrate the golfer. From the tee, the presence of the out-of-bounds on the right instinctively draws the player's aim away to the left. But the further left the tee shot, the more imperceptible becomes the target of the green. And what a target. The front of the green rises alarmingly on to a narrow shelf and again, the angle of the green in relation to the approach shot means that any stroke slightly overhit will skitter through on to the dreaded road. That really should be enough but nature has conjured up one more impossible trick in the shape of the Road bunker on the left of the green, "eating its way into its very vitals" as Bernard Darwin once described it.

On such a stage have walked many players, some to rise to the challenge the Road Hole presents, others to suffer a severe mauling. It seems entirely appropriate that the hole played a major role in the achievements of Bobby Jones during his unsurpassable year of 1930. That year the Amateur Championship, a title Jones had never won, was held at St Andrews and after some narrow escapes Jones found himself facing Cyril Tolley in the semi-finals. It proved to be one of the classic encounters of all time containing, as Jones wrote later "the completely brutal ferocity of man-to-man contest". The pair arrived at the 17th all square, Tolley having won the 16th, and then came the stroke that provokes controversy even to this day. Jones's second shot struck a spectator standing at the back of the green and was, some people say, prevented from running on to the road. Other people present swear it would have stayed up anyway, but the upshot of it was that Jones halved the hole and went on to win the match at the 19th. The following day he easily disposed of Roger Wethered in the final to complete the first leg of his impregnable quadrilateral.

Although ifs count for nothing in golf, the question remains as to if Jones's second had run onto the road he would surely have lost the hole and perhaps the match and the first leg of his Grand Slam. Today there would be no cause for such conjecture over the fate of that shot for the crowd are kept back behind the wall beyond the road, leaving the ball to chart its own unfettered course.

Thirty years later in the Centenary Open Championship, the Road Hole proved to be the stumbling block in Arnold Palmer's quest for the title. He played the hole in four strokes more than the winner, Kel Nagle, and lost by one to the Australian. The hole is anathema to Palmer for it goes against the very foundations of his attacking principles. Some 18 years after his début at St Andrews, Palmer was still trying to bludgeon the Road Hole into submission when he was tied for the second-round lead in last year's Open Championship. But again the hole won as Palmer drove out-of-bounds and took seven. "It's a good hole, a tough hole," said Palmer, "you have to play safe and I try to do something different every time and it just doesn't work. I try to make it a par-four and I'm not really sure it is a par-four." The next day Palmer again drove out-of-bounds for another seven.

The Road Hole also spreads its malevolent influence beyond its boundaries for I am sure the reason Doug Sanders took five up the 18th in the 1970 Open Championship was because he had escaped disaster on the 17th. His second shot to the 17th in the final round finished in the Road bunker, leaving him a splash shot of the utmost delicacy to a pin set tight to the hazard. Sanders executed the stroke brilliantly and his four was safe. Such was his relief that he even tempted fate by discarding his lucky tee peg for the drive up the last, feeling perhaps that nothing could prevent him from taking the title. Thus scorned, the fates wrought their revenge on Sanders's second putt.

A year later the Road Hole was part of a happier occasion as Britain won the Walker Cup for only the second time. David Marsh clinched the victory with a marvellous second shot to the 17th which finished on the green and so enabled him to defeat his opponent and make Britain's position impregnable.

And so we come to last year's Open Championship and once again the Road Hole played the major role in the outcome. The hole played to an overall average of 4.8 strokes throughout the Championship and there were just seven birdies gleaned by the world's best players. The highest score was nine taken by Japan's Tsuneyuki Nakajima who was on the green in two, putted into the Road bunker and took four to get out. That completed an unenviable double for Nakajima, the previous April he took 13 on the 13th at Augusta in the United States Masters.

Only Ben Crenshaw tamed the Road Hole in that Open, recording three pars and a birdie and even Jack Nicklaus had to be content with three fives and a four. Nicklaus played the hole as a par-five, hoping to get his second shot up the crest and on to the flat portion of the green. "If it doesn't make the top," said Nicklaus, "you're still better off there than in the Road bunker or left of the bunker where you have no chance at all." In his final round Nicklaus stuck to his game plan and from below that mountainous approach, struck one of the greatest long putts ever witnessed to within one foot of the hole.

Another casualty was Severiano Ballesteros who, two strokes ahead of the field in the second round, drove hugely out-of-bounds down the 17th. From his second drive, he struck a memorable 4-iron which pitched just over the Road bunker and stayed on the green but it still meant a six for the Spaniard and he was never a factor from there on.

Ballesteros regards the hole in much the same way as Palmer, whose attacking instincts he had inherited. "I think maybe it is the most difficult hole I ever play," said Ballesteros in his broken English, "they way they put the flag I think maybe one day they put the flag on the road instead of the green." Should that unlikely event ever occur, there is no doubt in my mind that Ballesteros would still go for it, for the challenge of the Road Hole, like the Old Course itself, is eternal.

GOLF AT ROSEMOUNT

R.C. Robertson-Glasgow

It's a platitude, no doubt, that we don't know how much we love things and people till we are about to leave them; but how strongly is this old truth felt during the last day of holiday on a favourite golf course.

In those final hurrying hours we meet the member who has so often, and surely on purpose, forestalled us by five seconds in the reading of the only two magazines published since 1950. This egotistical monster proves suddenly to be an altruistic man. His face, which we had till now considered, if at all, as more than homely, is ennobled by benevolent charm as he offers us his opinion of the weather and the more modern of the two magazines.

Outside, on the course, the same miracle of realisation is at work. The tree at the 13th, which a week ago lost us the hole against old H., stands confessed, this last time, as a silver birch; a Lady of the Forest, slender and lovely, with head-dress still of gold. The loch in front of the 16th tee, home of many a scuffled ball and derisive moorhen, is suddenly seen as a mirror of the eternal woods and the far too early sunset.

Indeed, this golf course of Blairgowrie is a thing of beauty, which it is not so foolish as to show us all at once. Each hole is a discovery, divided by trees from its neighbour. Those who like the curlew calling and rabbits watching the stroke will like the 6th and the far 7th. Others, who prefer the sight of flowers adjoining another garden trimly made of clipped heather, will favour the 4th hole, which only the long and straight may reach in two strokes.

But, to counteract this beauty of seclusion and surprise, the architects in their wisdom placed the tees of two holes within sight or comment of the mere passer-by, the non-golfing laity. One is the tee of that 4th hole. Close behind runs a busy road, on which will stand citizens, prepared to encourage or criticise their friends before or during or after the stroke. Here, too, come mothers and aunties and nursemaids with small children, who may be calmed or entertained by watching "yon man hit his wee ba' into the woods".

Then there is the tee of the short 15th. Here, as the player meditates a shot of some subtlety, Juggernautical lorries suddenly rush past behind him, and someone shouts out "Fore". It is a traditional cry; remnant of half-forgotten days when golf, in England at any rate, was supposedly played only by Arthur Balfour and a group of deluded aristocrats in fancy dress, who, like the Marquis of Evremonde, drove like the deuce at anything or anyone they saw.

Yet, for the most part, this golf course of Rosemount, to use its old and true name, is a place of peace. On each side the hills in order stand, the Sidlaws and the Grampians. And sometimes, on an autumn evening, when "the breath of winter comes from far away", the wild geese fly creaking and honking over, on their journey from the North. They detach the golfer from his fiddling putt and give a perfect lesson in formation to *Homo Volitans*.

PEBBLE BEACH

Henry Longhurst

Next morning after a long gossip with Peter Hay, who came to America 40 years ago from Aberdeen and is now the doyen of West Coast professionals, we had a tilt at Pebble Beach. With one or two unforgettable exceptions the general scene is not quite so spectacular as Cypress Point but from the back tees it would, I think, with even greater certainty crush an indifferent golfer into total oblivion. As a generality I should say that American courses are less difficult than British – partly because the greens are softer and you can therefore play "target golf" most of the time but mainly because in the golfing season (and courses in the north are closed in the winter) there is little or no wind. Pebble Beach, hard on the shore of the ocean, is among the exceptions and the wind can blow in with immense ferocity. I am aware that the wind also blows in Texas, and this, according to Hogan, explains why the best golfers like Demaret, Mangrum, Burke and, though he does not say so, himself as well as the best and biggest of everything else in the United States, come from Texas. For most American players, however, golf is a still-air game.

Pebble Beach reminded me in many ways of a longer, sunnier, and more sophisticated section of that lovely, all too little known course on the west coast of Ireland – Ballybunion. In the technical sense I suppose there is no difference between driving out of bounds into the Field at Hoylake or over the little stone wall at St Andrews or into the Bristol Channel at Porthcawl or, as I habitually did for the first dozen years of my golfing life, the cornfield, the allotments, the Great Ouse, or British Railways (Midland Regions), which bound the course at Bedford. Yet, psychologically, there is all the difference between driving into these and driving into the ocean. Oceans are hazards on the grand scale. They make one's efforts so much more puny and insignificant than mere seas or rivers. At Ballybunion, in winter one of the wildest places in the British Isles, with the original Cruel Sea pounding away on the rocks, a high slice is swallowed by the Atlantic like a grain of sand. A big enough slice theoretically would see no land till it touched Long Island. At Pebble Beach a good hook from the 18th tee, missing the tiny atolls that dot the surface of the Pacific, would presumably fetch up in Japan.

For five holes, as a matter of fact, Pebble Beach reveals little of what is in store. Wandering soberly among the fir trees it leaves one wondering politely what all the fuss is about. One's score at this moment may well, though mine wasn't, be one under fours. At the 6th it comes out of its corner, as it were, and delivers four tremendous body blows in succession. The 6th, after a comparatively innocuous drive, leaves you playing a brassey to a green set high on a headland, over which the wind may be tearing with frenzy. Eating into the fairway on the right is what in Devonshire would be known as a "combe", thick with undergrowth and leading to the rocks. A ball slightly "skied" is caught by the wind and whirled away like a feather.

Across the lower slope of this headland on the far, or ocean, side is a fascinating little hole of only 110 yards, the shortest perhaps on any course of this calibre, but, whereas on most country club courses this would be the merest "pushover", here on the edge of the Pacific, with the spray forming a dramatic background to a tiny green surrounded almost entirely by sand, it can be anything up to a No.3 iron.

Having got past this, you then receive the full impact of this essential quality of Pebble Beach, its power to surprise. You drive uphill at the 8th, along the side of the promontory opposite the 6th – a most commonplace stroke with nothing apparently to play for except to move the ball along and keep it in play. Having done this, you trudge up the slope and reach the crest, where with any luck your ball is lying.

"Good God!" I remember saying. "Look at that!"

A few yards ahead the fairway ceased abruptly at the edge of a cliff perhaps 150 feet high. The cliff worked its way inland to the left, forming a bay perhaps 180 yards across as it curved away back again across our front. Directly ahead on the far side of this bay was the green – tightly trapped, for good measure, with sand bunkers. If ever there was a death-or-glory shot, this was it – and a full shot with a brassey at that. I contributed a couple of balls to the ocean – it is almost impossible not to look up too soon, in order not to miss a moment of the ball's spectacular flight across the bay, the result of which is of course that, half topped, it disappears instantly from sight – but my third was a beauty and I can see it now, soaring over the chasm, white against the blue Californian sky, and pitching with a thump on the green.

Innumerable people must have torn up their card at the 9th. Many, on looking back at it, must have recollected the same sequence – lulled into false security by the first five, softened up by the 6th and 7th, sent tottering by the 8th, and knocked out by the 9th. Even the great Byron Nelson was once battered into submission by the 9th and gave in after about 11 shots. It is a long hole, parallel with the beach, with the tiniest opening to the green for those who go for it with their second – on the left a sort of chasm, on the right our old friend and enemy the Pacific.

After this comes a mild respite, enlivened, as I have mentioned, by the prospect of being able to go home and say you have sliced into Bing Crosby's garden – I imagine that he has never had to buy a ball, being supported wholly by involuntary contribution – but you emerge from the trees again with a fine one-shotter into the teeth of the wind at the 17th, with the green on the edge of the beach, and then you work your way home, crescent-wise, along the 18th which I believe I am right in saying no one has yet reached in two. After which you ascend, bloody but unbowed, to further gossip with Peter Hay in a 19th hole which is adorned once again with pictures of the Masters old and new – Tom

Morris, Harry Vardon, Francis Ouimet, Hagen, Jones, and the rest who have helped to turn golf into the world-wide language that it is.

Much of the Monterey Peninsula has been developed by the energies of Mr Sam Morse and his son, John, who between them, by creating so many of the sporting amenities and selling off plots of land at prices which people can afford, have turned it into the perfect spot for retirement, especially for Army officers from the big West Coast stations.

The golfer, however, may lift his hat not only to Mr Morse and his son but also to a figure long familiar in England, especially around Sandwich and Deal, namely Douglas Grant. He had a considerable hand in designing both Cypress Point and Pebble Beach – which is perhaps why they are not merely spectacular but some of the finest and most "intelligent" golf in the world.

Of the two, Pebble Beach is sterner and slightly the longer, Cypress Point the more *sympathique*, as the French would say. By which I do not mean that it is easy, even on a calm summer afternoon. It is the difference perhaps between Sandwich and, say, Hoylake or Carnoustie. At Sandwich a good scratch amateur may, and sometimes does, go round in 68, though often enough he fails to break 80. At Hoylake and Carnoustie the same man *knows* he is not going round in 68 – today, tomorrow, or any day that yet remains to him. While I do not myself any longer trade in such figures, I feel that if, in what I am now pleased to call my prime, I had done a 72 at Cypress Point, I should have rated it with a 74 at Pebble Beach. Indeed they do say that, whatever a man's handicap may be at Pebble Beach, it is three strokes higher anywhere else.

GOLF AND GLORY

Sarah Ballard

The golf club is not Muirfield. "The golf club is the Honourable Company of Edinburgh Golfers, which was founded in 1744," says Major J.G. Vanreenen, Royal Engineers (Ret.), the very model of a golf club secretary. "You will appreciate that this is a gentlemen's club. Ladies are perfectly welcome as long as they meet our requirements: a handicap of 24 or better from a recognised golf club and that they play in company with a gentleman." The Secretary presses the fingertips of his right hand against the fingertips of his left hand and continues. "In other respects this is an entirely male-orientated golf club. It is also a very private golf club. Visitors are allowed to play the course Tuesday, Thursday and mornings of Fridays."

• • • • • • •

A certain breed of golfer collects golf courses as he might butterflies, travelling the world in pursuit of the rarer species and cataloguing his conquests for the bedazzlement of fellow collectors. Some collectors specialise in the rare and the inaccessible – golf courses that straddle the equator or cling to glaciers, that sort of thing. But for most golfers, collecting is a search for roots, the roots of the game and the roots of obsession. This sort of collection leads to Scotland and, once there, inevitably to Muirfield, where the British Open will be played next week for the 13th time. St Andrews is older, Dornoch is harder, Turnberry is prettier, but Muirfield is, well, admirable.

The roster of Open champions at Muirfield reads like a 20th-century golfing Hall of Fame: Harold Hilton, Harry Vardon, James Braid, Ted Ray, Walker Hagen, Henry Cotton, Gary Player, Jack Nicklaus, Lee Trevino, Tom Watson. Only one winner, Alf Perry, a club pro from Surrey, England, who rose to the occasion in 1935, would not merit a chapter of his own in a respectable history of the modern game. The great Bobby Jones is missing, but one would like to think, if only for the sake of symmetry, that is merely because Jones never happened to play an Open at Muirfield. (He did, however, play a British Amateur there in 1926 and lost in the sixth round.)

The Muirfield course opened for play in 1891, which makes it about the same vintage as many of the grand old courses in England, Ireland *and* North America. It was built in the era in which the game that had been exclusively Scottish began to spread like a brushfire to wherever Scots had emigrated or the English had set up colonial shop.

But Muirfield's roots go deeper than that. The course is just the latest home of the Honourable Company of Edinburgh golfers, a club that can document its continuous existence back to 1744. That makes it, as far as its members are concerned, the oldest golf club in the world. At least one other Scottish club, the Royal Burgess Golfing Society, claims to be older – but it doesn't have papers to prove it. The Honourable Company does, and facsimiles of them are on display in glass cases inside the rambling quasi-Tudor clubhouse at the edge of the village of Gullane (pronounced Gill'n), 18 miles east of Edinburgh.

The Secretary's opening remarks notwithstanding, Muirfield is a hospitable place, as "very private" clubs go. Every year, between 6,000 and 7,000 visitors play the course, some of them women. Once a visitor has passed muster he is encouraged to play golf as the Honourable Company does: that is, a round of "foursomes" in the morning, another in the afternoon, with the celebrated Muirfield lunch in between. Now, foursomes is a companionable game – one ball, two players, alternate drives and shots. And the golf course justified applause – Nicklaus likes it so much he named his Columbus, Ohio, course Muirfield Village, which, were it anybody but Nicklaus, might have been presumptuous. But it is lunch that makes a Muirfield outing unique. The members are proud of their course, but they are almost equally proud of the table they set.

"A very high standard of feeding," says the Secretary. "Smoked-haddock pie and a choice of two soups to start, three roasts, beef, lamb and pork, steak-and-kidney pie, and mince, a minimum of six vegetables and two potatoes, a choice of 15 puddings, sweets, as you call them – and a choice of a dozen different cheeses."

And how does anyone play 18 holes after such a meal? "Very competently," says the Secretary. A local golfer, Rory Hamilton, says, "It is an easy matter to sort out members from guests. Members wear tweeds with leather-patched jackets and have small helpings."

After lunch, tradition dictates coffee and kümmel or port in the cavernous Smoking Room, where towering windows overlook the 18th green. From those windows, it is said, the members frequently wager on their colleagues "toiling thirstily up the 18th fairway".

Next door to the Muirfield clubhouse is a small, comfortable hotel called, simply, Greywalls. Greywalls is as much a part of the total Muirfield experience as foursomes. During the summer months about 70 per cent of the hotel's 23 guest rooms are occupied by Americans, most of them golfers. During the Open, the Royal & Ancient, which administers the championship, allocates the rooms. "The secretary of the R & A goes to the Masters in April," says Henrietta Fergusson, the hotel's manager. "He nobbles the golfers and says, 'Do you want a room at Greywalls?' He starts at the top and works down the list. He uses up all 20 rooms, which is what they think we have. We like to set aside a few."

Greywalls was designed by Sir Edwin Lutyens in 1901 as a country house and its gardens were laid out by his partner, Gertrude Jekyll. Lutyens's work was the height of fashion in its day and is still prized for its graceful proportions. At one point the house belonged to a mistress of Edward VII, and at his request a small lavatory and exercise yard were built into a garden wall. Since then the space has been roofed over and turned into guest bedroom No. 17, but it is still known as the King's Loo.

Andrew Mitchell is the 26-year-old head chef at Greywalls. Mitchell comes from the village of Leven, near St Andrews, and grew up on golf. He has played Muirfield only one time, but he does play once or twice a week, starting at 6 am, on Gullane's short No. 3 course, which he can get around in 2½ hours. "I love it so much," he says. "You forget if you had a bad night and something's been sent back. It's so peaceful."

Mitchell's view of the Open will be from his kitchen window, which overlooks the 10th tee, 15 yards away. "At least it will be something," he says. Fortunately, Mitchell loves his work as much as his golf, because during the hotel's season, from April through October, he works 6½ days a week, and the "half" is eight hours. Mitchell's menu is as sophisticated as Muirfield's is plain.

On a magical evening in 1980, Tom Watson, who that afternoon had swept across Muirfield's rolling turf to a record 271 and the third of his five British Open titles, and his wife were on their way to dinner at Greywalls when they saw Tom Weiskopf and Ben Crenshaw, the US Tour's leading golf antiquarian, heading toward the golf course. High spirits and the irresistible lure of a Scottish summer twilight drew the Watsons across the croquet lawn and over the low stone wall that divides Greywalls from the course. There, with antique wooden clubs, the three golfers replayed the 10th and 18th holes, followed by their wives, a few spectators and a bagpiper they picked up along the way. At the 18th green this merry band was met by the club secretary at the time – Captain P.W.T. Hanmer – who scolded them as if they were errant schoolboys, which, for that happy moment, they undeniably were.

It was not until the Honourable Company moved to its present home that it was able to assert sovereignty over its own turf. Originally, the members played on the links at Leith, the old port of Edinburgh, where they shared five holes with four other golfing societies. Not for nothing was the club uniform a bright red tailcoat. A red coat was not only a badge of membership, it was also the practical equivalent of a hunter's red cap. The links of Leith, as elsewhere, were common lands used for many purposes besides golf, everything from grazing sheep to drying laundry.

In 1836 the Honourable Company moved from Leith to Musselburgh, farther east on the south bank of the Firth of Forth, but even there, where the club remained for 54 years and where the Open was held six times between 1874 and 1889, the members shared a nine-hole course with three other clubs. Only in 1891 did the Honourable Company finally acquire Muirfield, a "Hundred Acre Field" on the outskirts of Gullane in the district of East Lothian.

In the beginning, the Edinburgh golfers were a rollicking band of golf nuts, given to claret drinking and wagering among themselves. In Tobias Smollett's 1771 novel, *The Expedition of Humphrey Clinker*, a character described golf on the Links of Leith: "Among others, I was shown one particular set of golfers, the youngest of whom was turned of four-score. They were all gentlemen of independent fortunes who had amused themselves with this pastime for the best part of a century without having ever felt the least alarm from sickness or disgust; and they never went to bed without having each the best part of a gallon of claret in his belly."

It was expected of an 18th-century sporting gentleman that he put his money where his honourable mouth was. The club's Bett Book was instituted in 1776 to keep track of the matches and the wagers made on them. In 1783, the Bett Book records: "Mr R. Allan betts one guinea that he will drive a ball from the Castle Hill without the gate of the palisade into the Half Moon battery over the parapet wall."

We have no way of knowing whether Mr Allan regretted his boast the next day, but we can be fairly sure he at least attempted the shot, because to back out of a bet was a punishable offence. "Each person who lays a bett in company of the Golfers and shall fail to play it on the day appointed, shall forfeit to the Company a pint of wine for each guinea unless he gives a sufficient excuse to their satisfaction."

Claret is still the wine of choice among the Honourable Company, and the Bett Book is still in use. Six times a year the club holds a dinner at which matches are scheduled, and wagers on those matches are recorded in the Bett Book. According to George Pottinger, the club's biographer, "Most bets have been made on foursome matches, but when the wagery fever has reached its height at the end of the dinner, it is not unknown for bets to be laid on events like the University Boat Race."

At the turn of the century, East Lothian was already to Scotland what the Monterey Peninsula is to this country, a golfer's version of heaven on earth. Within a few miles of Muirfield, in the villages of Gullane and Aberlady and the small resort town of North Berwick (so fashionable in the 1880s it was known as the Biarritz of the North), were, and still are, seven courses, each with its own history and individual charms. No need for Muirfield visitors to sit idle on Mondays, Wednesdays and Friday afternoons. The Luffness New course in Aberlady has greens said to be the best in Scotland. The West Links in North Berwick is an antique beauty that runs nine holes out and nine back along the very edge of the Firth. And the No. 1 course in Gullane, where Babe Zaharias won the British Ladies' Amateur in 1947, is still good enough to be a qualifying site for the Open.

The 7th tee of No. 1 is at the top of Gullane Hill, the highest point for miles around. The view from there is worth the trip even if one doesn't play the game. "You can see parts of seven counties on a clear day," says George Morin, the Gullane starter.

A few yards from the tee but facing away, toward Gullane Bay, the Firth, and the Kingdom of Fife beyond, is a plain wooden park bench of the sort one comes across at pleasing spots here and there throughout the region. Most of the benches are memorials. This one has a small brass plaque that reads: "IN FOND MEMORY OF MY WIFE NORAH CRUICKSHANK, WHO DIED 5TH JUNE 1982. SHE LOVED THIS VIEW."

Muirfield has no teaching pro and no pro shop, but it does have a caddie master, Archie Imrie, and an electric golf cart, a concession to the decrepitude of a few of the aged members. "I have to give it some corn," said the caddie master one morning as he approached the shed with a gas can in hand.

"He means he has to feed it," said Martin McIntyre, a caddie from Aberlady who had been called to the course for a morning round. "That's one of his jokes. That's why he's a caddie master and not a comedian."

McIntyre once caddied for the president of Gambia. When the president wanted to relieve himself, McIntyre pointed to a facility beside the 11th fairway. "It took his bodyguards 20 minutes to check it out," he says. "I was sorry I'd opened my mouth."

Muirfield caddies are also Gullane caddies. Their hangout is a bench outside Jimmy Hume's pro shop in the village. Across the road is the 1st tee, and next door is the ruin of the old St Andrew's parish church, begun in the 12th century, abandoned in the 17th. One of the newer headstones in the graveyard that surrounds the ruin reads: "ERECTED BY THE GULLANE GOLF CLUB TO THE MEMORY OF JAMES DOBSON 1853–1924 IN GRATEFUL APPRECIATION OF THIRTY YEARS OF FAITHFUL SERVICE AS STARTER ON THE LINKS."

One of the Gullane caddies, David Cochrane (52), spent eight years in the merchant marine, and he recites his ports of call for visitors – New Orleans, Corpus Christi, Galveston, Los Angeles, San Pedro, San Francisco, and Guaymas, Mexico. Once a year, Cochrane carries the bag of a lady from Locust Valley, NY, who, he says, once played in the Curtis Cup matches between Great Britain and the US.

American golfers playing a Scottish course for the first time are sometimes disappointed. At first glance the course seems as flat and featureless as a municipal course in West Texas. No water, no trees, just crisp turf growing on a bed of sand dunes whipped by wind off the nearest firth. Muirfield is different only because it is separated from the sight of the firth and the surrounding towns by an ocean of scrub-covered dunes and the dark green density of Archerfield Wood, the 2,500-acre estate of the Duke of Hamilton, on the east boundary.

At Muirfield, the vague feeling of playing in a field rather than on a seaside links has not been to everyone's liking. Bernard Darwin, the great English golf writer of the first half of the century, and a traditionalist, found "something park-like about those lines of fairway, each between two lines of rough . . . I admire it very much but I cannot find in it the supreme charm and the supreme thrill that belong to some courses." But to the modern professional, Muirfield is one of the very best because it is "fair".

The front nine circle in a clockwise direction, enclosing the back nine, which zigzag more or less counterclockwise. No matter which direction the wind blows, all golfers get some of the best and some of the worst of it. At St Andrews, by contrast, where the course runs nine holes out and nine back in the old manner, a golfer who starts with the wind at his back can gain an advantage over a later starter if the wind changes direction and follows him home as well.

However fair Muirfield may be, it still must be played wisely, because small errors of judgement can result in big trouble, usually in the form of deep bunkers whose sloping edges will gather in a shot that is even slightly misplaced. Some Muirfield bunkers are diabolical, notably one left of the green at the par-three 13th. Not enough that the bunker is below the level of the green, it is also six feet deep with a vertical face. The intelligent way out is backward, to a steep slope that can carry the ball to the bottom of the hill. From there, at least a bogey is within reach. In such a bunker a golfer is likely to view as unfair not only Muirfield but life itself. "I call it a 3 or a 33," said McIntyre.

The 5th hole, the first of three fine par-fives, runs west to east along the northern boundary of the course. The prevailing wind at Muirfield is from the west. With it at his back in 1972, Johnny Miller scored a double eagle with a driver and a three-wood. With an east wind, the 558 yards, which rise gradually all the way to the green, are a long, hard slog. But the green is the highest point on the course, and if the golfer had avoided the seven bunkers that surround it, the views are reward enough.

The 9th hole has been called "one of the finest par-five holes in existence" and "an antique rubbish". Some say it was a great hole until a man named Tom Simpson redesigned it, placing a bunker in the fairway, 44 yards short of the green, which forces the safe second shot left, where it is menaced by a low stone wall and out-of-bounds. In the last round of the 1929 Open, Hagen, pursuing his fourth British Open title, mishit his second shot and wound up at the base of the wall. His next shot – left-handed, with a putter – rolled across the green and several yards beyond. He left his run-up six feet short of the pin and two-putted, for a bogey. The lapse was not fatal. He finished with 292, the first American to win an Open at Muirfield, and the last until Nicklaus in 1966.

Muirfield's finishing holes – the par-three 16th, with seven deep bunkers around an elevated green; the par-five 17th, a 542-yard dogleg with bunkers threatening the player who tries to cut the corner; and the par-four 18th, whose tee shot required steady nerves and cross-hair accuracy at the very juncture where, usually in the last round, they are the hardest to produce – are designed to draw the best from the best. They have before; no doubt they will again.

And when it's over, and the last skirl of the bagpipes has died away on an evening breeze and the setting sun has streaked the sky over the Firth of Forth with pink, admirable Muirfield will revert to its rightful owners, the pheasants, the rabbits and the tweedy gentlemen at the Smoking Room windows.

CARNOUSTIE

Bernard Darwin

Forfarshire, too, is a county of many courses. Barry, Broughty Ferry, Edzell, Monifieth, Montrose, and, best known of all, Carnoustie. Carnoustie is comparatively unknown, save by name, to the Eng3lish golfer, but very popular indeed in its own country. So much so that its popularity has rendered necessary an auxiliary course, and the auxiliary course has taken a piece of good golfing ground that could ill be spared. It is a fine, big, open sandy seaside course; very natural in appearance; and in places, indeed, natural almost to the verge of roughness; but it is none the worse for that, however, and indeed it is altogether a very delightful course.

There is one curious feature, in that the taking of some new ground has caused one hole to be of a completely inland character. Certainly this hole seems at first sight to be dragged in by the heels, but we readily forgive it its inland character, because it is really a very good hole indeed. This is No. 7, South America by name. It is a good long hole, well over 400 yards in length, and the green is on an island guarded by a ditch. The soil is completely inland in character – the green once formed part of an old garden – and as if to emphasise that fact, a solitary tree has been left as a hazard, and naturally plays a prominent part in the landscape.

Burns, *anglicisé* streams, are a great feature of Carnoustie. Indeed one friend of mine returned from a visit there declaring that he had got burns badly on his nerves, and that the entire course was irrigated with them. However, it is not so much burns as sandhills that are likely to cause our downfall at the beginning. Of these hilly holes, the 2nd, by name the Valley, is a really fine one, and decidedly one of the best on the course. It is dog-legged in character, and has a distinct flavour of some of the holes at Prince's, since with the tee-shot the player carries just as much of the hill in front of him as he dares, and gains a proper advantage for a bold and successful shot. The drive is directed towards a guide flag on a hilltop, and if all goes well we are over in the valley. Then follows a beautiful second shot up a narrow neck, with a bunker on the left and other troubles on the right; 385 yards is the Valley's length, and Bogey does the hole in four. It is certainly one of the holes that he plays in his best form, for he very often takes five over holes that are no longer and not nearly so difficult or so interesting. Of the other holes on the way out, most are decidedly long, except the 5th, which is a simple enough short hole, and South America, before described, is as good as any of them.

On the way home there is a somewhat awe-inspiring second shot at the 10th, where we have to carry a hill, out of the face of which two bunkers have been cut out and appropriately christened the Spectacles. The 12th has a pleasing name, Jockey's Burn, and the 13th has a pleasing putting green. The 14th, by name the Flagstaff, is a good long and narrow hole, where the hills crowd in close upon us, and we must keep straight along the valley. The best hole on the way home, however, is probably the 16th, or Island, where there is but one way to secure an easy and comfortable approach, and that consists of pushing your tee shot out to the right so that the ball comes to rest upon a very narrow neck. Take an easier route from the tee, and you will be left with as unpleasant a pitch as need be, and the greedy waters of a burn running between you and the hole. Burns play an important part at both the last two holes also, for one has to be carried from the 17th tee and another menaces the pitch on to the home green. There really is some justification for the nervous golfer who has water on the brain after a round at Carnoustie.

AMBLEHURST

Siegfried Sassoon

Over at Amblehurst, about four miles away, there is hazardless nine-hole course round Squire Maundle's sheep-nibbled park. The park faces south-west, sloping to a friendly little river – the Neaze – which at that point, so I have been told, though I have never troubled to verify it – divides the counties of Kent and Sussex. On the other side of the river is the village. Squire Maundle's clanging stable clock shares with the belfry of the village school the privilege of indicating the Amblehurst hours. My progress up and down the park from one undersized green to another is accompanied by the temperate clamour of sheep-bells (and in springtime by the loud litanies of baa-ing lambs and anxious ewes). The windows of Squire Maundle's 18th-century mansion overlook my zigzag saunterings with the air of a country family dowager who has not yet made up her mind to leave cards on those new people at the Priory. As a rule I have the links to myself, but once in a while "young" Squire Maundle (so-called because his 87-year-old father is still above ground) appears on the skyline in his deer-stalker hat, with a surly black retriever at his heels and we play an amicable round.

Without wishing to ridicule him, for he was always kind and courteous, I may say that both his features and his tone of voice have something in common with the sheep who lift their mild munching faces to regard him while he plays an approach shot in his cautious, angular, and automatic style. He is one of those shrewdly timorous men who are usually made a butt of by their more confident associates. Falstaff would have borrowed fifty pounds off him, though he has the reputation of being close with his money. His vocabulary is as limited as his habit of mind, and he speaks with an old-fashioned word-clipping conciseness. His lips are pursed up as if in a perpetual whistle. The links – on which he knows every tussock and ant-hill intimately – are always "in awful good condition"; and "That's a hot'un!" he exclaims when I make a long drive, or "That's for Sussex!" (a reference to the remote possibility that my ball may have gone over the river). But the best instance I can give of his characteristic mode of expressing himself is one which occured when I once questioned him about a group of little grey stones among the laurel bushes outside his stable-yard. After whistling to his retriever he replied, "House-dogs bury in the shrubbery; shooting-dogs bury in the park . . ."

Aunt Evelyn always enjoyed a game of croquet with him at a garden party.

But in my spontaneous memories of Amblehurst I am always playing by myself. The sun is in my eyes as I drive off at the "long hole" down to the river, and I usually slice my ball into a clump of may trees. I am "trying to do a good score" – a purpose which seldom survives the first nine holes – but only half my attention is concentrated on the game. I am wondering, perhaps, whether that parcel from the second-hand bookshop at Reading will have arrived by the afternoon post; or I am vaguely musing about my money affairs; or think what a relief it is to have escaped from the tyranny of my Tripos at Cambridge. Outside the park the village children are making a shrill hubbub as they came out of school. But the sun is reddening beyond the straight-rising smoke of the village chimneys, and I must sling my clubs across my shoulder and mount my bicycle to pedal my way along the narrow autumn-smelling lanes. And when I get home Aunt Evelyn will be there to pour out my tea and tell me all about the Jumble Sale this afternoon; it was such a success, they made more than six pounds for the Mission to Deep-sea Fishermen.

JONES, THE SOUL OF IT

Furman Bisher

Robert Tyre Jones, Jnr, made his first association with golf at the age of six. A man named Fulton Colville, practising chip shots in front of the boarding house where the Joneses had taken summer quarters on East Lake, noticed him sitting on the porch steps watching and addressed him: "Would you like to hit some, sonny?"

After a few attempts, made shyly and awkwardly, for he was a scrawny child, little Bobby was favoured with a gift. Fulton Colville drew an old cleek – that's something between a putter and two-iron – from his bag and handed it to him, and so the legendary voyage into golf was launched.

Fulton Colville's role in it was only as a walk-on, but Bob Jones later said, "Something inspired him to give me that club. I didn't have any interest in golf before them."

It wasn't long before the Jones boy was out on the golf course at East Lake Country Club banging his little cleek around along with his parents. East Lake is only six miles from the centre of Atlanta, but in those times it was a summer retreat for the cityites, a colony surrounded by forest and enveloped by solitude, perhaps a setting you would expect in one of Scott Fitzgerald's vintages stories. Businessmen placed their families in quarters for the season – the Joneses chose a Mrs Meador's – and joined them by trolley that ran out from downtown. It was there, under the guidance of an immigrant Scottish golf professional named Stewart Maiden, that little Bobby Jones learned the fundamentals of the game that transformed him from a scrawny kid into an epic of sport and an international personality, a blessing for which he paid his dues to game and society times over.

He became at one and the same time the symbol of the Southern Gentleman and the American Sportsman. Clifford Roberts has said of him, "We never have had an athlete who came close to matching Bob Jones in popularity." It was this popularity that became the cornerstone of Augusta National Golf Club and the Masters golf tournament. It bordered on a kind of sainthood, unofficial but unwavering.

Author Paul Gallico turned his back on sports writing for fiction with a bitter-sweet fare-thee-well. He wrote a book which bespoke his disillusionment with the games and the people he had covered, but one of these was not Bob Jones, of whom he said, "I have found only one who could stand up in every way as a gentleman and a celebrity, a fine, decent human being, and one who never once since I have known him has let me down in my estimate of him."

Robert Tyre Jones the Golfer was not a "Jnr" in the technical sense of familial procedure. His father made him so in defiance of custom. Robert Purmedus Jones regretted not having been named for his father. He passed on to his son the name of his grandfather, staunchly oblivious to the rule that dictates such a christening falls under the heading of "II."

They were the Joneses of Canton, Georgia. They originated in that small town 40 miles north of Atlanta and were in the mercantile business, graduating into textiles before the family became dazzled by the city lights of Atlanta. There, offspring Robert P. became an attorney. For many years he served as general counsel for Atlantic Steel Company. Being an only child, little Robert and his dad became great pals. Mutual admirers. "The Colonel," Bob called him, as did most of those close to his father.

And The Colonel was always there in the gallery when Bob was playing one of his major tournaments. Young Bob dedicated his book, *Golf Is My Game*, to his father and elaborated on their relationship later on. "One of the greatest gifts golf gave me was the enjoyment of many years of playful association with my father," he wrote.

And he *did* write it. It was *his* book. Bob Jones would not stand still for a writing "ghost", any third person-first person relationship. When a title once was proposed to him for the *Saturday Evening Post* with a by-line that would read, "By Bobby Jones as told to . . .," he sniffed. "Makes me sound like a damned illiterate who can't write his own name," he said, and refused.

He was indeed an excellent handler of the language. His literary talent bordered on the Oxonian, finely fundamental and excellently rhetorical. His breadth of interests is brilliantly illustrated in the way he went about his education. He earned a degree in mechanical engineering from Georgia Tech, studied English literature at Harvard, and later whisked through law school at Emory University in a year and a half. He could have been most anything he chose to be, except a sprinter. His feet moved considerably more slowly than his mind, and he often made jokes about his slowness. But then you don't have to run fast to play golf.

As a gentleman sportsman, Bobby Jones was a mountain among hillocks. First, though, he had to learn his lessons himself, and the miracle of it is that he survived to adulthood through a petulant youth of club-throwing, pouting, and childish tantrums that embarrassed partners and rivals. And once, if you can believe it, stalked out of a tournament at the holy of holies, St Andrews. But once reformed, his reformation was as enduring as it was drastic.

In one of the US Opens he entered a forest to play one of his errant drives. Emerging a few minutes later, he signalled that he was penalising himself one stroke. The ball had moved as he was addressing it, and the rule clearly calls for a penalty, whether the player is being witnessed or not. It was a matter of honour with Bob Jones, and he was flabbergasted when the act drew such a wave of admiration.

"Well," he said, "you might as well have praised a man for not robbing a bank."

When he beat Watts Gunn for the US Amateur championship in 1925, much was made of the fact that it was the only time two members of the same club had ever advanced to the final round. (And it has never happened again.) The fact is, Watts Gunn was there only because Bob Jones had talked his parents into allowing his younger friend to accompany him and The Colonel to Pittsburgh to play the tournament. Even lesser known was the story of an interception that took place on the back stairs of the clubhouse at Oakmont, where the two friends were staying. Watts had met a young lady in Pittsburgh who had aroused his interest. On the night before the championship match, Bob came upon his friend trying to slip down the back stairway for another date with his new friend. "Oh, no, you don't," Bob said. "You're going to march right back up to that room. You'll need all the sleep you can get for tomorrow." And Watts Gunn's date was suddenly broken.

The competitive part of Jones's life came to an abrupt close in 1948, after which he never was able to play golf again. Struck down by some dastardly fate that was of such a cruel disposition as to reach out and trip a mortal it seemed to have judged to have given too much. The ailment that invaded his person was a rare one that with a creeping mercilessness took away his ability to manipulate his limbs and eventually shrivelled him to a withered ruin of the Adonis that he had once been. "Syringomyelia" was its medical name.

Almost 20 years earlier, however, he had assured himself a place in the roll call of golf's immortals. There is no other achievement in sport comparable to winning the US Open, the British Open, the US Amateur, and the British Amateur championships all in the same year. In fact, this Grand Slam has become, at least by the perceived limits of foreseeable years, the Feat Impossible. The economics of golf have seen to that. Amateur players no longer carry that status any longer that it takes to qualify for the professional tour. There is no longer the lure to remain amateur that existed in Jones's day, when the golf professional was still only a few steps removed from the choreman of the shop. But Jones, fortunate to be backed by a well-to-do father, as an amateur accomplished the Grand Slam. Since his time, not one of the professional players has been able to achieve even the "Pro Grand Slam" by winning the Masters, the US Open, British Open, and PGA Championship of the USA in one year.

Shortly after Bob Jones completed the improbable foursome by sinking the putt that defeated Eugene Homans on Marion Cricket Club's 11th green, it being their 29th hole of play in the finals of the US Amateur Championship of 1930, his retirement took effect. Retirement had been lying in the back of his mind since 1926, to be executed only when he could find the proper stopping place. Here he was, barely out of college, retiring from competition in golf at the age of 28, removing from the centre ring of the game its stellar attraction. The next four years of

American golf were to be low in interest without him. For Jones it was simply the halftime in his life.

Those were times when society rode high and the living was opulent. The estate life and Gatsby's era. Sprawling hotel resorts and the rise of the American Plan. Endurance flying and flagpole sitting. Flappers and Clara Bow. The budding of radio and Atwater Kent. Gloomy Gil Dobie and "Hurry Up" Yost. The Volstead Act and gin made in a bathtub. Sinclair Lewis and the Spirit of St Louis. Yale-Harvard and Albie Booth against Barry Wood. The Charleston and rooftop ballrooms. Crooning. The Stork Club. Electric fans. And hickory shafts.

Clifford Roberts drove up to Knollwood Country Club one day in the middle of the Roaring Twenties, presumably in his Pierce-Arrow or Franklin. Knollwood was located in Westchester County, where New York's wealthy went to the country for the weekend. He was a member. Bobby Jones was playing a friendly match at the club that day, and Roberts was pointedly "dropping in" to take a look at this young man of whom he had heard so much. Other details of the day grow vague, but the two were introduced and discovered they had mutual friends, among them an innkeeper named Walton Marshall, who divided his years between the Hotel Vanderbilt in New York and the Bon Air Vanderbilt in Augusta. Neither had the faintest glimmer of a notion at the time, but with this meeting the first seed of the Augusta National Golf Club was sown.

"Our paths crossed several times after that. I saw Bob play in several tournaments. One I recall distinctly was the National Amateur at Baltusrol when he lost in the final round to George Von Elm," Clifford Roberts said. It happened that Roberts was president that year of the Baltusrol Golf Club, near Springfield, New Jersey.

Roberts dealt in investments and securities. Therefore, his life ran to the monied interest, and he turned up at those fashionable addresses frequented by outstanding figures of finance, industry, letters, and politics. One of these was the Bon Air Vanderbilt in Augusta, which in those times registered the finest clientele in America, it is said. As testament, President Taft and J.P. Morgan were frequent guests.

"I had tried Pinehurst two times and had the terrible luck to run into snowstorms both times. Augusta had never heard of snow, and I was encouraged to try this location. It was a choice wisely made, not only for the golf and the climate, but because of the accommodations. Walton Marshall was a notch above your average innkeeper, and the Bon Air was beautifully run. Everyone who came to Augusta stayed at the Bon

Air invariably, but, by God, you had to get your reservations in a year in advance. January and February were the height of the season. It was closed in the summer," Roberts said.

"You see, people travelled by train then. Florida was too far, actually wasn't even developed to any great degree. The main purpose of people who came was golf, and Augusta came to fit our needs perfectly. You can step right outside the clubhouse here at Augusta, and you're just 150 feet above sea level. The climate was temperate and the courses were good, and that was the reason Bob spent a good part of his winters over here, playing golf. Conditions were so much better than in Atlanta, which is about one thousand feet higher."

Wherever Bob Jones played, it amounted to an exhibition, as that friendly match at Knollwood had turned out to be. People came out to watch. It was so at Augusta as well. He appeared often at the two courses of prominence then, the Augusta Country Club and Forest Hills, but he simply couldn't play a round of golf in privacy.

Augusta National, as it turned out, was the product of impulse. Roberts knew that in the back of Jones's mind was the idea of building a golf course to his own specifications and his own taste some time, some place. As they talked of it one day, Roberts blurted out, "Why not here in Augusta?"

A beautiful blend of the minds took place on the spot. It was simply a matter next of finding the property location, a piece of property that Jones would approve. In the fall of the 1930, shortly after Jones had accomplished his Grand Slam, Roberts arrived in Atlanta with a lay of land in mind, requiring only Jones's visual approval and a plan of membership.

There is next this vision of Bob Jones walking from the doorway of the old manor house, which is block-shaped like a fortress, and standing for the first time on the grassy overlook that has since become the terrace lawn of the Augusta National Golf Club.

"The experience was unforgettable," Bob Jones wrote later. "It seemed that this land had been lying here for years just waiting for someone to lay a golf course upon it."

What they had come upon was a gentle, rolling spread of hill and valley with a spring-fed stream that only a near century of preparation could have put in such perfect condition to receive a golf course. The moment of Bob Jones's first view of it came in December 1930. By the next spring, having heard its ultimate call, the 365 acres of land began to come alive.

While America was still a wilderness, Indians had camped upon this land, attracted by the spring that is the course's source of water, that feeds the lakes and Rae's Creek. De Soto and his marchers are said to have passed through it in their search for the Mississippi River. What the prospective founders of Augusta National Golf Club found there was a former nursery not so tenderly attended for several years. A family of Belgians had settled the property in 1857, and the nursery they created there was the first known in the South. They were of noble heritage. Baron Prosper Jules Alphonse Berckmans, motivating force behind the nursery, was a man of many splendours. Scholar, horticulturist, landscape architect, botanist, and artist. He had arrived in this country in 1850, having taken his leave of Belgium for political and religious reasons upon which there is no elaboration. He was followed into the nursery business by his two sons, Prosper Jules Alphonse, Jnr, and Louis.

The Berckmans' nursery made vast contributions to American horticulture, and the Augusta National Golf Club has gone to great effort to preserve and showcase that bonus that came with its purchase. For instance, all the thousands of miles of privet hedge that grow in the United States can be traced back to the mother hedge that still thrives directly back of the practice tee near where all the monstrous wagons and trailers gather in a television community each week of the Masters. The wisteria vine that seems to writhe out of the ground at the corner of the clubhouse on the terrace lawn is said to be the oldest in the country. The massive oak that stands guard like some arrogant sentry over the entire spread, from clubhouse down the gentle hill to the focal spectating point where the 2nd and 7th greens and the 3rd tee abut, is over 200 years old. Markers are found about the grounds identifying the botanical significance of all the growth of historical note – tree, shrub, and flowering plant.

Old Berckmans had remarried, and at the time of his death in 1910 he willed the property to his young widow instead of the two sons. P.J.A., Jnr and Louis soon left the area and relocated elsewhere. The young widow, having no interest in the nursery, eventually sold the property and its commercial name, "Fruitlands", and for about fifteen years prior to its discovery by Clifford Roberts and friends, the acreage had suffered for lack of attention.

One of Augusta's most distinguished industrialists, Fielding Wallace, was appointed to handle the purchase for the Club and eventually became its first secretary. Also, he later became president of the US Golf Association. (Around Augusta, his designation by the man on the street was unique: "The man who runs the Chinese hair factory", for his company imported the hair of Chinese women by the bales and produced mattresses and other products from it.)

As the membership was being formed, one of the first moves made by Clifford Roberts and his group was to search for and locate the two Berckmans sons and induce them to return and spend the rest of their lives on the old family place. P.J.A., Jnr became the Club's first manager. Louis, having fared more prosperously, was able to become a dues-paying member and was appointed the Club's first treasurer. In the process, they made great contributions to the horticultural rejuvenation of the grounds. And so we have a story beginning with a happy ending, and all the peripheral segments of one broad narrative coming together in the fruition of the dream of one man and the vision of another, and for a poignant side effect, the reunion of two brothers with the old soil on which they once bounded about on shoeless feet.

We take our fade-out as Bob Jones makes his solemn pronouncement as to the nature of Augusta National Golf Club and what it was all about at its origin: "Our aim is to develop a golf course and a retreat of such nature, and of such excellence, that men of some means and devoted to the game of golf may find the Club worthwhile as an extra luxury where they may visit and play with kindred spirits from other parts of the nation."

It has been achieved, never veering from course.

"Unless I break down, I hope to participate every year, regardless of how I am putting or where I finish" – Bobby Jones at the first Augusta National Invitation Tournament (which would not become the "Masters" officially for four more years), March 1934.

He *was* the tournament, especially that first year. He made out the first invitation list himself. His name brought the highest price in the Calcutta pool. He made no move but what journalism reported on it. Wherever he went on the course, those men covering the tournament were always close at hand; but it was a different kind of star-media relationship than had developed in the age of television. First, the press entourage was significantly smaller, and Jones knew nearly all of them personally. Also, those writers were privileged to follow close at hand down the fairway and chat with him between shots. When Grantland Rice arrived, their official dean was at hand, and as O.B. Keeler reported in the *Atlanta Journal*, "He [Rice] ruled the tournament as of even greater importance than the National Open." After all, it was the only place in the world where the public could see Bobby Jones play golf anymore. That, as it developed, had not been achieved with ease.

"I had an awful time convincing Bob he should play at all," Clifford Roberts aid. "He wanted to be the host and an official. I told him he couldn't invite his friends to a game of golf and not play with them."

People responded. The opportunity see Bobby Jones play again at $2 a head drew them out in numbers estimated at 3,500, even exceeding expectations. Most of them were gathered around the 1st tee as Jones made his first drive, and they cheered loudly. He wore a checked blue sweater above knickers, with socks to match. Paul Runyan, with whom he was paired, was dressed in a tomato red sweater and matching socks. Jones out-drove the little professional by 40 yards.

"Jones Off in His Putting as Masters Starts."

The headline in the *Atlanta Journal* drove directly to the point. Just as Jones had feared, his conduct on the green was erratic. He was playing with an unusual handicap. His treasured companion of all those great years was missing. "Calamity Jane", his putter, had been misplaced, and he'd had to send to Atlanta for a substitute. He three-putted each of the last three greens. His score was 76 on the first round.

Jones finished that first tournament in thirteenth place, tied with Denny Shute, a PGA champion, and Walter Hagen, US Open, British Open, and PGA champion, and the most flamboyant professional of his time, with a score of 294 for the 72 holes. It was to be, as history turned out, Jones's best finish in the tournament created about and for him. Of all the rounds he played in 12 Masters never once did he break par. The scores of his final year, 1948, indicate a deterioration of the game that a man who demanded so much of himself could not long bring himself to tolerate. He shot 75–81–79–79 and finished out of sight at 314. By this time the press had mercifully turned its head and left him to his peace, such as he could find.

During the four years between his retirement from competition and his return in the Masters, Bobby Jones had managed to fill his hours with gainful ventures. Warner Brothers, the film producers, contracted him for a series of instructional shorts with a story, or gag line, including some of the movie idols of the time such as Richard Arlen, W.C. Fields, and Guy Kibbee. The Listerine Company sponsored him in a radio series of golf and how it should be played, teamed with his Boswellian companion, O.B. Keeler. He was syndicated in another instructional form through a regular newspaper column. And the A.G. Spalding Company made his involvement complete when he was contracted to serve the manufacture of sporting goods for a many a lucrative year as a designer and consultant on a line of golf clubs that bore his name. When his career on the course came to an end, he was not, then, bereft of activity. He also had contacts in the legal profession to develop, and later he bought two Coca-Cola Bottling outlets. And always, always, there was the Masters.

"One of the miracles of it is that a town of some 65,000 can absorb all these people with so little ripple" – Clifford Roberts, 1975.

For several of the earlier years of the Masters, the Bon Air Vanderbilt served the tournament, served Augusta National, and continued to serve a continuing clientele of America's social élite. It was the centre of tournament living. Fare was $5 per day, American Plan. Formal dress for dinner was required. Walton Marshall managed on. He was not one to break with, or even allow warpage of, tradition.

Curiously, though, as the golf tournament made gains in popularity, the hotel's prestige lost ground. In no way were these changes of stature related, except for the inescapable fact that expansion of facilities at Augusta National surely siphoned off some of the Bon Air's regular patronage. When the Second World War broke loose upon the nation, Augusta's face began to change, and many of the old standards and traditions changed with it. Resort hotels began losing guests to the burgeoning "second-home" movement. Americans began moving about by air. That brought Florida nearer in time, and as the palms, the beaches, and the balmy air became more accessible, so did it become more attractive. The tourist boom broke out, driving the alligators and the Seminoles deeper into the marshes and mosquito country. The piney woods atmosphere of the mid-Southern resorts lost some of its appeal.

The military had taken over the Forest Hills Hotel in Augusta and its golf course during the Second World War, and civilians never got them back. The Bon Air's demise was less abrupt and dreadfully more painful. It was an awful thing to watch, year to year, its death by deterioration, neglect, and flighty management. It sat there on its hill, a huge white ghost, seeming to cry out for someone to save it. In its halcyon years, natives "down the hill" had gazed upon the Bon Air with awe, watching the great people of America, tycoons, presidents, men of letters and nobility, come and go in their chauffeured livery. Now all barriers were down. The gasping old hotel begged attention. The townspeople moved about its premises with freedom, but found themselves disillusioned, for all the attractiveness and the lure of the glittering personalities were no longer there.

Forest Hills Hotel has now become Oliver General Hospital, a branch of the Veterans Administration. The Bon Air still sits in its crook of Walton Way at the top of the hill, but the world races by it unnoticing. It has become a residential home for senior citizens.

The Hotel Richmond sprang to the force as the Bon Air began to fade. It was located downtown on Broad Street at the war memorial monument, a place where drummers stayed when the Masters wasn't on. Making no pretence of trying to take the place of the Bon Air in the social life of Augusta, it provided only four walls, a bed, a place to eat, and the necessities of life found in the typical commercial hotel. The Barringers owned it at the time it was cutting its widest swathe as a host, but death and estate problems brought it down eventually, too. Now it is closed and has been succeeded by a stunning new modern hostelry called the Executive House. Otherwise, Augusta has become a motel town. The visiting patrons are now decentralised, strung out from Interstate Highway 20, which crosses Washington Road two miles west of Augusta National, to North Augusta, across the Savannah River, and all the way to Aiken, South Carolina.

Then we have the latest form of itinerant resident. He rents. Not a room, but a whole house. He blows in for the week of the tournament. The landlord and family leave town for the week and take a vacation, generously bankrolled by the rental fee. The one-week resident brings in his family, friends, business accounts, or shares with another family. Or as in the case of a tournament player, another golfer and family. Sometimes the house is a classic, on the columned residences out Walton Way. Sometimes it's a subdivision house without pretension. Sometimes it goes for $1,500 for the week. Nearly every afternoon smoke from charcoal cookery casts a blue pall over the backyard. A few drinks, a steak, to bed, and out to the course early in the morning for the player. For the watcher, a long night, a midmorning brunch, an afternoon of gallerying, and a party in the evening, maybe the annual church Southern Bar-B-Q at the old lodge on the lake Saturday, or the loftier and more formal atmosphere of dinner and dancing at Augusta Country Club.

House rental became popular when the Augusta Chamber of Commerce took this course to satisfy the rooming demands in the years when Augusta was being transformed from a hotel to a motel town, and quarters were short. It has stuck. Some of the tournament players have been renting the same house or in the same residential section for years. Look out the window and Gary Player may be jogging by. Arnold Palmer may be backing out of the driveway. Jack Nicklaus may be standing at the mailbox talking to a one-week neighbour. Just typical American family living with stars in the roles.

. . . .

People drive by that place every day never knowing of its share in the history of golf. It is a silent landmark, saying nothing, revealing nothing of its secret that Bobby Jones once lived there. The address is 3425 Tuxedo Road, dead centre in the section of Atlanta where the heart of old Northwest Side society beats. On a turn behind a white spiked fence, the columned mansion sits back from the street, almost out of sight of eyes that would be curious. Where Mr Jones lived, a Mr Brown lives now, an implied pseudonymic procession of occupancy as if the address itself seeks its own anonymity. When the Joneses lived there, the mailbox bore a simple black-on-white plate that said "Whitehall". It is not there anymore.

There were three children: Robert III; Clara, named for Bob's mother; and Mary Ellen, named for her own mother. To them "Whitehall" was home, though the name itself had no meaning whatsoever in their lives.

"Dad bought the house from a Dr Childs, and the name was on the mailbox when we moved there. Dad just never did bother to take it down." Mary Ellen Jones, now Mrs Carl Hood, wife of a banker, mother of one daughter, car-pooler, member of Lovett School PTA, speaks from a wing chair in the parlour of her home in that part of Atlanta known as Buckhead. "After his operation, we made it a habit to visit him every Saturday afternoon at five o'clock. Have a drink and talk to him about friends and things outside that he had an interest in. We'd go by every afternoon after a Georgia Tech football game and tell him how the team looked and how the new players were working out. He never lost his interest in Georgia Tech, but going to games was out of the question. On the other hand, he kept going to his office nearly every day until about a year before he died."

Mary Malone Jones was in charge of the religious affairs of the family, and being of Irish descent, the children were reared in the Catholic faith. Little Mary Ellen attended parochial school at Christ the King, and one day in her first grade class all the children were asked by their teacher, a nun, to stand and tell of their fathers and what they did. When it came Mary Ellen's turn, she stood and said, "I don't know, but he has an awful lot of blue ribbons, so he must have won something; but my brother and sister have a lot of blue ribbons, too, and they rode horses."

Bobby III and Clara rode in horse shows at summer camp. Kid stuff. Mary Ellen never had such an inclination, nor toward any kind of athletic games, for that matter.

"I never was a golfer, but when Dad was involved in building the Peachtree course, he hired Steward Maiden, his old teacher, as the professional," Mary Ellen says. "Then he decided Stewart Maiden needed some customers and that I should start taking lessons. So once a week for about a year, I took a lesson from Stewart Maiden, who was not inclined to be very gentle with his instructions. To his outspoken disgust, I was a very poor student. To paraphrase the title of Dad's book, 'Golf Was Not My Game.'

"I played golf with him one time in my life, Dad and I against Mother and my brother. A two-ball foursome at Peachtree. The course was still rather new and in an unrefined condition. It was a dreadful experience for him. I put him in poison ivy, honeysuckle, thickets, and brooks, places where he had never been on a golf course. Finally, I was so tired of it all I hauled off without caring and hit a drive on the 4th hole, a par three, and the ball stopped about two feet from the pin. He sank the putt. I said, 'I retire, I quit. I'm finished,' and walked back to the clubhouse."

Of course, most of Bobby Jones's golfing battles had been fought by the time Mary Ellen was born. The Grand Slam had been won. He still played the Masters, but that was not one of the wars, more a walk through the park with old friends and old foes. None of the great conflicts is any part of Mary Ellen's memories. The public's steadfast reverence for her father was there, but even this made no deep impression because she grew up with it.

"They took me to California when I was three months old, when Dad went out there to make those movies. My nurse told me of all the famous movie stars I had met, but I remember none of that." Being the daughter of a celebrated father has made few waves in her life, in other words. "With a name like Mary Jones," she says, wryly, "you can get by without stirring up much attention.

"It was not that way with my brother. Bobby had something to live up to, being the son of Bobby Jones, the great golfer. He always had that shadow hanging over him. It was like being the son of Red Grange and playing half-back. Bobby played well, but never good enough.

"Dad always had this desire for him to qualify for the US Amateur, then finish in one of the positions that would earn him an invitation to the Masters. So one year he qualified for the US Amateur. He flew out to Colorado for the tournament, full of fire and enthusiasm, ready to take that old tiger by the tail. Who does he draw in the first round? A kid named Jack Nicklaus. Bobby never made it to the Masters."

If nothing had yet certified for her the international esteem of her father, his notability, the near sainthood bestowed upon him, the confirmation came in October 1958, when Mary Ellen was invited along to St Andrews to witness his acceptance of the Freedom of the City. Just right off, no one was quite certain of the calibre of the honour until it came to light that only one another American had ever received it – Benjamin Franklin. The Joneses flew to London on a flight that almost became a disaster. The plane lost an engine and had to turn back to Gander, Newfoundland, as it approached the point of crisis over the Atlantic. They reached St Andrews a day behind schedule.

"It was one of the great experiences of my life. The ceremony was a moving thing. I was stunned. Younger Hall was just jammed. We were taken in through the back entrance and seated on a stage. I'll never forget Dad, how he got on that stage and up to the lectern with his two walking sticks. He was determined to do it without any help. It was painful to watch him. I thought he'd never make it, but he did.

"He had worked hard on that speech of acceptance, and it was beautiful. It became quite emotional at the end, and then he and the Provost were seated in a golf cart and they drove down the aisle through the hall. People were crying and reaching out to touch him, and to touch even us, my mother, my brother, and me. I felt like the Queen of England. Then almost in unison, purely spur of the moment, I think, they began sinking 'Will Ye No' Come Back Again?' well knowing that he never would. We walked down the aisle behind him, and I can still feel the tingles in my spine. It was moving."

As for the Masters tournament, it was only a glimmer out there on some distant horizon to Mary Ellen. She heard of it, read of it, knew of it as some peripheral event concerning her family, but her attendance was rare. "A good deal of the time, especially when Dad was still playing, I was away at college. Then I was married and had other interests and responsibilities. I do remember one year a bunch of us in our twenties rented a railroad car and went to the Masters, but that was more a big party than it was a junket of golf. I can't even tell you who won it that year."

Four years before he died in December 1971, so crippled he could no longer endure a journey of even 165 miles to the Masters, Bob Jones and his Mary gave up the responsibilities of house-holding for an apartment on Peachtree Street. Most of the last twenty years of his life he required full-time attendants who served as valet, hand servant, nurse, and chauffeur. His man's man at the end was one of distinguished bearing and manner named Hoyt. Being virtually immobile at this point, Jones required constant attention. Hoyt moved along with him to the apartment, there to watch over him as he awaited his appointment with death. Three days before he passed on, Bob Jones told a close friend, "If

I had known it would be this easy, I wouldn't have been so worried about it."

On a cold Saturday morning in December, Robert Tyre Jones, Jnr died. Two years later, almost to the day, Robert Tyre Jones III, only 47 years old, lurched forward and died of a heart attack in Nashville, Tennessee. In May 1975, Mary Malone Jones passed away. Now only the two daughters are left, and some destiny has drawn them close. Clare and Mary Ellen live not more than two blocks apart, and "Whitehall" is not more than a mile away.

Chapter 6

CADDIES

MAN'S BEST FRIEND OR
BEAST OF BURDEN?

Michael McDonnell

The last time I was in Wandsworth Prison I met an old friend who was surprised and delighted to see me.

"Hullo, Mister Mac. How are you? Could you do me a favour? Send me a golf fixture list? I'll be out of here in time for the Daks."

"Wingy" Pearson was a caddie, so named because he had only one arm. Nobody knew how he had lost the other one but the deficiency did not hinder his efforts as he worked for some of the best-known professionals in British golf. They, like me, had no idea what Wingy and his colleagues did during the winter – only that they reappeared, like daffodils, in the spring. I had gone to the prison to deliver a lecture on sport to the inmates and when I caught sight of my old friend, he was quite unabashed at his circumstances.

"I try to come in here every winter," he explained casually, "bounce a few cheques or something. Nothing too serious, mind. Just enough to put me inside during the cold weather. Can't beat it. A warm bed, three good meals a day. It really sets me up for the season."

"Wingy" had a point because life was tough in those days for him and the rest of his Runyonesque fraternity who answered to names like Tam the Goose, Tosher, Irish Joe, Punch, Spud and Binocular Billy. Their nicknames hid true identities for reasons best-known to themselves but not hard to guess. Many of them lived a hand-to-mouth existence, looking for a golf bag to carry, gambling or drinking the day's wages and then sleeping rough in some bunker or shed. They were dismissed as vagabonds, treated as beasts of burden and referred to openly and scathingly by professionals as "rats". They were, it seemed, the necessary evils of a Royal and Ancient game. But therein lay the paradox because these men formed such a fundamental part of the game that even the Rules of Golf gave them special mention and decreed for example that the caddie was the only person a player could consult in singles play for advice. That Rule 9–1 still applies.

Because the rules still regard a round of golf as a joint effort between player and caddie, with equal responsibilities, any infringement committed by the caddie incurs a penalty on the player, as if he himself committed it. It still prompts the caddie to talk in terms of "we" when things go well but "he" when disaster befalls. It means, however, that the caddie is obliged to know the rules, or at least enough of them not to get his client into trouble as happened in the 1971 Ryder Cup match in St Louis. There, a chance remark by Bernard Gallacher's caddie cost this Scottish professional the hole before he had even hit his golf ball. His opponent Arnold Palmer had struck a superb shot to the green and as Bernard stepped forward to address his own ball, the caddie whispered: "Nice shot Arnie. What d'you hit?" A vigilant referee overheard the remark and declared that Gallacher's "side" had asked for advice. Penalty: loss of hole. For such reasons, some professionals ask only two things of their caddies: "Keep the clubs clean and your mouth shut." The game is difficult enough without the added worry of an unpredictable assistant who could cost more than his fee in lost prize money.

The term "caddie" probably dates from the time of Mary Queen of Scots, a golf enthusiast who even found time for a game a few days after her husband Darnley was murdered in 1567. Her page boys were the younger sons of French nobility and known as "cadets". Quite soon, the street urchins of Edinburgh became known disparagingly as "caddies" as they ran errands and carried goods for shopkeepers and other customers. They also carried golf clubs for players and gradually the term was applied not just to youngsters but also to grown men who made a living in this manner from the game. Thus began the tradition of the caddie – a man compelled to live at secondhand because his livelihood depended on the imperfections of others and how well he could guide another ill-equipped human being round a golf course. In such terms, the caddie saw himself as the senior partner, and still does. He judges wind strength, chooses the club, dictates the target area and leaves only what he regards as the simple business of hitting the ball to his client.

A caddie can be tough, sarcastic, sharp-tongued and quite merciless with a client who disobeys his advice as witness the hapless young golfer who threatened to drown himself after a bad round. The caddie mumbled: "Dinna fret yerself. You couldna keep yer heid doon long enough."

One Hollywood feature film and at least two substantial books, one by Henry Longhurst, have been devoted to the wit and wisdom of golf caddies, whose talent for the *mots justes* at times suggest a profound insight into the nature of golf and mankind. The caddies became – and still are – the most colourful characters in the game. At the turn of the century such men as Big Crawford from North Berwick stood supreme. In any dispute, this huge man raised his fist and explained it was the only "referee" that mattered. At Musselburgh, the famous Fiery John was never seen without his Glengarry bonnet. He had been saddled with a malicious nickname because the truth of it was he was such a withdrawn man that J.H. Taylor imagined him better suited to the monastic life, "passing the years behind grey walls secluded from the distractions of the turbulent world".

These men cajoled, counselled, inspired and occasionally bullied their clients to better golf or at least to winning ways. Pawkey Corstorphine of St Andrews always offered the same advice: "Don't risk anything: we'll play wi' oor heids." It was but a short stop from this kind of wisdom to imparting instruction on how to play, so that many caddies, already paid for their labours and knowledge, became professionals.

Essentially, the good caddie is an excellent judge of a golfer because his day's wages can depend on "the bag" he picks up. He boasts rightly that he can improve anybody's score by following Corstorphine's doctrine of always playing within one's capabilities. It make good sense, which we all acknowledge, yet it brings a deadening realism to the game when most of us still dream of unfettered perfection and would rather not be reminded that we are not as good as we think we are, even if a more cautious approach may pay better dividends. But the caddie is in it for the money and knows that the better the result the bigger the pay.

In this respect nothing has changed over the years, although the modern caddie is very much a highly-paid man of his times. If he works for a touring professional he will earn a weekly wage, plus a percentage of his client's winnings (about five per cent, which means that in 1984, American professional Tom Watson's caddie earned over 25,000 dollars in commission which put him well within the top 140 money-earners on the American Tour). He will have his own home, car, bank account, credit cards and, more than likely, will hold an impressive university degree. He stays in the same hotels as the stars, travels with them and is treated as a colleague. True enough, he is still lured by the roving lifestyle, particularly those college graduates looking for a break after years of study. But these days it is first-class all the way – no more bunkers and sheds. The top professionals have acknowledged at last the vital importance of the caddie.

Jack Nicklaus has employed the same caddie in Britain for more than 20 years. Before he arrives each year for the Open, Big Jack informs Yorkshireman Jimmy Dickinson of his travel plans and expects a full survey and report of the championship course by the time he arrives. Jimmy, in common with most top caddies, has his own reference library of information on every major golf course, not in leather-bound volumes but pencilled in grubby notebooks. These are the battle plans that have helped Nicklaus to win three Opens in Britain. Some time ago, Jimmy permitted me to look at his notes on St Andrews. He had marked down every ditch, bunker and hollow of strategic importance. He knew the distance between every fairway water sprinkler and green. He had other landmarks – an old shed, a distant spire – that gave the line of play and also ensured he and his client always knew the yardage.

Such information is essential for the jet-set golfer, for whom every week can mean another course in another country. There is insufficient time to learn a course in all its moods. The professional, therefore, has perfected the art of hitting the ball with a precision that can be measured within a few yards. All he needs to know is the exact length of shot that confronts him. But this strategy also means that the caddie must carry out a reconnaissance trip before each round to determine the exact locations of the newly-cut holes on the greens. It is just part of his overall duties, that include, too, checking his client's starting time to ensure there has been no misunderstanding.

Another aspect of the successful caddie's role is that he has know the likes, dislikes, habits and foibles of the top players. Jack Nicklaus, for example, is a brisk walker and at times the faithful Jimmy Dickinson has to run to keep up with him: "He doesn't like to be kept waiting – even a few seconds. When he gets to his ball, he wants me at his side – with the precise yardage to be played."

Alfie Fyles is the most successful caddie of modern times. A decorator out of the golf season, he has carried the winning bag in six Open championships – five times for Tom Watson and once for Gary Player. He even received a £2,000 tip from a grateful winner at St Andrews in another contest. Fyles comes from the Lancashire resort of Southport, which is now acknowledged to be the "Caddies' Capital" since most of the best-known travellers live there. (Among them is Jack Leigh, who caddied for Australia's Peter Thomson in many of his greatest triumphs.) It is a stretch of Lancashire that contains some of the finest golf courses in the world, notably Royal Birkdale and Formby, and provide much work for caddies throughout the year. Fyles himself travels now only to the big events and is no longer interested in the week-to-week tournament grind round Europe. But he has seen the world's greatest players under intense pressure – whether on the brink of triumph or disaster. He knows how they react in such moments and what they need – or rather what they do not need:

"It's damned lonely out there in the middle of the fairway even though there are thousands of people behind the ropes," he says. "The golden rule is that you must never distract your man – either by rattling the clubs, falling behind, casting your shadow, or talking.

"I never speak unless spoken to. Tom doesn't need to be told what club it is. He knows what he is going to do. But there is a feeling that we are sharing the pressure out there. Even though nothing is said, he's aware that I'm on his side – and it's a real presence he can see."

None of this is self-delusion because Alfie and his colleagues remain in such big demand by the world's best players. Moreover, the caddie ranks are still filled with intriguing characters. Visit the caddie's pub at any tournament and you will probably rub shoulders with the concert pianist who never went back after a nervous breakdown (he says); the former world motorcycle speedway champion who drives round in a Rolls-Royce; the boss of an advertising company who just walked out one day; a shopkeeper who sold everything for the open road; a coal merchant, a carpenter, a few plumbers and some young men who have known no other career. These days, their winters are not spent at Her Majesty's pleasure. The British contingent head for Spain and Portugal to work for rich holidaymakers.

The advent of golf trolleys and motorised carts has not affected caddies because their expert services are still needed. In fact, a golfer feels – well – undressed without a caddie at his side. Could it be that Bernard Darwin, the great golf eassayist, got it wrong? He complained in 1954 about a caddie who asked 30 shillings for a round and wrote:

"Things have come to a pretty pass when a mere porter, who may know nothing of the game, can ask such prices.

"Whether he will do so much longer remains to be seen because the 'pram' or automatic caddie is cutting into his profits. He will have to come down in his demands or be counted with the dodo and the brontosaurus.

"In fact, if after a few years, some copy of this book remains on which eating time has not made a meal, the reader may wonder what sort of creature this caddie was, if indeed he ever really existed."

On Bernardo! You should be with us now to see the high jinks on the last green of an Open Championship. The winner embraces his caddie. Then he shakes hands with the opponent's caddie. The dodo may be dead. But the caddie is alive and well and living in the lap of luxury –

if he's good enough. And Wingy? Who knows? He never did get back in time for the Daks.

THEY ALSO SERVE WHO ONLY PACE THE YARDAGE

Bill Elliott

Suffolk Road, Birkdale, is an unlikely place to figure in the legend and folklore of golf. A ordinary little street with just 28 ticky-tacky houses, for the past 100 years it has been the home of ordinary working-class Lancastrians. What Suffolk Road has that no modern city planner could provide is one of the greatest backyards in the world.

It is called Royal Birkdale; and with its hills and hollows, wind and sun, it rightly lays claim to being one of the finest links courses.

But in the hungry 1930s Royal Birkdale was seen by the little lads who were growing up in Suffolk Road not so much as a fusion of God and man's art as a chance to earn some cash. A day spent humping a gentleman's bag meant an extra loaf in the house by teatime. In the fullness of time it meant also that Suffolk Road was able to lay claim to a significant share in no less than eight Open Championship victories. Jack Leigh caddied twice for Peter Thomson when he won the Open. Teddy Dalsall guided Johnny Miller to victory and Albert Fyles won with Tom Weiskopf. Overshadowing them all is Albert's brother Alfie Fyles, who has known the thrill of walking to the last green and certain victory *four* times.

His first taste of this sweetest of wines came with Gary Player at Carnoustie in 1968; but it is with Tom Watson that Fyles himself has been able to reach out and touch greatness. Three times – Carnoustie 1975, Turnberry 1977 and Muirfield 1980 – Fyles has coaxed and cursed his American master to victory. The most significant win for Alf, and for caddies everywhere, came in 1975.

"I've had some great moments, but that win with Tom gave me the greatest professional satisfaction because he had never played golf over here before, never even been in the country, so it was a hell of a challenge. Any chance we had of winning seemed to go by the board completely when Tom arrived too late for even a practice round."

Instead of feeling his way around Carnoustie for a couple of days,

Watson had to turn to Fyles and say: "Alf, I'm gonna have to lean on you this week. Hard."

And he did! Fyles's response, meanwhile, provided the perfect answer to those people who think a caddie's job is no more than a porter's role at a railway station.

"Tom not only asked me the yardage on every shot and where the best place to put the ball was, he asked me what club he should take. The man is a genius at the game but I've no doubt that a good fifty-five per cent of that Open win was down to me," he says with pride.

Yet the greatest sporting double act since Pat Taafe and Arkle almost ended right there in Carnoustie. The trouble was the money Watson passed over to Fyles. There wasn't enough of it.

"I though he was a bit mean at that time and so the next year I caddied for Gary Player again," says Fyles simply.

That was in 1976, the year Miller won by six strokes from Jack Nicklaus and a young Spaniard called Ballesteros. Watson missed the cut.

"I got a Christmas card and several letters from Tom before the next Open at Turnberry but I knew my worth and I was not going to budge," recalls Fyles. "Actually it was Tom's lovely wife Linda who got us back together again. She asked me to have a word with Tom and when she smiles I can't refuse her anything."

Tom and Alf talked, a new deal was struck between player and caddie and Alfie Fyles took a giant stride into the game's history, for it was at Turnberry in 1977 that we witnessed the greatest head-to-head duel of modern times.

On one side Watson. On the other, the King, Jack Nicklaus. After two rounds they were level. In the third they both shot 65. It was marvellous, magical stuff and few of us dared hope that the final round could be anything but an anti-climax. Fyles agreed.

"After I came in from that third round I said to friends that I'd just been part of the greatest golf you could see and that there was no way they could repeat that. But they did. Saturday they were just as good.

"I've never seen a crowd get so excited. In fact, at the 9th tee Jack and Tom sat down and told officials they wouldn't carry on unless the galleries behaved themselves. The really crucial point for us came at the 15th where Nicklaus was 14 feet from the hole while Tom was off the green and a long way away.

"When Tom's ball rolled in for a birdie I saw Nicklaus rock back on his heels as though he'd been slapped in the face. He knew then that this Open was not his."

It almost wasn't Alfie Fyles's Open either, for before he was to reach the 18th green the stocky little man with the rattling laugh was to be half-trampled to death.

"After Tom played his approach shot at the last, the crowd went wild again trying to get close to the green. A pro's bag is heavy – and suddenly I found myself flat on my back with feet hitting me everywhere," he said.

That incident left Fyles with a permanent memento of an Open victory – the only one he has, as caddies are not thought by the R and A to be worthy of a keepsake.

"Someone stamped on my right wrist so hard they ground my watch right into my skin. I've got the scar and the lump to this day, but it's a small price because I feared for my life at one point."

The 1980 victory at Muirfield was a mundane affair compared to Turnberry but once again the man from Kansas and the man from Southport proved themselves to be in a different class. "We make a good team," smiles Alf. "I'm fifty-five now and the only man who makes me want to carry on lugging those bloody great bags around is Watson. He's so solid, so good, that I believe we'll win at least two more Opens before I have pack this daft job in."

A daft job that started for Alf when, as an eight year-old, he used to hurry from his paper round to caddie at Birkdale for nine old pence a round and threepence off the caddie master. He earns more now, but still not a lot. Offer the job, the hours, the conditions and the pay to many people and they would run laughing for the nearest dole.

"Aye, in the old days we often had to bed down behind a green somewhere. We used to call it 'staying with Mrs Greenfields'. If you wanted a wash you stopped at the first pond. It's better nowadays but I suppose we are still modern gypsies. There's something in my blood that makes me want to be a travelling man.

"But you'd have to be even dafter than me to do this job for the money!"

LIFE WITH LYLE

John Hopkins

At any major contemporary golf tournament in Europe (and a good few in America as well), the interested spectator can see the tall, sturdy figure of Sandy Lyle. The big Anglo-Scot, who was born in Shrewsbury of Scottish parentage, is easy to pick out. He's probably among the leaders, which is no more than you would expect from one of the world's best players. He'll be supported by a large gallery from which, from time to time, will come shouts of, "Come on, Sandy" or "Well done, Sandy" or "Good old Sandy" because he is among the most popular of golfers in Europe. And by and large he'll remain impassive to all but the most outrageous of his own strokes.

Alongside Lyle will be a shorter man, burly with iron grey hair, a studious expression on his face, carrying Lyle's bag. His name is David Musgrove and since 1981 he and Lyle have formed the most successful partnership of player and caddie in the world of golf. During that time Lyle has won two major championships (the 1985 Open and the 1988 US Masters), eight tournaments in Europe including the Dunhill Masters in June 1988 and the Suntory World Match Play in October 1988, not to mention a further four in the US, one of which was the 1987 Tournament Players' Championship, an event that could be called the fifth major championship. Other players have won more titles in this time but no other partnership has been as successful and is an enviable as Lyle and Musgrove's.

They are two men who, though separated by 14 years, share a mutual respect, a love of golf and a wry, uncomplicated approach to the game and to life. "Who's got the best job in the world then?" Musgrove is fond of asking before he answers his own question: "Sandy Lyle, of course. Who's got the second best job in the world?" he continues. "Dave Musgrove." And he grins, his normally rather stern face dominated by its beetling eyebrows breaking in a wide smile that is as warm as it is unexpected. Musgrove is a yeoman of England, straightforward, honest to a fault and able to see through the pretences and fabrications of others quicker than the time it takes him to say hello. Spend an hour with him in a pub or waiting at a railway station and you'll find him asking many questions, listening intently to the answers, anxious to learn. Never mind that he left school with few qualifications, he's an intelligent man with a deep well of honest-to-goodness common sense.

His life revolves around Kirkby-in-Ashfield, near Mansfield, where he lives blissfully happily in the terraced house in which he was born. From the front room he can see the school he attended as an infant, the doctor's surgery he was taken to when he was ill and the dentist he has gone to for years.

Thanks to golf he has experienced a lifestyle dramatically different from the one he would have known had he remained a draughtsman. He's visited four of the five continents and stayed in luxury hotels he could otherwise only have dreamed about and, at present at least, earns far more than he had any right to expect. But there couldn't have been a better demonstration of how down-to-earth he is and how solid his values are than occurred at Christmas 1987.

Musgrove and his girlfriend Hilary were in Tenerife on holiday and much against his will had been prevailed upon to attend a sales breakfast given by timeshare salesmen, "timeshare touts" he calls them. The virtues of one exotic venue after another were extolled and the more exotic the venue the less impressed Musgrove became. Finally and with a growing sense of frustration a salesman turned to him and said: "Well, where would you like to live?" Musgrove didn't need to think for a moment: "Kirkby-in-Ashfield," he replied.

"This is what life is all about, isn't it?" he says, looking around his front room at home. "The heavy gang at Coxmoor [his regular golfing friends at his golf club] are more in touch with reality than the sort of posers one comes across so often in golf. What does it matter what sort of a room you've got in your hotel? You know, they're offering rooms in The Lodge at Pebble Beach, California, with fireplaces, and everyone's falling over themselves to get one. They're not lit, of course, It's just so they can say to one another: 'Have you got a fireplace in your room? You haven't? I'm surprised. I've got one in mine and I'm only paying $280 a night.'

"Where's the chuffing sense of reality in that?"

His eye is caught by a book he was given recently – *What They Don't Teach You At Harvard Business School* by Mark McCormack. "Three of the main headings he comes out with early in this book are: 'Listen aggressively', 'Observe aggressively' and 'Talk less'. But I can clearly remember the first two things my grandmother ever taught me. The first was how to tie up my shoelaces. The second was what the three brass monkeys who sat on our mantelpiece represented – Hear All, See All and Say Nowt. Here's McCormack who's spent thousands and thousands of dollars on his education and written all these clever words just to say the same thing."

Musgrove met Lyle during the Benson & Hedges tournament at York in 1981. He had been caddying for the Spaniard Manuel Calero but was out of work, Calero having missed the halfway cut. (At pro tournaments only the leading 70 scorers compete in the third and fourth rounds.) Musgrove was cooling his heels on the putting green when Lyle approached him. "Would you like to work for me for a while?" he asked as he stroked putt after putt towards a distant target. Musgrove was dumbfounded but recovered quickly enough to mumble agreement.

The agreement was in principle; details still had to be worked out. "The thing I don't want from a caddie is a yes-man," Lyle said.

"That's all right," Musgrove replied. "You've not got one. The last thing I am is a yes-man. There are two things I want from the golfer I work for: I can't caddie for a golfer who quits, and I want to be paid regularly."

A few minutes later, as he stood on the putting green contemplating his luck at getting a job with the most consistent money-winner in Europe, Musgrove was approached again. "Would you work for me in the US next year?" Nick Faldo asked.

If Musgrove was dumbfounded at Lyle's approach, he was speechless at Faldo's. From beginning the day with no work he had now found employment for the rest of the European season and the early part of the following year. "I always go to the Benson & Hedges with some friends from home," he says. "They drive me up, I supply them with tickets, car park stickers and so on. I said to them as we were going home that night: 'I've had the most fantastic day of my golfing life.'"

The meeting of Lyle and Musgrove was a meeting of two men outstandingly talented in their own fields. Lyle's ability had long been apparent. After a glittering amateur career he turned pro in 1977 and won that year's qualifying school. Finishing 49th in the 1978 order of merit was good enough to earn him the Rookie of the Year award. He leaped to the top of the order of merit in 1979 – when he also appeared in Europe's Ryder Cup team – and again in 1980.

Musgrove was a good golfer who had caddied off and on for nearly 20 years since starting as a 12 year-old at Hollinwell, the Nottinghamshire course near his parents' house.

"It was my mother who suggested it," he recalls. "When I got to between the ages of playing with Dinky toys and not knowing what girls were for, she said to me one day: 'Why don't you go caddying and make yourself useful?' Me and my friend Hugo Monro set out on our bikes to Hollinwell and halfway there we got caught in a cloudburst. My first memory of the famous Hollinwell golf club is going down the drive in the slashing rain, parking our bikes in a shed and drying ourselves as best we could.

"A lot of my friends did paper rounds or butchers' rounds. That always seemed too much like hard work to me, getting up early in the morning and distributing papers. Anyway, I used to earn as much in one morning's caddying as they earned in a week. I would get six shillings for a round and that was a lot of money for a 12½-year-old, which is how old I was when I first went there in August 1955."

Musgrove learned the rudiments of golf by watching the men for whom he caddied, as so many caddies have done before and since. He has hardly had a golf lesson in his life. "On a Sunday if there were no members about we could play the first four holes, walk across to the 17th fairway and play that as a par-three, and then go down the 18th. We used clubs from the pro's shop."

He is still a good golfer and has retained a single-figure handicap since 1967. Yet suggest to him that a handicap of eight is something to be proud of and he will snort with that streak of realism and self-deprecation that is typical of him: "I can't play golf. I can hit it forwards and upwards and generally finish a round with the ball I started off with, which is the main thing. I can scrape it round. But that's about all."

In the mid-1950s Musgrove was one of a group of boys who would gather on weekend mornings and while waiting to start work amuse themselves by putting pennies on the railway line near the golf course as the Master Cutler steam engine passed on its southward journey from Sheffield to London. Then they would report for caddies' duties at Hollinwell by 9 am.

"Most of the old caddies at Hollinwell have gone now. Every time I go home I hear of another one that has died. Dal Warren, who used to caddie for John Jacobs, died this year. Dal's brother Joe taught me the most, I suppose, of the humorous side of golf.

"He would say: 'You take the short cut when you can.'

"I asked him once, 'But what happens when they hit the ball and you never see where it goes? Then what do you do?' His simple answer was, 'You have to stand there and confess you haven't a clue where the hell it is.'

"Another caddie, Charlie Cherry, was a good player. The man he was caddying for once at Hollinwell asked: 'What club is it?'

"'It's a six-iron,' said Charlie.

"'I can't get there with a six-iron.'

"'I could get there with a six-iron,' said Charlie.

"'No you couldn't.'

"'Yes, I could, I'll show you.' And he did.

"Another one was old Foster Chapman. He was caddying for Smiler Greaves, so-called because he never smiled. Smiler was also known as the

Spangle Man because after 12 holes he always used to give out Spangle sweets.

"Foster Chapman was broke and hadn't been able to buy any cigarettes for a week. Smiler made the mistake of throwing his cigarette down on the ground while he played his shot. As Joe Warren said: 'Foster Chapman's hand came out like a cobra and grabbed this cigarette and hid it for later.' Smiler, meanwhile, hit his shot on to the green and couldn't understand where his cigarette had gone.

"Then there was old Dr Sparrow. After six holes he'd tell his caddie to go and find him some balls in the woods. When the caddie brought some back old Dr Sparrow would be able to start again."

Musgrove worked as a draughtsman for the National Coal Board, and for several years he took part of his annual holiday to go to the Open and caddie. He worked for Jean Garaialde, the French pro, at St Andrews in 1964 and for the last two rounds they were paired with Tony Lema, the winner.

In 1971 he caddied for Roberto de Vicenzo, the great Argentinian, in the Open at Royal Birkdale. "In the third round we were paired with Mr Lu," recalls Musgrove. "On the 13th, a par-five, Roberto hit a drive and a six-iron and reached the green, and Mr Lu hit a drive and a screaming three-wood and his ball just reached the green. Roberto three-putted and Mr Lu holed his for an eagle.

"Going up the next hole, Roberto turned to me and said: 'They put me out with a Chinaman to improve my English.' At which point Mr Lu suddenly disappeared over a boundary fence to try and find a toilet. 'Hey,' Roberto shouted at me. 'Lu go and make shit.'"

While still caddying part-time, Musgrove left the Coal Board in 1966 to join the aerospace engine division of Rolls-Royce at Hucknall, near Derby, also as a draughtsman. Six years later, in January 1972, he took a decision that changed his life. He was offered voluntary redundancy. To a man who had lived his life in a rented house, the security of continuing with a firm as large as Rolls-Royce was appealing. On the other hand, Musgrove, by now in his late twenties, was a good golfer and he knew that if he didn't take this chance to try his luck as a caddie, then he would never do it. It wasn't a hard decision to make and he hasn't regretted it for a moment since.

For four years from 1976 Ballesteros and Musgrove were a regular partnership during which time Ballesteros won the Open at Royal Lytham in 1979. But not the least of Musgrove's qualities is a pride in what he does, and after several tumultuous years with Ballesteros he could no longer tolerate the abuse that was heaped upon him at, it seemed, almost every turn. Caddying for Seve at the Open at Lytham was hell, he was to say later. "Three weeks later he was still chewing me out. But there were also wonderful moments with Seve. He is so gifted it's not true."

But a change there had to be, and in Lyle, Musgrove found the perfect employer. "Sandy is the best bloke in the world to caddie for," Musgrove said in the *Sunday Times* after his victory in the Open at Sandwich in 1985. "I'll tell you what my life's like with Sandy – my wages must be the best on tour, must be, and when I stay at his house at Wentworth he brings me tea in the morning. That can't be bad, can it?"

The two of them go through a well-rehearsed routine before every shot. Lyle stands alongside Musgrove and the golf bag. They talk quietly for a moment. For a golfer and his caddie this is a moment as intimate as confession for a Catholic. This is when a caddie must enjoy his boss's confidence or he is on his way to being fired. At this moment the caddie must know the answer to anything he is likely to be asked. He must know what to say and, just as important, how to say it. He mustn't talk too much. The caddies must know whether his employer needs a little boost in confidence. Some caddies have been fired for talking too much at this moment, just as others have been fired for saying too little.

At first all Lyle asks for is the yardage. Sometimes, as on the 9th hole of the last round of the 1988 US Masters for example, the yardage suggests the club he should use. "How far is it?" Lyle asked Musgrove who was standing by the bag waiting.

Musgrove had already taken his yardage book out of the back pocket of his overall. "A hundred and seventy-three yards," he replied.

"In that case it's a seven-iron," said Lyle.

The decision was simple. There was no wind worth taking into consideration, no other factors to influence the shot. It was the distance for a seven-iron, and so a seven-iron it was. As Lyle moved to address the ball, Musgrove lifted the big white bag out of Lyle's sight. Moments later the shot came to rest two feet from the hole. A birdie three was inevitable.

That particular shot, however, was a formality. Lyle's mind was made up as to the club he wanted and the distance he wanted to hit it the moment he was told the yardage to the hole. The skill of one caddie over another comes in helping his player choose the right club for the distance. He might say, "It's a soft five," or "If you take eight, then it's got to be a good one."

There are those who say that in this respect Musgrove is the great controller. He chooses the club, tells Sandy how to hit it and then stands back and awaits results. "Some people think I do everything bar hit the ball," says Musgrove. "They make him sound like a robot controlled by me. That's not true. I say things to him and he says things to me. I give my opinion when he asks. I don't tell him what to do. It's not like that at all."

It is undeniable, however, that part of the skill of a caddie as good as Musgrove is knowing when to interfere with his player's club selection and when to keep quiet, and when and how to give those brief few words of encouragement.

Take the 12th hole of the last round in that 1988 US Masters at Augusta. Lyle, having bogied the 11th, had just hit his tee shot into the water on this beguiling short hole. After leading the tournament for nearly 40 holes, he was now certain to forfeit his position. He was furious with himself as he strode off the tee, showing all the signs of getting himself into a state. At this moment Musgrove needed two heads. One to count the distance from the tee to the dropping zone, thus working out how long a shot Sandy's third shot would be, the other to reassure his boss.

Born like most of us with only one head, Musgrove nevertheless had to handle both issues. "I'm trying to do two jobs at once," he says. . . . "I've got to keep a cool head, otherwise we'll never make another mistake. I was trying to measure from the tee to wherever he was going to drop, but at the same time I'm trying to calm him down. I told him: 'Don't worry about what's happened. That's done, ancient history. Just make sure you get a five.'"

Lyle took his medicine on the par-three 12th, failed to birdie the 13th, narrowly missed a birdie on the 14th and by the 15th was getting anxious again. It was time for Musgrove to step in once more.

There was a lull in play and Musgrove, part-time psychiatrist and counsellor, first drew Lyle's attention to the view. "I wanted to get his mind off the golf for a moment." Then, as the players began to leave the green, Musgrove performed a second piece of man management with such skill it suggests he has a future in dealing with lots of people and not just one when he decides to give up humping golf bags around the world.

"Look, Sandy," he said, putting his face close to Lyle's to emphasise the importance of what he was saying, "you've lost your lead and you're chasing now. A weight's been taken off your shoulders. Put that to your advantage. Let somebody else do the work for a change and we'll chase them."

History records that Lyle stood on the 16th tee needing to complete the last three holes in two under par. He did so; and the US Masters, one of golf's four major titles, fell to a Briton for the first time. It's as impossible to say that he wouldn't have done it without Musgrove's solid sustaining presence by his side as it is impossible to say he would have.

The Oxford Dictionary definition of the word caddie is, "*a*. a lad or man who waits on the look-out for odd jobs (def. 1730), *b*. Golf. A boy (or man) who carries the club etc. (def. 1857)."

One version of the word's origin is that it comes from *cadet* in French, the word used in France at that time to mean an officer apprentice, i.e. someone not commissioned. The Scots adopted the word cadet and with their burr it became known as caddie or cadie, meaning messenger or errand boy. The earliest drawings of caddies depict men standing with a bunch of clubs under their arm.

Whatever the origin, the implication of the word caddie is someone to serve, to fetch and carry, to help and advise, a person best described as a cross between a valet, confidant, messenger, bag carrier, companion. In the autumn of 1988 Lyle and Musgrove celebrated their seventh year as a partnership. In that time Lyle has been at his lowest ebb, when his wife Christine announced she was leaving him, and at the peak of his powers, winning the Open in 1985 and the US Masters in April 1988. In their years together Musgrove has been a constant in Lyle's life; certainly Lyle spends more time each day with him than with anyone else apart from his companion Jolande Huurman.

If Lyle has been good for Musgrove, then Musgrove has been good for Lyle. He is the first to say that it's the player who hits the ball, who holes the putts, who does the difficult part; but he is always there, ready. He knows the starting times, has packed the golf bag with items ranging from dozens of tees, several pencils, both waterproofs and a spare sweater, a dozen balls and a yardage chart of the course. Musgrove has yardage charts of 38 American courses, 12 maps of courses in Europe done by a firm called Strokesaver and a further 66 yardage books he has compiled himself using his own measuring wheel.

Only once has Musgrove made a serious mistake while working for Lyle. It came during the 1987 Phoenix tournament in the town of that name in Arizona, USA. The two of them had played golf with friends the day before the tournament and Musgrove borrowed an eight-iron from Sandy and forgot to replace it. "We got out the next day in the tournament, weighed the shot up for an eight-iron and couldn't find the club. I finally twigged where it was.

"That's probably the worst mistake I've made with Sandy. I've never overslept. That's the game, isn't it, to be there on time and ready to go. You can only be late once. My whole day is geared to getting up in the morning to be ready for playing whatever the time. The player has probably come 3,000 miles as well. You can't make a muck up then."

The traditional concept of a golf caddie is of a man burly enough to be able to carry a 50 lb golf bag. He'll probably have tattoos on his forearms, will drink a lot, perhaps spend nights on end sleeping rough. Income tax is what everyone else pays; the only VAT he'll know is VAT 69 whisky. The old caddies were wonderful characters, likeable rogues many of them, who lived on their wits and drank their savings. These were the men who invented the rhyming slang that remains a part of a caddie's vocabulary. "Fruit and veg" is a wedge. "You'll need the furniture" means you'll need a wood, "Lady Godiva" is a driver, "Tom Mix" a six, "Garden Gate" an eight, "Doctor's Orders" a nine.

"The image of a caddie is of a man with no collar and tie who can't speak properly," says Musgrove. "That may have been the case once but it is less so now. The increase in prize money has made caddying for a top-class pro a lucrative proposition, so there is more competition than there once was. The pressure is greater and so are the rewards. A missed putt can lose a player £5000. One shot saved can earn a caddie enough to live on for a month. It's become serious business.

"Some of us just want to do our job properly. It doesn't start on the 1st tee and end on the 18th green, you know. That's why we want to be able to get into the clubhouse locker-room to collect the clubs in the morning and return them in the evening – to do our job better. I don't want Sandy to have to do anything more than change his shoes."

A GREATER HONOUR KNOWS NO MAN

G. Gunby Jordan with Don Wade

The Mid-Pines resort in North Carolina was, in the mid-1930s, a place where all the formalities of the era were religiously observed on the golf course. It was during this period that a group of gentlemen from Philadelphia's Main Line came down for a golf vacation.

On the first day of play they were assigned caddies from "The Yard" and, arriving on the 1st tee, made what was not a very auspicious start. The first three men dribbled their drives barely off the tee, and the caddies gave themselves looks that indicated that this was going to be an extremely long and tedious day.

Prospects did not improve when the final member of the group prepared to play. He teed his ball and made two of the stiffest and most awkward practice swings known to man. He then addressed the ball and hit it all of 170 yards, right down the heart of the fairway. His caddie was overcome with both joy and relief.

"Look at that son of a bitch hit that ball," he yelled, and, by all accounts, never was the gentleman from Philadelphia ever accorded a tribute he held dearer.

IF YOU'VE SEEN ONE, YOU'VE SEEN THEM ALL

G. Gunby Jordan with Don Wade

Early in his presidency, Dwight Eisenhower was able to sneak out for a round of golf at the exclusive Burning Tree course outside Washington. The President was playing badly, and his caddie, an old man who had been at the club for as long as anyone could remember, was trying his best to be helpful.

"Baldy, swing slower," he would say.

"Baldy, keep your head down," he would offer.

"Now, Baldy, you've got to shift your weight," he implored.

To his credit, President Eisenhower took the advice in the spirit offered, but it soon became too much for one of his Secret Service bodyguards.

"Now listen here," he said to the caddie. "That's the President of the United States you're caddying for, and you mustn't speak to him like that. You must address him properly."

The caddie was understandably mortified, and the next time Ike missed a shot, he went out of the way to do the right thing.

"Now, Mr Lincoln," he said, "swing slower."

THE WIT OF THE CADDIE

Peter Dobereiner

For golfers there is nowhere in the world so rich in history, legend and myth than St Andrews. Pilgrims imagine that they can detect the history, legend and myth in the very air they breathe as they step on to the 1st tee of the Old Course under the lee of the forbidding clubhouse of the Royal and Ancient. It is powerful stuff this H, L and M, and not to be inhaled, for it plays curious tricks with the imagination.

The visitor gazes down the first fairway and muses, "Jeez, this is where it all began back in the 15th century. All the giants of golf have stood on this very spot and the place has not changed an iota in 500 years." All of which is rubbish, of course. In living memory St Andrews has changed out of all recognition. Not much over a century ago the golfers here were having to negotiate their way through cricket matches, football games, women spreading their washing out to dry on the whins, and men snaring rabbits on the links.

It is virtually certain that golf did not start at St Andrews. In his otherwise authoritative history of the town, Professor Douglas Young abandons the disciplines of scholarship to assert that a St Andrews University student invented golf. Such evidence as exists suggests with overwhelming circumstantial force that the game was imported from Holland, either by returning soldiers who had been introduced to it during Continental campaigns, or by Dutch merchants who plied a regular trade to St Andrews. (From the harbour in the Eden estuary they would have to pass along the links to the city, and the golfers among them would surely have recognised a likely area to follow their pastime.)

Be that as it may, we have no accounts describing Scottish golf for another 200 years and then it occurs in the court records of Kelso where it states that a Thomas Chatto was killed by a blow under the ear from a golf club, wielded by a man who was playing golf in a churchyard. Was that the game we know and love?

If we cannot evoke the past by looking out across the links, perhaps we may draw historical inspiration from the R and A clubhouse. It positively oozes a sense of permanence, dignity, statesmanship and stuffy respectability. Surely that noble institution remains as an inviolate symbol of the game's past glories? Well, I hope not. It was born in a pub – the brainchild of a group of raffish drunkards – as a tourist promotion stunt. At that time the town of St Andrews was in a bad way. Once the ecclesiastical capital of Scotland, the city had been unfrocked; its cathedral was in decay from the ravages of man's intolerance and the Scottish weather; the University was in decline; the city was in debt. Golf was its only viable asset. It was the local obsession, rivalled only by a club devoted to the pursuit and study of fornication, some of whose members may have been among the founding fathers of the golf society. At all events, the purpose was to pull in visitors.

That welcoming tradition was completely lost on Andrew Kirkaldy, an outspoken professional to the R and A. Sent to greet two visiting Americans he met them at the station, accompanied them in silence to the 1st tee and then whacked a belting drive towards the Swilcan. Kirkaldy stepped aside and grunted: "Beat that, ye buggers." Kirkaldy was, of course, a former caddie and much of the history, legend and myth of St Andrews concern what the locals mistakenly refer to as the wit of caddies. I can just about bear to repeat two examples.

A visitor on the 1st tee of the Old Course surveyed the prospect ahead and remarked, "Aha, a drive and pitch." He then took an almighty swipe with his driver and made glancing contact with the top of the ball, sending it rolling a few yards forward. His caddie muttered, "Now for one helluva pitch." The late Henry Longhurst liked to tell the one about the ecclesiastic golfer who ripped a gigantic divot out of the sacred turf, at which his caddie asked with withering scorn, "Shall I put it back or will you keep it for the harvest festival?"

As a young professional anxious to observe the rituals of his craft, Hugh Lewis plucked a handful of grass and tossed it in the air, in the way he had seen the big boys test the strength and direction of the wind. "What club do you think, caddie?" he asked, as the grasses were blown directly into the caddie's face. The man slowly bent down, tore out a sizeable turf, threw it full into Lewis's face and answered, "I don't know."

Doug Sanders played straight man to a star-turn caddie during a recent St Andrews Open in an incident which is still causing nightmares within the BBC. Exchanges between players and caddies are normally privileged, like communications between a solicitor and client, but a TV microphone clearly picked up the following dialogue.

Sanders: "What's the club?"

Caddie: "Six."

Sanders: "Six? A seven maybe."

Caddie: "Naw! You don't want to be ****ing well short."

Thus was the ultimate obscenity fired through the ether into millions of homes around the world. There is, alas, no TV record of one of the most turbulent days in the history of the city since the sacking of the cathedral. Two enterprising caddies travelled to Prestwick to meet the flight of two American competitors for the Open and were duly engaged. However, on arrival at St Andrews the players discovered that their British agents had already fixed up caddies for them. By now it was too late for those first two caddies to find bags and they repaired to the caddies' pub near the last green and recounted their tale of misfortune. Through no fault of theirs they had been denied work for potentially the most lucrative week of the year. Caddies are a clannish bunch and when the championship was over, and everyone was in funds, they passed round the hat and collected a goodly sum for the two unfortunates. Ah, the nobility of man. It was a gesture to warm the heart. It was also an opportunity, or so thought the two caddies who had actually carried the bags of the Americans that week. They slipped out of the pub and presented themselves to their guv'nors at the hotel. "We just thought you would feel better about that little misunderstanding," they said, "if you knew that we have taken care of those caddies who met you at Prestwick. Their families will not go hungry, after all, because we have shared our wages with them, the wages you gave us."

"That was a fine gesture," said one of the golfers, "but not necessary. You see, we realised that the mix-up would put those guys in a fix so we paid them their full whack."

Two highly indignant caddies returned hot-foot to the pub where the beneficiaries were by now advanced in drink. Words of a nature resembling the one used by Doug Sanders's caddie were exchanged. Chairs were bounced off heads. Pint pots whistled through the air. The ventilation of the public bar was immensely improved by the abrupt passage of heavy bodies through windows. Vital fluids, including blood and Glenlivet, were split *ad lib* and the battle raged long into the night.

It would be wrong to end on such an unsavoury note. After all St Andrews is a serious and dignified city, as befits the home of an ancient university. Here was the birthplace of logarithms and of another important work of scholarship, by Professor Tait, father of the noted Amateur champion, Freddie. The Professor worked out mathematically that the greatest distance a golf ball could be hit was a carry of 190 yards. His son, knowing little of the laws of science, then went out and hit a record drive, with a carry of 250 yards.

Let us leave the last word with the ladies and take up Shelley's plaintive cry, "Can man be free if woman be a slave?" At a women's championship the heavens opened and a group of lady spectators sought refuge from the storm by huddling against the Royal and Ancient clubhouse. After a while the stately figure of the R and A's *major domo* appeared, under a large umbrella. "Praise be," they thought, "the members have taken pity on us. The age of chivalry is not dead after all. Fie to all that talk about man's inhumanity to man" (or woman, if you want to be pedantic). "They are not the curmudgeonly, bigoted misogynists they have been painted, but compassionate and tender knights of the links. Beneath those patched and shapeless tweed jackets beat human hearts, and warm ones. Never mind if they only offer us shelter in a cellar where they keep the empty gin bottles, they are going to relax their rigid principles and permit us to enter those sacred portals."

The *major domo* smiled politely. "Ladies, I have a message for you."

"Here it comes," they thought. "The historic moment of truce in the war between the sexes is at hand. The Angels of Mons should be present at this hour."

"The members ask," continued the *major domo*, "that you do not stand in front of the windows; you are blocking their view."

There is truly no substitute for enduring traditions like that.

Chapter 7

GREAT CHAMPIONSHIPS

Dan Jenkins

He first came to golf as a muscular young man who could not keep his shirt-tail in, who smoked a lot, perspired a lot and who hit the ball with all the finesse of a dock worker lifting a crate of auto parts. Arnold Palmer did not play golf, we thought. He nailed up beams, re-upholstered sofas, repaired air-conditioning units. Sure, he made birdies by the streaks in his eccentric way – driving through forests, lacing hooks around sharp corners, spewing wild slices over prodigious hills, and then, all hunched up and pigeon-toed, staring putts into the cups. But he made just as many bogeys in his stubborn way. Anyhow, a guy whose slacks are too long and turned up at the cuffs, who matches green shirts with orange sweaters, a guy who sweats so much, is *not* going to rush past the Gene Littlers, Ken Venturis and Dow Finsterwalds, the stylists, to fill the hero gap created by the further greying and balding Ben Hogan and Sam Snead. This is what most of us believed around 1960, even after Palmer had won his second Masters, even after he had begun to drown everyone in money winnings. This was a suave new godlet of the fairways, a guy out of Latrobe Dry Goods?

We were, of course, as wrong about him as the break on a downhill six-footer, as wrong as his method seemed to us to be wrong: hit it hard, go find it, hit it hard again. We knew we were wrong one day when the bogeys suddenly went away. No one understood why or how, except that Palmer willed them to. And now he had become a winner like none we had ever known. He was a nice guy, of all things. He was honestly and naturally gracious, untemperamental, talkative, helpful and advising, unselfish of his time, marvellously good-humoured; he had a special feeling for golf's history and he was honoured by its traditions; and with all of this he remained the gut fighter we insisted he be, a man so willing to accept the agonies of pressure and the burdens of fame that for a few years we absolutely forgot that anyone else played the game he was dominating and changing.

He actually started *being* Arnold Palmer in that summer of 1960, a stupidly short time ago, it seems. He became the Arnie of whoo-ha, go-get-'em Arnie on a searingly hot afternoon in Denver when, during the last round of the US Open, he exploded from seven strokes and 14 players behind to win. Two months earlier he had finished birdie-birdie on national television to win the Masters and now he had created another miracle – again on national television.

Much has been written into the lore of golf of how it was that day, of the epic 65 he shot in the final round at Cherry Hills, of the day that really made him, but not by anyone who had lunched with him, kidded him, and then happily marched inside the gallery ropes with him, scurrying after Cokes, furnishing cigarettes, and hoping to put him at ease.

During lunch in a quiet corner of the Cherry Hills locker room before that round, Arnold was cheerful and joking as he ate a hamburger, drank iced tea, and made small talk with a couple of other players, Bob Rosburg and Ken Venturi, a writer named Bob Drum, and myself. He talked of no one else who might win. All he seemed concerned about was Cherry Hill's 1st hole, a comparatively short, downhill, downwind, par-four. It bugged him. He thought he could drive the green, but in three previous rounds he had not done it.

"It really makes me hot," he said. "A man ought to drive that green."

"Why not?" I said. "It's only 346 yards through a ditch and a lot of high grass."

"If I drive that green I might shoot a hell of a score," he said. "I might even shoot a 65 if I get started good. What'll that bring?"

"About seventh place. You're too far back."

"Well, that would be two-eighty," Arnold said. "Doesn't two-eighty always win the Open?"

"Yeah," I said. "When Hogan shoots it."

Arnold laughed and walked out to the 1st tee.

For a while I loitered around the big clubhouse waiting for the leaders to go out, as a good journalist should. In the process of milling around, however, I overheard a couple of fans talking about an amazing thing they had just seen. Palmer, they said, had driven the 1st green. Just killed a low one that hung up there straight towards the mountains and then burned its way through the USGA trash and onto the putting surface. Got a two-putt birdie.

I smiled to myself and walked out onto the veranda and began edging my way through the spectators towards the first tee where the leader, Mike Souchak, would be going off presently. But about that time a pretty good roar came up from down on the front nine, and seconds later a man sprinted by panting the news that Palmer was three under through three.

"Drove the first, chipped in on two and hit it stiff on three," he said, pulling away and darting off to join Arnie's Army. Like the spectator and a few thousand others who got the same notion at the same time, I tried to break all records for the Cherry Hills Clubhouse-to-Fourth Fairway Dash. We got there just in time to see Arnold hole his fourth straight birdie.

Wringing wet and perishing from thirst, I staggered towards the 5th tee, stopping to grab a Coke at a concession stand. I ducked under the ropes as an armband permitted and stood there puffing but excited. Arnold came in briskly, squinted down the fairway and walked over. He took the Coke out of my hand, the cigarettes out of my shirt pocket and broke into a smile. "Fancy seeing you here," he said. "Who's winning the Open?"

Palmer birdied two more holes through the 7th to go an incredible six under, working on an incorrigible 29 out. But he bogeyed the 8th and had to settle for a 30. Even so, the challengers were falling all round him like wounded soldiers, and their crowds were bolting towards him, and the title would be his. Everything would be his now. Later on, somewhere on the back nine holes, I remember sizing up a leader board with him and saying, "You've got it. They're all taking gas." "Aw, maybe," he said, quietly. "But damn it, I wanted that 29."

There have been other major victories, as we know, and scores of lesser ones, and precisely because of him the professional tour has tripled, quadrupled in prize money. He has become, they say, something immeasurable in champions, something more than life-size, even though he has turned into his forties, the hip hurts, and a lot of other big ones have slipped away.

This is true, I think. He is the most immeasurable of all golf champions. But this is not entirely true because of all that he has won, or because of that mysterious fury with which he has managed to rally himself. It is partly because of the nobility he has brought to losing. And more than anything, it is true because of the pure, unmixed joy he has brought to trying. He has been, after all, the doggedest victim of us all.

LET'S GO FOR BROKE!

Peter Thomson and Desmond Zwar

It is a tired, crumpled but enthusiastic Press conference that packs the tent waiting for Lee Trevino, the winner of the 1968 United States Open. Anti-climax as someone announces: "You're all invited to a

Margarita party tonight at the Blue Sombrero. Lee wants you all to come along."

Amidst speculation about the contents of a Margarita (in fact: 1 fl oz tequila, 1 fl oz triple sec or curaçao and 1 fl oz lemon juice, shaken well with ice and strained into pre-chilled salt-rimmed large cocktail glass), in strides the happy little Mex.

The reporters clap, and Trevino, hatless, sits down, bags under his eyes. "OK. Shoot!"

"What's a Margarita, Lee?"

"I dunno. I've never drank one."

From a New Yorker: "Foist question is howdya get to the Blue Sombrero?" A mock-puzzled Trevino: "Where's that?"

"That's where you're holding your party."

"Who? ME?"

Bob Gorham, PGA Press Secretary, trying to bring a more serious note to the conference: "Lee, the fellows would like to know how you feel, what it means to you and so forth."

"Well, I'm a little nervous. But I feel great. I mean show me a guy that wouldn't feel great that's just won the Open. It's something that has happened that I never felt would happen to me. Before I knew it, at the 12th hole, I had a four-shot lead!

"This tournament means a lot to me, moneywise and everything else." (Conservatively, the Open is reckoned to be worth more than one million dollars to the winner.) "As you know, I now have an exemption from the PGA for five years' (qualifying) for the Open win. Now I get to the World Series of Golf." A grin breaks out over the tanned face: "Probably now I've got to winning the US Open they'll discontinue the World Series of Golf. Ya know, that's like ownin' a pumpkin farm and they knock off Hallowe'en!

"You guys," he beams at the reporters, "have been great. You've wrote a lot of funny stories about me, I've toldya a few funny ones. I'm about the happiest Mexican in the world, I guess."

"Howdya wife take it?"

"Claudia? She saw me on TV. She's probably cryin'."

"When will you have the money (300,000 dollars) down to her?"

"Oh I should have it there by Wednesday, if not she'll call. And that's the truth! That's no joke," he says.

"Going to the last hole my caddie said: 'Let's birdie this hole. Let's go for broke.' I had a poor lie and I said: 'You know I wouldn't want to be remembered as the US Open champion and layin' up with a wedge. So

I took a six-iron out and tried to move the ball and it just skimmed out a little bit to the left and I was still in the rough. I took a wedge just to try and get it on the green. I swung it as hard as I could and it ended three feet from the hole and I knocked it in for par.

"On the 17th? Well, on my second shot, me and my caddie were discussing about how far it was and I wanted to hit a one-iron. 'No don't hit a one-iron. You may go over the green,' he says. 'Just hit a two-iron.'

"'But I'd hafta hit it too hard.' I said.

"'Well hit it hard then.'

"I swung as hard as I could and missed it. But he has all the confidence in the world. He said: 'No problem. Just chip it up and one-putt.' This kid, you know, if it hadn't have been for this boy, I wouldn't have won the golf tournament, believe me. And I don't even know if he plays golf! His name is Kevin Quinn and he's 18."

"Where is he, Lee?"

"Outside, waitin' for the cheque."

Trevino, relaxed, sipping his beer from the bottle, is enjoying the chat. "He talked to me all the way around. It was unbelievable. You would think I was the caddie and he was the pro! He had me under control the whole way round. After I birdied 12 I said: 'Hold me down! Just hold me down!'

"Then he made his one mistake. I think he was chokin' a little bit on the 15th tee. I teed up the ball and said to Kevin, what d'you think? He said: 'A five-iron.'

"'A *five* iron [165 yds. Par 3] You gotta be kiddin'. I might go over that TV tower!'

"'A smooth five,' reckons Kevin.

"Bert hit an *eight*!"

"He *did*?"

"So," says Lee Trevino, "I drew an eight and I hit it and hit the pin."

Q: Do you always take your caddie's word – even a kid?

"Well yes. He controlled me pretty well when I was practising and everything and I took his word. You know, when you're playing for this much money there is so much pressure and you're out there front-running, you want a little encouragement and you want somebody to reassure you – say, "Yeah, that's the right club." He only made one mistake all week and that was on 15 when he tried to put a five-iron into my hand."

Lee Trevino caddied himself for six years. Next question: The money? He's going to buy back the Alamo and give it back to Mexico. Golf? Started playing it with a broomstick "swinging at horse-apples and you know what they are". Then he found a discarded golf club, a few balls in the rough and he used to hit balls about a cow pasture where they burned the hay. "So twice a year they would cut the grass to make the hay and I'd have my own country club." He went to work at a driving range at a par-three course "and the owner brought me up like a son and gave me my first set of golf clubs. I owe everything to him."

"When I first started winnin' those 3,000-dollar and 4,000-dollar cheques last summer, I said, 'Say, how long's this been goin' on out here?' "

Lee and his wife live in a small apartment in El Paso at a motel at the country club he once worked for and now – through his golf success – part-owns.

"It's a kitchenette," says Lee, going into the details for the Pressmen, "I have two rooms on each side. Me and my wife and my little girl sleep in one room and the maid sleeps in the other bedroom. The dogs sleep in the living-room. In three weeks my 30,000-dollar Spanish-style house on the 18th fairway will be finished.

"Wuz I married before? Yeah. I get rid of them when they're 21. I have a son six years old, who lives at Columbia, Missouri. I communicate with him twice a week, I call him on the phone. At Christmas time I flew my little boy, his mother and her husband down to Dallas – they couldn't afford to come down there. I flew 'em down and it was worth every penny of it, believe you me," he says, pudgy face screwed up in sentimentality.

What about contracts?

"I have no golf-ball contract, no golf-club contract, no shirts, no nuthin'." ("In other words," he could have said, "I'm wide open!")

And Little Lee Trevino, the newest millionaire, takes his last swig of beer from the bottle and plods out again through the admiring crowd. To the outside world. And a new fame. And the sky's the *limit*, Gringo!

•   •   •   •   •   •   •

Still there in the Press tent, red cap pushed back on his head, showing fair hair, caddie Kevin Quinn tells how it was done: "Yes, at 15 I was real nervous. I didn't know what I was talking about! After that hole we just made sure we got to the green, we got to the middle of the fairways and we were not going to get into any trouble.

"All you have to do really is remind him of the obvious. He knows," allows Kevin, who works nights at Kodak and is still studying business at school, "how to play the game more than I do. What I did was remind him . . . 'there's a little wind coming across . . . make sure you keep in the fairway here . . . stroke the ball.' You keep bringing up these little things that keep him concentrating. When he got tense? We just talked. I don't think he was really tense at all. When he started out this morning he was just a little tense, I guess, but once you start hitting the ball you loosen up," said caddie Kevin Quinn, 18 long years old.

• • • • • • •

Sunday night in Rochester. They are cleaning up at Oak Hill after the Open. Lee Trevino and the Press are whooping it up over *"Margaritas"* at the Blue Sombrero, celebrating the most popular win in years.

At the same time, Mr Billy Casper is arriving at the Rochester Mormon Church to speak at a "fireside".

What manner of man is this? On the golf course a day or two ago he had said: "I think I'm playing well . . . because I am a happy man who has found a deep inner peace."

The Mormon religion, he tells reporters, has shown him his true identity, his purpose: "To do as much good for mankind as is humanly possible for one man to do."

(Mr Casper invites us with our tape-recorder, to the "fireside", to hear what he has to say.)

The service is in a packed, new A-frame church with Scandinavian-style white pine ceiling, a stage, a choir and an organ. On the stage sit the dignitaries, wearing lounge-suits, the Mormon Bishop, Mr Casper in a dark suit and dark tie, legs crossed and Mr Gary Warren, his right-hand man.

After hymns, a number by the quartet, a short introduction by the young Bishop, Mr Casper rises to speak . . .

"I have," he says in his deep, quiet voice, "been a member of the Church for 2½ years. And it seems like every week there is something new, a happening that strengthens my testimony . . ." The Casper attitude, so well-known on the golf course, is there again. Head slightly tilted back, mouth set in almost grim line, the eyes looking down over sharp, prominent nose at the congregation.

He tells of a tour he had made with a well-known Californian sports columnist to a Rochester religious centre, hallowed by the Mormons. "A day later my wife called me. She was in tears. I asked her what was wrong. She then proceeded to read this column that the gentleman had written.

"And . . . [almost brokenly] it was most beautiful. I'm sure that in time all of you will be familiar with this column on his experience he received that afternoon. He is not a member of the Church. I saw him this morning on the practice tee as I was practising, and . . . I thanked him. On behalf of the Church of Jesus Christ of Latter-day Saints.

"Back in 1959," says Billy Casper, to a background of babies crying at the rear of the church, "I went to Salt Lake City. Almost immediately we arrived at Salt Lake City we found there was something very special about it. And as we became acquainted with people we found there was something very special about the Mormon people. They had such a wonderful spirit . . . a great fellowship. We found the family as a unit. The youngsters weren't shoved off to watch TV while we were in the home. They were a very special part of the evening.

"We developed a very close relationship – a very warm relationship – with Mr Hack Miller, sports editor of the local paper, the *Deseret News*. He would periodically come to tournaments on the tour and always, when he came to a tournament, he had a pamphlet, a tract, or a book. And always we would have dinner together and we would sit and talk. My wife was there and she did most of the talking as she was the one most interested in Mormonism.

"I had no religious background. I had gone to Sunday School about once or twice in my life. But I believed in God.

"As she and Brother Miller talked I would sit in a corner, half-listening. I was always more interested in golf – what I was going to shoot the next day.

"I think that at that particular time in my life if I had to make a decision between my family and my profession, it would have been a very difficult decision. In 1965 I went to Las Vegas for a tournament and Brother Miller brought to Las Vegas a book called *Meet the Mormons*. This is a very beautiful pictorial book – a wonderful missionary too. The reason it appealed to me is because I was an extremely slow reader and didn't care to read, and I could look at the pictures and get the message." He smiles down over the rostrum and the Brothers and Sisters smile too.

"A week after returning from vacation in Hawaii it was arranged for Mormon elders to call on us.

"Two gentlemen came to the door, sent by Hack Miller. We sat down, and they asked if we would be interested in taking lessons. I said yes. So I called my two children and my son, Billy, and we started into the first lesson, and to my amazement my children knew more about the Gospel of Jesus Christ than I did.

"I then went off to a tournament, and I had a suitcase *filled* with Mormon literature as I travelled. I was now starting to read and study it . . .

"In San Diego on January the 1st, 1966 we were baptised into the Church. For a number of years, previous to this, I had been faced with several questions. The main question was: 'What am I trying to accomplish while I am here on the face of the earth?' There were two others, 'Where did I come from?' and 'Where am I going?'

"I can testify," he says evenly, "that I know the answer to these questions now, and I have found them in the Gospel of Jesus Christ.

"Almost immediately I found that there was something different. I knew that I would not be able to receive a Calling in my work because I travelled between 7½ and 9 months of the year. Yet I knew that I wanted to advance in the priesthood and I had a conference with my Bishop and I suggested that maybe I could give my time and effort in each of the cities I went into, by talking to the members of the Church about my experiences through my testimony; he thought this might be a good idea."

(And now to golf.) "In the first week of January, I played in the tournament at San Diego (I had played in the tournament for 13 years and never won it) but I teed off that last round on a cold, windy, misty day, and I shot 64 and won the Championship by four shots."

The fact that his religion meant no coffee or tea, alcoholic beverages or smoking, was a help to him in his golf. "If I drink coffee or tea, I definitely feel shaky on the 1st tee.

"I had," he says, "encountered Arnie's Army many times. But I had a letter from a Mormon who said: "Brother Casper, now you are a member of the Church of Jesus Christ of Latter-day Saints, no matter where you travel in the world you will find your family. And your family numbers approximately 2½ million!"

"And how true this is. Wherever you travel you have a family.

"Later in 1966 I found that I was engaged in the US Open in San Francisco. I had shot 137 in the first two rounds and played quite well. So had another fellow – who had an army – he had shot 137 also. In the third round I had shot 73 and this gentleman had shot 70. So I had a three-shot deficit. As Mr Palmer and I played the front nine of the last round, I had increased my deficit to seven. As we started the back nine I had made up my mind that I was going to try and make pars and birdies. I made a par at the 10th, I parred the 11th and birdied the 12th. So did Mr Palmer. The 13th, I made another par. Mr Palmer lipped and made a bogey.

"So we came to the 14th. Five holes left and I was five shots behind. My young son, Bobby, aged five, was at home being looked after by friends. He was seated in front of the TV. And just as the tournament came on he went out. And when he came back, Sister Leininger, who was looking after him, asked what he was doing. He had gone into his room to say a prayer for his Daddy.

"On the 14th hole Mr Palmer's putt went into the hole from 40 feet, and spun around and sat on the lip." (Laughter).

"That gave him a par. And I made a par. So we had four holes left and I was five shots behind.

"On the 15th hole I played a shot into the middle of the green and Mr Palmer now was more interested in breaking Ben Hogan's low-score record for the United States Open. He needed one birdie going in, to break this record. And this particular hole was a short par-three, a potential birdie hole, and the last was par-five which was another potential birdie hole.

"And he went right for the flag – as he always does. But his shot didn't come off quite proper, and it went into the sandtrap. He came out. I putted my putt and it went into the middle of the hole. As I watched, I thought to myself: "If Mr Palmer misses and makes a bogey, he loses two shots. He is no longer five ahead then, but three ahead.

"And he missed.

"The next hole I wound up getting a birdie. Mr Palmer wound up making a bogey – *two more shots*.

"Bobby was gone again! And when he got back, Sister Leininger said: 'What have you been doing, Bobby?' He said: 'I've been in to say a fresher prayer for my Daddy.'

"At the 17th, I drove first, and drove out into the right rough. Arnold drove, and drove into the left rough. And he played out of the left rough into the right rough. And I played out of the right rough into the left rough.

"From there, he pitched the ball within seven feet of the hole. And I pitched the ball within three feet of the hole. He left his putt short and made a bogey. And I made my putt. All of a sudden, in eight holes, seven shots had dwindled away.

"We both made par on the 18th hole and it meant that there would be a play-off on the following day.

"I got home about midnight from a local church service and my wife cooked me dinner. I had had nothing since breakfast. I was up at 8.30

am and off to San Francisco to play in this play-off. And I shot 69 and Arnold shot 73.

"I was the leading money-winner that year. I received an award as the Most Outstanding Player in 1966. I had won four tournaments. I had been able to fulfil three goals – to win the San Diego Open, to win the US Open again and to be the leading money-winner.

"And I felt that all this was brought about because of the inner peace which I received from the Gospel of Jesus Christ. The things that seemed important before were no longer important things. Now my family and my Church were the important things. The Gospel of Jesus Christ touched every phase of my life. I found as we travelled we experienced great love and fellowship from the members of the Church.

"Now," he concludes in a low voice that gives the impression Billy Casper is close to tears, "we have had a very choice experience here in Rochester.

"Being able to experience your fellowship. Being able to visit the Sacred Grove . . ." A silence of some 10 seconds, then:

"I know that I have a Father in heaven who lives; that He does answer my prayers. For He answered the prayers of a five-year-old boy in 1966.

"And I know He does answer your prayers, and my prayers . . ."

THAT SMALL COLOSSUS:
HOGAN AT CARNOUSTIE

Bernard Darwin

As long as golfers talk championship golf, 1953 will be recalled as Hogan's year. Indeed, I think it would have been even if he had not won, so entirely did that small colossus bestride and dominate the tournament.

It was Hogan that sold the tickets in their thousands to the great joy of the authorities and filled the huge park with row upon serried row of shining cars; it was Hogan that produced what was, I think, the greatest crowd of spectators that I ever saw at a championship; and it was Hogan that every single one of them wanted to watch. Hardly anyone there had seen him play before since, when he was here in 1949, he was still too ill to play, and in less than no time anyone with any knowledge of golf came back overawed and abashed by the splendour of his game.

There were to begin with certain local patriots disposed to speak of him as "Your man Hogan", and to murmur that he might do all manner of things on American inland courses, but let him wait till he comes to play over the great Carnoustie course in a Carnoustie wind. Yet even those parochial critics were soon convinced, for they knew golf and were too honest not to admit that here was such a player as occurs only once in a generation or indeed once in a lifetime. As soon as the one Scottish hope, Eric Brown, had faded away I think the whole of that vast crowd wanted Hogan to win. This is not to say that Dai Rees, the ultimate British hope, who had played most gallantly, would not have been a most popular winner. He certainly would, but the feeling that the best man ought to win – there was no earthly doubt who that was – overrode all other sentiments.

And what a wonderful win it was! He did what Bobby Jones, Hagen and Sarazen had all failed to do at the first attempt. He came here weighed down by his immense reputation, and for the first two rounds his putting was unworthy of him and he seemed to have got the slowness of the greens a little on his nerves so far as he has any nerves. Yet when he once began to take some of the chances which his magnificent iron play gave him, when the putts began to drop so that we said "Now he's off!", and it was almost a case of in the one class Hogan and in the other class all the other golfers, it was a measure of his quality that having been hard pressed for three rounds, sharing the lead with one very fine player, and having all sorts of others hard on his very heels, he yet managed to win with something like ease.

It is an impossible task to give anything like an impression of the player to those who have not seen him, but one can perhaps pick out one or two points. Hogan stands decidedly upright with his weight rather forward on the left foot and the right foot drawn a little back. He holds his hands decidedly high, the right hand notably far over, and the right wrist almost arched. The swing is rhythmic and easy and not as long as I had expected from the photographs. The club at the top of the swing may in fact go a little past the horizontal, but if so the eye – or my eye – cannot detect it. The impressive part of the swing comes in what the books call the hitting area. Then the clubhead appears to travel with such irresistible speed that it goes right through the ball and far past it before it begins to come up again. He has, incidentally, a good deal of power in reserve, and when he really means to hit out, as he did with his two wooden clubs at the long 6th hole, his length is very great indeed. I suppose, however, it is his iron play – particularly his long-iron play – which is most striking. It is that which gives him so many chances of threes because he hits so appallingly straight. When we were all waiting behind the home green for his iron shot to the 72nd hole and Hogan, no doubt giving the out-of-bounds on the left a wisely wide berth, finished up eight or nine yards to the right of the pin, somebody remarked: "He's dreadfully crooked, isn't he?" It was a true word spoken in jest. Eight yards to the left or right of the pin was definitely crooked for Hogan.

His putting is, to me at least, the least attractive part of his game, as far as looks are concerned. He has the ball very far forward opposite, or almost in front of, his left foot, with his right foot back, and the whole attitude has something of stiffness. But if ever there was a case of handsome is as handsome does, this is it, for he hits the ball a wonderfully solid blow. The ball does not trickle away at the end of the putt; it goes right in, and when a putt is particularly crucial he seems positively to will it into the hole.

Hogan is a compelling subject, and I have been running on about him like "a new barrow with the wheel greased". So I must do scanty justice to others. There is Locke, for instance, who lost the championship but lost it like a champion: his first round of 72 when the north-westerly wind was really blowing hard, was splendid, but he seemed to make just too many inaccurate iron shots. I think I have never seen Rees play better and I think his temperament was in as good order as his golf. His finish of two threes in the second round swept us off our feet with a wave of enthusiasm. I suppose that on the whole he did not play the finishing holes as well as the others. As he came off the green at the end of his last round, having tied with the leaders, but knowing that Hogan would catch them, he exclaimed sadly: "The 15th and 16th again!"

Eric Brown's two 71s showed his quality. I think he is a little too easily disturbed and not quite philosophical enough to win through at the moment. The one who seems to have the perfect temperament is the young Australian, Peter Thomson. He has now been second twice and he is only 23. As far as anyone can be sure to be a champion he is, and a most worthy and popular one he would be. The South Americans Cerda and de Vicenzo, acquired much merit. Either is just about good enough to win.

Finally, in a quadruple tie for second place was our now old friend Frank Stranahan. He not only played very, very well, but with tremendous courage. He provided one of the most dramatic moments of the tournament in the last round. He seemed out of the hunt so far as winning was concerned, when suddenly it was discovered that he was piling one three upon another and wanted a four at the home hole to be home in 33 and round in 70. The case was altered with a vengeance and when he holed his long putt for a three – he holed a chip for a three at the very same hole in the morning – and got his 69, it looked as though anything might happen. "We have seen the putt which won the championship," said one very shrewd friend in an ecstasy of excitement. When we reckoned up what the others had to do it had seemed very possible. "No, I think Hogan will just do it," I said, or I think I said, but I didn't think he would do it by four whole strokes. If there was one hole more than another that made that last round of Hogan's it was his three at the 5th, where he holed his chip from a nasty rough place on the back of a bunker. No doubt it was a help, but he was in an unstoppable mood. Carnoustie certainly showed itself a fine, stern examination paper for champions. Only the best could get full marks there.

LONG LAGS IN THE BRITISH OPEN

Sam Snead with Al Stump

Before I went to Scotland for the British Open of 1964, I'd never met anybody with a "sir" or "lord" in front of his name. So I still wonder how the London newspapers expected me to know it was a duke sitting across the aisle on the train to Edinburgh and the North.

Because of the duke, things got a little hot for me in British golfing society.

Down home in the woods, I wasn't short of ancestors and relatives myself. Mostly we were proud of Aunt Maggie Mathews, who gave birth to 20 children, including stillborns, and my great-uncle John. Big John Snead stood 7 feet 6, weighed 365, and died of fever in the Civil War after killing a few companies of Union soldiers with his bare hands.

We might have been plain people, but we were unusual. One of my great-grandmothers lived to be 106 years old and could still outshuck anybody in a cornfield when she was past 90. But no Snead ever ate tea and crumpets or got a look at royalty, except me – and in my case it was just a long-distance glimpse of King George VI when he'd galleried the 1937 British Open, which was my first trip out of the USA.

In 1937 as a kid contender I'd finished 10th with an even 300 shots at Carnoustie, Scotland, in the Open. In 1946 I was primed to do better. But then along came the duke, and then a whole mess of more trouble.

Along with Lawson Little, I rode a gully-jumper train up from London. We passed places with names like Kirkintilloch and the Firth of Forth and then we slowed down past some acreage that was so raggedy and beat-up that I was surprised to see what looked like a fairway amongst the weeds. Down home we wouldn't plant cow beets on land like that.

"Say, that looks like an old, abandoned golf course," I said to a man across the aisle, tapping his knee. "What did they call it?"

You'd have thought I stabbed him. "My good sir!" he snorted. "*That* is the Royal and Ancient Club of St Andrews, founded in 1754! And it is not now, nor ever will be, abandoned!"

"Holy smoke," I said, "I'm sorry." But how could I tell that I was looking at the most famous links in the world, the course that Bob Jones said he respected most? Until you play it, St Andrews looks like the sort of real estate you couldn't give away.

He was so insulted, this Duke Something-or-Other, that the British papers made a fuss about my remark and from then on I was dodging reporters who had the knife out for me. The only place over there that's holier than St Andrews is Westminster Abbey. I began to think the whole trip was a mistake. In fact, I'd tried to avoid entering the British Open in the first place.

A few weeks earlier in New York, I'd met with L.B. Icely, the president of Wilson Sporting Goods Company. I used and endorsed Wilson equipment and drew top royalties for it, and Icely had a say-so about where and when I played. Icely listened to my arguments against going, then said, "No, Sam, we want you to enter. It's time you won a big title overseas. The prestige will be terrific."

What did I want with prestige? The British Open paid the winner $600 in American money. A man would have to be two hundred years old at that rate to retire from golf.

But Icely was firm about it.

"Have you seen me putt lately?" I argued. "It's awful. On the greens my mind just seems to leave my body."

"In this Open at St Andrews the greens are double size. Big as a barnyard," said Icely. "They'll help you get your touch back."

I complained that a centre-shafted putter, such as I used then, was illegal in the English championship and that I hated to switch to a blade putter.

"Mr Walter Hagen," came back Icely, "has done fairly well with a blade. He won the British Open twice at Sandwich, and also at Hoylake and Muirfield. I suggest you talk to Walter."

Hagen had the answer for my miserable putting when I saw him. "Just start hitting the ball above the equator," he advised.

"Goodbye, Walter," I said.

Hagen was no help. In advising me to hit the ball slightly above the centre line, he was looking for end-over-end rotation, or over spin. But I'd long ago learned that too much over spin hurt me more than it helped. When the ball contacted the hole, whether on the right or left lip, it had a better chance of dropping without heavy topspin. I'd often discussed this with Ben Hogan. As Ben argued, "Given a lot of topspin, the ball retains too much energy at a point where you want it to die and often worms its way right out of the cup." Using Hagen's method, I'd seen many a ball go half in and flip out. And I'd topped far too many putts, also.

Whatever was wrecking my putting in 1946, it wasn't because I failed to try and catch the fat of the ball with a square action and apply a medium amount of over spin.

Once Icely had put down his foot, I went to England. And the jinx was on me all the way. Leaving New York, our Constellation sprang an engine fire on take-off and we stopped on the runway with smoke pouring into the cabin. All of us in there came popping out like ants. In London, which was still in bad shape from the war, you couldn't get a good meal or a hotel room. People were sleeping in the street. Carrying my golf bag, I knocked on the door of a private home in Kensington Road and asked to rent a room overnight.

"I'll be leaving in the morning. I'm going to St Andrews."

"So I see," the owner said. "Having fun while the rest of us are on rations."

"Fun, hell," I said. "You should see me putt, mister." He slammed the door in my face.

At another house, a guy who looked like Boris Karloff with a monocle rented me a room for one hour for seven dollars. After one hour of sleep, I was kicked out and someone else got my bed. I slept in a depot and then caught the Edinburgh train. On the train, I began to get a light-headed, dizzy feeling. I thought it was from the beans and porridge I'd eaten – there being no other food available. But an Englishwoman explained it. "You've been drinking a lot of our tea, haven't you?" she asked. "Well, it's quite strong these days, and undoubtedly you are suffering from a tea jag, which bothers most strangers. It's quite similar to being inebriated. Don't worry, in time it will pass."

Now I knew I'd putt myself out of the Open in the first 18 holes.

Next came Duke Whoozis, and the insult I gave the Royal and Ancient course, without meaning to. After my remark that it was a pretty run-down old weed patch, the London *Times* gave me a good jab:

"Snead, a rural American type, undoubtedly would think the Leaning Tower of Pisa a structure about to totter and crash to his feet."

After that came caddie troubles. The way most golfers tell it, St Andrews caddies are the world's best and can read the grass right down to the roots from Burn Hole, which is No.1 on the Old Course, to Home Hole. Mine were a bunch of bums. I had four caddies in four days. One of them whistled between his teeth when I putted. After letting him go, I drew a fellow in sailor pants who couldn't judge distances or carry. On one hole he slipped me the three-iron and said, "That's the ticket, mate." The shot left me 30 yards short of the green. The next hole he clubbed me with a five-iron. This time I refused his advice, took a seven-iron, and even then landed over the green in a bunker. "Mate, you're sunk," I said, and gave him back to the caddie master. Then came "Scotty", guaranteed to be St Andrews' best.

Scotty went to jail for drunkenness the night before the Open started, leaving me to figure the course for myself.

The gigantic double greens were a break for me. One of them measured almost two acres in size. I knew that nobody in the field, including the great Henry Cotton, Bobby Locke, Johnny Bulla, Dai Rees, and Lawson Little, would get close enough very often to hole with one putt, which would help equalise my poor work around the pin. I thought that if I could beat them from tee to green, I had a chance to finish in the money. As it turned out, I never was longer off the tee. On No.10, 312 yards, I drove the green three times in four rounds; on No.12, 314 yards, I drove the green two out of four.

But it was the heavy-blade putter I was using that put me in a three-way tie for first place with a total of 215 strokes when the third round ended. I couldn't believe what was happening.

Later on I saw that a habit of mine on long putts had paid off. From 25 feet or more distance, I've never believed in going for the cup. On long-approach putts, any time you aim to make them you'll either overcharge by 10 or 15 feet or fall far short and wind up three-putting, the reason being that from 25 to 75 feet no one can make a 4¼-inch cup his target with accuracy. From far out, I pick a line and adjust speed *to* the general area of the hole. Closer up, I go directly *at* it. I want my lag putts to die within easy second-shot distance of the cup.

There's another percentage involved here. A putt travelling fast enough to overrun by two or three feet must hit the cup almost dead center to go in, whereas a putt stroked up to the cup and no farther may fall in even if it's an inch or more off line from centre.

A cup has a front and rear door and two side doors – four entrances. By not charging too hard, you take advantage of all of them.

Walter Travis, who was such an uncanny putt master that the British barred his centre-shafted Schenectady mallet from their country for 40-odd years, didn't agree with that theory. He took dead aim every time. Billy Casper, one of the best putters today, does agree. Doc Cary Middlecoff thinks he can hole every long putt and goes for broke. Lloyd Mangrum, one of the half-dozen best on the greens I've seen, tried to drop 90-footers but advised average golfers to aim for a two-foot circle around the pin. There's little agreement on this, but after the British Open I never questioned this part of the game.

In the final round, a St Andrews Bay gale made every putt a guess. It was so bad that balls jiggled and oscillated when you addressed them. Flory Von Donck, the Belgian, had a downhill 20-footer with the windstorm behind him. Von Donck turned his back to the cup, putted uphill away from the target, and then, as the ball rolled back down the hill, a sudden gust swooped it 15 feet past the hole. Others who tried to drop approach putts in that wind wound up chewing on their mufflers when their long rollers were blown every which way.

All I wanted was to be reasonably close and to lag for the safest possible position on my second putt. With the green sloping toward me (in any kind of weather) I'd rather be three feet short than over. It's 2–1 easier to make a 36-incher from an uphill lie than from a downhill or sidehill lie. Putting uphill, you take a firm, natural grip. Downhill, because of the extra momentum you'll get, you loosen the grip, and without realising it you can get sloppy. On the No.10 hole, from 20 feet away, I eased up to within 18 inches and dropped it for a birdie. On the No.12, from 30 feet, I did the same thing. With the 40-mph wind behind me, I stroked extra easy on those slick, dried-out greens. Against a crosswind, I allowed for a big break, up to six feet on long putts.

On No.14, Hell's Bunker, a Scotsman stuck his whiskers in my face and said, "You can shoot sixes from here on in, laddie, and win."

I checked this with Richards Vidmer, the *New York Times* reporter, who carried a walkie-talkie radio.

"No, six a hole isn't safe," said Vidmer. "But you can take it with fives. Cotton, Rees, and Von Nida have blown themselves out of it. But Bulla and Locke are still close."

With that news, I gambled a bit on an eight-footer at Hell's Bunker and got it for another birdie. At the par-four 16th, some genius had placed the pin on a little shelf at the rear green guarded by a steep incline. My

30-footer climbed the grade, then rolled part way back to me. Next time I putted stiff to the flag, but the result was three putts, five strokes, and a bogey.

On the Road Hole, No.17, the gale took my pretty nine-iron pitch, right on the flag, and swooped it 25 feet away. Again just lagging up, I was paid off for being cautious. The wind provided an extra few turns and in she fell – my longest putt of the tournament.

"He could use his bloomin' puttah on every shot and win!" somebody in the crowd shouted. That was music to my ears. Back home they'd been saying that I couldn't roll a marble into a manhole with both hands.

The Road Hole won the Open. All I had to do was play out No.18 in 7 shots – and I took 4 – to finish ahead of Locke and Bulla. I'd been half drunk on tea, and had gone without sleep and a good caddie, but my 290 score beat all four of Walter Hagen's best totals in this tournament, two of the three winning scores of Bob Jones, and the best by Tommy Armour, Jock Hutchison, and Denny Shute when they took home the cup.

The purse of $600 was such a joke that I decided then and there not to defend the title. My travelling expenses alone were over $1,000, and nobody but me picked up that tab. On top of that, all my hitting muscles "froze" in the icy wind at St Andrews. For days I ached in every joint.

Then there was my caddie friend, "Scotty", who got himself sprung from jail and begged me to give him the winning ball. "Maun," he promised, tearfully, "I'll treasure it all my days."

That ball was worth some cash, and Scotty proved it. An hour later he sold it for fifty quid. So he made more off the Open than I did.

For years afterward, British and American writers panned me for passing up the British Open, but like I've always said – as far as I'm concerned, any time you leave the USA, you're just camping out.

MY COLOUR OF GREEN

Severiano Ballesteros with Dudley Doust

"He is something else, this young Spaniard, and all things being equal he has an excellent chance of becoming one of the authentically great golfers of all time."
Herbert Warren Wind, the American golf writer, in the *New Yorker*, 26 May 1980.

• • • • • • •

Ballesteros was to travel many times to America before returning with the prize he most coveted – a major US crown, preferably the Masters. The word "Masters" was in the language of his childhood: it was his window on the outside world. His uncle, Ramon Sota, played at Augusta six times – first in 1964, finally in 1972 – and tied for sixth place in 1965, the year Seve was eight and still chipping with stones and, perhaps significantly, the year Nicklaus scored a 271, a Masters' low-scoring record which Seve later would challenge.

The moment he first set foot on the course in 1977, Ballesteros felt at home: the Augusta National Golf Club, while on a grander scale, is similar to the lush, rolling, pine-covered Real Club de Golf de Pedreña. "When I saw it, Augusta gave me a very familiar feeling," Ballesteros recalls. "These were my trees, my colour of green, and I said to myself, 'Seve, one day you will win this tournament.'"

Golf Digest seemed to share this notion in their cover question: "Can This Teenager Win the Masters?" The query wasn't altogether fair. Since the Masters was first played in 1934 only two men (Horton Smith in 1934, Gene Sarazen in 1935) had won it first time out and, even more impressively, the youngest player to win the classic event was the greatest golfer ever to play in it, Nicklaus, who captured the title at 23 in 1963. What is more, in 1977 Ballesteros was only lately released from the Spanish Air Force and therefore fairly rusty.

Pointed out as a prodigy, Ballesteros felt under pressure. He nearly succumbed to it for, on the very first day at Augusta, while over-straining to smash a practice ball out of the grounds, he pulled a muscle in his back. He was also suspicious. "The Augusta people are trying to test me," he muttered darkly when he saw he was drawn to play with Nicklaus on the first day. "They want to see how I can take pressure." Ballesteros talked nonsense, for his pairing was meant to be honorific: Europe's best player on display with the world's best.

Ballesteros was introduced on the 1st tee as the holder of the Dutch Open championship and leader of the British Order of Merit and he stood, eyes down and emotionally impervious. "I was okay until I noted the sharp contrast between the green grass and the white tee marker," he recalls. "That put a very strange feeling in my stomach. I suddenly realised I was playing in the Masters."

Ballesteros opened the championship uncertainly, with a 74 and 75. As the second evening descended he sat in the players' lounge, watching the last players toiling on television, worrying over missing the midway cut. "Don't worry, you'll make it," I remember telling him. "You're only five strokes over par." The remark angered Ballesteros. "Yes," he snapped, "but if I was five *under* par I would be leading the tournament." He settled down and finished on 291, three over par, 15 strokes behind the winner, Watson, and joint-33rd. All the same, it was an impressive début.

Ballesteros's Masters education continued in 1978 when, three under par after three rounds, he played the last day with Gary Player, both lying seven shots behind the leader, Hubert Green. It was to be a memorable day. Player made the turn in 34, useful but nothing spectacular, then scored two more birdies and was only three strokes adrift of Green as he walked purposefully down the 13th fairway with Ballesteros. "Seve, I want to tell you something," he said, and gestured towards the crowd thronging beyond the distant ropes. "Those people don't think I can win. You watch, I'll show them."

He did. In one of the most spectacular finishes in Masters history, Player scored seven birdies over the last 10 holes to nip Green, Watson and Rod Runseth by a stroke to win the title. Player's fight, and his remark on the 13th fairway, left an indelible impression on the young Spaniard. It reinforced Ballesteros's own siege mentality. "I think Player maybe likes to think people are against him so he can fight harder," Seve said later. "I'm like that. The more against you are the crowd, the more you want to prove something." For himself, Ballesteros's own battle that day brought little reward, a 74 for a shared 17th-place finish.

In 1979, Fuzzy Zoeller won after a playoff with Watson and Ed Sneed. Sneed had let a three-stroke lead slip away over the last three holes, a collapse that would haunt Ballesteros. The Spaniard finished tied for 12th spot, seven behind Zoeller. He felt he could win in 1980.

Accordingly, the Spaniard began to draw up his battle plans. His first rehearsal, with the Masters pointedly in mind, took place in the Suntory World Match-Play championship in the autumn of 1979 on the West Course at Wentworth, near London. Trees crowd the fairways at Wentworth, as they do at Augusta, and in the interest of keeping the ball in play the Spaniard shortened his swing for more control. Ballesteros-watchers could see it clearly: Seve had chopped as much as eighteen inches off the top of his backswing. Under pressure in the championship – Ballesteros lost on the 40th green in the semi-final round to the Japanese Aoki – he resolutely retained his new, short and serene swing. This act of restraint was on of the most crucial triumphs of his entire career.

Back in Pedreña during the winter he continued his rehearsal, tossing balls willy-nilly into the pine trees and playing out. He drilled himself in big, high shots that curved left, the necessary shape for Augusta, where 11 of the 13 dog-legs swing in that direction. Yet he was unhappy. His swing had been built partly in the image of Nicklaus's, with a break or "cock" of the wrists in the takeaway. Ballesteros was finding that this action reduced his control of the clubhead, a discovery that Nicklaus had made too. Therefore, in the evenings the Spaniard stood in front of a full-length mirror in the farmhouse stables, down among the cows, and reconstructed the takeaway. He explained: "I wanted to see myself take the club back more in one piece."

Ballesteros also began exercising on a "Gravity Gym" machine, a fixed trapeze device with pads and canvas loops which he had first seen the previous autumn in Graham Marsh's home in Perth, Australia. Three sessions a day the Spaniard dangled from the device, twisting and lifting himself as many as forty times a session, stretching and building the muscles of his imperfect back.

On rare departures from Pedreña, Ballesteros dated a television presenter in Barcelona. It was through her that he met a psychiatrist interested in what the Spanish call "sufrologia", a form of positive thinking. A 30-minute cassette tape was made in which the doctor's soothing voice speaks to Seve who listens through a plug in his ear. "What the doctor says to me is private," Ballesteros says. "But it helps me to relax and convinces me I am good."

Sound in body and mind, Ballesteros now turned to the heart of the game, especially at Augusta: putting. Augusta's green could be harrowingly fast, he knew, but apart from household carpets there was only one fast surface at hand: the Pedreña beach, with the tide out. The beach wasn't as undulating as Augusta's greens, but that didn't matter. "I was interested in the pace. I wanted to get the pace of Augusta in my mind," explained Ballesteros. "Also, on the beach, it was difficult to find the line of the putt and that made me practise my concentration."

At the beginning of March 1980, Ballesteros began the final phase of his Masters preparation by travelling to America for three Florida tournaments. He missed the cut at the Doral-Eastern Open at Miami but tied for 15th at the Jackie Gleason Inverrary Classic and came joint 3rd at the Tournament Players championship at Sawgrass. He passed up the next two events and, a week before the Masters, moved into Augusta.

The Augusta National Golf Club is something special. After St Andrews, it has the most famous course in the world, and probably the finest one inland. It certainly is the most colourful, with 65 stately magnolias that march up the long drive to the clubhouse and blazing azalea, yellow jasmine and other pungent flowers and trees that lend their names to holes. The fairways are invitingly broad, the greens enormous and subtly contoured, as one might expect of such an admirer of British seaside links as Bobby Jones, who devised Augusta. With no rough to speak of and only 44 bunkers, the most dangerous natural hazards are the flowering dogwood and the longlead pines.

Ballesteros's first problem in 1980 was to "get his distances" – that is, to pace off the distances from landmarks, such as an isolated tree or sprinkler head, to the fronts and backs of greens. In the past the distances had been got by his regular caddie, Marion Herrington, but Herrington got them in yards. Ballesteros, a Continental European, thinks in metres, and he would have to add 10 per cent to convert the yards to metres. Such mental arithmetic was imprecise and wasted time. Yards wouldn't do in 1980. Ballesteros therefore paced off his own distances and entered them into a booklet he kept in his hip pocket.

Next Ballesteros studied placement of his tee shots. All Augusta's holes, save perhaps the 2nd, are reachable in two shots and most are dog-legs; therefore, a high premium is placed on playing into a position that "opens up" a green. To this end it is important at Augusta to "think a hole backwards". Nicklaus does. On practice days, he can be seen at the front of greens, staring back over the rolling waves of fairway, considering where his approach shot should come from. Ballesteros did the same.

Ballesteros finally studied the greens. Augusta's are not only big and racy but they hump and roll and fall away in the most frightening manner. A downhill putt, merely touched, can run off the green. "In practice," Ballesteros said later, "I spent much time looking for places where I could putt uphill at a hole." The Spaniard also noted that the greens, after a wet spring, were slowish for Augusta. Some were notably slower than others.

Ballesteros was ready. Publicly, he would make no predictions. Privately, he was bubbling with confidence. "Give me a three-stroke lead with three holes to play," he told a friend, referring to Sneed's collapse in 1979, "and I'll win."

On the afternoon before the first round, Nicklaus customarily calls together the world's press to explain his and Augusta's current form. This time Watson, Nicklaus's heir presumptive, beat him to it. Watson called *his* press conference. The Kansas Citian's press conferences, while less patronising, are every bit as informed as Nicklaus's. Watson felt he was in good form, except in one department: "My driving's a hair-line off."

As for Augusta, the recent weather had left the fairways and greens "a little bit skinny" of their usual lush growth but the soft course would play long. The usual key holes, the par-fives, were therefore even more crucial this year but, for Watson, the biggest psychological hurdle came at the 14th, not one of Augusta's usually remarked holes, but one that immediately follows the tensions of Amen Corner, the trio of tough holes at the far end of the course. You could pay dearly by emotionally relaxing on 14. He felt the most interesting hole this year was the new 8th. Because of the new contouring of the approaches to the green, the course was now one-third of a shot tougher than in 1979. The field was strong, however, and he estimated the winning score would be 278, 10 under par and slightly below average over the past decade.

Who would win? Such big hitters as Andy Bean and Ballesteros – and Nicklaus, "because he knows where to hit the ball round here" – must be favourites. What, Watson wondered aloud, was the line from London? The British Press dutifully found out: Ladbrokes fancied Watson at 5 to 1, followed by Nicklaus at 8 to 1 and Ballesteros at 12 to 1.

Watson's puzzling remark about the "new" 8th hole adding "a third of a stroke" to the course bears expansion. To the casual visitor, the Augusta National course appears to be sacrosanct. It isn't. In an effort to keep up with the improvements in the game over the past 30 years, the ground staff had made well over 150 alterations, a remarkable number in the conservative world of golf. A tee has been elevated here, a bunker shifted there, greens relocated and recontoured, ponds dug and filled, trees cut down and replanted. "I don't know a course in the world, except maybe Nicklaus's at Muirfield Village," Watson once said, "that undergoes such regular revision as the Augusta National."

And so it was with the 8th. The hole, 530 yards long, mostly uphill and bending left past a colourful wood, had shown up on the computer as the easiest par-five at Augusta. Something had to be done. The job, as usual, was left to the Tournament Improvements Committee, a powerful body which includes such former Masters winners as Gene Sarazen, Ben Hogan and Byron Nelson.

The problem was easy to identify, and no one saw it more clearly than Nelson. In the old days – before 1956 – the green had been guarded by three massive mounds rolling back along the left from off the green. If the ambitious shot was overdrawn, and if the flag was tucked back left, a player was set the difficult task of approaching over the mounds for a crack at the flag. What is more, three smaller mounds had guarded the approach on the right front of the green, creating a flattish bowl.

"It was one of the most unusual greens I ever played, and one of the most challenging," says Nelson, who in 1942 effectively won his second Masters with a play-off eagle three there against Ben Hogan. "If you were accurate you could use the mounds. If you weren't, they could use you." In 1956 the mounds were removed to allow spectators a better view down the fairway from behind the green. "Without those mounds," Nelson goes on, "you could hit just about any old shot off the fairway, as long as you stayed out of the trees." After the 1979 Masters the Committee decided the green area had to be restored to its original configuration and, working from plastic models, the job was done through the summer. By 1980, as almost always, the course was just a little different for the Masters.

• • • • • • •

The opening day dawned clear and bright, with a marauding breeze, but not enough sun to warrant the white peaked cap Ballesteros wore when he appeared on the first tee at 12.12. Frankly, he looked odd. The cap, obscuring those dark, expressive eyes, muted his glamour. He wore it for reasons: to block out gallery distractions and, more cunningly, to reduce the glare of Augusta's crystalline white bunker sand. He was dressed conservatively in a white shirt and dark blue trousers. "I feel calm in calm colours," he says. "I don't want people to watch me the way I dress. I want people to watch me the way I play."

As the 1979 Open champion, Ballesteros was playing the star role in his pairing. His partner was Craig Stadler, "the Walrus", a corpulent irritable American with a drooping moustache. In past years, Ballesteros had set out, all guns blazing, aiming his big drive over the corner of a distant bunker and, perilously, played hide-and-seek with a stand of pine trees out to the right. This year, having noticed how Trevino played the hole, he settled into his stance, slightly closer than usual to the ball, aimed down the left side of the fairway and, gently swinging in an outside-inside plane, faded his drive into the middle of the fairway. A crisp pitch, two putts, and the Spaniard was away with a par.

Ballesteros was a model of wise, easy power throughout the round, missing only one fairway off the tee – in contrast to his fabled last round in the 1979 Open at Lytham where he hit only two – and when he erred he did not strike back as he might have done in the old days. He probably never played a more impressive round in his life. At the end of the day, his 66, six under par, shared the lead with the Australian David Graham, who reigned as American PGA champion, and Jeff Mitchell who, as a West Texan, ought to have played well in the wind. The favourite Watson played without distinction for a 73 and Nicklaus, troubled by the wind, scored a 74.

The weather on the second day was blissfully bright, with barely a breeze. Ballesteros was paired with Larry Nelson whom, in the 1979 Ryder Cup matches, he had called lucky to hole a long chip shot. The American team and Press had made a meal of this careless remark. After Lytham, they felt, who was calling whom lucky? At Augusta, neither man would rekindle the fuel for the Press. They played with friendly, mutual respect.

The Spaniard's golf that day was pure theatre. At moments it was the old Ballesteros: he jumped at the odd ball, sending it screaming off line, then punished these mistakes with great, lashing recoveries. He scored birdies off his three most hideous drives of the day, the last one worse, by acres, than his fabled "parking lot" drive at Lytham.

The build-up to that nightmare drive began on the 15th when, subduing the 520-yard hole with a drive and a 3-iron, he scored a birdie. It put him nine strokes under par, three clear of his nearest pursuer, Graham, who had just reached the 6th tee. Pumped up with adrenalin, Ballesteros called for his eight-iron as he stepped on to the tee of the watery, 190-yard 16th. "No," said Herrington, "It's a little seven-iron." Ballesteros relented and pounded his ball eighty feet past the pin, leaving himself an ugly downhill putt. As he left the tee, a nearby explosion of applause signalled Graham's birdie on the 6th green. Ballesteros three-putted to fall back to a single stroke advantage over the Australian.

Herrington was horrified by his mistake. He apologised to Ballesteros. The Spaniard, eschewing the tenet by which he always shifts the blame away from himself, replied, "Don't worry. It was my fault." Ballesteros was seething with himself when he reached the 17th tee. He snap-hooked his drive. The ball veered left, clicked through the top of a pine tree, bounced into the adjacent 7th fairway, skipped between a pair of bunkers and ran up on to the elevated 7th green. It came to rest some ten feet from the hole – the wrong hole.

Ballesteros climbed to the green where he met Graham and his playing partner, Andy North. The situation was bizarre. Here was the Spaniard, ten holes ahead of his nearest rival, on the same green. What's more, Ballesteros's ball was in Graham's direct line to the hole. "Nice drive" said Graham. "Would you like to play through?" Ballesteros, embarrassed, marked his ball and, as soon as the green cleared, dropped clear without penalty. Once, twice the ball rolled away and finally Ballesteros set it in place.

He surveyed the prospect before him. Clearly, such a shot had never before been contemplated in the 46-year history of the Masters: high over the corner of a massive scoreboard, over a gigantic hump and on to a hidden green. In all, 150 yards. Crowds were cleared from behind the green. Spectators, blundering across the path of the shot, were startled to be shouted back. Many cowered, scattered. "Are you going to make a birdie?" a fan asked. "Yes," said Seve.

The Spaniard took a precarious footing and smashed his seven-iron shot over the edge of the scoreboard, crouched and listened. Silence. Then deafening, distant applause. Ballesteros was away, half-sprinting after it, his fans surging behind him. It was Palmer in the Sixties, all over again. "Waa-hoo!" Then from one Southern throat came the curious drawl, "*Olé!*"

Ballesteros found the ball only 15 feet from the hole and, smooth as milk from a pitcher, he poured in the putt for the birdie he promised. Nelson, bemused, later remembered the Spaniard, a fixed look in his eye, marching toward the final tee. "When Seve gets going he starts walking fast, he's got different thoughts on his mind," Nelson commented. "Seve is a rare kind of guy. He's an excitable golfer who can concentrate."

The pyrotechnics were done for the day. Ballesteros scored an untroubled par on the finishing hole for a 69 and a midway total of 135, which put him four strokes clear of the field. In his wake, on 139, lay Graham and Rex Caldwell, a journeyman American. The two giants of the game looked lost in the crowd, Watson on 142 after another 71; Nicklaus on 145, also having returned a 71, a total that by only a single stroke escaped the 36-hole cut.

Nelson, after scoring a workaday 72 with Ballesteros, reckoned that Watson and the Spaniard were heirs-apparent to Nicklaus. He compared and contrasted these two princes of golf. "Tom and Seve are totally different in their attitude," he said. "Tom is more involved in technique and perfecting his swing. It's in the back of his mind to score well, sure, but what he's concerned about is hitting the ball perfectly as a means to this end. Seve is different. He just wants to shoot lower scores than anybody else."

There had been lower 36-hole Masters scores shot than Ballesteros's – Raymond Floyd's 131 in 1976 was the lowest – but on only three occasions had players held a more commanding lead at this point: Floyd in 1976, Nicklaus in 1975 and Herman Keiser in 1946 – all were five strokes clear of their fields. The Spaniard was set fair. "Seve is going to have to be caught," said Graham. "I don't think he will back up."

The Masters was now taking shape: unless someone mounted an attack and kept pressure on him, the confident Ballesteros might turn on the steam and, like a distance runner or cyclist, break away from the field. The weather, only a mild wind and enough rain to soften the green, prophesied low enough scores for such an attack to succeed. It would be a fascinating day.

Gibby Gilbert, nine strokes behind, made the first move. He birdied four of the first seven holes before Ballesteros teed off, closing the gap to five strokes. In itself, this was not worrying, for Gilbert still had the more difficult home half of the course to play. But who next might make a run at the Spaniard?

Ballesteros opened the day with rickety bogey-birdie-bogey-par then hoiked an ungainly drive, "almost between my legs" off the 5th and straight into a stand of pines. As luck had it, the ball came to rest precisely where the ground staff had recently uprooted a tree. Only Seve could have found such a place. If on the previous day the Spaniard, after dropping off the 7th green, played a shot no man ever had played before in the Masters, his ball lay this time where no player had ever trod: in the rough in the little valley at the bottom of the 6th fairway and, as he faced the unseen and faraway 5th green, hard against a rising wall of pine trees.

Ballesteros, nearly 250 yards from the green, could not play towards it. "Seve, maybe here you are going to take a double-bogey six," he said to himself. "But even if you do, you're still going to be one shot ahead. Keep calm. Don't get mad."

Calmly, Ballesteros selected a pitching wedge, opened the face flat, and with a vicious slash sent his ball climbing steeply over the trees and back into the fairway. A long pitch and two putts later and Ballesteros had a five, possibly the most satisfying bogey he had scored in his life. Nonetheless, his lead was now only two strokes from Graham, his playing partner who birdied the hole, and Caldwell.

Ballesteros is most dangerous when wounded, and on the next hole, a par-three that drops like a stone to a wildly rolling green, he nearly scored a hole-in-one. His seven-iron shot off the 190-yard hole, pitched nicely short of the flag, ran up and twitched away from the cup for an easy birdie two. He was back in command, three strokes in front; yet he had scored only par in his six holes for the day.

In retrospect, many holes appear crucial in the winning of a tournament but none, even during what was to be an eventful final day, could have been more important to Ballesteros's Masters victory than the 8th on the third day. The 8th – where the green was remodelled by Byron Nelson; Ballesteros came into it after parring the 7th.

As the Spaniard walked towards the tee his confidence returned: glancing up at the big scoreboard he had seen that Watson almost certainly was gone. The American had bogeyed the 11th, had taken a triple-bogey six on the short 12th (by blocking his tee shot into Rae's Creek) and lay 10 strokes behind him. Graham was now four back, Caldwell three.

Ballesteros cracked a big drive, 285 yards and nearly all carry. He could not see the green from his ball but, consulting his hip booklet, he reckoned the pin to be 224 metres (245 yards) away, almost all uphill. He walked forward, had a look and took a decision. He wouldn't bother shaping his shot off the mounds; he'd just fly it string-straight, covering the flag all the way. And that's what he did: struck a stupendous three-iron, high and straight. The ball dropped light as a feather on to the green, and came to rest six feet from the hole. Seve stroked in the putt for an eagle three.

The effect of the three-iron blow was devastating. Graham, who over the past few holes had appeared to be playing slowly in an intentional attempt to break the Spaniard's pace, was shattered. He dropped a shot on the hole and was not heard of again. With that eagle to help him, Ballesteros made the turn in 35; one under par, and playing with almost unremarkable brilliance he came home in 33 for a round of 68. This put him at 203, distantly followed by the chubby American Ed Fiori, who had come in with a 60 for a 210 total. Graham (72) was in joint-third spot, along with Newton, Andy North, the 1978 US Open Champion, and J.C. Snead, the legendary Sam's nephew, all on 211.

The 1980 Masters seemed over bar the shouting, and the counting. With a seven-stroke lead and standing 13 under par, Ballesteros had raised prospects of a record victory. He could not only become the youngest man ever to win the Masters, being 80 days younger than Nicklaus was when he triumphed in 1963, but he could join the exalted company of Nicklaus, Francis Ouimet and Bobby Jones as the only men in history to win two or more major championships by the age of 23. Further, the Spaniard could set another record by winning by a wider margin than Nicklaus's nine strokes in 1965.

Not surprisingly, Ballesteros said he would first see to his victory before taking on other targets. Seve, no doubt about it, was stuffing the Yanks in their own back yard, and the foreign players rallied round him. From the blunt, warm-hearted Newton, who was to be paired on the final day with the Spaniard, came a surprisingly virulent defence in a broadside delivered over television.

"I've read some of the newspaper articles this week and, you know, it's almost as though you guys are waiting for Seve to blow it," snapped Newton, glaring at the camera. "I've also heard some pretty snide, completely uncalled-for remarks from some of the players. They say he's lucky and a "one-putt Jessie" and all that (bleep) . . . America's considered to be the tops in professional golf and here comes a young 23 year-old and he's taken some of the highlight away from your superstars. But, you know, the guy's a great player and the sooner Americans realise it the better." With that, Newton turned and went back to the putting green.

Ballesteros looked remarkably composed. "Come to dinner," he said to a journalist from London. "Only we don't talk about golf, okay?" He had invited eight friends to dinner, mostly Spanish, mostly male. He does not seek attention but when later he appeared in the living room of his rented house, dressed in a yellow shirt, all eyes drifted to him. Ballesteros radiated golf that night although there was only a single golfing item in the room: an antique, hickory-shafted putter which lay on the otherwise empty coffee table: a birthday gift to Seve from Rhena Barner, Ed's wife. Guests wandered by, however, and as though it was a talisman which had been blessed by genius they picked it up, waggled it and looked askance at Ballesteros.

It was a buffet dinner and towards a pretty female American journalist, much liberated, he was courtly, guiding her through the queue and putting her firmly at the head of the table. Towards Señor Jose Santiuste, the elderly gentleman to whom he had given his 1979 Open championship ball, he was deferential. Among his fellows, he was lusty and jovial – they indulged in great teasing of accents, and made much play of *cojones*, the Spanish measure of courage.

One minute Ballesteros was joking about Spanish football – the national team had recently been thrashed by England – the next he was watching *Saturday Night Fever* on television in the den, quite outside the mainstream of conversation. Then he was gone. It was 10 o'clock. He lay on his bed, the cassette ear-piece plugged into his ear, listening to the soothing words of the Barcelona psychiatrist.

13 April, the fourth day, and Ballesteros and Newton appeared on the 1st tee prepared to drive off at 1.48. Seve started in irrepressible form. With the most delicate of pitches he birdied the 1st, then the 3rd hole, to increase his lead to 10 strokes.

At about that time Jim Armstrong II, the club manager, was in his office with Seve's manager. What size Green Jacket would Ballesteros require? 42, regular. In the certain belief that such a standard size could be borrowed from the pro shop, Armstrong went on to explain the rights and responsibilities surrounding the Green Jacket. A new champion was entitled to wear it off the Augusta National Golf Club premises only for his tenure as champion and only at social golfing functions. Thereafter it would be kept for him in a cedar-lined closet in the champions' locker room. Ballesteros would have permanent privileges to that locker room. Armstrong had begun to itemise the other prizes that would come to Ballesteros: the $55,000 first prize, of course, and a silver humidor bearing the signatures of all the players. Crystal vases for low daily scores, Thursday and Friday; a pair of crystal goblets for the eagle ... then news came from the course. Ballesteros was falling apart.

The Spaniard had played cast-iron golf since the 5th and made the turn in 33 to go 16 under par for the tournament and 10 clear of Newton – and of Gilbert, who was moving down the 11th fairway. As the young Spaniard stood on the 10th tee the low-lying holes beneath him must have looked like El Dorado.

The golden vision soon turned to dross. On the 10th green, a speedy threadbare surface, Ballesteros three-putted and Newton, with a par, closed the gap to nine strokes. Ballesteros righted himself on the 11th, but Newton birdied. Eight strokes. The Spaniard thought – almost nonchalantly – that his chance of breaking the tournament record of 217 strokes was slipping. ¿y que? so what? Augusta's 12th is "the most demanding tournament hole in the world", according to Nicklaus. A one-shotter at only 155 yards, it is tucked at the end of the famed Amen Corner, just over Rae's Creek, and against a tall backcloth, and players standing on a sheltered tee have no way of reading the air currents high above the green. A well-struck shot can abruptly hold up and drop like a stone into a bunker in front of the green or, worse, into the creek.

Year after year, Masters aspirations drown in the creek. 1980 was no exception. A triple bogey had finished Watson's hopes on the previous day and Weiskopf, en route to his 85 on the opening day, had put five balls in the creek, an all-time record, and taken 13 on the hole. The Spaniard studied the heaving pines in the distance and planned his shot: he would start his ball left and let the wind bring it into the flag.

He set himself solidly, aiming left, and took his six-iron into the backswing. At the top of his swing a thought suddenly struck him: *go straight for the pin.* As his club started down, it happened: his leading hand, the left one, tightened on the grip. He fractionally let up, "blocked-out", and the ball flew to the right.

Ballesteros watched, feeling helpless as the ball pitched into the bank, stuck, then trickled down into the creek. There was no calling it back. The Spaniard, who rarely swears, did so now. Electing to drop out of the water under one stroke penalty, Ballesteros meticulously dropped the ball over his shoulder in the correct line between the flag and the point at which the ball entered the water. He chipped to the back of the green, just to be safe, and carefully two-putted. A double-bogey 5. Newton too another birdie: the three-stroke swing closed Ballesteros's gap to five strokes. It was a comfortable enough lead, but one that was moving alarmingly in the wrong direction.

Off the next, elevated tee, Ballesteros punished his drive, drawing it nicely round the dog-leg. From there, he pondered the shot: 162 metres (180 yards) over Rae's Creek which at that point lay crooked in front of the green. A four-iron? The choice struck him as dangerous; he needed more club. He called for his three-iron. Herrington felt it was wrong but said nothing. Ballesteros thought: hit the ball softly, get control of your power again.

His decision was disastrous. Swinging unnaturally slowly, Ballesteros hit the ball "fat": that is, he struck the turf a full two inches too far behind the ball. The clubhead dug in. The ball climbed feebly into the air, fell short of the green and skipped into the creek. Walking up the fairway, Ballesteros felt the eyes of the crowd on him; suddenly he experienced the same sense of embattlement that he had witnessed in Player on the same fairway in 1978. *These people don't think I can win. I'll show them.* He lifted out of the water, as he had done on the previous hole, and dropped the ball over his shoulder. The referee asked him to drop it again. *This man is trying to put me off!* thought Ballesteros, and he lost his temper.

"Sir," he snapped sarcastically, "Are you *sure*, sir?" Yes, the referee was sure. Ballesteros dropped again. His chip was once again safely strong but, putting back down a slope, he hit the hole and the ball snapped away. He finished it off for a bogey six – against *another* Newton birdie, his third on the trot – and the Spaniard's lead was down to three strokes. Meanwhile applause mushroomed up ahead: Gilbert had birdied the 14th hole; and the American was now four strokes behind and closing in. You are *stupid*, Ballesteros said to himself. What are you doing? You were comfortable but now you are in trouble. You can lose this tournament. You must work hard.

Newton cracked a perfect drive up the 14th fairway. Ballesteros hooked his. The ball swerved left into trees. At that point a curious incident took place as Ballesteros moved up the fairway. A spectator shouted at him, point-blank: "Come on, Jack! Go, Jack!" The image of a rampaging Nicklaus came into Spaniard's mind. It did not occur to him that the man might be shouting in support of Jack Newton.

"The shout was like a knife in the heart for me," Ballesteros recalls. "I looked at the man and made a big expression in my eyes. The crowd, the referee – and now this guy. I didn't know whether people were against me or not, but that was how I felt and, let me tell you, it helped. I am like Gary Player. The more the crowd is against me, the more I want to prove something."

Ballesteros's shot needed shaping and with a six-iron he shaped it perfectly round a tree, over a greenside mound and into the green, 25 feet past the flag. It was a glorious stroke, one that Newton later said won the Spaniard the Masters. Ballesteros nearly ran in the putt for a birdie, but settled happily for a par. It left him three ahead of Newton and, as news drifted back, also three ahead of Gilbert, who had just birdied the 15th hole.

Augusta's 15th, par five or 520 yards, travels over a lumpy fairway which, just beyond the driving area, falls away to a pond in front of a sloping, elevated green. It is a fine, frightening hole, the frequent scene of competitors, trouser-leg rolled, knee-deep in water. The tee itself presents a view of half of Georgia.

Ballesteros smashed a 310-yard drive to the perfect position, the right-centre of the fairway. "Give me a birdie and we can take it home," said his caddie. The Spaniard selected a four-iron, an ambitious club with water just short of the green, and gave the ball a might lash. He hit it fat, as he had so calamitously done on the 13th fairway. Herrington muttered, "Good shot, sir," which sounded strange to the Spaniard.

Herrington was right. It was a good shot, settling softly down on the green, inside Newton's ball, and some 20 feet from the pin. As Ballesteros reached the green he lifted his hand to the applause and glanced at the scoreboard. Herrington, he thought, wasn't right this time: a birdie here might not take home the title. Gilbert had birdied the 16th to draw within two shots of the Spaniard.

Newton putted first. His stroke, on Ballesteros's line, sped eight feet past the hole. It not only showed the Spaniard the way, it also showed the green to be dangerously fast. Accordingly, Ballesteros played a cosy tap. Even so the ball limped on and on, four feet past the hole.

Newton, playing first, missed his return putt. Ballesteros put his down. A birdie against Newton's par, lifted him four clear of the Australian, three of Gilbert. *Give me a three-stroke lead with three holes to play,* he remembered saying on the eve of the tournament, *and I'll win the Masters.*

All that now stood between him and the title, the Spaniard felt, was the 16th, where water stretches nearly the whole way from tee to green. For safety, he drilled a firm six-iron past the pin. Then he gently tapped the first putt, holed the second. "It's finished," he said, turning to his caddie. "The tournament is ours."

It was. Ballesteros, keeping an eye on the scoreboard, cruised safely into port. He scored two solid pars on the home holes, to finish with 72 for the day and 275 for the tournament, three under Watson's forecast. At 23 years and four days, Ballesteros was the youngest Master of them all.

MEN CALL IT FATE

O.B. Keeler

This is written the Sunday morning after the conclusion of the 1930 British Amateur Championship at St Andrews with a happy sort of night journey in between – those British had a luxurious special train at the St Andrews station waiting for those in a hurry to get to London, and with a large party of Americans aboard, it was not unlike a football train home after your side has won.

Bobby Jones had won the British Amateur Championship at long last. I think he was happier over this victory than any other since he broke through with a major triumph in the US Open Championship in Inwood in 1923. I talked with him after he had been rescued by a squad of big Scottish policemen from about 15,000 admirers at the 12th green, who apparently had determined to take the new champion apart to see what made him tick, and brought back to the hotel. There was a band at the home green to play him in but the band got involved in the crowd and never sounded a note.

Bobby said, "There has been nothing in golf I wanted so much. I can't believe it really happened."

But when word came that they were ready to present the cup, Bobby apparently convinced that he was not dreaming, brushed his tousled hair hastily and went out to face the huge gallery for the last time – out to the same small veranda where he stood in 1927 to receive the Open Championship trophy.

The story of the 1930 British Championship seems to me to confirm, or at any rate, strongly support a sort of hypothesis that had been forming in the back of my head for years – that golf tournaments are matters of destiny, and that the result is all in the book before a shot is hit. Looking back over Bobby's eight matches, you may see crisis after crisis in those furious encounters with Tolley, Johnson and Voigt where the least slip in nerve or skill or plain fortune would have brought defeat to Bobby's dearest ambition. Yet at every crisis he stood up to the shot with something I can define only as inevitability and performed what was needed with all the certainty of a natural phenomenon.

"The stars are with Bobby in this tournament," said a man with whom I was walking. "His luck is as fixed as the orbit of a planet. He cannot be beaten here."

It sounds absurd to say this but it is the gospel that at the very moment my companion made this remark Bobby in the semi-final round was one down to George Voigt, in the last of the 18-hole matches, and had just blown a four-foot putt at the 15th green which would have squared the match. From the 16th tee, George's drive went into the bunker, known as the "Principal's Nose", and the match was squared. On the most treacherous hole on the course, the famous Road Hole, George's ball was stone dead for a birdie four, and Bobby with an iron second none too good had a putt of four yards for a half. All I could think of was that it was the same length and with much the same borrow as the historic 12 foot putt he had holed at Winged Foot the year before to tie for the US Open. The stroke and the result were also a fair replica; the ball rolled easily to the front of the cup and fell in.

Bobby had something rather curious to say about the putt too.

"When I stood up to it, I had the feeling that something had been taking care of me through two matches that I very well might have lost, and that it was still taking care of me. I knew that however I struck that putt, it was going down."

There was another putt earlier in the week that meant an incalculable saving to Bobby. On Thursday afternoon, he came to the home green with the US Amateur Champion, Harrison "Jimmie" Johnston, one up on the heels of the most spectacular rally of the tournament. Bobby, going along in his accustomed mode, gradually had put the gallant Jimmie under, and as they left the 13th green, Bobby was 4 up with 5 to play. The gallery began to drift away in search of more excitement. The few thousand who remained got the excitement.

Jimmie took back the long 14th with a birdie four, smacking a long iron dead. Bobby threw away the 15th, finally missing a four-foot putt for a half. He got a half at the 16th and was dormie 2. Jones very properly played the Road Hole for a par, leaving the burden for Jimmie, who shouldered it handsomely by producing a magnificent birdie and a win. At this stage I recalled very vividly a match Jimmie had played in the Western Amateur Championship in which he was 5 down and 6 to play and had won the next six holes and the match. One glance at Johnston showed he was in precisely such a humour now. Another slip by Jones, another birdie by Jimmie, and the US Open Champion would be out in the sixth round. If Johnston squared the match on the home green, it was certain he would win the extra holes.

The strain was working on both the players. Jimmie's pitch to the 18th ran and ran to the upper left hand corner of the green, a good 30 yards from the flag. Here was a great chance for Bobby, who needed only a half, but he needed it about as much as he had ever needed anything in his life. But he too was wavering and his pitch was almost a duplicate of Johnston's, going to the same distant corner, perhaps two yards nearer the pin. Now it was up to the putting.

Jimmie putted first, a good one, 30 inches from the cup. Bobby's estimate of range and grade for once was faulty, or his deadly touch for once was gone. The ball, apparently on a good line, died eight feet from the pin. There remained a downhill, sidehill putt, but with the same inflexible certainty that marked the other crises of the week, the putt went down. Bobby said it was the longest eight-foot putt he had ever seen, and Jimmie's the most remarkable rally.

"I gave him one hole," he said, "but remember he took the others."

No more fitting combat was ever arranged than that in the fourth round between Jones and Cyril Tolley; the British Amateur Champion defending his title and the US Open Champion, attacking with all his skill and courage and determination. What an utterly amazing battle it was – these two fine sportsmen probably were the greatest exemplars the game has ever seen of the casual demeanour in competition. Neither Jones nor Tolley condescended to reveal by the slightest trace or symptom of eagerness his intense desire and his concentrated will to win. In this attitude I should say that Tolley was even more casual than Jones for Bobby could not by any trick or superior power of the will keep his face from growing grey under the furious strain nor his eyes from sinking deeper into his head. But not in one gesture or in one pose or in one hurried or wilfully delayed shot did he betray the terrific strain under which he played and finished and pulled out a match that was squared six times. Never more than a single hole separated the combatants, so that at times one might have guessed them not to be contestants in a desperate, living and undecided sporting event, but rather actors going through well rehearsed roles in some tremendous drama.

Only once did Bobby take more than his usual swift deliberation on a shot – his second on the diabolical Road Hole, where they were square for the sixth time, and Tolley slightly ahead on his drive, left Bobby to guess first on the ominous problem of the shot to the long, narrow green with the horrid road along the other side. A bold shot for the pin ran a risk of catching the deep pot bunker in line with the pin, or going over the green into the road. Bobby stood there for a long half minute pondering. Then he motioned the stewards to move the gallery back from the rear of the green, well to the left of the bunker, I was standing with Dr Alistair McKenzie, the famous golf architect. He shook his head.

"It's a very bold conception," he said. "It will take some clever playing."

The gallery at this time numbered around 12,000, and the stewards could not get them very far back of the green. There may have been a shade of destiny in this. Bobby hit a truly great iron shot, aimed to pitch deep in the swale and run up to the back of the green. The ball hit just where he intended it to hit, but it went up on the big bound into the gallery Jones had asked to be moved back. It might have been down below the 18th tee, it might even have been in the road. "Men call it Fate."

Anyway, and uncompromisingly, it was a break in luck. The pressure on Tolley was vastly increased and when the big fellow's iron was short of that wicked bunker, I could see nothing but a win for Jones. I felt that no man living could execute so deft a pitch as would clear the bunker and stop anywhere near the hole, cut in that absurdly narrow plateau green.

See how a golfing situation can change. Jones's simple little approach was eight feet short. Tolley, pitching with the most exquisite delicacy stopped his ball within two feet of the flag, the finest shot he ever made, he assured me afterwards. One minute, Jones had the hole and inferentially the match in his hand; in another minute he was putting for his life, a perilous eight-foot putt with his adversary comfortably and convincingly established for a half. Here was another crisis but again the putt went down.

Two drives close to 340 yards on the 18th, two chips, neither too good, and a half in par. Close play by the US Champion at the 19th;

loose play by the British Champion, whose pitch was far outside and whose approach left him open for the stymie which ensued; and the great bout was ended.

But these three hard earned victories were not the only close calls that Bobby had during the week. The trouble with the British Amateur Championship is there are so many golfers in it whose names are not in the stud book. In his first match with Sidney Roper, an ex-coal miner, Bobby started 3–4–3–2–4 against Roper's par of 4–4–4–4–5, and was three up, and that is the way the match ended, 3–2. Bobby was never able to increase this margin by a single hole. I have seen Bobby hot before but I had never seen anybody stand the blast and show no signs of folding up as Roper did. Bobby said he had been told that Roper would shoot steady fives at him. He shot 15 fours and one five.

Sid Roper learned his golf on the public course at Bulwell Forest a few miles from Nottingham, where Robin Hood used to operate on opulent travellers and remove purses from them. I told Bobby this.

"He darned near removed me from this tournament," was the rejoinder.

The biggest first-round gallery I ever saw witnessed the shot the US champion confessed was the best he ever produced – the 120-yard pitch from a bunker into the hole for a deuce at the 427-yard 4th hole. Bobby's drive went into the Cottage Bunker, around 300 yards from the tee, never laid down to catch drives. I was standing at the back of the green as he waded down into the bunker. The ball lay perfectly clear on the wind-blown sand. Up came a feather of sand instead of a divot. The ball, obviously struck as if from turf, came on in rather a steep pitch, hit in front of the big green; the spin took hold promptly and the ball rolled slower and slower and dropped in softly without touching the flag stick.

"They ought to burn him at the stake. He's a witch," said one man in the gallery.

Another said, "I came 8,500 miles to see this tournament, and that shot is worth the trip."

That shot will stand up like Washington's monument at St Andrews, where Scotsmen know and love golf. Generations unborn will hear about it with Caledonian unction.

Despite Bobby's success in working through seven 18-hole matches, he still did not like the short route. It was curious to see with what a different attitude he attacked the longer problem. Where he had mixed superbly brilliant golf with decidedly blue splotches in these short-route engagements, he set about the 36-hole final round with Roger Wethered, a former British Amateur Champion, in the workmanlike manner that characterised his best medal-play performances.

He went the 30 holes of the match two under fours. Roger played bravely but was not able to endure the pressure exerted by the great medalist over the long route.

After observing Mr Jones in 25 national championships, never had I seen him steal a show with such amazing spectacularity. Every day he in some way managed to produce the Big Feature of the day. He was a long time winning the British Amateur, but when he did, he extracted every sensation, every emotion the great drama had to offer.

A BRAW BRAWL FOR TOM AND JACK

Dan Jenkins

Go ahead and mark it as the end of an era in professional golf if you're absolutely sure that Jack Nicklaus has been yipped into the sunset years of his career by the steel and nerve and immense talent of Tom Watson.

You could argue that way now, in these hours after Tom Watson has become the new king of the sport in a kingly land; when Watson has already become the Player of the Year, not to mention the future; when he has done it in the most memorable way in the annals of golf; and when he has done it for the second time in this season to the greatest player who ever wore a slipover shirt – Jack Nicklaus.

You could also say it very simply with numbers. In the last two rounds of last week's British Open, Tom Watson shot 65 and 65 to beat Nicklaus by one stroke. Oh, by the way, they were playing together. Oh yes, and another thing: Watson's 72-hole total was 268, which was a new record by only eight shots. And, incidentally, the victory gave Watson his second major title of the year (and the third of his fresh and exciting career); he had taken the Masters, of course, standing up to Nicklaus in a slightly different type of pressurised situation. And, let's see, the British Open gave the handsome young Watson his sixth win of the year and some $300,000 in tour earnings.

But all of that doesn't even begin to examine what the stakes were on the gorgeous links of Turnberry on Scotland's west coast in the most atmospheric, ancient and some would argue, most treasured of golf's four major tournaments. Actually, what took place was the most colossal head-to-head shotmaking and low scoring in the history of golf.

Tom Watson and Jack Nicklaus started to lap the field on Friday, when their identical rounds of 68–70–65 had given them a three-stroke bulge on the nearest pursuers. But just when everyone was ready to concede that Friday's duel had outspectaculared anything ever witnessed from the days of the gutta-percha ball to those of the Apex shaft, Tom and Jack went out and did it all over again in Saturday's final round, spinning out the overwhelming and unbelievable drama and suspense to the very last delicate rap of Watson's putter on a two-foot birdie putt, which gave him a second consecutive 65 to Nicklaus's shabby, horrid and humiliating 66.

On each of the last two days, Watson came back from what looked to be certain doom to catch Nicklaus and finally do him in. Watson just would not go away, not in the face of Nicklaus's birdies, or his icy stare or his mighty reputation. When Watson was two strokes behind in the third round, he fought back to tie Jack, and in so doing broke the Nicklaus rhythm and the tempo of his short putts. Then on Saturday Watson came back again twice, once from three strokes down tie, and again from two back, finishing the round with four blazing birdies over the last six holes.

Watson was in fact two shots behind the premier player of the game with those six holes left. Who can give Nicklaus two shots over six holes and beat him by one? Who could even contemplate it? Only Tom Watson in this day and time, a Tom Watson who has the best complete game in golf and has been showing that he has it all year. A Tom Watson who has the most reliable, solid swing around, who has the well-educated patience to hold himself in control, the strength and vigour of youth, and now the confidence and determination to make himself worthy of the No.1 role he has seized.

Here's how it was at the most torturous time of all, out there at the par-three 15th hole in the last round after Watson had just stabbed Nicklaus through the front of his yellow sweater with a 60-foot birdie putt from the hardpan 10 feet off the green. That astonishing shot hit the flagstick and dived into the cup and brought Watson into a tie once more.

They went to the 16th tee and Jack and Tom looked at each other. The blond and the redhead. Yesterday and today. Then and now. Dominguin and Ordóñez.

And Tom smiled at Jack. "This is what it's all about, isn't it?"

And Jack smiled back and said, "You bet it is."

They parred the 16th, and so it came down to the last two holes, as most knowledgeable people had been thinking it would. The 500-yard 17th was a pushover par-five, an "eagle hole", surely a birdie hole. The 18th was a bothersome par-four. Anything could happen.

But now it was time for the grand final shot out of Watson's bag that would unglue Jack and make him commit the tiny but killing error that would be the difference. Tom absolutely stung a perfect three-iron right over the flag and onto the green at the 17th, where he would be putting for an eagle from only 20 feet – a sure birdie, in other words.

This had long since been match-play, and the pressure was now on Nicklaus. What Watson's shot did, coming in the wake of so many others that had been hounding Jack, was bother Nicklaus just enough to make him press a sloppy four-iron that not only missed the green but also left him with an evil chip shot. Maybe only a fighter like Jack could have got that chip as close as he did, within four feet of the hole. But the mortal damage had been done.

Watson had a cinch birdie and Nicklaus had just a working chance at one. Only the day before, shots by Watson had forced Jack to miss a couple of short putts of the kind that he has never blown before but will now find himself fearing more frequently. Nicklaus missed that four-foot putt and for the first time all week Watson was alone in the lead.

When they went to the 18th, Watson struck a crisp one-iron off the tee into perfect position and then nailed a seven-iron that struck into the flat like an arrow in the ribs of the bear. A sure birdie.

It was marvellous showbiz that Nicklaus recovered from a desperate and awkward drive to reach the green in two and then sink a 40-foot birdie of his own. Fine curtain call and all that, but the putt was pure luck, the kind that only drops when you need it the least on the final hole of a major championship. Jack knew Tom had already won it, just as he probably had a deeper feeling of impending tragedy on all those earlier holes when he was unable to lose Tom. And Watson ended the drama by tapping in from two feet out.

After Watson said all of the nice things about how hard it is to keep concentrating and trying not to make any mistakes against a Jack Nicklaus, it was time for a more telling reaction. In a certain amount of privacy, Jack shook his head and said, "I just couldn't shake him."

With that, Nicklaus looked off in thought with something of the expression of an aging gunfighter. He did not say he had been expecting *someone* to come along one of these years. But the look seemed to indicate that he had finally met him.

It might be well to speak of where this all took place. For years, golfing enthusiasts from various continents had wondered if the British Open could be played at Turnberry, certainly the most scenic of Britain's links courses, and they had wished the Royal and Ancient would attempt it. Many an official within the R and A itself had wished it. But Turnberry presented serious problems as a championship site. No town, no roads, no hotels, among other things.

Turnberry, when it was not functioning as an air base during world wars, consisted of one massive hotel up on the hill overlooking the RAF runways, the Firth of Clyde, in which fishermen still hook onto crashed Hudson bombers, the island bird sanctuary known as Ailsa Craig, and the gleaming lighthouse out on the point, which had long since become Turnberry club's logo.

All the objections to Turnberry as a site might have been valid before the British Open had regained its reputation as one of the Big Four in golf, before the Arnold Palmers and Jack Nicklauses had turned it into something other than a rickety event in which Peter Thomson beat half a dozen guys from Stoke Poges. The people would come streaming in to see it nowadays, no matter what the R and A figured. And how right it was.

Each day the great grandstands scattered over the dunes were filled by 10 am and thousands more were tromping through the whin and heather as if a Mark Hayes wearing his Amana hat or a John Schroeder were real people. They stormed the tented village, as it is called, that hodgepodge of commercial exhibitions featuring everything from shooting sticks to pork pies to cashmeres at discount. Only in this championship among the Grand Slam tournaments can the spectator see players from as many as 27 different countries. Leap over a burn in the British Open and you can go from a Severiano Ballesteros waist-deep in non-Spanish flora to a Baldovino Dassu neck-deep in non-Italian fauna.

To the British, the charm of Turnberry's links lay in the fact that its holes are closer to the sea than those of any of their Open courses. At a Carnoustie, Muirfield, Birkdale, or Lytham, for example, you can't even catch a glimpse of the water from a tee or green. You can see it at St Andrews, but there is no way to strike a ball into watery oblivion without a hydroplane. Ah, but Turnberry. The water is always there, furnishing a series of backdrops, washing up against a competitor's concentration.

The best of Turnberry is bound up in its golf, and, delightedly, the rest of the world learned about that last week. Although it got caught in a warm calm that produced the lowest scoring in the 106-year-old championship's elegant history, Turnberry earned its way into the R and A's Open rota both with the record crowds it drew and the breathtaking action it provided, and not just from Tom and Jack.

It has never been any secret that if you could catch one of the famous old courses in England or Scotland in a dead calm, you could scorch it. Unlike American layouts, wind is 50 per cent of the danger, as much a part of linksland golf as a pot bunker or gnarled heather. The necessity of wind to British golf is why the Open has always been staged on courses by the sea – to ensure the sternest test. But throughout the four rounds there was no wind at Turnberry.

And so with hundreds of spectators wearing no shirts at all instead of the customary Open garb of topcoats and rain gear, and with the course looking more like a Farrah Fawcett-Majors than a Lotte Lenya, the players leaped at it with glee and daring. The result was a raft of scores that would have sent old Tom Morris staggering dizzily toward a barrel of ale. It was so easy that a couple of American tour regulars, John Schroeder and then Roger Maltbie, led the first and second rounds. Schroeder with a 66 on Wednesday and then Maltbie with 71–66–137. These were Americans who would have looked more at home at the Quad Cities tournament. It was their first time over, even though Maltbie's mother is Scottish and his dad had been a flyer stationed in Scotland during the big one. The British considered them unknowns, unaware of Maltbie's three victories on the US tour.

It was in Thursday's second round that Turnberry began to take some real lumps. Hubert Green came very close to going around in a figure as weird as a California licence plate. He went seven under par through the first 13 holes. Then mistakes got him when, as he later admitted, "a 59 crossed my mind". He settled for 66. At more or less the same time, however, Mark Hayes was out there shoving Turnberry inside an Amana refrigerator. Hayes plays golf in hiding, pulling a brimmed hat down over his shy, almost terrifying modest, expressions, and although he is a superb golfer who makes his own clubs in Edmond, Oklahoma, and is one of the new wave of young stars, words flow from his lips every other eon. With a cross-handed putting style he was trying out for only the second time in competition, he flattened Turnberry with a 63.

It was the lowest single round – by two strokes – ever shot in the world's oldest major championship. Back in 1934 a golf ball had been hurried into production after Henry Cotton's 65 at Sandwich – the Dunlop 65, of course. And now Hayes had shot 63 and everyone was goofy over it. Except Mark Hayes. He was another American in the British Open for the first time and he didn't know about the record, which would have been even lower if he hadn't started thinking cross-handed and chosen the wrong clubs on the 18th hole and finished with a bogey. Surrounded by a mere 900 million members of the Press, then, Mark Hayes was asked what his reaction was to his monumental feat. He sat there. He looked down. He thought. Finally, he said, "I have a lot of trouble figuring out the distances over here."

That was it. The *Eagle* has landed. If I have but one life to give. Give me liberty or give me. Lafayette, we are somewhere. And so forth. Mark Hayes has shattered Britain with a 63 and Amana had not sent a poet with him to Turnberry.

All of this ushered the Open into Friday and Saturday and what were to become two of the grandest, most thrilling and astonishing days that the sport has ever known. As single days in competitive golf went, Friday 8 July and Saturday 9 July 1977 had to rate right up there with such other landmarks as the last round of the 1975 Masters, when Nicklaus outlasted Tom Weiskopf and Johnny Miller; with the final day of the British Open in 1972, when Lee Trevino cut the heart out of Nicklaus. Nicklaus's shot at the Slam, and Tony Jacklin; and certainly with the last 18 holes of the 1960 US Open at Cherry Hills when Arnold Palmer left wounded soldiers all around Denver.

History will most likely see it as better than any of those. Better than any golf – ever. The display that Tom Watson and Jack Nicklaus put on at Turnberry over those last excruciating, compelling, agonising and interminable 36 holes can only be summed up by quoting from that old RAF monument sitting out there on Turnberry's back nine.

Somewhere on the granite it says, "Their name liveth forever more." Well, if theirs doesn't, there's not a kidney left in a pie in Ayrshire.

NICKLAUS GOES FOR BROKE

Al Barkow

At Muirfield the plan was to leave his great mace, his driver, in the bag, use it only sparingly. He would not need it much. The fairways were fast-running, and the ball would roll substantially after landing. And old Muirfield has so many ageless, unplaned little knobs poking up to freckle its surface that no one can be sure which way a ball will bounce off them, especially with the harder-hit driver. So Nicklaus would use his one- or two-iron, or three-wood, to get a softer descent and to keep the ball out of the long grass. He could afford the loss of distance. He was using the smaller British ball, and with any ball could hit those shorter clubs as far as most men hit their drivers. Muirfield was a lady to be not assaulted but caressed.

Thus he played for the first three days – restrained, conservative petting. It was taking much of the buff of the polish of promise that had begun the week, but that was Nicklaus's way. He won with massive, relentless, all-front sweeps, not the commando raids of Arnold. Yet this time the plan was not working. That is, it was and it wasn't; Jack was only one shot behind the lead after 36 holes, but his plan had been devised for windy weather, not without a century of good reason, and it was calm – calm and warm. Almost as if he believed reality would conform to his plan, on the second day of play he had overdressed and had to shed a woollen turtleneck sweater.

Muirfield was not co-operating, and neither were some of the golfers, two of whom approached old Muirfield as though she were a young harlot with her pants down. In the third round, Lee Trevino and Tony Jacklin shot 66 and 67 respectively. A "piece of cake", Jack said of the course, but he stuck to his diet and had a third-day 71. With one round to go, he was six shots behind Lee, five behind Tony, both formidable champions themselves. Would Jack scrap the plan he had so doggedly held to? He would have to, wouldn't he?

On the 1st hole of the last round came the answer. The 1st hole at Muirfield is possibly the toughest on the course, a long par-four played through a narrow alleyway slinking between mother's grabby arms. Jack had been using his one-iron from the tee, but now, with his back to the wall, he pulled his bludgeon driver from his bag. When he took the cover from its head, it was the dragon slayer unsheathing his mightiest sword. A bright metallic click in the open air of Scotland and the ball was away – long, long. Gone was the little controlled fade. The ball had the more natural draw at the end of its trajectory. The night before, Nicklaus had told friends, "What the hell. I'm going for broke. I either shoot 82 or 62." The game was on.

He parred the 1st, playing a short-iron second shot. At the next, a short par-four where he had also been playing his iron from the tee and using an eight-iron for his approach, he again bared his driver. With it he mauled the ball to within 30 of his own steps from the green. He had little more than a long chip shot left, and he played it well – to within

10 feet. He birdied. At the 3rd, again going to his big stick where he hadn't before, he nearly drove the green. Another birdie. He was now into what was to be one of the most absorbing, impassioned 11 holes of golf this writer and many other had ever witnessed.

With every shot Nicklaus played, both the jaded and the initiates to golf were burbling more and more with excitement and running after the big blond, who himself had begun to exhibit the current he was generating. For a big man, Nicklaus has a short stride, making him appear to be walking faster than he really is. But now the step did have more ginger, and he was difficult to keep up with. Always a courteous golfer, at one point Nicklaus showed some impatience at having to wait for his playing partner to hit a shot. Perhaps it was more surprise. It seemed he didn't realise that in fact there was another person playing golf with him. The fellow was Guy Hunt, a little-known English professional, and to his credit he played fine if unnoticed golf in the eye of the tornado.

No one could keep up with Jack's storm of birdies, either, and as he completed the 9th hole with another birdie, his fourth of the day, and dashed to his rooms in the Greywalls Hotel just behind the 10th tee to have his daily mid-round "relief stop", he had drawn into a tie with Jacklin and Trevino. "Bloody marvellous!" "Keep it up, Jacko, I got me a fiver on you, mate!" were some of the cries from the gallery.

A fine, low-running six-iron approach at the 10th set up another birdie, which he got, and a big smile came over his face. Coming from six back, he had the lead, was five under par going for the moon. At 11 Jack pitched his second shot to within six feet of the cup. Another birdie coming up. Hot damn, he may get his 62. There was a palpable silence around the green as Nicklaus prepared to putt. He stood over the ball stock still, a block of heavy concentration. But an instant before he would take the club back, with the timing of a desperate hustler there came a tremendous roar from afar. Not too far. The 9th hole, to be exact. Trevino and Jacklin were paired together and on that hole at the time. One of them had just done something big. It was more than a birdie. The roar had a deeper resonance, was more sustained. The scream of an eagle. The 9th is a par-five reachable in two, and eagleable. We learned soon after that Trevino had indeed chipped in . . . for a three, an eagle. Nicklaus stepped away from his ball, reprepared himself.

All quiet again, and Jack was once more just ready to stroke his putt when yet another howl came from the 9th green, this with an even greater, throatier gusto since it was for the British hero, Jacklin, who holed a long putt for his own eagle. No one knew better than Nicklaus what had transpired two holes away. Jack knows the scream of an eagle. Again he stepped away from his ball, this time shaking his head. He half smiled and said, "Geez". Those who heard the remark could not help but smile. The man wasn't all computerised birdie-maker after all.

But back to business. That little putt. He would need it now to hold a tie with Trevino. After those two interruptions, did the putt get a few feet longer, the hole smaller? We would now see the stuff of which Nicklaus was made. Steel. He again set himself, deliberately. He eased the putter back as only Nicklaus seems able when under pressure – slowly. He eased the blade through, and the ball went dead into the hole. The roar at that matched at least one of the preceding.

Then, dimly at first, later more noticeably, we could see that Jack had lost, or had decided to back away from, his aggressive stance. With the lead, he reverted to his conventional form, letting others make the mistakes. He went back to using safe irons from tees. He had birdie chances at 13, 14, and 15, but missed. The putts had not been hit with quite the same authority as before. The thrill was ebbing. At 17, a par-five he could have reached with a three-wood and an iron, he did use his driver. Strange, because here he didn't really need it. And he hooked it badly into deep grass on the slope of a fairway bunker. He played out far short of the green, but hit a fine six-iron to within 12 feet of the hole – a birdie chance. The putt slid by, and as he waited crouched beside the green for Guy Hunt to putt out, Jack's head hung weighted down as if by a stone, his body elastic gone limp.

Still, he was not out of it. Trevino and Jacklin were only one shot ahead of him, although they had the 17th to play and you had to expect at least one of them to birdie the hole. So why not recharge himself for one more big play at 18? It is a strong par-four that Jack had been playing with a one-iron from the tee and another to reach home, which meant it was also a very long hole. He should go for the driver here, I thought, shorten the test as much as possible, and enhance the chance for a birdie by leaving only a short iron to the green.

But no, he didn't. He played a one-iron and a five-iron. All right. The second shot was 35 feet or so from the cup. Not a real birdie chance, but surely he would give it a good run. Again, no. He left the putt short – *short*. He said later that he played a one-iron from the 18th tee because of the percentages. He wasn't that confident with his driver (hadn't used it enough all week), and he played for a sure par on the grounds that the other fellows would still have to play the hole. If neither birdied 17, Nicklaus didn't want to bogey the last hole and lose the tournament should Trevino or Jacklin also bogey it. This is also why he didn't charge the last putt.

A Kantian critique of pure reason – good golf sense, good management. Then Trevino chipped in at 17 to save par, and after seeing that, Jacklin three-putted from inside 20 feet to fall out of contention. Trevino, who grew up in the discomfort of a fatherless, poor home, to whom management meant seeing the piece of cake and taking without hesitation, bashed his driver on 18, stroked an easy 7-iron to the green, and walked away with the title by one stroke over Jack.

When it was over, I could not help feeling that Nicklaus had somehow betrayed the deeper spirit of competition, that on the final hole he might have revived that brief but galvanic 11-hole departure from character and torn head-on into the last hole with all he had. Sure, his great success in golf comes from careful control of his mental and physical powers, but he had shown a flash of daring, a blood-and-guts Nicklaus transported beyond common sense. It had worked, and it was good. But he didn't do it again, and as I drove slowly back to Edinburgh through a Sunday twilight, I felt a selfish disappointment at being deprived of a memorable sporting moment.

BEST SHOT OF MY LIFE

Dave Anderson

In sports, the burden of excellence for the best athletes is that they're expected to win the best championships. If they don't, their skill is suspect. So is their nerve. So is their place in history. And in golf, the United States Open is the best championship, the most difficult to win, the most prestigious.

"If you don't win the Open," says 80-year-old Gene Sarazen, who won it twice, "there's a gap in your record."

Tom Watson has been aware of that gap in his record during his reign as the world's best golfer over the last six years. He has won three British Opens, two Masters and nearly $3 million in prize money on the PGA Tour, but that merely made the Open more important to him than it is to perhaps any other current golfer.

"To be a complete golfer," Tom Watson once said, "you have to win the Open, you just have to."

But now that burden and that gap no longer exist; now he's a "complete golfer". Tom Watson won the Open yesterday over the treacherous Pebble Beach Golf Links with a two-under-par 70 for a 72-hole total of 282 that included one of golf's most memorable shots. From the rough to the left of the green at the 209-yard 17th hole that borders the jagged rocks of the Pacific Ocean shoreline, he chipped his ball 16 feet into the cup for a birdie two only moments after Jack Nicklaus had finished at 284 with a 69.

"That was the best shot of my life," the new Open champion said later. "And winning the Open makes me feel my career is one plateau higher."

Tom Watson now is up there on a plateau with the best golfers in the history of the game. At age 32, he has won six major championships – three British Opens, two Masters and now one United States Open. And in four of those triumphs (the 1977 and 1981 Masters, the 1977 British Open and yesterday's classic confrontation), he conquered Jack Nicklaus, whom most golf historians consider to be the best of this or any time.

"When it got down to Jack and me, I called upon old memories," Tom Watson said later. "And they were pleasant memories. In a small way and a large way, that helped me to win the tournament."

Just as Jack Nicklaus had to suffer as the villain who dethroned Arnold Palmer two decades ago, so Tom Watson has had to struggle for popular acceptance in the shadow of the Golden Bear's record. And yet, in their *mano a mano* duels in major tournaments, Tom Watson has won on all four occasions. When the new Open champion walked off the 18th green yesterday, the four-time Open champion greeted him with a smile.

"You're something else," the Golden Bear said. "That was nice going. I'm proud of you. I'm pleased for you."

In the interview tent, Jack Nicklaus was told that Bill Rogers, who had been paired with the new champion, had suggested that if Tom Watson were to chip 100 balls from that spot in the rough off the 17th green, he would not hole even one ball.

"Try about 1,000 balls," Jack Nicklaus said.

But when Tom Watson was informed of what Bill Rogers had said, the new Open champion smiled.

"Bill didn't see the lie," he said. "I had a good lie."

And when Tom Watson was informed that Jack Nicklaus had mentioned that he couldn't duplicate that shot with 1,000 balls, the new Open champion smiled again.

"Let's go out and do it," he said. "I might make a little more money."

When that chip with a sand-wedge rolled into the cup for a one-stroke lead on Jack Nicklaus that he increased two strokes with a birdie four at the 18th hole, Tom Watson had produced one of the most memorable shots in golf history. That chip shot will be talked about along with Gene Sarazen's double eagle in the 1935 Masters, with Jack Nicklaus's one-iron that clanked off the flag-stick on the 17th at Pebble Beach in the 1972 Open, with Jerry Pate's five-iron to the 18th green at the Atlanta Athletic Club in the 1976 Open.

"That shot," Tom Watson said later, "had more meaning to me than any other shot of my career."

That shot meant that Tom Watson no longer had to answer questions about why he hasn't been able to win the Open, the same question that the now 70-year-old Sam Snead is still asked. Just as Sam Snead is the best golfer never to win the Open Championship, Tom Watson had been the best current golfer not to have won it. But when Tom Watson arrived in the interview tent last night, he had a new question to answer.

"Why," he was asked jokingly, "haven't you ever won the PGA championship?"

"Now it's Arnold Palmer," he replied, laughing, referring to Palmer's inability to win the PGA throughout his illustrious career. "Before it was Sam Snead, now it's Arnold Palmer. But tonight you can ask me all the questions you want about the PGA."

When he shared the 54-hole lead with Bill Rogers Saturday night, Tom Watson had been asked how he would spend the time until he teed off yesterday in the final round. He talked about how he would watch the *Sesame Street* television show with his 2½-year-old daughter Meg.

"We'll count," he said. "but not up to seven or eight."

In golf a seven or eight is disastrous. Through four rounds here, he never had a seven or an eight; he shot as high as six on a hole only twice. And yesterday when he returned to the interview tent, he was asked what he had done in the hours before the final round.

"I watched *Sesame Street* with Meg," he said, grinning. "They only counted up to two."

He was alluding to his two at the 17th hole, the two that was created by the "best shot" of his life, the two that put him "one plateau higher" among all the famous golfers, the two that won the Open for him, the two that will be remembered as long as golf is played.

Tom Watson had produced a memorable shot in a moment of crisis in a dramatic duel with the best other golfer of his time in the world's most important golf tournament. That's winning the way a champion is supposed to win, a champion now without a burden, a champion now without a gap in his record.

BRILLIANCE HAS ITS REWARD

Derek Lawrenson

Monday 18 July, 1988. There should not be a golfer alive who does not have that date etched on his heart, the day when Severiano Ballesteros delivered unto us THE ROUND. A performance over 18 holes at Royal Lytham and St Annes that was so special, so sublime, it deserves its own place in Open lore, an inch above every other great round that anyone else has ever played in the 117-year history of the world's most important golf event.

Monday finishes to Major Championships are traditionally tepid affairs. Monday is the day when everyone is usually cleaning up and nobody turns up. Everyone is a little mad because flight arrangements have to be cancelled, with work plans thrown into disarray. This was one Monday when all the inconvenience in the world found its consummate reward. Observing the Lytham plaque commemorating a shot played by Bobby Jones in the 1926 Open, the gifted American writer Dan Jenkins wrote: "It would not be possible to commemorate Seve's 65 with plaques, for it would render the course unplayable."

There have been lower rounds than Ballesteros's 65 on that day. There have been rounds where more putts have been holed, more accurate iron shots played, more fairways hit from the tee. But no-one has played so well in the context that Ballesteros played so well that day. And great rounds are all about context. Lots of golfers can shoot 63 in the first round of the Mundane Open. But who shoots the joint-lowest final round in Open history, the lowest round of the week by no less than two shots, to walk off with the glittering prize? Severiano Ballesteros did, and the most naturally talented golfer of his generation described it thus: "It was the best round I have played in my life so far. Perhaps once every 25, or maybe even 50 years, a man plays that well." Ballesteros knew instantly what he had done, and time will only enhance the achievement.

But behind every great sporting deed, there is another who deserves credit, because no one ever pushed back the barriers of human excellence without another egging him on, testing him to the limit. In Ballesteros's case, that man was Nick Price.

Price had begun that momentous day with a two-stroke lead and said to his caddie, Dave McNeilly: "If we just shoot 69 today we can forget the rest." He had thrown away The Open at Troon six years previously. This time he showed what he had learnt. He did indeed shoot 69. Indeed, he would have shot 68 but for charging his putt at the last in a desperate attempt to achieve parity, and missing the return. But even a 68 would not have been good enough. Price, the leader on day four, could therefore have shot a score lower than anyone else had achieved on the first three days and up to that point in the final round, and still have lost. It needed a good player playing as well as he could to bring out the great in Severiano Ballesteros.

But there is another context in which the Spaniard's round has to be placed. Silly as it seems now, there were many who believed that Ballesteros would never win another major championship. Even Seve had his doubts. Ever since Augusta in 1986 when he hit his second shot to the 15th in the final round into water to lose that Masters, he had lost the quality of total self-belief that ultimately had taken him to the top.

"When I lost in a play-off the following year, I began to wonder whether my time . . .' Ballesteros never completed the sentence. It was as if he could not believe the heresy he was speaking. Yet it was true. Ballesteros thought he had lost the winning formula. The smooth putting stroke went, the flashing smile with it. We got the brooding Spaniard. The señor had lost his nerve.

Before Lytham, Ballesteros watched videos of himself from 1979. He watched videos of himself in 1988. He saw what everyone else had noticed. The scowl had replaced the smile. Ballesteros took a vow, to relax, to fall back in love with golf.

This latter facet is easier said than done, of course, but this is how Ballesteros approached Lytham in 1988. It helped that he began The Championship with three straight birdies. At one point he was five strokes ahead of everyone else, and threatening to build an insurmountable lead.

But at the start of the final round, the outcome was far from certain. There was Price and Ballesteros, there was Nick Faldo and Sandy Lyle. The chances then were high that, given a leaderboard of such quality, someone would produce something special and in the end it was the most gifted player of them all performing as only he can.

Faldo and Lyle have brought us all unbounded pleasure over the last two years, but on this day they played bit-parts. Faldo had shot 18 pars on the final day the previous year and won. This time he shot a level-par round and finished six shots adrift. Third place, however, represented a worthy defence of his title. Lyle slipped to a 74 to finish seventh.

So it was Price and Ballesteros, and from the 7th hole onwards it was a match-play duel to rival that played out by Jack Nicklaus and Tom Watson at Turnberry in 1977. Both had birdied the par-five 6th, and at the next, another long hole, Price hit a majestic three-iron second shot to within six feet of the cup. Ballesteros did similarly with a five-iron. It was to be like that from then on. Whatever Price did, he found Ballesteros did so as well. Both holed for eagle threes.

Ballesteros then picked up his fourth shot in three holes with a birdie at the 8th and now the pair were level. Seve parred the 9th to be out in 31, and Price, without hardly doing anything wrong and a great deal right, had seen his lead disappear. But he took strength from the fact that he was playing well, and he kept on playing well. He birdied the 10th. So did Ballesteros.

Then Ballesteros birdied the 11th as well to be six-under. He was ahead for the first time. Then he was not. He bogeyed the 12th. Even gods have their off-moments. Moment was the operative word. Both players birdied the 13th. Price's second shot finishing no more than inches from the hole.

Remarkably, the two most miraculous shots of the whole day were still to come. When Ballesteros won at Lytham in 1979 he had done so after driving way right into an area being used as a public car park. He got a free drop and went on to make an outrageous birdie. This time he showed what a more complete player he is now. A perfect drive was followed by a near-perfect second, a sand wedge that finished inches from the hole. Another birdie, and he was ahead once more.

Price still would not give in. Both players parred the 17th, and when Ballesteros missed the 18th green, with the Zimbabwean safely on in two, the first five-hole play-off in Open history appeared a distinct possibility.

Ballesteros's ball was sitting down in a heavy collar of rough on the left-hand side of the green. It was not a straightforward shot under any circumstances, and particularly these. Ballesteros had thrown away major championships in the previous two years. Would he do so again?

Some chance. The 15,000 crowd (absenteeism must have been high in Lancashire on that day) held its breath. Ballesteros carefully took his stance, opened the blade of his sand wedge, and played the shot so perfectly that the ball burnt the edge of the hole before finishing inches away.

The Open was his. There was a clenched salute. There were kisses for the crowd. There was a gracious remark for the runner-up, Price.

This was the Ballesteros of old, returned to us once more, with still more tricks from a unique repertoire. How good it felt to have him back.

Chapter 8

IT'S ALL IN THE MIND

GAMUT OF EMOTIONS

Robert Tyre (Bobby) Jones

Golf has been called "the most human of all games" and a "reflection of life". One reason that we enjoy it and that it challenges us is that it enables us to run the entire gamut of human emotions, not only in a brief space of time, but likewise without measurable damage either to ourselves or to others.

Much has been made of the drama of championship golf, and there is no doubt that it can be intense. But within more meagre limits, ordinary everyday golf can provide the same challenge and drama. Even here, we have all the elements of a gripping experience that can be lived through to the fullest and then dismissed at the end of the day.

On the golf course, a man may be the dogged victim of inexorable fate, be struck down by an appalling stroke of tragedy, become the hero of unbelievable melodrama, or the clown in a side-splitting comedy – any of these within a few hours, and all without having to bury a corpse or repair a tangled personality.

BEST FOR IDIOTS

Sir Walter Simpson

The more fatuously vacant the mind is, the better for play. It has been observed that absolute idiots . . . play steadiest. An uphill game does not make them press, nor victory within their grasp render them careless. Alas! we cannot all be idiots. Next to the idiotic, the dull unimaginative mind is the best for golf. In a professional competition I would prefer to back the sallow, dull-eyed fellow with a "quid" in his cheek, rather than any more eager-looking champion. The poetic temperament is the worst for golf. It dreams of brilliant drives, iron shots laid dead, and long putts held, whilst in real golf success waits for him who takes care of the foozles and leaves the fine shots to take care of themselves.

SEAMUS MACDUFF'S
BAFFING SPOON

Michael Murphy

"How'd ye lik' to hit a few wi' Seamus's club?" he said quietly. He walked over to the open space where he had been hitting his shots and held up the shillelagh. "Come," he said, waving me toward him with an abrupt decisive gesture. I looked back at the cliff edge. The face was gone. I peered intently at the place where it had been, then scanned the entire perimeter of the ravine wall. There was no face to be seen.

"It's gone," I said

"Ye see," he answered, "the fire plays tricks there on the rocks. Come hit a few."

I was relieved – and disappointed. I wanted to see the mysterious figure of Seamus MacDuff in the worst way by now.

He handed me the gnarled stick, cradling it on its imaginary cushion as if it were a sceptre. I waggled the stick carefully, gradually lowering it into the arc of my golf swing until I was swinging it with a full sweep. It had amazing balance. "It's incredible how easily it swings," I said. "Did he make it himself?"

"Claims he made it from an old shillelagh." He was watching me with amusement. "Do ye want to hit one now?" Without waiting for an answer he teed up a featherie on the sandy ground. "Now, Michael," he said as he put the ball on a tiny mound of earth, "try to hit it clean without hittin' any rocks. Seamus'll gi' me royal hell if we hurt his baffin' spoon."

I eyed the primitive target and swung. The ball exploded from the club and I looked up to follow its flight. I could not see where it had landed in the dancing shadows.

"Ye missed the taraget," he said with a broad smile, "but ye hit it good. Seamus woulda' been proud o' ye. Heer, hit another one." He teed up the other ball.

I swung and hit it squarely. "Where did it go this time?" I asked, peering into the shadows.

"Ye hit it on the other side o' the taraget this time, but yer swingin' good." He was grinning broadly now. "Ye're the first person I've seen wi' Seamus's club beside maself. Ye make a funny sight."

I held the shillelagh up in the light. "I feel funny holding it. I swear it wants to swing itself."

"Come, let's find the featheries," he said, walking off toward the target. I followed him down to the white circle. It was painted with some kind of whitewash. I could see that it had been painted over many times.

"Has he repainted this?" I asked, pointing to the crusty markings.

"Been usin' it for yeers. It washes off each winter in the rains." He picked up the balls and led me back to our imaginary tee. "Michael, come heer," he said, "I want to show ye somethin'." He had me take my customary golf stance in front of a ball he had put on the ground. "Now, I want ye to try somethin' slightly different this time, will ye do it?" He looked at me hopefully, cocking his head to one side. His large blue eyes caught the flickering firelight. I could see my reflection in them, he was stading so close, a distorted image of my entire body wavering like flame. "Would ye like to try it?" he repeated the question, fixing me with that slightly cross-eyed double-angled look. I could now see two images of myself in the mirror of his eyes, each one slightly different from the other. I nodded that I was willing. "Awright, now," he said quietly, raising a long finger. "When ye swing, put all yer attention on the feelin' o' yer inner body – *yer inner body*." He whispered these last words as if he were telling me a secret.

I looked at the shifting reflections in his eyes. To this day I can vividly remember my reaction. It was as if an immediate split occured in my mind. A part of me instantly knew what he meant; another part began to question and puzzle. I looked at him dumbly, without answering, as the two attitudes formed themselves.

He leaned toward me and took my arms in his hands. "Close yer eyes," he said soothingly. Then he lifted my arms – I was still holding the shillelagh like a golf club – and moved them through the arc of an imaginary swing as a golf professional does with a student, whispering again the words, "feel yer inner body". My questions and puzzlement quieted and I fell into the rhythm of his movements, slowly swinging the club and sensing what he meant. It was like the state I had discovered that afternoon during our round of golf – a growing power, rhythm, and grace, a pleasure that had no apparent cause. Yes – perhaps you have had that sense of it – a body within a body sustained by its own energies and delight. a body with a life of its own waiting to blossom.

"Do ye see what I mean?" he murmured as he swung my arm back and forth. I nodded and he backed away. "Now try to hit the ball tha' way," he said.

I adjusted my stance and waggled the club, focusing my attention on the sense of an inner body. When I swung I topped the ball and it bounced high in the air.

He nodded with approval. "Good, good," he said loudly, "ye stayed right in it, now try another."

I took my stance and swung again. This time the ball flew toward the target but fell short. "Ye did it again. Good!" he said decisively. "Now stay wi' tha' feelin'." We found the balls and repeated the exercise. He seemed oblivious to the results as he studied my attitude and "energy". He claimed that my state of mind was reflected in an aura around me which he could sense. "Yer *energy* was good that time," he would say, or "it wavered on that one." He was as definite about these statements as he was about my physical form.

Our lesson continued for half an hour or more, some twenty or thirty shots, while I practised that indubitable awareness of my "inner body".

The experience went through stages. At first there was a vague yet tangible sense that there was indeed a body closer to me than my skin, with its own weight and shape. It seemed to waver and bounce and subtly change its form, as if it were elastic. Then – I can still remember the feeling so clearly – it changed to an hourglass: my head and feet were enormous and my waist was as small as a fist. This sensation lasted while we looked for the balls and returned to our tee, then it changed again. My body felt enormously tall, I seemed to look down from a point several feet above my head. I told him what I was feeling. "Now come down heer," he said, calmly putting a finger on my breastbone. "Just come down heer." I returned to my ordinary size and shape, and continued swinging.

I was aware that part of my mind had suspended judgement, that many questions were simmering still. But it felt marvellous to swing that way, so absorbed in the pleasure and feel of it. And it was a relief not to worry about the results. I could have gone on for hours.

But he ended the lesson abruptly. "Enough for now," he said, putting a finger on my chest, "rimember the feelin'. Yer inner body is aye waitin' for yer attention." We added some branches to the fire, which had almost died out, and leaned back against a pair of rocks. I glanced up the cliff, but no face was there, just the writhing shadows on the canyon walls. I felt marvellously alive, as if I were floating in some new field of force, but the questions that had been suspended began rising like vapours.

This state I was in was too good to be true, too easily come by, I began to wonder how soon it would fade after Shivas and his colourful admonitions were gone. Anyone would feel good around him, getting so much attention, being led into adventures like these. Dark and true premonitions, I felt an edge of sadness.

TIME TO CHANGE HIS TACTICS

Derek Lawrenson

The Australian winger David Campese said recently that rugby has a habit of kicking you in the guts. In the immediate aftermath of a thrilling 118th Open, it is tempting to consider an addendum: if only golf would treat Greg Norman so leniently.

Golf kicks Norman from pillar to post. In other sports, good fortune tends to measure out equally with bad. The Royal and Ancient game offers three categories: lucky golfers, unlucky golfers, and a stratum below that belonging solely to Norman.

The more pleasure the Queenslander brings, the more it seems he is denied a place in the history books. The more he mocks great golf courses with the majesty of his talent, the more he is denied the ultimate prize. The day they introduced a four-hole play-off to The Open you could guarantee would be the day Norman birdied the first hole of it.

Watching Norman these days is to recall those cartoons where an angel sits on one shoulder stressing good and a devil on the other advocating waywardness.

The angel blesses Norman with the ability to hit the ball miles and earn enough money to rip down a $2 million home and build a $5 million one in its place. The devil's influence means the home has more swimming pools than the trophy cabinet has major championship replicas.

The angel gives him scores like 64 at Royal Troon, and 63 at St Andrews. The devil's say ensures these scores do not add up in the final countdown.

Heaven help us if Norman possessed an intense personality like, say, Nick Faldo. They would probably have led him off to the funny farm long ago.

And yet, and yet . . .

The circle is not quite complete. For while you can argue quite accurately until you are blue in the face that Norman brings pleasure in grotesque disproportion to the majors he has won, the fact remains it would not all have happened to a Faldo.

If Norman could trade an ounce of his aggressive flair for an equal deposit of Faldo's course management qualities, then all the bad luck in the world would not matter. He would now be the proud holder of at least five major titles.

His friends put it another way. Good friends are candid to a point and Norman's are no exception. The Open revealed all.

Ironically, Norman let us in on all this after one of the highspots of his career. He had just broken the course record with a final round of 64. How good was it? Put it this way. Had Mark Calcavecchia not birdied the last, had Wayne Grady dropped one more shot, it would have been the lowest final round ever to win The Open.

Still, that was far from Norman's mind as he basked in the glow of a special performance. He had opened with six straight birdies – surely the best start ever made to a round in The Open – and now he shared his secrets. He had taken the advice of the aforesaid friends. Needless to say, this being Norman, these were no ordinary friends.

Jack Nicklaus had told him to put more brain in his game. Tom Weiskopf had advocated more finesse. Norman talked proudly of how he had followed their advice, and how it had paid off.

Well, for a while anyway. For in the play-off that followed we saw once more the good, the bad and the unlucky Greg Norman. Sheer ability gave him two birdies for starters. Sheer fate decreed these would fall in an extended rather than sudden-death play-off. But it was sheer bad play of the kind that had so alerted Nicklaus and Weiskopf that ultimately cost Norman this title.

Norman failed to heed Weiskopf's advice about finesse at the third play-off hole, the 17th, and Nicklaus's on the subject of the little grey cells at the last.

At the 17th, Norman trundled a straight-forward pitch 10 feet past the hole and missed the putt back. At the 18th he smoked a drive into a fairway bunker 325 yards away. Norman protested that he did not think it in range. He protested too much.

A little more mental activity here would have told him that the bunker was well within range. Certainly Calcavecchia had thought about it. He said: "The first time round I was five yards short of it with a drive that was far from being my career best. And Greg is 15 yards past me every time."

We learned a lot about Norman in The Open week. And the thing we learned most of all is that here is a player who either cannot, or will not, change, and who at 34 is wrapped up in an irreversible image.

It is an image that has brought Norman all the wealth he needs, and friends only too happy to indulge his whim for fast transport.

It is an image that blesses him with one of the more amiable personalities in golf, a sunny disposition that for most palates overrides the occasional excesses of ego.

Most of all it is an image that, when firing on all cylinders, propels Norman to golf of a standard that few players in history, let along today, could hope to match. Not for nothing did Tom Watson describe Norman's 63 at Turnberry in the 1986 Open as "the finest round played in a tournament in which I have been a competitor".

We all know about Norman's image. And in golf terms it is summed up in the title and the first lines of an instructional book he wrote. Called *Shark Attack – Greg Norman's Guide to Aggressive Golf*, it begins: "There are several good ways to swing at a golf ball, but only one good way to play golf – aggressively."

And all this may be enough in life and would be enough for the vast majority of us. But there is a downside to the image. That opening paragraph is a frontline contender for the biggest load of codswallop ever written about the game. Aggression without finesse, without brain, means you drive into bunkers on the final hole of a play-off. It means you try to make a chip for a two, instead of playing for a three, and end up making a four.

"Norman must be hurting inside," Calcavecchia said after his Open win. Sure he hurts. The American described his pitch shot at the 12th on the final day that went in on the fly as a "miracle from God", and Norman witnessed at first hand so many of those in recent years that he could add another Gospel to the Bible.

But maybe someone up there is trying to tell him something. Maybe someone is displeased that a very great talent is not realising its full potential, and that maybe these "miracles from God" are the sport's way of trying to get Norman to see the whole picture, and not just the death and glory one.

Maybe golf, often described as the fairest of sports, is acting fair in the case of Norman after all.

THE INNER CONFLICT

Liz Kahn

By the end of the 1977 golf season Tony was at a low ebb and still thrashing around uncomfortably in a depression, although no one had ever suggested or acknowledged this fact.

When, as a top-level sportsman, you become unable to perform at your particular sport, the chances are that you are either reacting to a low state brought about perhaps by over-exposure, or you may slide into a depression through an accumulation of circumstances that become extremely painful, particularly when you continue to subject yourself week in and week out to the very thing at which you are unable to succeed.

It is possible that you may play yourself out of a depression or low state of mind, and regard it as just being a bad spell. On the other hand, when disaster compounds itself to the extent that you can no longer produce the desired results because the effort has become too great, then it is clear that the pace has proved too fast – the mind and body have reached an exhausted state.

It was not that 1977 was a complete disaster, far from it. In January, Tony was competing on the American Tour and played very well at Tucson, where he was in contention in the last round and finished tied-18th. The following week he raised his game to come second to Tom Watson in the Bing Crosby tournament at Pebble Beach, where he and many others were disappointed not to see him the winner. He took six up the final hole and Watson pipped him to the post by one shot.

Because of his relatively low-key performance over the previous few years, the element of doubt crept in concerning his ability to handle the big occasion and subconsciously Tony allowed himself to be affected. He maintained, however, that his club choice of a one-iron, instead of a driver, off the 18th tee at Pebble Beach in the final round of the Crosby, was one that he would not change given the moment again.

At the end of the season Tony won the English Professionals' Championship, which was dismissed lightly as containing little competition. This is never true since to win a four-round tournament you have to play well as there is always someone in the field who can have a great week or great round and beat you. Nick Job, with a 66 on the last day, nearly did just that. Neither the Press nor Tony put too much store by his win. He was not, he said, enjoying his golf due to his continued putting problems.

So far as Tony was concerned his state of mind all revolved around his putting, since this was the one area in his game over which he had no control and which was causing him so much pain. "I felt like quitting in 1977 – I definitely thought, who needs the aggravation? There's a difference between doing something unpleasant each day or feeling like you were shackling yourself and letting some bastard whip you. I was hurting myself and not just doing something I disliked. It was taking so much out of me, there was no point, it became stupid. I really wasn't playing golf. As soon as I walked on to the tee the shutters came down and I didn't enjoy anything. I was waiting for all the bad things to happen, waiting for the situation where I knew that I would have a putt and get myself worked up into such a state about it that I could't hit it, or at least when I did it would go sideways. I just felt there was no way I could get the putter through. I could always take it away but I couldn't control the path of it coming through – my hands would go. I tried all sorts of positions and the last thing I was thinking about was holing the putt, which should be the first thing to think of instead of my obsession with putting a good stroke on it.

"People were writing to tell me what I could do with my putting but I couldn't do what anyone suggested. Anyway I know more about the golf game than 99.9 per cent of the guys out there, especially the amateurs. I've played with all the great players. I've dissected the game, I know what a strike is, whether my hands are too low, too high, too far back; all about rhythm, timing, weight, and eye over the ball. Christ, I had hundreds of letters and none of it was to the point. What these people didn't understand was the fact that I knew all the time, but it was a question of getting on a green and doing it – because it was between my ears, my mind wouldn't let me do it.

"I've always had the most vivid dreams about golf, and they were not good either. I would hit the ball and it would go into a sink. There I am in a washbasin, and the ball is sitting in the plug-hole. Then I'm in the sink trying to get the club back, but I can't because the sink is too curved. I have to get it out of the plug-hole and finally I wake up in frustration trying to do it.

"In another dream I've putted, and the ball goes under a wardrobe, and there I am flashing about with my putter, trying to get it out from under the wardrobe.

"Then I was playing golf with my Dad, and someone threw a ball from behind a hedge and said, hit this one, it's a good one. The ball was called a "Missileite", and when you hit it, the ball went forever – like a missile.

"On another occasion I was playing with some other guys and hitting off a tee. There were sliding aluminium doors in front of the tee and they were open when the other fellows hit, but when it came to my turn they closed the doors until they were only a foot apart. I had to tee off and I was thinking, shit, I've got to get through that little gap.

"In one dream I had, I couldn't swing the club back because there was a wall behind me, so that I couldn't generate enough clubhead speed to hit the ball.

"Usually I dream during tournaments but never about winning – my dreams all are on the negative side."

"It may sound stupid but I couldn't think through the barrier – it was as though someone had just put a block there. I was terrified every time I stepped up to a putt. The rest of my game was so natural because I never thought about it – only what happened on the putting green. However well I played it meant nothing in relation to my score. It was a fight, an effort, just like an ice wall and there's no way to get over it. That's what I was up against every time I walked on to a green. I got to the point that when I was over a six-inch putt I visualised muffing it, I couldn't knock the ball in smoothly. Every single part of every game was an effort because I had a conflict between a will to want to do it and an almost bigger will not allowing me to do it. It was desperate. I thought putting was the most important thing in the whole world and, honest to God, I wondered if I were sane. I would say to myself why on earth do I want to put myself through this anguish and torment all the time when it seemed that nothing good ever happened. It was just miserable."

Tony's misery over his putting and mental problems finally made him recall a woman, now around 50, whom he had met in South Africa in 1965 and 1966, named Réné Kurunsky. He searched out and found an old letter from Réné with her telephone number in Johannesburg and he picked up the 'phone and dialled it. "A native girl answered and told me she would be back later so I knew she was still there. When I got through again, she said, 'Tony, my Tony, what's up' – just like that after 12 years. I told her I was desperate with my game and she had been the only one who had really helped me when I was playing in South Africa all those years ago and my putting had been terrible. She had told me I was allowing myself to build barriers and worrying too much. She said that if I didn't stay in the present, I would go into a low and worry about the past or future. Réné told me to look at trees, at my feet moving, to make myself aware of the present. It was commonsense and it worked.

Being positive, you are what you think you are, you will win if you set out to win, you can do anything with a firm belief in your ability.

"I've always known I had the ability, although it can stagnate and waste if you misuse it, and now I'd got all the channels blocked. During my depression I had all this ability within me and I wouldn't let it come out. You want to burst and there's no way you can relax enough to allow it to happen, you're so uptight.

"The first thing Réné said to me on the telephone was, what are you trying to do when you get on a green? Trying to make a good stroke I replied, and she said that's bull for a start. You're supposed to get the ball in the hole aren't you? So why don't you try to do that instead of making a good stroke? That was the first indication to me that I'd been barking up the wrong tree, that I'd got myself into such a state and so blind, I never even realised my objectives were wrong."

It just so happens that Réné Kurunsky is a Scientologist. After the telephone call, and after trying a new approach to putting, Tony decided, on her recommendation, that he would spend a few days at the College of Scientology, founded by American Ron Hubbard at East Grinstead, Sussex. In November 1977, he spent about £1,000 for Vivien and himself to go along and be "audited". Impatient by nature, Tony tried to run the sessions, to tell them he hadn't any problems other than his putting. Tony's personality does not allow him to admit to any weakness or chink in his armour, and with such people, self-analysis can prove very painful. But finally the treatment began to work, the concentration and attention accorded him were attractive. "I liked to do an hour's session every day," Tony admits indulgently. Then with more practical sense: "But it's a joke what they charge. I thought it was extortionate, nothing more nor less – it worked out at £25 per hour. But I think they've got something going there, whatever it is.

"I sat in a room with a woman – she doesn't tell you anything, you explain yourself in the end and they ask you questions. It's very clever – actually it's marvellous, it really is. She asked me all sorts of questions about my early life and my parents – all bull – any problems I may have had I accept in that regard. For instance, if I had arguments when I was growing up it didn't bother me, nothing bothered me. I never lay in bed worrying or got frustrated about it. I thought all the questions were leading up to something but they weren't. So I protested and said this is all bull, I'm doing nothing but talking, you're writing all sorts of notes and I'm getting nowhere. I want to get on to the areas where I can benefit and that's on the golf course where my thinking is bad.

"So they sent another woman who asked me what bothered me most, and I replied my putting. She asked what happens, and we went into all that, and even though you're talking to non-golfers it doesn't make any difference. They love their job these women. It's a very interesting job with the mind – to ask the right questions in order to get the answers you want.

"I went into another session with the first woman and she told me to imagine all the things that could happen on a putting green. So I went through a list of about 20 things, like, it could get dark when you walk onto it; the hole could heal up; it could get windy or rain; the grass could turn blue. She kept saying yes, and eventually I said, well you can imagine anything can't you – the ultimate answer. Straight away she says, thank you. And you realise the fact that this is the whole point, you can imagine anything, good, bad or indifferent and I was imagining the worst of everything. When you're as low as I was you forget all about the good side. Then that session finished.

"Next, I was asked what is your problem? Well I can't putt. What part of your problem can't you face? Well I can face any part of it. I know, but what part can't you face? Any part I replied, and again the same question. Then you start delving deeper into your mind and ultimately I said, well I'm negative and she said, thank you.

"You won't admit that to yourself, but having done so it did me a power of good. I came away from there feeling so much more aware of every aspect of everything. Although the woman drove me bananas at times and it pissed me off the hours I spent, I enjoyed it because you use your own mind. What does postulate mean? she said. I'd say, well . . . and then she gave me a dictionary and told me to look it up . . . it means to imagine you can – postulate you are going to win this tournament.

"The belief in Scientology is that we're all a spirit first. Réné always reckons I've got a fantastic spirit which makes me what I am. Your spirit is your soul – a *thetan* – and it goes on, and has gone on forever. It is in your body which will die, and it will go on. There are certain things in your mind you can't fully explain, thinking maybe it's happened before, or deep, deep things that are almost too much to believe they happened in your lifetime. Children, when they say things to you, sometimes have an understanding deeper than is possible. If you accept that the spirit goes on, the mind is just meat and believes what it is fed. The spirit is the person and the mind can get in the way.

"The problem is that sportsmen need to be more childlike because there's no fear in children. The same as if I want to throw something

I throw it naturally, I don't have to think about it, I let it go. When we're childlike and let it happen rather than make it happen, that's when it will happen right. My reaction to what had been fed into my mind had affected my thinking, my clarity, but I benefited immediately I admitted I was negative.

"With Severiano Ballesteros I can feel and sense when I'm near him that he is thinking totally clearly – there's no purpose other than getting the ball into the hole. Maybe that will change with the years, with experience and happenings, or maybe he'll retain it and understand what makes it happen as he develops. Jack is probably the only one who has done that. Gary is close too.

"In Scientology you are forced to use areas of your mind that have lain dormant. I read a lot and know most words, but the most important thing is never to use a word you don't fully understand. While we were at the College, we weren't allowed to drink and you're supposed to have seven hours' sleep a night and never go hungry. I felt fantastic after five hours' auditing a day for four days, not just about my problem, but I was so aware of everything.

"Viv went though she had no need to go, but they said it's nice if she does and she did 'life repair'. She didn't need it, she's as happy as Larry, she could ask them questions, but she enjoyed it. At the end they tried to get me to go on another course, but I thought, look out, they're getting their claws into you. I'm a pro golfer not a Scientologist, so I didn't want to get involved. But I've never seen a happier bunch of people who sometimes work 12 to 14 hours a day. Scientology means the 'knowledge of wisdom'. Ron Hubbard was the founder and he's been knocked like any individual who wants to be different. He may be right or he could be wrong, but he's a bloody smart cookie.

"When I went to the College, or Saint Hill as they call it, I thought there would be a magic answer. A lot of it's a waste of time. I waffled on about every damned thing that came into my head and none of it was relevant. I'm the happiest guy in the world with healthy kids, a marvellous wife, a lovely home, comfortably off, healthy and fit. But I really enjoyed digging into my mind – I got a natural high from it. The only other time I felt anything like it was playing at Dalmahoy, when I won the Wills Open by seven shots, and in one round I felt that I could put the ball wherever I wanted. I shot 65 and putted like a fool, but I was on a higher level of concentration and it was fantastic.

"Ron Hubbard is incredible. The millions of words he has written mean he's putting down in black and white the finer feelings that

I would have. He's using all the right words that I wouldn't begin to know, but had I taken a different path I would like to have been that clever – to be able to put on paper in a logical, sensible way, exactly the things that one feels. He's more right than anything I've read, or am likely to believe in.

"Writing this book on Tony Jacklin will take hours and hours to put together, and then people will interpret it exactly how they wish. Why can't they read what is written? Scientology is reading the absolute and understanding all of it.

"Anxiety takes you into the past, says Ron Hubbard. The important thing is that you've got to think about the past in order to be anxious. I don't suppose most people would think in those terms and sometime in my life I may be able to help someone else. When you get anxious, it's because of something that has happened before. In golf terms, you become anxious about a shot because you know all the variables.

"When I was at my lowest ebb, gaining that knowledge was an important factor, an aid to helping me out of it. It gave me a greater understanding of my problem – and there was no question that I did have a problem.

"In my bad spell I sometimes criticised myself and would think others were lucky, which was bad. I should have been doing something else to get my mind straightened out.

"I'm not a religious person, but Scientology is as close as anything I've come to that I would believe in concerning the spirit that is in every individual.

"Take the Bible – it's a marvellous fairy tale. It's just a great story of good, giving indications to everyone how good God is, Jesus is, and the fact that all these marvellous stories should make you pure. The stories all have morals but I think they are open to many interpretations.

"Everybody needs to believe in something. If they haven't a strong belief in themselves, they need something else to hang on to. They are lectured by preachers and priests in a search for inner comfort.

I believe in something – maybe it's me, and someone will say, you selfish bastard. Well I'm sorry, but that's the way I am. Young people are apt to try to beat the world, and if you're not selfish and trying to do that one thing, you'll be eaten. You may wear a few different hats, but life is for the takers.

"It's not just myself that I believe in, it's more than that but it's difficult to define – maybe it's a superior being. I don't know whether anyone knows what it is.

"I know when you're dead, you're dead, and that's it, forget it. What will happen is that the soul is the memory that one leaves behind. Whether you go out with a machine gun and murder people, or you lead a good life, isn't going to make a scrap of difference as to whether you go to heaven or hell. Going to hell means that everyone you have left behind thinks you've gone there.

"I'll never be blotted out, will I? I'd like to think I was going to get my three score years and ten, but if I died tomorrow I wouldn't regret anything. There's nothing at this stage of my life that I wish I had done. It would bother me if someone died and had not known the full value of knowledge, fun and experience in their life, because I think every human being deserves the chance to take it.

"But after you've done everything and maybe become a genius, you have to remember you're flesh and blood, and people die – that's the only inevitable thing. As long as you live your life with that knowledge, you can't be too disappointed when it happens."

TIME FOR A CHANGE OF LIFE

Pat Ward-Thomas

A golfing acquaintance recently declared that he had reached the change of life. He was, of course, referring to his golf and not to a bizarre circumstance of nature. When I sought explanation he said that the time had come when he was inclined to remember the good shots in a round rather than the bad, thereby achieving some consolation for his efforts, however paltry the overall outcome might be.

This was surprising. The last time we had played in the same match his attitude had been quite different. He had played far below his best until about the turn, when he produced a remarkable recovery stroke. The ball was on a steep, downhill, sandy lie. Between it and the flag, no more than 20 yards away, was a deep bunker, above which was a sheer little shelf to the edge of the green. It would be hard to conceive a more testing stroke: it had to be thrown up very steeply so that it would land softly. The slightest under-or over-hit would be fatal.

Gary Player, as skilled in shots from sand as anyone I have seen, could not have played the shot better. It fell gently and rolled to within inches of the hole. Whereupon his partner remarked that it made up for some of the previous errors. But the hero would have none of it, declaring that nothing could really compensate for them. From a practical viewpoint he was right; but why, as he came to realise later, not savour the triumphs, few though they may be, and forget the tragedies?

Many golfers never progress beyond this stage and sensibly recognise that in all probability they never will. In a way they are to be envied because they return to the clubhouse not dissatisfied with their round. Perhaps their driving was steadier than usual, they may have mastered a hole that normally defeated them, one or two long putts may have fallen, maybe a bunker shot finished dead or a rare victory was won against an old rival.

A few such happy moments are sufficient to make their day even though they may have taken an awful number of strokes. They will have crowned the joy of treading smooth turf, the feel of the summer breeze, the music of birdsong, the sense of escape from mundane reality and the pleasure of being with friends. And when the round is done, how eagerly they look for someone to whom they can impart the glad tidings.

Occasionally it happens that the listener is a much more accomplished golfer and is equally anxious to unburden himself, but for very different reasons. He is seeking a sympathetic ear into which he can bemoan the strokes that spoiled his day. "It's incredible," he will way, "but I had a six at the 8th, the easiest hole on the course, fluffed a chip and took three putts. Admittedly, my five-iron to the 11th was pushed into the bunker, but it didn't have to finish in a heelmark. You know how well I've putted lately – well, I missed three from inside four feet. The greens are a bit rough, but 78 was terrible the way I was hitting the ball." The permutations of misfortune, real or imagined, are infinite.

The victim of this recital, having no idea of how many strokes he himself had taken, could retort that he would happily settle for so few problems and would give anything to go round in 78. If ever he did pass such a landmark he would be in ecstasy, but if thereafter he did so fairly often he, too, would probably find himself dwelling overmuch on his mistakes, thinking that the 78 should have been 75, and so on, down the scale. Once a golfer has reached the stage where horizons are clearly defined and ambition sharpened, he is less likely to be satisfied with his handiwork.

Wise is the golfer who remembers that every round, however low the score, includes one or two shots that are not perfectly struck. For the great player they may only be slight errors of timing or judgement, but a matter for regret nonetheless. Accustomed as the tournament golfer is to striking the great majority of his strokes truly, he will naturally recall the few that were not, but will accept them as part of the unforeseeable day-to-day variations of form. The club golfer who is often restricted to one weekly round or less finds such a philosophy hard to acquire.

HIDING YOUR FEELINGS

Bobby Locke

I hope I have been able to put across a very important point, that my success in golf, apart from my ability to play the game, has been largely due to my psychological outlook. I hope I have made it clear that I try to avoid all extremes, and anything that is likely to disturb my mental outlook and in turn destroy that vital factor of relaxation.

I had a good lesson in avoiding extremes as a youngster in a South African competition. In a final – it was the Transvaal Amateur Championship – I met a golfer named Hugh Lyddon. The people I was staying with in Johannesburg made me go to bed early, at about eight o'clock. I could not sleep, and got up next morning feeling wretched. What was fatal was that I started the game feeling that it would not matter if I lost a few holes as I could always win them back. Right enough, I lost some holes, but I could not get them back. I was beaten.

I require a minimum of six hours' unbroken sleep to give me sufficient strength for a good day's golf. I find it is absolutely no good going to bed early if I am not tired and my brain is active. I always like to get to bed about 10 o'clock when I am reasonably tired, and it is just about that time it is easiest for me to drop off to sleep. I then rise the next morning about 7 am. Golf does not enter my mind when I am going off to sleep, though I suppose that when you are at the top it does remain in the subconscious mind.

Another reason why I take so much care to hide my emotions is not to give anything away to the other fellow. I learned as a boy that I must watch my opponent's reactions. In 1934, I had just turned 17 years of age and had reached the final of the Transvaal Amateur Championship. On my way to the final, I met another 17-year-old boy in the semi-final. I was four down with six to play, and naturally I thought all was over. I holed a long putt for a birdie four on the 13th hole, and taking a glance at my opponent, noticed signs which told me immediately he was shaken. He became pale and walked much faster to the next tee. The result was a bad drive for him, and I won another hole back. His expression almost admitted defeat, and as luck was on my side, I beat him at the 19th hole. I then left the course and turned this event over in my mind so many times that I realised that when playing big golf I should have to watch my opponent's reactions.

I have been called many things by various people when I am playing, because my expression never changes – "poker face", "muffin face", etc., but that is due to a determination never to convey to my opponent what my inner feelings are. I can quote an example. Sam Snead visited South Africa in January–February, 1947, and out of 16 matches he won two, we halved two and I won 12. A month later I arrived in America, and they all wanted to see the "man from the jungle" who had beaten their Sam Snead. When they saw my swing, they were not impressed. They said I over-swung with the club and that one day I would over-swing so much that I would stay there. They were frankly uncomplimentary, but said I was a nice guy – until I started taking the money! These boys, I think it is true to say, underestimated my ability. After my third round in the Masters tournament, when I had a 70 against Nelson's 72, my mind flashed back to Bobby Jones's book. He said there, "Play for par and if you do, your opponent will be matching you and will then make mistakes." This is what happened, and I had them fighting me. As I said before, they completely underestimated my ability, but when I got on top of them, I just kept hammering away, my rusty old putter doing more than its share, with the result that I had them disturbed mentally. I noticed this particularly when I played two or three of the leaders – I won't mention names. If things were going well with them, they would smoke one cigarette every three holes, but when I had them on the run, it was three cigarettes a hole. When I saw them chain-smoking, I said to myself, "Keep up the pressure and you will be all right."

One other fellow, when in difficulties, conveyed his feelings to me by not being able to stand still and continually scratching himself. Another man whom I beat fairly regularly showed clearly how he was feeling. Each time I holed a long putt, I glanced across and a white line, about half-an-inch wide, would appear down the side of his face. I knew then he was wounded.

There is a player in America who has the same temperament as mine. I used to watch his reactions, but could learn nothing from them as to how he was feeling inwardly. If this man holed a 35-foot putt or missed a 12 inch putt, his expression never changed. He would merely tap his ball into the hole, lift it out and walk quietly to the side of the green. He never batted an eyelid. He is Johnny Palmer.

My opponents never know when I am on the defensive. Golf, I can assure you, is not all attack. Tactics enter into it, but only I know what is going on in my mind.

THE YIPS

George Plimpton

One evening in San Francisco I heard for the first time about the "yips" – a phenomenon talked about rather uneasily by the pros, and with wary respect, as one might talk about a communicable disease ravaging the neighbouring township. The yips (a name invented by Tommy Armour, who had them) was the term given the occupational malaise of golf – a nervous affliction that settled in the wrist and hands, finally, after the years of pressure and the money bets and the strain. It was what ultimately drove the pros out of the game to the teaching jobs at the country clubs, setting the balls on the tees for the girls in the Pucci pants who came down for their two free gift lessons of the summer.

The legs don't give out, as in so many other sports, or the wind, or the sense of timing, or the power, but the *nerves*, so that one could see the hands of great golfers beset by the yips tremble visibly on the putting greens, the greatest names in golf completely at the mercy of short putts of four, five, six feet.

I said I had never heard of such a thing.

Dave Marr told me that he had seen Byron Nelson stand over a four-foot putt at Florida's Seminole golf course, and, finally after swaying back and forth several times, he had stabbed at the ball desperately and sent it *40 feet* past the hole.

At that same club, Seminole, Craig Wood had them so badly during an exhibition match, which should have relaxed the pressure, that he hit the first nine greens right on target in regulation strokes, but then putted so badly that his first-nine total was *44*. His dismay was such that he refused to putt out at all during the second nine; when he reached the greens he stopped and picked up the ball and stuffed it in his pocket and walked on to the next tee. The rest of his foursome, sympathetic, allowed him double gimmes, the regulation two putting strokes, and marked him down as such.

There was someone, a curious youngster, unaware of the ravages that the yips are capable of committing, who had gone up to the golfer and had the temerity to ask: "Why aren't you putting out like the others, Mister Wood? I mean, I don't understand . . ." and then he had stopped in mid-sentence because Wood had such a murderous look on his face.

It seemed to get them all. Leo Diegel had an awful time with nerves. He fussed around with a pendulum stroke with his putter but most people though he was afflicted with a spastic tic. A great golfer, he never had the right mental equipment and he knew it: "They keep trying to give the championship to me," he once said, "but I won't take it." In the British Open in 1933 at St Andrews he faced an incredibly short putt, just a foot or so, and he wandered up to it shaking like a leaf and stubbed it past the hole to lose the championship. (Others have reported that poor Leo missed the ball altogether – perhaps it was the next one he stubbed past?) Vardon, at the end of his career, in 1920, when he was in his fifties, got the yips. They were blamed on two attacks of tuberculosis. He called them the "jumps" and recommended putting in the dark as effective treatment. Apparently it didn't work. Gene Sarazen (he eventually got them, too) recalls Vardon as the most atrocious putter he had ever seen. He didn't three-putt, he four-putted.

Rod Funseth . . . said that one of the saddest examples of the yips he had seen were those infesting the person of Jon Gustin, who was known for owning one of the prettiest swings on the tour. Funseth went on about him at some length. Apparently, he was a great dresser – he had been a former flag-bearer in the Honor Guards in Washington. Very snappy. "So you had," Funseth said, "the fine combination of a great swing, smooth and pretty as Snead's, and a guy who *looked* great as a golfer, like he stepped out of the advertising pages of *Esquire*, and yet what would happen, because of those yips, was that he would stand over the ball to swing – his irons, drives, putts, any shot – and his hands would come back, but the *club head wouldn't*. It would stick there right behind the ball like it was cemented to the ground."

"Lord Almighty," I said.

"He had to give up the tour."

"Well, I would think so."

"Worst case I ever saw."

"No cure, I don't suppose, for the yips."

"Golfers who have the yips *try* to cure them, God knows," Funseth said. "Gene Sarazen found one – at least one that worked for him. Watch him in the Senior tournaments. He steps up to the ball and hits it all in one motion – almost like he's hitting a shot off a polo pony. He doesn't dare stand over the ball, because he knows he'll freeze. Snead had the idea you could drift into a sort of 'pleasant daydream' to get back to the fundamentals of the practice swing. And then I recall that Bobby Locke had an idea that the yips could be cured by holding the club very loosely."

But Locke at his best also felt that the putter should be held as gently as possible so as to maintain the maximum of "feel". "If the yips had him bad, why you wouldn't be surprised to see his club just slip out and fall on the grass. Really no thing to have," Funseth said. "There's no sure cure. The yips can get so bad that you hate the idea of being in the lead in a tournament – where the pressure can bring on an attack. You begin to crave for a fair round, even a mediocre one, where the pressure isn't so stiff."

The great distinction to make was that there was no similarity between the yips and "choking" – though every once in a while the younger pros, who looked on the yips as something that couldn't possibly happen to them, would say that yips was just a fancy word that the older pros thought up to hide the fact that pressure gets to them too.

"Who told you that?"

"Oh, one of the younger professionals."

"That figures. If you want to see choking on a vast scale – I mean, what the caddies call the Apple Orchard for the big lumps that turn up in the throat – and if you want to see the eye-staring and those clammy foreheads, then you got to take in the qualifying tournament that the rabbits play in. Ludicrous. Or you'll see one of those kids play in the high 60s for a round or so in the Open, and then what happens to him? The pressure gets to him. He skies to an 80. He chokes. He's so scared he damn near closes his eyes when he swings."

Someone said: "Pee Wee Reese, the shortstop, used to have a good phrase for the choke. He'd say, 'I know I'm choking when I'm chewing and can't work up a spit.'"

"Sometimes a particular hole will cause a choke – a choke hole," said Marr. "Like the 18th at Cypress. It's like walking into a certain room in a big dark house when you were a kid – you get this fear that hits you."

Johnny Pott said: "That's why we spend so much time on the practice tee. You're down there trying to groove the shot, to tone up the muscle memory, so that when you get out on the golf course and the pressure's really on – the choke at hand, and you can sense your eyes popping, and the jaw shaking – the muscles can still perform in their usual groove and you can get your shot off. You practise to get the muscles moving almost automatically."

"Doesn't that work for putting as well?"

"No, because muscle memory doesn't have anything to do with putting. Take Sam Snead. He's got the most famous swing in golf – you wouldn't find a differential of a millimetre in the circle of his swing if you took a thousand stop-action films of the guy. Perfectly grooved. Great on long putts, where the demands on muscle and swing are slightly more. But short putts! Give me someone out of kindergarten! His hands come back fine, but then the blade seems to go out of control just at the stroke. Sometimes he hits the top of the ball so that if it drops, it bounces every which way to get in there. Snead has had the yips for years. That's why he took that pro's job at Greenbrier way back in 1937. He thought he was going to have to quit the tour because he had the yips so bad. Or take Hogan, the most tragic case. Best tee-to-green player there ever was. Ever. I mean he puts the ball *there* off the tee, then *there*, just where he wants, then *there*, right on the green. You might as well *give* him those shots. But once on the green his troubles begin. He had those two holes to go at Oak Hill – just par-par, that's all he had to do to tie for the 1956 Open, but the yips got him. You know the guy got ten thousand letters from people trying to help him."

"Ten thousand!" I said.

"That's right."

I once asked Claude Harmon about those ten thousand letters, and whether he thought I would get an answer if I wrote Ben Hogan and asked him what the most ridiculous of the suggestions received had been – I thought that might be interesting.

"You wouldn't get an answer," Harmon said, looking at me sharply. "Because I'll tell you one thing. Hogan would have *tried* every damn one of them – I don't care how 'ridiculous' – to rid himself of those things.' He repeated what I had heard so many people say: "If only Hogan could have putted – Jesus, he'd've made every record in the book look silly."

Hogan's miseries with the yips reached a climax in the 1954 Masters* when, leading the field, he went to pieces on the final holes of the tournament. He three-putted the 13th, missed a four-foot putt on the 15th, three-putted the 17th, and then came to the 18th needing a six-foot putt to win the tournament. Claude Harmon said that Hogan went off to the side of the green and he made about one hundred practice strokes

---

*It's doubtful that Hogan had the yips this early. I think his final 75 was merely a poor last round – by Hogan standards. He went out in 37 and came back in 38, so there was little difference in his play on the last nine holes and missing a final six-foot putt to win is standard procedure for most golfers!

with his putter, all markedly different – changing his grip, the position of his hands on the club, the stroke itself. When Harmon asked him about it later, Hogan said that he had been trying to find a stroke, any stroke at all, in which he felt comfortable – a last-minute desperate search – and after the experimenting at the edge of the big crowd around the green, he had taken one of the styles back out on the putting surface and, perched over the ball, he used it, and not surprisingly he missed the putt.

Claude Harmon had an interesting notion that a golfer's control over those shots, putts especially, which were conducive to the yips, was at best fragmentary since the ball travelled over the *ground*, and was at the mercy of irregularities and worm casts and the rubs of the green and beetles sticking up their heads to look round and minuscule pebbles and so forth.

"Even a machine will miss half the time from six feet. It's been tried," Harmon said. "Golf is really two games. One is the game in the air. The golfer can lick that part of the game. It sounds like quite a feat – I mean, you've got to get all those parts of your body moving absolutely correctly to send that ball off the tee at over 200 miles an hour. But once the ball is up in the air, there's not much that can happen to it. The air is a medium a golfer can control, as easy as fish in water: he can move the ball in it just where he wants to – fade it, or hook it to his liking, if he's good enough – and he's never going to be surprised unless he makes a mistake himself. Or unless he hits a bird. But the other part of the game is across the ground. It sounds easy. You hardly move a muscle to hit a putt. A child can do it easier than nothing. But the medium controls the ball, that's the difference; the golfer can get the ball moving, that's all. After that, the ball moves and turns and dies by reason of the ground surface. What you can't control gets the best of you after a while – death and taxes, the old song – and that's what the yips are."

Harmon's story reminded me of Bernard Darwin's anecdote about the famous billiard professional who saw his first game of golf and remarked on it as interesting enough, but wondered why (as he said) "do golfers on the green first knock the ball up to the hole, and *then* put it in."

Some golfers felt that any prolonged absence from the game resulted in such a loss of confidence that an infestation of the yips would result. Bobby Cruickshank remembered that when his great rival* Bobby Jones returned to competition in 1934 after a four-year layoff, his putting had

---

*No one was Jones's rival: he was too much better than any of his contemporaries – including even Walter Hagen, who seldom won if Jones was in the field.

deteriorated to such an extent that he wandered around the Masters that year asking his fellow golfers if they could spot what was wrong. "It looked the same," Cruickshank said. "I mean you'd see him address the ball, then set the putter in front of the ball, and then at the back of the ball again, and then the stroke – that was the famous procedure he went through. But you could see he had no confidence."

Claude Harmon told me of a more recent example of the damage a layoff could do – the decision of Mike Souchak to take his family for a month's vacation on the beach after he had a remarkable succession of wins and near-wins on the tour. "I told him he was crazy. You got to keep at it. When he came back it was gone – it had floated away on him, and what he had was like the yips."

Occasionally, though, one heard of cures. Roberto de Vicenzo, at one time afflicted with the yips so badly that he had the reputation of handling the spookiest putter on the tour, had been able to do something about it. It had not been easy. In the throes of the disease he had changed putters every week, picking out a new putter every time he went into a pro shop. He looked in a closet at home in Argentina not long ago and found 50 putters standing there, a total not counting many he had given away. No one of the putters seemed better than another. Each seemed utterly unreliable. In 1967 in Australia he blew an 11-shot lead in the last 14 holes because of his putting and lost to Alan Murray in a play-off. He talked about an occasion in England when his putters had let him down – his accent heavy, his big hands moving artfully in the air to describe his meaning, his chair squeaking under him, his face expressive under the white baseball-style golf hat he wears to cover his thinning hair.

"In the British Open, in 1965, I think, we are playing the final day, which is 36 holes, and in the morning I am leading. I have had one bad green, number 9, which I three-putt in the morning, but I still in very good position. So we come to number 9 in the afternoon and I say to myself, 'Roberto, you no three-putt this green this afternoon, do you?' I didn't. I make *four* putts. I was so mad I wanted to break all my clubs and quit the game and never play again. I had no confidence. I look at the cup and she look like a little spike mark. I tell myself, 'Roberto, you no can put the ball in there.' So I lose my confidence and I lose the tournament right there."

Vicenzo's cure turned out to be a matter of self-application – finding the right type of putter, the correct style of hitting a ball with it, the regaining of confidence, and practice, endless practice. Many golfers go through an equivalent regimen of experiment and practice without finding the answer: Snead had tried a number of putters and such grotesque putting styles – the "sidewinder" in particular, in which he faces the hole and strokes the ball just off the outer edge of his golf shoe – that only his great grace as an athlete keeps him from looking ludicrous. Vicenzo was lucky. He found his putter two years ago. A mallet putter that he says is appropriate for his big hands. He watched other golfers' putting styles and decided that all the good putters (with the exception of Billy Casper and Doug Ford) use their *arms* primarily in the putting strokes, not the wrists, which had been his style. So he changed his style and found his sense of "feel" increased immeasurably. His confidence began to return. He practised endlessly – especially to get what he refers to as the "head in rhythm . . . to work the head and the hands at the same time". He began to collect some tournament wins – notably the British Open, and then a close run at the Masters which he would have taken to a play-off had he not handed in a mistotalled score card. But he was phlegmatic himself about the future. "The putt is a funny game. You can't think you got it for always. You can lose it tomorrow. But for the moment," he said, "I feel better when I step onto the golf course. I no feel scared to step onto the green. Not any more. Or maybe for the time being, eh?" (It was. Roberto "retired" early in 1976. Poor putting was the reason for his decision. However, he is still competing.)

Another older player I talked to about the yips was John Farrell, once the great rival of Bobby Jones and now a teaching professional in Florida. He said that if you play in competition long enough you're sure to get the yips. "Walter Hagen," he said. "If you had to vote for the player with the best temperament, well you'd *have* to vote for him. Hell, he had such confidence that there wasn't a shot that held any terror for him: they used to say that when he had a particularly tough shot to make, and he'd stepped up and made a great one of it, why then he'd whisper at his caddie, 'Did I make it look hard enough?' and give him a wink, y'see. Well *he* got them. The yips. He got them so bad that he tried strokes and grip styles you could scarcely *believe*: cross-handed putting; or sticking the elbows way out so that the wrist action was throttled down and his whole body moved as stiff as a derrick. He even tried putting in the dark – thought that might cure him. Nothing did. . . ."

I asked the question I had put to the others – if there was any connection between the yips and losing one's nerve.

"It's that you lose *nerves*, not nerve," Farrell said. "You can shoot lions in the dark and yet you can quiver like a leaf and fall flat over a two-foot putt."

"I would think," I said, "that years of experience standing over two-foot putts, and gaining all the knowhow of reading greens and distance, and the competition – that all of that would be to a golfer's advantage . . . confidence."

"Oh, I wouldn't want to be so sure as that," Farrell said. "I always remember Waite Hoyte, who pitched for the Yankees, you'll recall, and what he used to say about 'experience'. He said experience *punishes* you. A veteran player *knows* what can happen to him: he comes onto a pitcher's mound and he knows the batter waiting for him can pop the ball right back to the bullpen where he's just come from for a home run. He's gone through it before. So he's something of a fatalist. It's the same in golf. 'Experience' punishes you as you continue with the game. That's why in golf we speak of someone being 'competitively young' or 'competitively old'. Craig Wood, you see, he was 'competitively young' at 43 because he started playing serious golf when he was well into his thirties. Then on the other hand Bobby Jones was 'competitively old' at 23 – he had started at 15, you see, which gave him early 'experience' but it aged him good and quick as a golfer."*

"Experience," Farrell went on ruefully. "I won the Open in 1928 at Olympia Fields, and then in 1929 I missed the cut at the Open at Winged Foot. Dropped from the tournament and I had *won* the year before! D'you think *that* experience did me any good! Well, I'll tell you. The next year at Interlachen, Minneapolis – in the 1930 Open which Bobby Jones won to fetch himself the Grand Slam – I stepped up on the 1st tee with the 'experience' gained from those bad rounds the year before, and what did I do but get myself an eight on that first hole. I managed to pull myself together after that and I finished eighth behind Jones, but don't talk to me about *experience*. Snead can't win the Open because of his memories – missing that two-footer in the 1947 Open. Palmer won't win the PGA. He has that block. No; it's the kids, the strong young golfers who have it all. They make great big errors – I mean, a kid like Marty Fleckman coming up with an 80 after leading the Open into the last day in 1967 – but he's at the age when mistakes are easily forgotten; those kids' imaginations aren't jumpy with crucial flubs – y'know, disaster, that's what they don't know about. Not yet, It'll come. They'll get there. Experience will come. Oh yes."

---

*Not so. Jones retired at the age of 28, having won the British and US Open and Amateur Championships in a single year – 1930. In 1925, when he was 23, his greatest achievement (including winning each of the three British Opens for which he entered) lay ahead.

Chapter 9

HAVE CLUBS
WILL TRAVEL

Mark Wilson

After four hours of final practice in the Georgia sunshine edging his own game to an acceptable state of sharpness, Arnold Palmer was unceremoniously resting his aching feet on a table, and soothing a parched throat with a liberally iced soft drink amid the many splendours of the East Lake Country Club at Atlanta. Then suddenly he publicly declared the outcome of a Ryder Cup series as tantamount to a foregone conclusion. He did so as if it was the most natural thing to do, and in a manner that suggested it was only right and proper for all to know before paying entrance money.

Alligator shoes, fine alpaca cardigan over a tailored shirt, and light-weight slacks impeccably cut, the American team captain, dollar million-aire and fairway idol, fitted perfectly into the extravagant surrounds of a paradise clubhouse as he faced the 1963 Pressroom inquisition seeking his thoughts on what the October morrow would bring. "Aw, come on fellas," he playfully rebuked for having been asked how strong the British opposition was expected to prove. "Now you know me better than that. I can't guess how good they are going to be out there. But I'll gladly tell you the message I've just given my boys in the locker room – and that is there aren't 10 golfers from the whole world who could possibly beat us right now."

To some listening British ears – our own captain John Fallon had contented himself to a "We are determined to do our very best" pronouncement in contrast – such extreme forthrightness jarred almost the senses of propriety. But experience of the flamboyant American golf scene, so often dedicated to having the best whatever the cost, soon teaches understanding of moments like these. Palmer's expression of unmitigated confidence was sincere and completely justified, as events proved, but in any case nothing less would have been publicly acceptable from him. Modesty can be read as another word for pessimism.

East Lake, a name long familiar as the home course of Bobby Jones, fits snugly into the "Think Big" pattern. It sets itself the highest standards; obviously enjoys its costly living to them; and unquestionably thrives upon the policy in every sense. When the Ryder Cup was played there the club's well vetted golf membership totalled around 1,000, and that left a waiting list of so many more eager to pay the £300 entrance fee that anyone over 40 years of age was credited with scant hope of living long enough to be given the opportunity of parting with his money.

It should not, of course, be thought that East Lake is representative of all American golf, though there are many more country clubs which will claim equal standing. It bestrides a level, however, to which the remainder aspires. The thousand or so who wallowed contently in its opulence as members included, by my findings, some of the nicest, most generous and resourceful people ever to have graced the game. Even so, living with them was an arduous business; for common to them all was an insatiable desire to welcome each visitor to the very limit of his endurance, and so resolutely is this pursued that only the hardiest of guests is likely to survive more than a couple of days without having to seek a hiding place in which to rest up for a time.

Southern hospitality knew no bounds at East Lake, extending far beyond customary conviviality and the unrestricted use of Thunderbird automobiles driven by women members specially uniformed for the purpose. The assorted problems of the British intake, players and camp followers alike, were seized upon and seen solely as a challenge to the club's ingenuity in solving. Three personal instances, quite unrelated to the normal affairs of a golf centre, may help to illustrate. Immediately upon arrival I discovered my need for a private telephone in the clubhouse with which to make my constant and personal calls to the *Evening Standard* in London. Having just before this faced a considerable installation delay at home in Britain, I posed my problem with trepidation.

Minutes later a club member associated with the Bell company of America was found and brought to me. He listened to the problem and then, almost with embarrassment, declared: "If only I'd known about this before lunch, Mr Wilson, you would have had that telephone this afternoon. Now we have to wait till tomorrow, but it will be there by breakfast time, I promise you." It was, too! Having once got my telephone, problem two arose somewhat automatically. On the opening two days of the match the time factor dictated that I would need to be on the line giving the nearest thing to a running golf commentary for the first hour of play. Only that way could I make the last editions of the evening newspaper in London. But how does one stay with a trans-Atlantic call and at the same time see what is going on about a golf course? Well, that poser cost East Lake no headache, either. The local television station was fully covering that first hour on both days

– so a TV set was wheeled in to keep my telephone company.

After all this, problem three was small enough, but the solution was no less big and generous, and certainly more personal. Seeing me without a match for a cigarette, a welcoming member passed his lighter, and then refused to accept it back despite every argument presented. "No, sir," he insisted. "I've got another on me." I found they enjoyed doing that sort of thing at East Lake. It comes under the heading of Southern hospitality, to which every visitor is entitled.

The East Lake membership pays dearly for its golf, but it gets a full measure of what it demands: the best, the very best. To gloss over the facility range, there is a clubhouse born of the "If we haven't got it then it's not worth having" way of thinking; two magnificent championship courses; lakes for yachting and fishing; a swimming pool built to precise Olympic standards; and a downtown multi-storey social headquarters which leaves nothing wanting for the pursuit of enjoyment other than a well stacked purse. Four restaurants were operating in the clubhouse by my count at the time of the Ryder Cup, though when another visitor claimed to have seen a fifth through the tinted windows, no one was prepared to argue against him. It was a big place. There were, for instance, rooms for reading, writing, talking, sleeping, games, cards, television and so on.

But oh! the men's locker room. Here was the *pièce de résistance*. Here, 50 yards long, was one huge expanse of wall-to-wall carpeted extravagance. "Some place for changing your shoes in," joked a British player taking his first look. The joke was on him. You don't change your golf shoes in the East Lake locker room after play. A coloured club servant takes them at the doorway for instant cleaning – and in exchange you collect a throw-away pair of paper slippers. Needless to say, anything and everything a man could possibly want to revitalise himself after a round of golf is there for the taking.

On one glass shelf in the softly lit washroom I counted fourteen different brands of hair oil, cream, eau de cologne, deodorant, aftershave lotion and talcum powder. If you didn't feel fresh after going through that lot then you certainly smelt it. Yes, they know how to live at East Lake. And I don't blame them, either, for after a day's golf with a group of the members in the Georgia heat I felt entitled to any aid science had ever devised for body restoration. We moved a few miles to Druid Hills, another course of superb beauty, of rolling fairways bordered by pines, and large expanses of water. The clubhouse was less pretentious, not being a country club; more on the Sunningdale style as I remember.

Georgians, I discovered, take their golf quite seriously. There were rituals to be observed, the purpose of which appeared primarily to be for starting an argument on the 1st tee and thereby ensuring a needle match with stakes to suit. To Mulligan or not to Mulligan is the first question. The high-handicap members of our party stood out for the right to have a second penalty-free drive to start the game if dissatisfied with their first; the better players naturally opposed such levity with the rules, but in this instance they lost. But the greatest argument of all had yet to come.

Despite the fact that all had official club ratings, and played each other every week, my companions quite comfortably spent another 10 minutes bargaining for extra strokes. The winner last time out was arbitrarily penalised two shots while someone else was conceded an additional one purely on his word that he had not been to bed the night before. Two others agreed to play level after one of them had put paid to the bantering with a solemn speech in front of the clubhouse. He raised a hand for silence, and then, in a deep Georgian drawl, announced: "Sir, I'll tell you one last time what you are gonna get off me. You'll gonna get 14 clubs, five hours of my precious time, and as much conversation as you want. And not a damn thing else." The Nassau style of wagering, so much for the front nine holes, the back nine and the whole round, plus inducements for eagles, birdies, longest drives, single putts and, it seemed, anything else that could be dreamed up, left me baffled from the start.

Eventually the match began at 9.10 am. Five hours and twenty-five minutes later, at a hazy, scorching 2.35 in the afternoon it finished. Every player had holed out on every green, meticulously kept a card and a book of the wagers. During the whole of this time the sun had blazed to a point when the temperature topped the 100 mark. I came off the home green utterly dehydrated, and upon returning to the air-conditioned comfort of the East Lake clubhouse by fast car, promptly enjoyed the most exquisite 80 minutes of my whole life – just sitting on the floor of a shower under a constant stream of cool, cool water.

During the match itself I became aware that I was cheating, or rather my young coloured caddie was doing so for me. Whenever one of my shots strayed into the woods which bordered the fairways he would instantly hare off at great speed. On reaching the spot I inevitably found him standing over the ball which offered both a magnificent lie and an easy recovery line through the most convenient gap in the trees. When this had occurred four or five times I decided something must be done about it, though I was anxious to avoid an embarrassing scene with the caddie who would doubtless deny what was obvious. So I approached my East Lake opponents, told them my fears and heartily apologised. Then one confessed in return: "Don't give it a thought, sir. We had a word with the boy at the start and told him to make sure you enjoyed your game." "But that's cheating," I mildly protested. "No sir," retorted my companion with feeling. "That's Southern hospitality."

American caddies include some tremendous characters, as the British team at East Lake discovered. There was one coloured fellow there who was never seen without an expensive-looking cigar in his mouth. And thereby, as they say, hangs a strange tale. Six months before the match a group of fund-raising top US tournament players had staged an exhibition at the club and this young man had carried for one of them. "What's your name then, son?" he was asked. "Poe, sah," he replied. Joked the youngster's newly found idol, "Any relation to Edgar Allan Poe?"

The caddie's surprise was such that he is reported to have dropped his bag on the ground. Then with an innocence matched only by his truthfulness, eyes popping, chest swelling, he blurted out his answer: "Why, sah, ah IS Edgar Allan Poe!" To the everlasting credit of the professional he said no more, and for a young coloured boy life began anew that moment. He must be a famous caddie, even the top players had heard of him, and from that day onwards he never took to the East Lake course without a cigar in his mouth, a status symbol for all to see. Like Palmer, like East Lake itself, like so much of the American golf scene, Edgar Allan Poe had got the message: THINK BIG.

HOW IN THE NAME OF BOEING . . .?

Raymond Jacobs

Long distance travel, unless it be by yak or some equally improbable vehicle, is no longer the rarity that permits dining out on the strength of the experience. Perhaps this is because the jet age has removed so much of the sense of accomplishment from travelling; it is difficult to feel that a vast distance has been covered when nothing has been seen of the intervening territory.

The paradox of this is that although the airlines persist in telling us that jet aircraft have made the world a smaller place the opposite is true. The fact that you can leave Prestwick at 5 pm (our time) and arrive in Vancouver at 10 pm (their time) and be on the first tee, albeit twitching involuntarily, twelve hours later, undoubtedly reflects the speed at which the journey has been made. But it is even more a reminder that you have in fact come 8,000 miles, not in five hours, but, due to the time difference, in thirteen. Physically you are at the Pacific Ocean; in every other sense you are somewhere back near the Atlantic.

There is the further reflection that this is the kind of thing the Palmers, Nicklauses and Lemas of this world do for a living. Sometimes, for the appropriate inducement, they will travel half-way round the world for a single tournament, and they, of course, are expected to produce, as usual, scores in the 60s before they zip up the cover of their giant golf bags and, additionally weighted down by dollars, steal silently away to the next oasis in the sun. And so you tremulously prepare for the opening drive, your head feeling as though it were tightly packed with cotton wool, through which the thought struggles to the surface – how in the name of Boeing do they do it?

Having taken into account the comatose state in which I played their course, the members of the Shaughnessy Golf Club, of Vancouver, will not, I trust, take offence when I record that there is next to nothing of their course that I remember, except that, fortunately, it was pretty flat, wound through trees, and was very new. There was also, as I remember well and with gratitude, a hut close to the 9th green, where a healing glass, as the Irish put it, helped to restore the tissues. Further refreshment of the senses was made available by, on the one hand, glimpses of the Pacific and, on the other, the snow-dusted mountains which stand, as it were, in Vancouver's back yard.

These mountains are the cause, so it is said, of the moist and temperate climate which Vancouver enjoys – and means that, as in Britain, it rains a lot – but on this March day the entire panorama sparkled in the sun and, though this is another story, it was possible later to ski on slopes only a 20-minute car drive from the centre of the city.

But if the course is remembered only darkly, the scenery is not, and the clubhouse is etched even more clearly in the mind. It is a fetish of golf in Britain, and particularly in Scotland, that clubhouses should be as primitive as possible, the only concession to affluence being the terse notice, "Cigar butts should not be dropped in the urinals". Amenities, as the town planners would say, have improved in recent years, but in very few instances is there the Byzantine opulence which is the hallmark of the trans-Atlantic clubhouse.

This, of course, is at least one of the reasons why golf in Britain and again, especially in Scotland, is so astonishingly, almost ridiculously, cheap. The country club, in its many-faceted glory, is a rare phenomenon and so there are few of those curious, exclusive social enclaves which have provided such a rich field of study for American psychologists, sociologists, and novelists. It is rare for the hero of a 600-page paperback not to experience one of the many crises of his life at the Saturday night dance at the country club, where, in John P. Marquand's phrase, "values of competition assume new and romantic lustres".

Indeed, Mr Marquand's book *Life at Happy Knoll* sets out for the uninitiated the *raison d'être* of the country club. "A self-reliant British subject," he writes, "might be surprised to discover that now some millions of Americans find in their country clubs escape from reality, dreams of wish-fulfillment, means of avoiding the drudgery of home life, areas for the entertainment of their children, as well as a place where conventional outdoor sports may be pursued. . . . There is food and sympathy at the country club."

I would not willingly abuse the hospitality shown to me at the Shaughnessy Golf Club by suggesting that its members have joined, at not inconsiderable expense, merely to escape from reality. But to someone who had hitherto regarded a clubhouse as an unprepossessing place where one changed one's shoes and drank, but in the main avoided the food as far as was polite to do so, the magnificence of the furnishings, the splendid bar arrangements, and the quality and quantity of the food served only to underline the shortcomings of many of our establishments.

The lounge, for example, contained as vast an expanse of deep-piled carpeting as the office of a typical tycoon in a Hollywood technicolour spectacular. The furniture was in proportionate scale, and made one positively nervous to sit on it. The food in the dining-room was up to the standard one would expect to find only in a good city restaurant, and the service – largely, as I recall, by members of the sizeable Chinese population in Vancouver – was as obliging as it too often is not in Britain.

The bar was unlike anything I had seen before, or rather it was the system that was unfamiliar. Built into the back of each member's locker was a rack big enough to hold three or four bottles – whisky, rye, gin, etc. These were then carried to the table and ice and the mixings were bought according to taste and need from the barman. Hard cash never seemed to change hands, everything being on the chit system, a method of payment which is painless at the time but which has an unpleasant habit of rebounding on the bank account when the bill is presented at the end of the month. Still I suppose that if you can afford golf in that style, agonising reappraisals of one's financial soundness because of a bar bill seem unlikely to occur very often.

Even allowing for the Spartan conditions which prevail in so many British clubhouses it is doubtful whether such pomp and circumstance are either necessary or desirable in this country, where in any case the majority of clubs exist for the game only and none of the activities which are an integral part of the trans-Atlantic club. The Americans and Canadians have taught the British a thing or two about the game in their time, and no doubt will continue to do so, but there are some innovations we can do without.

Still, everyone has their own ideal of what a clubhouse should be and I would like to suggest mine. To begin with it must be built on a single level and have a view, standing on top of a rise like the hotel at Turnberry, or the *ante-bellum* mansion which is now the clubhouse of the Augusta National GC, where the famous Masters' tournament is played annually and which must be one of the most unassuming establishments ever designed for a wealthy and exclusive membership.

Such a site would allow a flattering opening drive and a tough uphill hole to finish, for the course, by the way, would, as at Muirfield, have the first nine holes forming a clockwise perimeter inside which the second nine would more or less double back, thus bringing the 1st and 10th tees and the 9th and last greens all within two minutes' walk of the locker-room door.

In this room, in addition to the customary adjoining ablutionary arrangements, would be my greatest concession to un-Puritan luxury. Instead of the dismal discomfort of cold, dark brown linoleum, there would be underfloor heating and wall-to-wall carpeting, as there also would be in the lounge and dining room. I would leave it to the house committee to decide whether spiked shoes would have to be removed before entering this temple of comfort, but in any event there would be no hardship involved in walking even in bare feet on a floor thus covered compared with the chilly alternative that is usually found.

The dining-room would be staffed by waitresses, if possible as appealing as the ones which somehow always seem to be around at Muirfield, and the food would be unexotic, but as substantial and reasonable in price as it contrives to be at Prestwick. All I ask of the bar is that there are enough people behind it to satisfy quickly the needs of those on the paying side.

All these amenities may not add up to anything very out of the ordinary and would certainly not put my clubhouse on that now lonely and narrow eminence reserved for five-star hotels. But I venture to suggest that a good many clubs could do more for the creature comforts of their members and, since every club is becoming more and more dedicated to the task of finding more and more money, what better way to increase revenue than to make the clubhouse attractive enough to persuade members to stay longer, come more often and, of course, spend their money?

OVER THE WIRE IS OUT OF BOUNDS

Pat Ward-Thomas

The first real opportunity for many of us to play games was late in 1941 when some 400 RAF officers were sent to Warburg, near Kassel, where for almost a year they were together with 2,500 Army officers and men, most of whom had been captured in Normandy. Although the camp was a swamp of mud and cinders there was at least space.

The Red Cross and YMCA had now become aware that prisoners needed books and sports equipment as well as food, and supplies were forthcoming. A football pitch, almost full-size, was levelled and a League of six clubs, five Army and one RAF, with second elevens, was formed. The matches were intensely competitive, and the standard of play quite high, especially by the NCOs' team. The atmosphere was akin to a Cup-tie at home and playing in front of a highly critical and wildly excited crowd of 1,000 or more was a unique experience for all of us. Betting was rife and large amounts changed hands, either in the well-nigh valueless German Lager Marks or cheques to be settled after the war.

We were so remote from real money that it soon ceased to have much significance. I never took part in the gambling schools, preferring the quieter and more predictable pastures of bridge; not so a friend of mine who could not resist baccarat or chemin de fer. At one point he was £1,600 ahead and I begged him to hang on to half of it, a considerable sum in the Forties, but within days he had lost the lot.

The Warburg camp was closed late in 1942. Some went to open Stalag Luft III but I and others returned to winter resorts in Poland. Those journeys across Germany were ghastly. We were packed into ancient wooden third-class carriages often for two days and more. At night two would try to sleep on the luggage racks, two on the floor and the rest curled on the seats. I have often been reminded of those dark days when incarcerated in a huge modern aircraft, the quintessence of travel discomfort, but at least your destination usually is known, the food is better and you can get a drink.

Eventually I reached Stalag Luft III which housed the great majority of British, American and Commonwealth Air Force officers. In 1943 there were three compounds, strictly separated; two more were added later to accommodate the growing numbers of Americans. From the sport viewpoint the east compound, where I resided, was the most remarkable in that, in spite of it being the smallest, 330 by 130 yards, games were more highly organised there than in the others.

We were fortunate in having several gifted games players in our midst. Ted Edwards, a New Zealander, was an All Black trialist; Derek Heaton-Nichols, whose father was South African High Commissioner in London at the time, had played cricket and rugby for Natal, and Colin Maclachlan, a Midlands county rugby player, was also an Association footballer of League standard. These men were a strong influence in quickening the interest and raising the standard of our games. They were all taken prisoner within a few weeks of the war beginning. Edwards was shot down on 6 September, the very first officer to be imprisoned from either side. Later others of above-average or even first-class ability in various games, notably cricket and golf, appeared.

The camp was in a clearing within a pine forest, its surface loose sand blackened with pine loam. A constant battle was waged to try to make level pitches but they soon became loose and rough again. Football and rugby were extremely strenuous, especially as the normal seasons were ignored and games were often played in temperatures approaching 90, literally in a bath of sand and sweat.

Rugby was comparatively short-lived. The games became too violent as people unleashed their frustrations, and the Germans did not take kindly to an increasing number of injured players in their sick quarters, but before rugby was abandoned it did help a spectacular rescue of a man from a tunnel.

The Germans held their check parades in the morning and afternoon on the football pitch where the prisoners were assembled in companies of five ranks deep. One such fell in daily within a few yards of the wire and as the parades usually lasted about 20 minutes a tunnel was begun, the sand being dispersed among members of the company. Eventually the hole was big enough for a man to be put down and sealed in during a morning parade after the company had been checked, and brought up in the afternoon before the counting officer reached that company.

On one occasion the Germans did not hold an afternoon parade but the man had to be extricated from the tunnel. He could not have lived through the night. The football pitch was in full view of two guard towers and any group suddenly gathering for no apparent purpose would arouse suspicion. A rugby match of about twenty a side was organised and after a while a huge scrum formed over the entrance of the tunnel. The sand was scraped away, the trap lifted and the man safely rescued. The tunnel was then sealed again. Fortunately the German guards knew nothing of the rules of rugby, though the ingenious attempt to escape eventually failed.

Soccer continued with unabated fervour. A League was formed with eight clubs, each bearing a famous name – Aston Villa, Wolves, Arsenal (for whom I kept goal) and so on. The size of the pitch, 80 by 40 yards, restricted the teams to seven players, but as each club had four sides some 200 or more people had at least a game a week. As at Warburg the competition was intense. League matches were usually played in the evenings and hundreds would look forward to it as eagerly as they do at home.

Sports equipment of various kinds gradually began to arrive and the choice of games to expand. Under the Canadian influence softball soon became popular and when ice-hockey sticks appeared a rink was levelled and banked. When flooded it swifly froze in the harsh winter and a good supply of skates enabled many to learn to skate to the amusement of the less intrepid. The hockey sticks, often made of hickory, were soon at risk as a source of shafts for home-made golf clubs.

Each summer an athletics meeting was held, involving prodigious labour in levelling a track of 220 yards. The sand was harder near the wire where people constantly walked and inch by inch a five-lane track was made. On the great day of the meeting the camp almost had a gala appearance. For weeks the athletes, of whom I certainly was not one, trained and considered their diet and some fine performances were recorded.

When coconut matting came from England our hosts were persuaded to lay a concrete cricket pitch: this was in two sections with a gap of some six yards in the middle so the bowling of bouncers was frustrated. The ball would hit the soft sand short of the concrete and trickle tamely towards the batsman. Perhaps it was as well for the balls were hard.

For six weeks cricket was played for about eight hours a day, then the matting went to another compound for its turn. The boundary on one side was a hut within thirty yards and many a tea party was rudely interrupted. Somewhat naturally windows were left open. We had among us an Australian, Leslie Dixon, who had played Sheffield Shield cricket for Queensland not least, I believe, when Bradman scored 452 not out. Leslie was far too lively for us and rarely slipped himself. Aidan Crawley gave us glimpses of the talent that had made him an outstanding England-class batsman for Kent and the Gentlemen. All in all we had some reasonable cricket, a wonderful boon to those who had been starved of it for so long.

Other games such as basketball and deck tennis also had their enthusiasts and I have not the slightest doubt that during the summers of 1943 and 1944 in the east compound at Sagan there was more concentrated and varied sport taking place in a small area than anywhere else in the world, or for that matter at any time in history.

To an outsider the camp on a high summer day would have presented an astonishing spectacle. Everywhere men, as scantily clad as was decent, were throwing, hitting or kicking balls from morning until sunset. Many of us became almost totally immersed in playing, thinking or talking about games. However humorous or trivial they might appear in retrospect the activity involved was healthy, amusing and above all a distraction, an escape from the ever-lurking threat of anxiety, foreboding and depression.

From my viewpoint, and that of many others, the most significant happening during this period was the appearance of a hickory-shafted lady's mashie. It came into the possession of Sydney Smith, a journalist of repute with the *Daily Express*. I came upon him one day as he was chipping a peculiar-looking ball back and forth. He had made it by winding wool and cotton round a carved piece of pine and covering it with a laboriously sewn bit of cloth. Although the ball bore no resemblance to a real one, and would travel only about sixty yards, it gave us a wonderful echo of golf. Hour after hour we would play, objects of incredulous stares. When others wanted to take part Sydney would say, "Make a ball and then you can." His words heralded a revolution beyond our imagining.

In almost no time men were making much improved balls, more durable and tighter-wound than the original. Then one crafty fellow wound strands of rubber round his ball and straightaway was the longest hitter in the camp. Within a few weeks a score of people were involved, including several good players. The best of these were Danny O'Brien, a Scottish player who reached the last eight of the first English Championship after the war. George Murray Frame, who had a low handicap at Troon, and Oliver Green, now Director of the Woburn Country Club, probably were next in the ranking.

The Sagan golf club was born but we needed a course. To say that we laid out one is something of an overstatement. All we did was choose places for tees and suitable objects to hit for holes. These included tree stumps, poles, an incinerator door and a tiny fir tree about 18 inches high. As the poles were quite high many a hole in one was recorded a dozen feet or more from the ground.

When the membership had grown to 12 we had our first competition, a knockout, and Hugh Falkus, well known after the war for his nature broadcasts, and I reached the final. Falkus, no golfer then but gifted with strong hands and a deadly aim, was expert at hitting the "holes", such as they were. The fir tree caused some discussion because we thought that its little trunk had to be hit, whereas Falkus would claim to have holed out if his shot whistled yards past the tree but grazed a leaf in passing. Fortunately Falkus was not as deadly as usual in our match and I became the first Open champion of Sagan.

As interest grew evolution was swift. An 18-hole course was planned and in such a confined space involved some dangerous if fascinating shots. One blind shot over the kitchen hut, controlled by the Germans, had its perils and the fire pool made a splendid hazard for the 18th. It was deep and filthy but this did not deter two madmen from diving in to retrieve a ball on a freezing winter day. The air was alive with balls of all manner and shapes whistling about the camp. Our activities were watched with interest, scorn and at first tolerance, but it was soon obvious that the course would have to be smaller. Hole after hole was played over tiny gardens, a few yards square, where it was possible to coax vegetables into life. The horticulturists were far from amused when a golf ball decapitated a cherished tomato plant. Sunbathers were also in danger. One man was hit on the bare body with a full shot from no great range and was furious when the striker exploded with laughter. One unfortunate creature's peaceful morning shave in front of his window was interrupted when a half-topped tee shot crashed through the glass. On another occasion a German *Unteroffizier's* morning constitutional in the *Abort* at the end of the kitchen buildings was disturbed by the crash of glass all around him accompanied by the inevitable mirth. Someone had shanked. No action was taken save we were asked to move the tee. Such incidents were fairly frequent and we feared that a serious complaint might be laid against us.

Meanwhile the first green or rather "brown" had been fashioned by Norman Thomas. With the loan of a spade from the Germans this did not take long. An area of about 8 by 10 yards was cleared of stones, stumps and roots and the ground levelled, covered with good yellow sand and kept smooth with a home-made squeegee. The surfaces were fairly true and quite fast after rain. Eventually we had browns for all nine holes of the new and shorter course which measured some 850 yards. The longest hole was 140 and the par 29. The course record still stands at 57 and is unlikely to be broken.

At first the Germans regarded the shaping of little banks and bunkers with suspicion until they realised that there was nothing ulterior in our motives. Mistakenly, they thought otherwise after Eric Williams and his two companions had achieved the only successful escape from our camp by means of the famous Wooden Horse. The tunnel was discovered later the same night but the German attempt to hold an identity check was frustrated by deliberate fusing of the lights in one hut. This made them more angry than usual and clearly they decided on a show of strength. The next day the whole camp was assembled and surrounded by some 200 soldiers with machine guns at the ready. Had there been further signs of insurrection I think they would have fired. Fortunately they calmed down and the only victim was the golf course which seemed an obvious means of dispersing sand from the tunnel. This was understandable because for months the Wooden Horse had stood between the wire and our sixth "brown". The course was flattened but a few weeks later the Germans were persuaded that it was innocent, which it was, and head brownkeeper Timmy Biden and his helpers restored the course. The excavation of yellow sand was forbidden; the browns became almost blacks and their surfaces not so true.

The planning of the course was a natural development, the evolution of ball manufacture truly remarkable. Once rubber had been introduced it became one of the most precious commodities in the camp and the fervent golfers would make all manner of sacrifices to get it. Prisoners were allowed quarterly clothing parcels from home and many was the plea for gym shoes, air cushions, tobacco pouches and the like which were ripped to shreds on arrival. The man with rubber to spare or to exchange was every golfer's friend. The effect on our golf was no less than the Haskell banishing the guttie forever. The age of the string ball was dead.

Within no time ball-making had become almost an art form. The Scottish craftsmen of old would have nodded approvingly at the ingenuity, skill and patience we devoted to the task. Most of the balls had a solid rubber core, some hollowed to hold a small bit of lead. Several feet of rubber were necessary. This was stretched and cut with razor blades or scissors into very narrow strips which were wound round the core as in an ordinary ball. Experience alone taught one the correct tension. Too tight a winding produced a wooden effect when the ball was struck or would cause the rubber to snap. If too slack the ball was like a pudding. At the same time we strove to make the ball 1.62 inches in diameter and 1.62 ounces in weight. Delicate experiment usually made this possible.

The earlier balls of string and wood were covered with cloth, or Elastoplast coaxed from the officer in charge of medical supplies, but this process was soon abandoned. The new covers were made of leather cut into two figures of eight, similar to those covering a baseball. These were carefully sewn with thread or twine, which was not readily available, or strands of cotton strengthened with wax or German boot polish.

The leather, often obtained by cutting good shoes into pieces, varied in thickness and quality. It was usually advisable to soak and stretch it before cutting the figures of eight according to tin patterns, cut to a fraction of a millimetre of the right size. These had been shaped by one of the experts, possibly Norman Ryder who produced a detailed thesis on ball-making for the benefit of the embryo practitioners. Very soon balls of astonishing quality were appearing from the, so to speak, benches of Ryder and others. An Australian, Samson, was highly skilled and one example of his work is in the Royal and Ancient museum at St Andrews. It is precisely the same weight and size as a real golf ball, perfectly symmetrical, with cover stitching that would do credit to a machine.

I did not rank with Ryder, Samson, Graham Hogg and others as a ball-maker but mine were fairly close to the true mark. Shortly after the war Reginald Whitcombe and Alfred Perry played an exhibition match at Stockport, then my home club. I asked them to hit the balls I had brought back; they did so with drivers and both flew some 200 yards. Years later I asked Nicklaus to try one. He refused for fear that it might burst, but to this day the one I have still bounces well. The other is in the Museum of the United States Golf Association in New Jersey.

Such is my incompetence in matters domestic that my wife Jean still finds it hard to believe that the balls really were my own work. As far as I can recall making one took me about six hours as against Ryder's estimate of four. Many a man laboured long over his ball and sometimes, within moments of going on to the course, saw it soar out of bounds over the wire. If he were lucky a passing guard might throw it back, and the guards on the watch towers occasionally used their field glasses to aid the search, but if the ball were lost there was ample time to make another.

The perimeter of the camp was protected by a high double-stage barbed wire fence. Any attempt to climb this could be met with a bullet but inside the main fence was a strip of no man's land bordered by a low tripwire. Entering this area was forbidden but so many balls for the incessant games went in that the Germans provided a few white jackets. Donning one of these was tantamount to giving parole that no attempt to escape would be made and the balls could be retrieved.

During these early months of golf the little mashie, often in the hands of strong, unskilled players, must have hit several hundred thousand shots. That it survived was a rare tribute to the quality of the hickory and the firm of Patrick of Leven who, I think, were the makers. In the confusion when we were suddenly evacuated as the Russians advanced early in 1945 someone must have taken it with him. I hope so: it deserved a place of honour in a museum. I brought back the first steel-shafted club to reach the camp. It bore the name of Gilbert Heron of Oslo and mighty useful it proved as an aid during our march in the snow, lasting a week, to Luckenwalde, the final camp for most of us.

As the golfers wrote to various countries pleading for clubs a good supply was forthcoming. Norman Thomas and I had been adopted, in a manner of speaking, by a most attractive Danish girl, Doreen Wessel, who wrote to us and sent parcels. One of these consisted of ten clubs. Sadly, I never met the angelic Doreen, who married an American and went to live in Grosse Pointe, Michigan.

Our joy at the arrival of these clubs can be imagined. All were hickory but in good condition and the pressure on the little mashie was greatly eased. Such had been the demand for clubs as the golfing fever spread that home-made affairs began to appear. Some were extraordinary contraptions fit for a museum but their creation revealed remarkable skill and patience. The shafts usually were carved from ice-hockey sticks and the heads fashioned from sections of water jugs or stovepipes melted down. The latter were found to be strong enough without being too heavy, and were not constantly breaking, but the Germans objected to their use and that source was abandoned. Of the clubs that survived regular use one was the work of a Canadian, Don Elliott, a useful golfer and of necessity a powerful one. His club, known as "Abort Annie," weighed about 20 oz but the best of these efforts was made by Lee Usher, an American from Iowa. As I recall his club was well balanced and strong.

In the autumn of 1943 I wrote to the Royal and Ancient at St Andrews, giving a brief account of our golf and asking if they could spare a few clubs and balls. A copy of the letter was sent to Bernard Darwin who wrote of our efforts in one of his *Country Life* commentaries. He mentioned instances of golf in unusual places in the First War including a prison camp where young airmen were armed with cleeks. "So erratic were their shots that on one occasion the German commandant, a portly and pompous old colonel, advanced to the middle of the playground, possibly to protest, and was driven into highly undignified flight. The airmen were no respecters of persons and pursued him relentlessly with a creeping barrage of cleek shots. He did not apparently bear any malice; so there must have been one German colonel for whom something good could be said." We ventured no such liberties at Sagan, at least not intentionally.

Darwin ended his article by assuring readers that arrangements had been made by the R & A to send clubs and balls through the Red Cross. They arrived and among them was the steel-shafted driver. Naturally its use was forbodden except for practice swinging but I used to feel it longingly and wonder whether I would ever hit a shot with it. The chance came one bitter winter day when everyone was inside and the camp deserted. I went to a far corner, almost trembling with anticipation, and teed one of the real golf balls which had come with the clubs from St Andrews.

The driver had an extremely whippy shaft like those which Bing Crosby used and was quite unsuitable for me. However, I made a good contact with the ball which soared away out of sight in a great slice over the kitchen building. Anxiously I waited for any indication that it might have hit something and then came the inevitable plonk and tinkle of broken glass. The ball had crashed full pitch through a window and so startled the people in the room that they flung themselves to the floor. In the deep winter silence they thought that a bullet was responsible. Greatly embarrassed I went to apologise, prepared to face any anger if I could reclaim the precious ball. It was given back to me but my stroke was the first and last ever hit with a driver at Sagan.

By 1944 pleas for clubs had borne rich fruit. They came from many countries, mostly neutral. One man received several new steel-shafted irons and eventually we had about 100 clubs. Real golf balls were considered too dangerous to use except on special occasions such as an exhibition match when the course was cleared and the camp warned. And so in the naive belief that the balls would be less hurtful leather was substituted for the gutta-percha covers. Miraculously, no one was seriously hurt even though it was quite common for people to hit shots back and forth to one another, within a few yards of passers-by on their circuits of the camp.

Within a few months of the golf starting over 300 people had played the course. Although the number on it at any one time had to be controlled the fever did not abate. All day long men were swinging clubs, practising or talking golf. O'Brien and Morgan particularly, and other lesser experts, were much in demand for giving lessons and several prisoners, who had never previously touched a club, were quite competent golfers when they returned home. After all they had reasonable tuition in the basics of grip, stance and arc of swing and opportunity of practice. It was amusing to hear embryo golfers talking of draw and fade, weight transference, backspin and so on, within a few weeks of starting to play.

Hitting approaches of up to 100 yards or more to the minute browns was splendid training and I remember my first round or two on a proper course after the war. The greens looked enormous and I wondered how anyone could possibly miss them, but that illusion did not last long. Nevertheless many learned a great deal about the game and had also grown accustomed to playing in front of crowds. Quiet and well-behaved though they were when an important match was in progress, one was always aware of critical eyes and that, as most golfers will agree, is a great aid to concentration.

Competitions of all kinds and challenge matches were frequent. In one such O'Brien and Samson challenged any pair in the camp to a 36-hole foursome and two 36-hole singles for a stake of £50. The backers chose Morgan and Frame to play for them but after winning the foursome they lost both singles.

In writing an account of this match for the camp newspaper (a few sheets pinned to a notice board), I began to think that reporting games was the profession for me. Later that summer I wrote the story of the golf in our camp. Several of us thought it might be of interest at home but had no idea where to send it, then someone suggested Henry Longhurst.

Everyone enjoyed his book, *It Was Good While It Lasted*, and he looked an amiable soul from his pictures. First it had to be censored by the Germans and some unfortunate fellow had to plough through 14,000 words. Only one part, where I had made an oblique reference to the Wooden Horse, was deleted. The Germans probably thought the story reflected a contented life for the prisoners; it may have done. There was no point in my being critical of the conditions if the story was to reach England. It was duly mailed to Longhurst care of his publishers but little did I imagine that it would be a step towards fulfilling a dream.

The winters in East Germany were too harsh for the regular playing of outside games but most people found pursuits enough to pass the time. Many plunged into serious studies because by then it was possible to take exams in numerous subjects, not least law. I have no doubt that many a career was founded in those dark years. Study was not easy in densely crowded quarters and needed exceptional determination and concentration if it were to be worthwhile.

Neither of these gifts was my strong point but I did pass a Royal Society of Arts examination in Spanish of about O-level standard. The exams were as strictly invigilated as any at home and I was quite proud of my certificate, small achievement though it was. My teacher was John Tilsley, a prisoner since 1939, who had taught himself Spanish while in Germany. He started a class and bravely contrived to pass on his knowledge but there were no Spanish speakers in the camp and we lacked practice in conversation.

For many of us bridge was an enormous boon, indeed a salvation in the winter. I had little idea of the game when taken prisoner although both my parents were good players. At first our bridge in the camps was pretty moderate to say the best of it but after a while many of us studied in earnest. The works of Ely Culbertson duly arrived and became our bibles. Day after day we would play from early afternoon until midnight when the lights went out. There were various regular schools, some more earnest than others, but those in which I was involved played with all the thought and concentration we could muster. Difficult hands were analysed, often long after the session had ended, and gradually several of us became above-average players as I realised after the war.

For a long while George Murray Frame was my most frequent partner, his bridge as steady as his golf, and given a reasonable balance of the cards we were usually victorious. We mastered Culbertson's system of asking bids, long since supplanted by cue bids, but we found it invaluable not only for bidding slams but for stopping short when they were not safely makable. Heaton Nichols and Jim Margrie were two other devotees. For two years I kept a record of my bridge, which is of interest regarding slams. In just over 2000 rubbers with various partners I made 24 grand slams and 238 small slams. Obviously we missed some which were makable and bid others which were not, but over so long a period the average is probably a true guide. Every other form of cards was played in the camp but I always preferred bridge. Ultimately the superior player will prevail even if the margin between him and the others is only slight.

One winter five of us played almost every day, cutting for partners after each rubber. One man was less reliable than the rest and inevitably was the only loser. We played for what now would be 10p a hundred, a considerable stake then but enough to prevent careless play. I think I won about £70 paid by cheques written on scraps of paper, all of which were honoured after the war.

Early in 1945 we were happily involved in a game when the Germans came rushing in and told us that we had until dawn to leave the camp. The longed-for Russian advance had reached the Oder not far to the east of us. The next morning we trailed off into the snow, not knowing where we were going and carrying what we could on our backs or on rapidly-made sleds. A vast amount of stuff including, someone estimated, over two million cigarettes, was left in the camp. The journey was not pleasant but had its diverting moments.

The second night out, hundreds sought refuge in a church and I remember the mad scramble for a space to sleep. I managed a choir stall but one enterprising fellow made straight for the altar, knowing that it offered space for only one. He moved the cross to one end, hung his things on it and slumbered in peace. Little fires were alight in the churchyard as people heated tins but when we left the next morning there was no mess, nothing out of place, no trace that the old church had truly been a sanctuary.

We spent another night in a glass factory which at least was warm, and the last of the journey in a stable on the Graf von Arnim's estate. The next morning brought a rare surprise in the shape of the Gräfin. From notes made at the time and forgotten until I ventured upon this book I recall that she was attractive, in her thirties, petite with light wavy hair and clear grey eyes. She was wearing a sports shirt, a brown tweed coat and short riding boots. Years of enforced abstinence had not entirely dulled my awareness of feminine appeal and she was the first woman I had spoken to in over four years.

German guards were at hand but I chatted to her for quite a long while. She spoke freely of the Nazis, of the war and of their estate, and of how they would have to leave it soon in an Alfa Romeo towed by two horses because they had no petrol. One of the mares in the loosebox where we were talking was about to foal and as she crooned to it in German I realised that it was a different language to the coarse tongue I had been hearing for so long. She was apprehensive of the Russians, the local Communists and the Nazis; we are between three stools, she said.

The war seemed utterly remote in the morning stillness with the park, wintry and bleak, the lake and the great old trees all suggesting peace. On the top of the castle was a figure holding a spear which to me seemed a brave symbol of the dying world beneath. The incident depressed me and I wondered what would become of her, but soon we were in cattle trucks on the way to Luckenwalde. It is strange how memory can reject the unpleasant and until reading my brief notes I had forgotten that the conditions were "the bloodiest I have ever seen – two hundred in a room with only two fires and three-decker beds. Many people with dysentery, sickness and exhaustion. Felt OK myself; in fact the worse the conditions the better mentally I have usually been." Food was desperately short, a greater hardship for recent prisoners than for us, and I cannot remember any games but we could see the fires of Berlin, a dreadful, awesome sight.

Although the end of the war was near we became increasingly uneasy when the Germans tried to evacuate us to the south. We were taken to the station and loaded into cattle trucks (*hommes* 40, *chevaux* 8). The corridor between Russians and Americans was narrow and under constant bombardment; our chances of passing through unscathed were remote but fortunately no engine was available and the journey was abandoned. I cannot recommend a cattle truck for sleeping quarters. We were packed in and the doors locked throughout the night. Tins were the only means of catering for calls of nature and once I was wakened by a warm stream on my face. A friend, as it happened, was stumbling past me intending to pour the contents of his tin through the window, but in the darkness had failed to notice that the bottom of the tin was punctured.

During the lovely spring days we heard that President Roosevelt had died and then to our relief came the order to return to the camp. The guards by then mostly were elderly *Volksturm*, Dad's Army types, and several times on the walk back to the camp we stopped so that they might rest. There was nothing aggressive or unpleasant about them and we pitied their immediate future. The Russians were very near and the only course for the old guards was to flee – which they did soon afterwards, leaving the camp unprotected. This was an eerie time for it seemed possible that some bloody-minded character might take it upon himself to have a go at us. One night a fighter aircraft screamed low over the camp, cannons blasting, and I well remember the crashes as men toppled out of the top bunks, but the shells fell far away.

A few mornings later we were woken by the sound of Russian tanks and armoured vehicles roaring into the camp and had a first sight of their formidable fighting females. The Russian attitude was not unreasonable. We were allowed to wander freely outside the camp but soon learned to identify ourselves quickly as British or American; there were several instance of others being shot. When we heard that the war in Europe was over a few of us gathered in what had been a German officer's house to hear Churchill's VE Day speech. Most of the group had been prisoners for four years and more and had become thoroughly cynical and jaded in their outlook. As the great voice died away there was no excitement, no explosion of joy and relief. As I recall it the silence was broken by a harsh voice saying, "Well that rat fuck's over!"

For millions it was but not quite for us. Days and weeks passed without sign of repatriation. An American convoy of 100 trucks came from the Elbe hoping to take the British and Americans away. Maybe they neglected to ask permission from the Russians; we were in their territory. Whatever the reason the Russians posted armed guards by the trucks to prevent anyone boarding them. No one did but many left the camp and made their own way to the Elbe about 100 miles away. As far as I know most of them arrived safely, but I and other old lags were taking no such chances. We might have done had we known, as I heard after reaching England, that the Russians were considering repatriating us by way of Odessa or, worse, making us work because apparently Russian prisoners had been made to work in France or somewhere. Happily we knew nothing of this and the early summer dragged on.

Every day civilian refugees of numerous nationalities streamed into the camp. Many from Berlin were striving to get to the south, among them an English girl named Thomas who had married a German before the war and had survived the final bombardment of Berlin. If I remember rightly she had children with her; and I have often wondered how she fared.

At last the Russians relented and took us to the Elbe in trucks. We were handed over to the Americans who, as I recall the week we spent with them, were kind enough without being over-welcoming. Many of us looked pretty scruffy and to some Americans must have appeared as a bunch of "Goddam Limeys". We were very browned off by then and one heard remarks such as "We've been prisoners of the Germans, the Russians and the Americans but wait till the British get hold of us!" As it proved we need have had no fears; the reception centre at Cosford was splendidly organised. The Americans flew us to Brussels where we expected to wait for a night, but just as some of us were planning to celebrate our first glimpse of civilisation we were hastened on our way home.

One memory of those strange times which will never fade was of the flight back to England. For years one had longed for the day when the English coast came into view again, never doubting that it would. As we crossed the North Sea on a perfect evening late in May, I stood behind the pilots of the Dakota waiting for the coast to appear and feeling nothing but a massive anticlimax.

For years one had lived a cocooned sort of existence, completely screened from all the normal problems of everyday life. Short of escaping one had no control over one's destiny. One never had to think of taxes, rates, bills, transport of any kind, looking after a family, pursuing a career or tending a garden. If the Germans wanted to shuttle you round the country there was nothing you could do about it.

Gradually one came dangerously close to being so conditioned to life as a prisoner that any interruption was resented. I became sharply aware of this one day in 1944. Very occasionally the Germans organised walks outside the camp; the prisoners signed a parole that they would not attempt to escape and little parties with a guard would go out into the country for two or three hours. I went only once because it disturbed life's trivial routine and I was relieved to be back in the camp again.

That evening in the aircraft I knew there was no retreat from reality and that I had to face whatever lay ahead, to make decisions and to accept responsibility. The prospect was disturbing yet, emotional though I am, there were no tears, no lump in the throat as we crossed the coast.

We landed at Dunsfold in Surrey, and almost before I trod at last on English soil a WAAF armed with a flit gun or some such weapon squirted powder up my trouser legs and jacket sleeves. We may have looked odd but we were not lousy. Neither did a long night train journey to Cosford quicken a joyous sense of return but, as I have said, the reception was most efficient. Within 12 hours I was released on six months' leave and a cousin, who lived in Wolverhampton, collected me. I stayed the night with him but not until I joined my parents the next morning was I fully sensitive to the impact of homecoming.

In writing about prison camp life I have dwelt on the lighter side because the games had a decisive influence on my future. I have said little of the frustration, the horror of the unknown sentence, the awful loneliness of spirit which could lead to despair and the anxiety about family, particularly for those who married shortly before being taken prisoner and scarcely knew their wives. There were no visits from friends or relations and no journalists or reformers eager to record complaints. I sometimes wonder what those who show far greater concern for the welfare of vicious criminals than for their innocent victims would think of the conditions endured by prisoners of war.

GOLF IN IRELAND

Peter Dobereiner

I worry about Ireland. Every time I go there I am like a puppy having its first encounter with a hedgehog. The experience is at once fascinating and perplexing and frustrating. You cannot move in Ireland without running your nose on to the sharp spike of paradox.

The saddest paradox is still to come. The country's main asset is its haunting and timeless beauty. And in order to survive Ireland must attract the tourists in such numbers as to destroy the very quality that makes it attractive. Who wants to visit a Silent Valley echoing to the blare of motor horns? Or march across a Connemara bespattered with caravans?

The Irish know it is happening and they recoil from the prospect of their land becoming no more than a view from a motel window and themselves picturesque figures to animate this landscape. They know they are eating their seed corn. Except in this case, being Irish, they are distilling it into their peculiar brand of anaesthetic. As a result they live in a mood of haphazard gusto and strictly day to day.

When I go to Ireland I normally order a hire car in advance, so that it is waiting for me on arrival. In theory, that is. In practice, I have lost count of the number of times I have been told: "Sorry, sir, we have no reservation in that name." On the other hand, whenever this had happened, I have invariably and without compunction been given a car reserved for someone else.

Experiences like this are inescapable. The Irish like to tell the story of the German industrialist who set up a factory in Ireland. He set out with

Teutonic efficiency to establish his business and was soon on the brink of insanity. Whenever there was a wedding, or a funeral or a coming-of-age party in the neighbourhood the entire factory staff simply took the day off, mostly being distantly related to each other and joined by an even stronger bond if they weren't: free booze is thicker than blood. Faced with the choice of losing his mind, or his factory, or both, the German sensibly decided that if he couldn't beat them, he must join them. He became an Irishman by association, a sort of honorary second cousin, and joined the festivities at every opportunity. He went to all the wakes and cried and drank and called for another chorus of "Molly Malone und her veelbarrow mit". And the odd thing was that despite all the unscheduled stoppages the productivity per head was higher than in any of his other factories in Europe.

There must be a moral in there somewhere. About four times a year my golfing work requires me to visit Ireland and on every occasion, as the date approaches, the prospect produces an irrational excitement. Part of it is a forboding amounting to a racing certainty that such plans as I have been foolish enough to make are going to be irrevocably wrecked. Partly it is the realisation that many of the most memorable experiences in my life have been in the company of Irish men – and many of the near-disasters, for that matter, in the company of Irish women.

Before each trip I give myself a lecture. Ireland is a fully paid-up member of the twentieth-century community of nations. Its technology is as advanced as anybody's. I tell myself firmly that Ireland is no different from any other civilised country. All that Pat and Mike rubbish is just comic patter of professional entertainers and has absolutely no relevance to the Ireland of the Seventies.

Thus, freed of all received misconceptions about the place, I arrive, briefcase in hand, ready to do business. And so it is that I am always caught off balance by the sheer Irishness of the place.

It happens suddenly. Once, within 15 minutes of landing, I was driving into the interior with my resistance getting lower by the minute from the bliss of driving on roads virtually free of other traffic. Thanks to what I take to be a national pastime of breaking off signposts so that only a stump remains containing one or two letters, I became lost. Nothing unusual in that.

The only living creatures I could see were an elderly man and a pig. He was standing in the middle of the road and was trying to stuff the struggling creature into a sack. (Don't ask me; I haven't the slightest idea.) I asked if he could direct me. "Let me see, now," he said, repeating my destination two or three times. "Lisburn . . . Lisburn now." He screwed his face into a frenzy of concentration. At last he seemed to get it straight in his mind, and drew a deep breath in preparation for what were obviously going to be pretty complicated instructions. He fixed me with a look which implied that if I hoped to grasp the theory of relativity with one gulp, I'd better keep my wits about me. I responded with due attention.

"You carry on along this road."

"Along this road."

"And then you come to a town."

"A town. Got it."

"And when you get into the town, you turn . . ."

"Yes?"

"Nowhere!"

And so it was. Absolutely straight ahead. For a while I turned over the theory that he was a plant, paid by the Irish Tourist Board to give local colour to susceptible visitors. But it happens too often.

The same day another stranger directed me to carry on until I came to a fork and then go straight ahead. You'd need an army of unemployed actors to work on such a scheme. It has to be genuine.

Irishness flourishes in many forms. No doubt it still drives creative men like Shaw to emigrate in gloomy frustration. In small, well-rationed doses I find it engaging. In retrospect: you may be wondering what all this has to do with golf. It is simply this: whereas Irishness can be tiresome in the extreme to a visiting dynamic businessman anxious to get on with the job, it is perfectly attuned to golf. The game is leisurely, paradoxical and depends for enjoyment on social contact. So is Ireland. It is a perfect mix. The people, the climate and the lifestyle all conspire to improve the golf and give it a unique flavour.

At this point a small personal confession is necessary. When the Irish talk about their own whimsicalities, it can be mawkish but at least they have every right to pull their own legs. For a foreigner to do so can all too easily sound patronising or superior. I am aware of the danger and so must quickly point out that when it comes to what the efficiency experts call Organisation and Method I am a complete non-starter.

The clerks in the booking office of my local station are no longer surprised when I put a pound on the ticket counter and ask for twenty tipped. And, like others before me, I have been known, on arriving at Charing Cross in my Sunday-go-to-meeting suit, to telephone home to ask where I was supposed to be going. So, if I make gentle fun of Ireland

I can assure you that Ireland, in the form of my many friends there, takes ample and justified revenge.

With that preamble out of the way, I can progress with my story which began with a kindly editor ordering me to go and play a round at Portmarnock with Harry Bradshaw. I had two projected trips to Ireland coming up, the first to Belfast and then later to Dublin. Obviously it would be much more convenient to visit Portmarnock while I was in the nieghbourhood on the Dublin visit.

Needless to say, when I got to Belfast I telephoned Harry and said that I believed we were supposed to play golf, and how about Thursday? It says much for him that by not so much as a tremor in his voice did he betray any surprise at a lunatic calling him up to keep an appointment six weeks early. "Sure, that will be grand," he said. It was months later that I discovered I'd got it all wrong. Those who have never seen The Brad hit a golf ball have missed a unique experience. The Irish do not take kindly to regimentation. They are too individualistic.

So while the English and Scots, and to a large extent the Americans, work to mould their golf into a classic style, the Irish pay little attention to correctness of form. They are not concerned with how they look so much as how they score and while it is true that they do not have correct golf coached into them, it is equally true that they don't have natural ability coached out of them.

As a result, most of the Irish professionals have "faulty" techniques. Christy O'Connor commits the cardinal sin of flicking at the ball instead of keeping arms and club in one solid entity through the ball. Wristy Christy has never lost a moment's sleep over this fault from the time he became the first man to win a four-figure cheque on the British circuit to the time he won a record £31,532 in the 1970 season. Jimmy Kinsella uses a driver with two shafts, one hammered down inside the other, thus putting superfluous weight in all the wrong places. He wields this absurdly unsuitable weapon with an action which led me to describe him as the only man who plays golf without a backswing. His method is a compromise between a convulsion and a lunge. It is a hopeless parody of a golf swing and the only redeeming feature about it is that he hits the ball farther and straighter than most professionals.

Paddy Skerrit, by comparison, is almost orthodox except in his temperament, which is totally unconventional. Concentration, as we are constantly being reminded by the experts, is half of golf. You can tell that the great players are concentrating by the way they prowl around, scowling and cursing. They toss bits of grass into the air to test the wind and pace off distances and ask the galleries to keep quiet and swear at photographers and make dozens of practice swings. Skerrit seems to imagine that you can play golf without any of these preliminaries. He never scowls. Even when his ball goes into a bunker he just gives a wry smile and hits it out. Otherwise, he simply looks at the target and makes his shot. Just like that. Dammit, he makes golf look like a game.

But none of them is quite so eccentric as Bradshaw. Possibly someone once told him that it cost two penalty strokes if you raised the club above waist level. It would be just like the Irish to get confused with the rules of hockey. Anyway, that's the way he plays it and his attitude on the course is, if possible, even more casual than Skerrit's.

In appearance, Bradshaw looks like a country butcher, portly and ruddy faced and with a cap pulled in the manner of a guardsman so far over his nose that he has to tilt his head back to see out, peering from under his cheese-cutter. Even when he walks on to the tee and hits off, you do not immediately suspect that here is a vastly accomplished professional golfer. For a start, it all happens so quickly. He stoops to tee his ball, takes one glance up at the fairway and it has gone, dispatched with a flick from massive hands, straight but not long enough to suggest that he will give you much trouble.

On that perfect day, hot and with hardly a breath of wind, the 1st hole at Portmarnock looked easy meat. I felt confident that I could sail my drive way past my opponent's ball. I took out my spoon. I did not want to humiliate a great player whose best years were past. A suspicion of a hook took my ball into the rough. Bradshaw trundled his on to the front of the green. As luck would have it my ball tucked itself into a bank from which I could only hack it back onto the fairway and so it was just as well that the pitch finished close to the flag. Harry took one glance at the line of his putt and stroked the ball straight into the hole.

I consoled myself that you can't play against flukes. All you can do is plug away and wait for the luck to change. Harry chatted amiably all the while. We talked about the time when he should have won the Open. It was at Sandwich in 1949 and Harry's ball by a million to one chance had rolled right into a broken bottle. Would a referee have allowed him to drop clear?

The question is academic because Bradshaw did not ask for a ruling. He smashed the ball out of the bottle with his wedge, a venerable instrument with a brown enamelled shaft and the thinnest of grips. It had not brought him a fortune at Sandwich because he had lost the play-off against Bobby Locke but today it was enchanted. He was getting up and down from everywhere. Eventually it penetrated my thick skull that it was not luck at all. It looked like magic all right, but that superannuated wedge and an even older putter were murdering me.

The greens at Portmarnock are, quite simply, the best in the world and on that day they were superb. Even I holed putts from long distances but I could not live against this man. From 100 yards out he was guaranteed to get down in two. I blushed at the memory of having entertained a hope that with my handicap shots and a bit of luck I might give him a game. A little while previously Harry had been engaged to play a filmed TV match at Portmarnock against the redoubtable Billy Casper. As the day approached the members were torn between loyalty and the seductive odds offered by the local bookies. Harry was having back trouble. And even without that disability he was not as long as he had been in his prime.

Casper, on the other hand, was right at the top of his powers and arguably the most accomplished golfer in the world. One of the members put the agonising problem to Harry. Of course they all wanted him to win and they would be out there pulling for him. They honoured and respected him and wanted him to understand that nothing would ever change that situation but the time was fast approaching when the serious matter of putting down the bets had to be faced. The ties of friendship and loyalty were putting an intolerable strain on their consciences. "Don't worry about that at all," said Harry. "So far as I am concerned it won't make a scrap of difference if you bet on Casper." These generous words were as comforting as a papal absolution. "But," added Harry, "I can tell you one thing. I will win." There are sportsmen for whom such words would be meaningless, nothing more than a *braggadocio* attempt at self-reassurance. Coming from Bradshaw, as they knew full well, the statement meant exactly what it said. And, of course, he did win, much to the profit of the faithful who duly celebrated in fitting style.

Not that the Irish need much encouragement in such matters. After Bernard Hunt had won the inaugural Carroll's tournament, the tiles on the clubhouse roof were popping under the strain of the merry-making. In the early hours of the morning a policeman arrived to investigate what sounded like a revolution and the following exchange transpired:

"What's going on here?"

"We're celebrating a famous Irish victory."

"But Bernard Hunt is English."

"Sssssssh!"

Although incidents like this enliven the life of a golf correspondent, it is not Irish tournament golf which attracts me to Ireland. Tournaments, after all, are still work, even though they may be spiced with a certain element of novelty. My delight, and it is shared by everyone who has experienced it, is to play golf in Ireland. It is probably the last country in the world which can offer the type of golfing experience which used to be enjoyed by the wealthy and privileged in pre-war England and Scotland.

As I have already mentioned, driving a motor car in Ireland still retains an element of recreation. Motoring is a pleasure rather than a chore and this in itself is a bonus for the golfer. He can put his clubs into the car and be off, on the whim of the moment.

Unless you happen to choose a fashionable Dublin course on a summer weekend, there is no need for preliminary phone calls or formal letters of introduction from the secretary of your own club. You just arrive, pay a tiny green fee and the course is yours. To those who come from countries where golf clubs treat casual visitors as if they were suffering from infectious and fatal diseases the mere fact of being made to feel welcome is a refreshing change.

But the real change is the courses themselves. A wealthy and well-connected golfer in London can play some wonderful golf courses but they are basically of two types, heath or park. Edinburgh is rich in golf but again the choice is limited to links or parkland. Glasgow is the same. From Dublin, however, you are within half an hour's drive of all manner of golf. There are the majestic championship links of Portmarnock and Royal Dublin. There is dunes golf over the Island, lush parkland at Castle. You can play in the clouds among the mountain tops at Howth. Or, if your legs and lungs aren't up to such exertions, you can stroll over the flat clifftop fairways at Woodbrook. There are 30 clubs in and around Dublin and all of them of a different nature. Not all of them are great courses, or even good, mind. But different, certainly.

My own preference, however, is to get right away from cities whenever possible and to ponder on the larger spiritual issues, such as which is the greatest golf course in all the universe. I have narrowed it down to two: Royal County Down on the east coast and Ballybunion on the west. One day, after many more field trials, I shall arrive at a firm conclusion.

These two are, of course, big and magnificent links. Killarney is magnificent also. But, at the risk of sounding like a travelogue, I would urge that the itinerant golfer in Ireland should on no account neglect the small and out-of-the-way courses. Some of them are ludicrous and I remember one, which shall be nameless, where the men who built the greens were clearly working from the plans for tees. All the greens are exactly rectangular, like upturned cake tins. Others are gems. If you drive through County Kerry and take the right turning off the coast road down a cart track and then again turn down the right track from the previous track, you will, if you are lucky, discover Dooks. I found it by accident and since there was no one but sheep to whom I could pay a green fee, I slipped what I considered a suitable offering through the letter box of the hut which does a duty as a clubhouse and went out to play. Even at the time, it was a dreamlike experience, playing over the rolling hills and guessing, often wrongly, which hollow would harbour a green. I did not see another human all day.

Not that human contact is unrewarding on Irish golf courses. Quite the contrary, as my friend Mark Wilson discovered. He is, if I may say so without offence, one of those players to whom half the glory of golf is belting the life out of the ball. And being a powerful man he can belt it with stunning effect.

He went out to play one evening and engaged a caddie, a bright lad with flaming red hair and a keen interest in his master's golfing welfare. They came to a hole elevated high on a mountainside. The fairway, hard and fast, sloped away below and the fresh breeze blew directly from behind – exactly the circumstances to quicken the pulse of a belter. Mark caught the ball with one of his Sunday specials, right off the screws.

"Boy!" exclaimed the lad, "that was some drive." As they walked down the fairway the caddie kept emitting expressions of astonishment and admiration. "You certainly gave that one the business, mister." "That was a real beauty" and so on. As they came nearer the ball the lad's chatter became more and more excited. At last he burst out in excitement: "You've done it. I've seen them all play this hole – O'Connor and Joe Carr and all them big hitters. They none of them ever got this far. That must be the world record." He looked at Mark with hero-worshipping awe and added: "I never did see the like of that drive all my life." And for the rest of the round he kept up the reference to that Herculean drive. "Just give her one like you did back there." All of which was highly agreeable to Mark's ego and he tipped the lad liberally, ten bob over the odds, when they finished.

Later, Mark was talking to the club secretary in the bar and the conversation went like this:

"Good round?"

"Very pleasant, thank you."

"Enjoy the course?"

"Very much."

"Caddie all right?"

"Excellent."

"Which one did you have?"

"Ginger-haired lad, a boy of excellent judgement."

"Did you tip him well?"

"Yes, I did actually. Ten bob! Why do you ask?"

"At what hole did he tell you that you'd hit the longest drive he'd ever seen in his life?"

"Twelfth . . . you mean?"

"Everybody. Never fails. It's pretty hard not to get a long way off that twelfth tee. That boy will be a millionaire before he's twenty."

Finally, if anything I have written should persuade you to try Irish golf for yourself, please don't rush all at once. That would ruin everthing. Pick a companion, or two or three. And take care to choose men whose drinking rate corresponds with your own. Then sneak across quietly in twos and threes and sample the game as it should be played. As it was in the beginning – world without end (if we are lucky).

NOMAD'S LAND

Tim Glover

Shimmering on the horizon, in the middle of nomad's land, was what appeared to be a mirror image of a bedouin encampment. On closer inspection, the tents were of a massive scale and made, not of canvas, but of glass, concrete and sturdy steel.

No mirage. It was the heart of the Emirates Golf Club, seven interconnecting "tents", serving not only as one of the most original clubhouses in the world, but also one of the most outlandish: golf's answer to the Sydney Opera House. The Emirates were offering classic entertainment of a different kind.

The inaugural Desert Classic, on the outskirts of Dubai in the Persian Gulf, represented the Volvo Tour's most adventurous excursion beyond the boundaries of the EEC. The Arabian desert may seem an odd place to detour, especially on the heels of the Tenerife Open which had no sand to boast of but volcanic ash and rocks, and it would have been odder still but for an immaculate course which rewarded those intrepid enough to join the caravan to the Middle East.

"I was amazed to find it in such magnificent condition," said Tony Jacklin, who was playing in the tournament. "They spent ages trying to get Muirfield Village in the same condition for the 1987 Ryder Cup."

Four years ago the course, which measures 7,100 yards, was a pipe dream. The Maktoums, the wheels of the family industries oiled by the black gold beneath the sand, want to develop Dubai as a tourist attraction, hence the golf course. The sheikhs, however, would not sponsor the Desert Classic and the £250,000 prize money had to be put up by Karl Litten, the American who designed the complex.

It mattered not to Mark James. The 35-year-old, who was born in Lancashire and lives in Yorkshire, took the £41,660 first prize, beating the unranked Peter O'Malley at the first hole of a sudden-death play-off.

James, clearly at home by the green oasis, led at the half-way stage with rounds of 69 and 68 and his worst score of the week was a par 72 in the third. It left him two shots behind O'Malley's 70 going into the last round but another 68, to O'Malley's 70, took them into extra time on aggregates of 277, 11 under par and three strokes clear of the nearest challenger, Paul Broadhurst.

James and O'Malley returned to the 17th, the first extra hole, and whereas the Australian missed a birdie putt of around 10 feet, the Englishman, who hit a wedge to six feet from 124 yards, struck oil with his putt. It was the score that broke O'Malley's back.

"Whether I am playing for £1 or for £41,000 makes no odds," said James. "I don't need any inspiration." It was James's tenth tournament victory in a career that plumbed the depths two years ago. He underwent a form of rehabilitation, spending hours studying videos of the great swingers of the game, in tandem with his coach, Gavin Christie. "I haven't given up hope of becoming a world-class golfer," said James. "From tee to green I am just as good as anyone in Europe."

In addition to the cheque, James held aloft the Dalleh, a gigantic silver coffee pot which was the official trophy: coffee-making throughout the Middle East is a way of honouring one's esteemed guests.

O'Malley, who failed to get his Tour card in 1987, won £27,760 which should ensure his presence at far more European events in the years to come. Broadhurst (25), from Atherstone in Warwickshire, gave an equally astonishing performance to take third place and £15,650. He turned professional last year after winning the silver medal for being the leading amateur in the Open Championship at Royal Lytham. The Desert Classic was his third Tour event.

If there was a criticism of the course it was that the greens were too hard, not in terms of difficulty, but in firmness. They were too hard in both senses for Ian Woosnam. In the absence of Seve Ballesteros, who turned down the offer of considerable appearance money, Woosnam was, as it were, number one seed in the desert. In the first round, on his 31st birthday, he lost his head, or at least the head of his putter, during a 74 and thereafter never really got in a telling blow.

An indication of the course's pedigree is that, in spite of it being in near-perfect condition, only 25 players from the field of 120 bettered par in the first round.

To counter the obvious geographical problems the course, which if untended would rapidly revert to desert, is sprayed with up to a million gallons of water a day. The hybrid grass was implanted from Georgia and to keep it alive desalination plants were built. The brine is turned into water and it is pumped 50 miles from the Gulf to the course. To protect the layout from sandstorms, banks of trees were planted around the entire complex. The Emirates Golf Club, which was officially opened 12 months before the Desert Classic by the late General Zia, charges £1,500 for individual membership and there is a waiting list. "At the end of the day we hope to have a nation of Arabs playing golf," said Terry Duffy, English director of tour operations. That day will be a long time coming. Of 2,000 members, only two are Arabs.

IS IT TRUE WHAT THEY SAY ABOUT AUGUSTA?

Chris Plumridge

Even if you are an itinerant golf-writer possessed of a fair degree of low animal cunning standing on the 1st tee of Augusta National Golf Club you don't want to come up with an airshot. Even if you're partnered by Joe, Jerry and Dick from Des Moines and it's the Monday morning after the epic Watson–Nicklaus chase of 1977, you still can't shake off that clammy feeling in your stomach. And even if the people watching are a fellow journalist come to jeer, plus those busy packing up the hot-dog stand concessions, you still find your lips moving in a silent plea to the almighty that He, for once, will allow you to make reasonable contact with the ball.

Some people say that waiting to drive off that 1st tee is the finest laxative in the world, but I'll just have to take their word for that. When you arrive at the course and are told you are on the tee five minutes ago, joining up with Joe, Jerry and Dick (from Des Moines), you don't have too much time to think. You just grab a caddie named George, run to the tee, put a ball down and hit it out there to the brow of the hill. Maybe that's the way to avoid thinking of the fresh air, the clammy feeling and the exercise in prayer-delivery.

It's the history that gets to you. All those immortal names, all those azaleas and dogwoods, all those breathtakingly beautiful holes, all wrapped up in the legend that was Bobby Jones and is now the legend of the US Masters.

It was Jones of course, in partnership with the famed architect Alister MacKenzie, who was responsible for the creation of Augusta National out of the 365 acres that was formerly Fruitlands nursery. In his grand design, Jones wanted a course that would examine fiercely the acknowledged professors of the game, yet still afford maximum enjoyment for the less-gifted player. Thus the mile-wide fairways, the huge greens and the minimum of bunkers provide the handicap player with generous maximums for his poor shots, and if he or she is content with one-over par golf, then Augusta is the ideal course to exercise that contentment.

If, however, the player is hunting for pars and birdies, then those wide fairways and massive greens require a precise placement of each shot, and when you're playing to Masters Sunday pin-positions, you need more than precision: you need a slide-rule.

After a week of watching the Masters being won and lost, it's easy to fall into the trap of thinking that maybe this course is not quite all it's cracked up to be. You see so many superlative shots, so many putts dropped, and all done with comparative ease, that you tend to forget the problems the players have to face.

That illusion is immediately dispelled the moment you walk onto the 1st green, sight down a putt with more turns than a corkscrew and with a touch as light as your nerves will allow, send a ball six feet past the hole. Even though you hole the return, you cannot believe a green could be so fast.

You still cannot believe, after two good shots down the 555-yard second, when your pitch lands by the pin and bounds on to the back fringe.

Tom Weiskopf thinks of the 3rd as a second-shot hole played from the right-hand side of the fairway. If your drive is left, he maintains, the pitch to this 360-yard hole will kick away to the right, leaving an impossible downhill putt across that table-top green, a putt that can accelerate right off the green into a bunker. Weiskopf was correct: you don't want to be on the right of this green, but he's never had to calculate for the rank ineptness of this correspondent, who thinned an eight-iron along the ground and up the fronting ridge to within 15 feet. Two putts later it was three straight pars and eat your heart out, Ben Hogan. Jack Nicklaus maintains that the 220-yard 4th plays shorter than it looks and a great many experienced players think it's a wood for the tee. Even from the middle tee, some 20 yards nearer, it looks a very long way. When you see your shot with a four-wood finish over the back of the green and nearly out-of-bounds, you get the feeling that perhaps Nicklaus knows a little more than you, but then he's had 19 Masters to find out.

Hardly anyone goes to the 5th, which is set high on a ridge above the main action below. This lack of attention resulted in three putts from what seemed infinity with two levels. The short 6th is where Billy Joe Patton, the American amateur, holed in one in 1954 during his chase of Hogan and Snead and it was also where, in 1974, Art Wall completed two of his run of three consecutive twos. This British amateur was happy with his par.

The idea on the 365-yard 7th is to drive it straight down the funnel of trees and flip a short iron up onto the green lying above you. There is another way to play it and that is to hit a high, looping hook over the trees towards the 3rd tee, and then hit an eight-iron to the green. What you mustn't do is put your second above the hole, because the downhill putt will mean you'll three-putt just like I did. Slog it all the way uphill on the 530-yard 8th and then start the downhill run on the 440-yard 9th, where you're almost certain to be playing your second from a downhill lie across the valley. That's the first nine and the best is yet to come. Can the nerves stand up, or will the heat get you first? The 10th is a 485-yard par-four and just beautiful. Called the "cathedral of pines" because of the giant sentinels that surround the green, this hole requires a draw from the tee to reach the flat land at the bottom and shorten the approach. The second is then played over an artistic splash of sculptured bunkers to a green with the softness of cement. When you walk on this green it feels like walking on Ryvita: crunch, crunch go your feet and zip, zip goes your ball.

Ray Floyd, joint Masters record-holder with Nicklaus, likes to keep his drive on the 445-yard 11th down the left side. He wants his drive there so he's hitting his second across the water that flanks the left side of the green. Gary Player also favours this particular approach but Doug Ford, Masters winner in 1957, banked on a drive down the centre and hooked a second which he aimed to bounce off the banking on the right of the green. Strategy is the key on this hole and water on the left is a foretaste of what is to come on the 12th.

So much has been written, said and sworn about the 155-yard 12th, that when you stand on the tee all the stories come flooding back just to confuse your thinking. You remember hearing that the worst place is to be in one of the bunkers at the back of the green, because then you're blasting out from a downhill lie towards Rae's Creek. You remember reading about the dogwood tree on the right of the green, and if it's moving then the wind is blowing. You remember the story of how Sam Snead, in 1952, put his tee-shot in the creek, dropped out, skulled his pitch into the front bank and then chipped in for a four. You remember all this folklore and when you've taken five different clubs out of your bag, you finally keep one and swing on another prayer. Up it goes and you watch. The dogwood tree is moving and it's going to be short – no it's not, it's too long. Glory be, it's on the back fringe and two putts later you have your three, which feels like a minus two.

You play the 485-yard par-five 13th as a par-five unless you're one off the pace in the Masters. Otherwise, you lay up short of the creek that meanders in front of the green, and you pitch up to a pin that's so tight to the edge of the ditch it almost seems afloat. This is where Tony Jacklin saw a water-mocassin and it's a hole full of venom. So it's amen to Amen Corner, and on to the 420-yard 14th with its rolling green of drunken borrows. The rule here is to be at the back of the green with the second.

When you reach the 15th you remember you've seen it on TV, but it never looked like this. Drive to the crest of the hill and think of Gene Sarazen and the 1935 double-eagle. No wonder the cameras cluster, waiting hopefully for a repeat performance. The pros always try and go for the green over the water, because to lay up means facing, as Nicklaius says, the "toughest pitch in golf" from a downhill lie to a front-of-green pin-position. If, like me, you hit a fat four-iron second when your caddie's telling you it's only a six-iron to lay up, then you too will face the toughest pitch in golf. Get it anywhere on the green and give thanks.

Bath-time awaits on the beautiful, scenic, 190-yard chocolate-box 16th. Water all the way between you and the green, which tends to make the hole appear shorter than it is. Don't fall into that trap. Hit a four-wood all the way and to hell with the pros hitting a five-iron.

Remember that the 17th at 400yd plays longer than it looks, and take a club more for the second, and when you three-putt for the sixth time in the round just reckon that's about par.

The 18th is only one of two holes at Augusta that dog-legs to the right (the other is the 1st). It's 420 yards long and uphill all the way. By now you're drained by the heat, but you manage to get the drive away reasonably. George hands you that old four-wood and tells you to hit it right of the pin, which you can just see above the big deep bunker on the left of the green. You hit it straight into that bunker and George rolls his eyes heavenwards muttering about a dumb so-and-so who can't hit it where he's told.

You find yourself in the very same bunker where Jack Nicklaus found himself 24 hours earlier. He, you may remember, failed to get down in two, and that was the end of his chase of Tom Watson. It's the first bunker you've been in, which isn't so surprising as there are only 44 on the entire course. The sand is firm but powdery underneath; if you dig too deep your club may come out in Vladivostock. Keep the club low and hit right through. Up she pops and nearly goes into the hole. Hey Jack, where are you?

And so the walk over hallowed ground is finished, the communion with the ghosts past. Was that Horton Smith who brushed by me as I chipped at the 4th? Could that brightly clad figure behind the 7th green be Jimmy Demaret? Was that Byron Nelson standing by the bridge across Rae's Creek at the 12th? There was a man by the 16th green hitching up his trousers: could it have been Arnold Palmer? Was that soberly dressed man on the 10th Ben Hogan? It could have been, because he didn't say much.

All those names, all those memories are with you during a round at Augusta National and the course brings them sharply into focus. Is it true what they say about Augusta? Believe me, it is. In spades.

Chapter 10

ARCHITECTURE

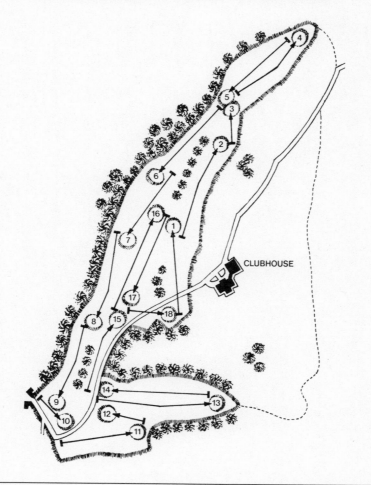

Henry Cotton

I have had a struggle to make good in my chosen profession; life has been one big competition ever since I decided to try and become a good golfer. It is not that one doesn't get helped along; I have been helped and encouraged by many loyal friends but I had to do most of the work myself. I am too honest to say that I did it all alone but there were no team-mates as in soccer, cricket or rugby. Golfers just have their clubs, a ball and themselves and strive to beat the course and the conditions – not forgetting all sorts of outside influences.

Most of us like competition – we thrive on it – in fact, the champions seek it; it is their life. I enjoyed it although for some years it was undermining my health, but it was a price I had to pay, because I ignored the fact that I had to eat and rest properly in order to do any good. I learned this the hard way and given another chance, would count proper feeding more important than practising. A man has only one body for his lifetime and though surgery is progressing towards replacement of worn parts, there are not yet any guaranteed spares.

In the life stories of modern players which the boys new to the headlines have written for them, there is a sort of down-to-earth frankness. Yet somehow, I do not get the feeling that beneath all the surface comradeship they express, they show the underlying, human feeling of jealousy. But it is there. It is true that in the hurly-burly of the tournament itself – just another tournament to the also-rans, but "the best tournament I have ever played in" to the winner – there is not much time for the players themselves to brood; it is their wives who suffer.

They sit on a verandah sewing, knitting or just talking, taking up positions in groups according to the husband's or family friendships; but somehow it seems to sort itself out into an order of precedence (champs with champs). When the "father of the family" misses the money again, it is a silent, unhappy car or caravan group which treks to the next stop, always assuming, of course, that the money is lasting out.

This kind of suffering was not for me. I did the American tour as an excited, enthusiastic young professional of 21 or 22, but it was all new and so different then. Less crowded, too, with no pre-qualifying, but not, I decided, the life for me. I wanted to compete, but on my own terms as it were. Living in a suitcase, worrying about laundry coming back in time and eating every meal in some cheap restaurant or at the bar counter of a drugstore, could not be my destiny, I hoped.

I wanted to be the best player in the world for my own satisfaction. I knew that it was part of things that the public and my friends should help me to get some rewards for my efforts, but I could never get around to go hunting all over the world (although I still liked travelling) just to win money at the price of my health and discomfort. People who do the "nine to five" life, up on the "rush hour morning", back on the "teatime crowded", want to get away from the monotony and for their annual holiday they want to travel. Life in the sun all the year round; it must be heaven, they think.

It is the sort of life many people dream about, but once the novelty has worn thin, the endless moving-on becomes a strain and even the successful ones soon look 10 years older than they are. Many of them would settle for the "nine to five" life and lots of wise ones get out and go into normal business before "it gets them".

Long before my 50th birthday I decided that winning wasn't easy any more and that I had lost the urge to practise, because it tired me and made me a bore at home. I came back from a day's golf or practising, teaching or playing and just wanted to sit in a chair and rest quietly without talking or reading, whilst the "battery" got a recharge. I did not want to discuss life at home with all its silly, to me, little incidents of late food deliveries, staff, shopping prices and, of course, fashions. I was becoming the ideal bore!

Golf was and still is my life, but the tournament appearances were out for there is not much real consolation when one could claim to have been a potential winner for 25 years, to find only "supporting roles" and ever to be known as wonderful for one's age. I played one a few more times to take a close look at some of the new boys because, having had the crowds following me for years and now being on the other side of the fence, I found appraisal of a player's talent vastly different in the two cases.

A second shot with a five iron, say to within seven yards of the pin, always looks good to the spectator but from the player's end, it may look mediocre. In fact, at one time, I would have been quite disgusted to be so far away. I am a generous spectator, often giving praise for strokes which are really very ordinary but my wife, "Toots", on the other hand, who has watched so much golf played by all classes of players, is brutally honest in judging shots she sees. She will not give any credit unless it is a *good* shot and she will not accept mediocrity in anything, particularly in golf, a game she knows and understands so well. She is in short a better spectator than I am.

Having made golf courses as a young man, I turned again to construction work. In 1933 I designed one of the first financially successful par three courses in Britain at Sandown, Isle of Wight, which was built for a Mr Kennedy and called Brown's course (using "Brown" as for everybody). It has made money ever since and is still going strong 32 years later. I like to think that is so because it was well made and well run. I teamed up after the war with Sir Guy Campbell and did a small amount of work with him; but there was very little to be done, mainly owing to a lack of money.

In the last five years, however, golf has suddenly begun to boom and I drifted into this side of the game on my own quite instinctively. Because there are people who have made golf courses over long years, there is competition in this field too, but I am used to competition. In Britain (much less than in Europe) golf-course architects have rarely been given full opportunity to make a course as they wish, being limited either financially, by the ground available, by the soil, by the committee or by all of these. Everybody, in fact, who gets into office at a golf club fancies himself as an architect, and there are few clubs in this country upon which a captain or president has not left his mark on the ground with some structural alteration to the layout, sometimes good, sometimes bad.

I often dream of making a Pine Valley over here, of making the hardest course in the world. Perhaps not one that I would enjoy playing now – though I still like to have to play nominated strokes – but certainly one I would have enjoyed trying in my prime. The bigger the challenge, the better I liked it.

Today the best courses are more often made on the Continent where more money is available and where architects are given a freer hand, but it was my good fortune to make the Canon's Brook course at Harlow New Town in Essex where Sir Richard Costain, Chairman of the Development Corporation, gave me complete freedom from the beginning. It was built in three years, as land and money became available, and without any rough at all, but it is long and will, I think, be found pretty testing when tournaments are played from back tees. I hope to see the "tigers" go at it one day.

In America, two top golf architects, Robert Trent Jones and Louis Sibbett Wilson, became involved in a slanging match about their work.

It could have been like the Sarazen-Hagen feud or the Bob Hope-Bing Crosby one; all good friends behind the scenes. "Wilson is a fine architect," remarks Jones "but he dog-legs too much, sometimes at 14 out of 18 holes. "Jones is a nice fellow, friend of mine," says Wilson, "but his work gives the impression of too many straight lines."

Jones is so busy, say some other critics – at times he has as many as 25 jobs going at once – his work is rubber-stamped, but Jones denies this and says: "It takes a better man to design a course than to build one. Any civil engineer can manage the clearing and the drainage." Wilson maintains: "It takes a better man to build a course than to lay one out." The opposite view.

I find that whilst the design is all-important, a course is destined for ever to be played a certain way, but a working knowledge of the construction side, earth moving, seeding, drainage and clearing is more than essential and already I have the pulse on all of this – and in several countries too.

Golf is a sport that needs competition; played solely for exercise, it is but half a game in a way. It needs the challenge of an opponent or a course and the person who kids himself about his skill is only getting half the fun. Whether it be a simple par three course or a great championship links, it is still a challenge and I love competition.

I have had opportunities to travel recently to various parts of Europe without my clubs, taking only drawing equipment, coloured pencils, rulers, paints and camera and it is a stimulating challenge. I enjoy helping clients make more courses available for more golfers for their numbers undoubtedly will increase and I hope that my various designs will give them all pleasure, because I believe that golf courses can be built so that everyone can have fun.

THE BRITISH
LINKSLAND COURSES

Sir Guy Campbell

British golf was first played over links or "green fields". The earliest of them were sited at points up and down the eastern seaboard of Scotland, of which Dornoch, Montrose, Barry, Scotscraig, St Andrews, Elie, Leven, Musselburgh, North Berwick, and Dunbar were, and Dornoch,

Barry (Carnoustie), and North Berwick are typical. Nature was their architect, and beast and man her contractors.

In the formation and overall stabilisation of our island coastlines, the sea at intervals of time and distance gradually receded from the higher ground of cliff, bluff and escarpment to and from which the tides once flowed and ebbed. And as during the ages, by stages, the sea withdrew, it left a series of sandy wastes in bold ridge and significant furrow, broken and divided by numerous channels up and down which the tides advanced and retired, and down certain of which the burns, streams and rivers found their way to sea.

As time went on, these channels, other than those down which the burns, streams and rivers ran, dried out and by the action of the winds were formed into dunes, ridges, and knolls, and denes, gullies and hollows, of varying height, width and depth.

In the course of nature these channel-threaded wastes became the resting, nesting and breeding places for birds. This meant bird droppings and so guano or manure, which, with the silt brought down by the burns, streams and rivers, formed tilth in which the seeds blown from inland and regurgitated from the crops of the birds germinated and established vegetation. Thus eventually the whole of these areas became grass-covered, from the coarse marram on the exposed dunes, ridges and hillocks, and the finer bents and fescues in the sheltered dunes, gullies and hollows, to the meadow grasses round and about the river estuaries and the mouths of the streams and burns. Out of the spreading and intermingling of all these grasses which followed, was established the thick, close-growing, hard-wearing sward that is such a feature of true links turf wherever it is found.

On these areas in due course and where the soil was suitable, heather, whins, broom and trees took root and flourished in drifts, clumps, and coverts; terrain essentially adapted to attract and sustain animal life.

Nature saw to this. First came the rabbits or "cunninggis" as an ancient St Andrews charter describes them; and after the "cunninggis" as naturally came the beasts of prey, followed inevitably by man.

This sequence had a definite effect on these wastes or warrens. In them the rabbits bred and multiplied. They linked up by runs their burrows in the dunes and ridges with their feeding and frolicking grounds in the straths and sheltered oases flanked and backed by whins and broom. The runs were then gradually worn into tracks by foxes, and man the hunter in his turn widened the tracks into paths and rides. Generations later when man the sportsman, having adopted golf as a pastime, went in search of ground suitable for its pursuit, he found it waiting for him, in these warrens, almost ready to hand. In form it was certainly primitive but it supplied lavishly what today are regarded as the fundamental and traditional characteristics of golfing terrain.

The rides leading from one assembly place to another made the basis of each fairway; the wild and broken country over which the rides threaded their way provided the rough and hazards – rough and hazards that would now bring a blanch to the faces of the most accurate and phlegmatic of our "Professors", and the sheltered *enclaves* used by the "cunninggis" for their feeding halls and dancing floors presented the obvious sites for greens.

Shortly the original layout of nature, interpreted and completed by beast and man, not only hallmarked golf as a point-to-point game, but from then on became the blueprint and sealed pattern for every links and course constructed by intention; indeed it remains today the ideal of all quality design.

As a complete and concentrated example of these "combined operations", the alliance between nature, beast and man (the foundation of our first links with a governing influence on their descendants here and all over the world), the area known as St Andrews links is outstanding. Its coastline back in the dim ages started from the cliffs guarding the Scores, then ran inland and below what is now known as the Station Hill, and continued along under the high ground of the Strathtyrum estate policies to where the River Eden makes its break for the sea at Guard Bridge – a perimeter extending from east through south, south-west, west to north-west. As the sea retreated from it the process of natural reclamation progressed until today the links area is bounded by a long belt of fertile farmland, an expanse of saltings, the Eden estuary and St Andrews Bay.

What is now the Old Course was primitively in existence when the University was founded in 1414. As today, it then "pointed" generally north by west and south by east in the shape of a hill-hook. Then, however, it occupied the narrowest of strips between the arable land on the west and a dense mass of whins that spread east to the high ridge of dunes flanking the sands. So narrow a strip that until towards the middle of the 19th century there was room only for single greens; at first 11 and later nine. Accordingly in the full round, eventually of 18 holes, golfers had to play to the same holes both going out and coming home, with priority in approaching to, and putting on them, at the call of those homeward bound. The nine holes all had names which were used both going and coming home, i.e. "The Heather Hole out", "The High Hole home", a custom that still continues.

With the advent of the gutta ball the game became so popular that the old method, as it were, of flow and return along the same pipe, became impossible. Consequently six of the nine greens were extended laterally so as to allow two holes to be cut upon them, thus establishing the double greens for which the Old Course has so long been famous. A new site for the 17th green was established due north of the Road hole and just west of the Swilcan Burn.

The three single-hole greens were and are the 1st, the 9th or End, and the 18th or Home. When the 18 separate holes were first played the original nine holes were used on the outward half, and the six holes on the extended greens and the newly sited 17th green on the return journey. This caused two "crosses" in play, one between the 1st and Home holes, and the other between the 7th or High hole out and the short 11th or High hole home. Before long the course was sampled in the reverse order, or "right-handed" going out and coming home. Leaving only one "cross", between the 7th and 11th holes, was found so satisfactory that this layout – the right-hand course – came to be accepted as the "official" presentation for all major events, although up to the First World War the right-hand and left-hand courses were used alternatively a week at a time, except during the high season.

In this connection and as a fact historically interesting, the Amateur Championship of 1886, won by Horace Hutchinson, was played at St Andrews over the left-hand course. It happened by chance. The week for the great event coincided with the turn of the left-hand course, the Old Course was so prepared, and play in the tournament was begun over it, before authority was aware what had occurred. Accordingly, the Amateur was continued and completed over the left-hand course for the first and only time. This has been recorded by Jack Tait – Freddy Tait's eldest brother – who was himself a competitor, and for the occasion acted as the special correspondent of the *Times*.

Incidentally this "alteration" of course presentation was due chiefly to the representations of Old Tom Morris, the curator of the links, who declared the "switch" was necessary to prevent constant wear and tear in defined areas – the Old Tom who said to a golfer deploring the taboo on Sunday golf, "Weel, sir, the links want a rest of the Sabbath, even if you don't."

This "spreading" of the Old Course (for the width of the fairways was also extended sufficiently to provide a distinct route for both the outward and homeward journeys) was not the only change that time and the increasing popularity of the game brought to St Andrews links. In 1894 the New Course running parallel to and east of the Old Course was constructed out of the mass of whins already mentioned, but leaving a belt – now steadily and regrettably disappearing – to separate it from its ancient neighbour. Three years later a number of additional holes were made east of the New Course and close to the dunes or sandhills, which became the exercising ground of children and beginners under the name of the Jubilee Course.

Golf continued to gain fresh adherents year by year in such numbers that in 1912 the Town Council of St Andrews had a fourth course constructed on each side of the railway line, west of the Old Course and between it and the farmland, and the Eden estuary. This was named the Eden Course and is today a representative expression of modern golf architecture.

And year by year while all this was happening, the sea continued its retreat. Up till the First World War this was so gradual as to rouse little if any attention. But in the interval between the first and second cataclysms, the pace quickened at such a rate that by 1939 an entirely fresh tract of golfing ground had formed between the sandhills and high-water mark. A case for St Andrews links of *ein Drang nach Osten*. On this freshly surrendered expanse the Town Council prepared another full 18-hole course, during the Second World War, incorporating the holes of the former Jubilee Course under which name this latest extension is now known. Thus, thanks to nature, the co-operation of beast and man, and finally of man alone, nine-tenths of St Andrews links as today existing is devoted to golf, and supports four full-sized 18-hole courses – two of them used in championships – and three putting courses of 18 holes and generous dimensions.

This may seem a somewhat lengthy description accorded to one place, but it is justified because it crystallises the story of the origin, evolution and development of all similar areas in our islands: such as Carnoustie and Machrihanish in Scotland; Westward Ho! and Prince's in England; Harlech and Aberdovey in Wales; Portrush and Portmarnock in Ireland, and many other happy hunting grounds that will quicken the minds of the faithful golfers to and by whom they are known and held in esteem. And it is on such a foundation stone, historical in its laying, that the edifice of British links and courses has been built.

WHAT MAKES IT GREAT?

Robert Trent Jones

I've lived with this question for many years, both professionally and personally. Professionally, I have wandered over countless acres of virgin land – fording streams, climbing hills, wandering through woods – in all seasons of the year, everywhere. I have watched all the masters from Jones to Watson in the world's greatest tournaments, everywhere. Personally, I have hit thrilling shots over beautiful ponds close to well-placed pins. I have dumped bad shots into nasty little ponds and watched them sink to a watery grave, everywhere. In seeing and contributing to many of the world's great courses, I have spent a lifetime in observing, analysing, dissecting, and playing. I think I know what makes a great golf hole.

There is the legitimate "mother" of golf courses – St Andrews. It is nature's created "monster". Down through the ages its contours have been created by receding seas and swirling winds which have left in their wake plateaux for greens, pockets for traps and undulating fairways. The result is a grandeur, a rhythm of flowing line unique to itself in all the world. The first time Bob Jones at a very youthful age played St Andrews in a tournament, he blew up in despair. Later, his game and emotions under control, he came to love it.

The Old Course has probably had more effect on golf architecture than any other single course. It required thought and in turn rewards the thinking golfer. Conversely it penalises to distraction the player who does not think.

No course, however, should overpenalise. All golfers cannot be great players. The target area for an average golfer must be larger to offset somewhat his lack of skill. Where the direct route confronts him with a formidable hazard – trap or water – beyond his repertoire of shots he should be offered an alternate route less risky, less demanding, less toll-taking, but not limp in character or it becomes boring. Keeping the tingle of excitement, the exhilaration of the game, for all classes of players both male and female, is the test of a great golf course. To sum up, each hole must be a demanding par and a comfortable bogey.

It was about the turn of the century that the game, bursting with converts, required more and more courses to meet the popular demand. This required the services of specialists, creating the profession of golf course architecture. As the game moved inland the architects' model was the "linksland" – courses nature had nurtured. The mimicry was both good and bad, but the models were there. The beautiful rhythm of line made by the dunes along the sea, the natural hewn plateaux, were unlikely to be copied exactly. For a fertile imagination, with golf knowledge to match, the guidelines were there to adapt and create holes of outstanding character.

For architects and players alike had noted that some holes stood out as being superior – in interest, strategy or play and beauty – to be categorised in golf's honour list of great holes. Fortunately, what the earth's surface offers rarely repeats itself, except in dead flat land, so opportunities are unlimited for creative manipulation, be it on meadowland, on mountain valleys, or on the desert, each course can have distinctive features all its own.

I believe that the vitality of the game of golf is that it offers man his own personal challenge for combat. He attacks the course and par. The architect creates fair pitfalls to defend its easy conquest. In a true sense, the game is a form of attack and counter-attack. New and improved instruments are created which, together with practice and skill may bring the course to its knees. The architect calls on his ingenuity to create a hole that will reward only for achievement.

The modern professional with his precision-made equipment, carpet-like and weed-free turf, low unpunishing rough, on many courses makes a mockery of par. The shattering of par without the proper challenge is a fraud; a diamond is valued only by its texture, cut and polish, so should be the standard of a round in par.

My name has been taken in vain many times on courses we have designed and/or remodelled for play in championships after some great players have been frustrated playing the courses. This was particularly true when we opened Spyglass Hill, on the fabulous Monterey Peninsula at Pebble Beach, California. The scores were high and the wails of anguish loud. Many have told me since it was the condition not the course that bothered them, and while tough, it was a fair and great course. Bing Crosby himself shortly thereafter shot a 77, and proclaimed it to be one of the world's great courses.

But emotions are part of the game, sometimes a very large part of the game. There's certainly exhilaration that comes with great performance. And just as certainly there's terrible dismay with a poor round. Golf, however, offers much more than perpetual battle between man and setting. Just to be out there, to walk and enjoy natural surroundings is *almost* enough by itself.

Aside from the battle, though, there is a tranquillising effect of golf.

Many courses are truly beautiful. Wandering through woods, observing a tormented sea, relaxing near a reflective pool, observing the majesty of a mountain range – all are part of the game. The seaside vistas of Dorado Beach, Maura Kea, Spyglass Hill, Kanaapali, Mid-Ocean are all inspiring in their sheer beauty; the mountains of Jackson Hole, Colorado Springs, Hot Springs, Jasper and Gleneagles are exhilarating and eye-filling in their beauty; Augusta National is an arboretum of placid beauty.

There are thousands of courses throughout the world with ribbons of trees lining fairways that are soul-satisfying to the golfers who play them. The greenness of the fairways, the menacing texture of the rough, the fearful aspect of the water, the carpetlike appearance of the greens – all become elements which, blended properly, make a great golf course.

However, while a great golf course should have beauty, it should above all else have great playing values. To me, the two are inextricably linked. Yet, holes should be fair. As the player stands on the tee, he should be able to weigh risk against benefit. If he decides to bite off a slice of pond on a par-five, for example, so that he has a chance of being on in two, he assumes the responsibility of perhaps a 230-yard carry dead straight, and a terrible penalty if he doesn't make it. The position of trapping tilt or contour of fairways as well as width or narrowness are factors to be considered as you stand on the tee.

As an example of what I mean, there is the 13th hole, a par-five, severe dog-leg left on the East Course at Dorado Beach in Puerto Rico. It is one of my favourites. The player may hit straight out to a relatively wide fairway. But to the left there is a pond of considerable width. Question: does the player attempt to traverse the short route, thereby placing himself in good position for a try at the green? Suppose he does, and makes it, is he going to be home safe in two? Here again, he is faced with a decision. The green is elevated, and protected in front by another pond about 75 yards wide. Behind the green, about 30 yards away, is the Atlantic Ocean. And the green is well surrounded by traps as well. The courageous and capable golfer can reach it. But he will have made two thoroughly superb shots.

On the other hand, the hole may be played conservatively as well. If he doesn't try to carry the first pond, but hits straightaway, he has an excellent chance of making par. In this case, however, he has no opportunity to try to make the green in two. His second shot must be played to the left which is the only approach by land to the green. The hole is fair to all, demanding to all to be sure, but it demonstrates clearly the rewards and penalties that should be innate to all great golf holes.

Just a word about the ultimate target: the green. To me, there's simply nothing more enjoyable than to play a shot to a well-placed, beautifully designed green where the guardian traps and contours are in harmony with a subtle pin position. Variety in green design is infinite – elevated, terraced, tilted, mounded contours, flank trapping on the sides, direct trapping or water in the front. Varied green designs contribute to the joy of playing a great golf course as they contribute to the misery of failure to respond to its demands.

What makes a great golf course? Like the human beings who play them, they vary widely in style and character, but possess character all their own. One thing to remember: great ones may be beaten, but never defeated.

OUTSIDE OF LONDON

Jimmy Demaret

Somehow, when you are fully aware of the part England and Scotland have played in golf history, you expect to get a special thrill trudging through the hallowed sand traps and strolling down the fairways on the courses where they invented the game. The Ryder Cup matches were played at Ganton, outside of London,* and I can best describe the course as a sort of Pennsylvania Turnpike with tees. You could have called me Hooker Demaret during those 1949 matches but I always managed to stay on the fairway anyway, by hook or crook. (That's a joke, son.) The British golf architects allow history to overawe them, in my opinion. Instead of placing bunkers where a bad shot is penalised, as they do in this country, the British let the obstacles remain exactly where the gophers made them centuries ago. You can push a drive straight down the middle 280 yards, and land in a big trap right in the centre of the fairway. They answer your complaints in tones of disbelief. "Fill it up and then build another some place else? Why, that hole was dug in the time of William the Conqueror!"

---

*Ganton is "outside of London" the way Nashville, Tennessee, is "outside of New York."

DESIGN FOR LIVING

F. W. Hawtree

To produce anything for public approval is a hazardous occupation at the best of times. To design golf courses is to abandon tranquillity for ever besides doing one's constitution a violent injury in other ways.

The golfer has to be serious about the game if he is to be amused by it. From his first stroke, he is ready to pronounce on the design of his course. One great golf architect affirmed roundly that nine-tenths of the laity's comments were based on "invincible ignorance". On the other hand, one of the great players said lately that "golf architects can't play golf themselves, and make darned sure that nobody else can". How can we bridge this gulf?

A possible common denominator is the Chairman of the Greens Committee, especially where he selects obscure pin positions, puts back tees, narrows the fairways or lengthens the rough. Often, being elected for a limited term, he opens up a few new bunkers as a memorial. But he is doing the job for love. The world of golf being pleasantly confined, the golf architect often finds that he is obliging a friend on the same terms. Perhaps this is the ultimate answer.

The golf architect does not expect sympathy and he will never get it. The golfer regards those who work in golf as butterflies. The golf correspondent is equally used to the pleasantry about life being one long holiday, but at least he gets a roof, a telephone, and a scoreboard. Try operating in the rain in 150 acres of farm land, with ploughed fields, barbed wire, thorns, ditches, and inquisitive bullocks for good measure. The probability is that in two hours you are expected to return, unruffled and free from mud with an outline layout and an opinion on which someone may be spending upwards of £100,000. Holidays last only a few weeks; but the golf architect suffers this kind of relaxation throughout the year.

You are standing on a railway station in Brittany. This is about as far away in Europe as you can get from Turkey, where you are due next day – but that is how your holiday has arranged itself. After eight hours on the train, you join the back of a taxi queue at the Gare Montparnasse with 90 minutes to get to Orly, where you are to catch a plane for Frankfurt. This happens in one of those periods when all the Paris taxi-drivers are feeling the homing instinct, and will accept commissions only towards their base. You reach the airport with just two minutes to spare. But don't worry –

the plane is an hour late, anyway.

It is 10 pm before you reach Frankfurt. A United States lieutenant meets you and takes you to the General von Stauben Hotel. You are on "invitational orders", so you get a room. Somebody else has got it, too. Five empty beer bottles indicate that he is a congenial type. You take the vacant bed gratefully. It is Oktoberfest and there are brass bands, dancing, and song in the ballroom, but fatigue eventually overcomes these distractions.

At 2 am, thunder awakens you. From the balcony, you observe that wooden benches are being removed from the ballroom and stacked in the yard below. An iron fire escape leads conveniently from one to the other. When all the benches have rumbled and crashed to the bottom of the escape, you go back to sleep.

At 3 am the lights go on, and the congenial type says, "Hi!" You say "Goodnight!" and leave it at that.

At 7 am, after this interesting night, you breakfast and go to the Rhein-Main airbase. A number of US airmen and civilians are hoping to move about the world in military aircraft. Some, like yourself, are going to Ankara, and eventually decide to travel by way of Evreux, in Normandy. An old hand reckons it will be a week before they move on from there, but those who have already spent a week at Frankfurt are willing to take the chance.

At mid-day, you embark. The pilot explains about the alarm bell which, he says, you cannot mistake (as if you would) and which need not worry you, because he has plenty of crew to look after the passengers. He doesn't say who looks after the crew. If you feel weary, he tells you, this will be due to lack of oxygen. You wonder how long you can last.

For political and technical reasons, your route lies via Luxembourg, Lyons, St Tropez, Sicily and Greece. So you are sitting with your lunch-box for nine hours, and it is 10.30 pm local time when you land at Turkey; in Izmir, not Ankara. Formalities to get a room are not enlivened by the strange music from a wireless set. Another old hand says they are playing their 78s at 45 down here.

Food is no longer being served in the Officers' Club, so you go to bed hungry in a cold bungalow where seven American officers telephone far into the morning for news of a plane out of there. Some ask for a call at 5 am. It is another short night.

After breakfast, you return to the airfield, where the 5 am starters are still waiting. At 11 am you leave them and walk up a ramp into the nose of a flying cathedral containing one five-ton truck, two tractors, mail bags, films, crates and, in the organ loft, a crew to take it all up into the air. Two hours later they put it all down again at Ankara. They go right round the world doing this.

Your reserved room has been taken, but you get in at another hotel. The Base Civil Engineer will be around to see you at once. He arrives at 6 pm, and rushes you through traffic which appears to be progressing by a series of U-turns. As you reach the site of the new golf course, night falls.

Any golf architect will recognise this kind of vacation. With minor variations, I enjoy it two or three times a month. But at least one gets variety and one is working with earth and things that grow. The job may well supply some elemental requirement of human nature. One day in Manchester . . . next day in Majorca; one day enduring a lunch lasting four hours; 24 hours later, glad to find an old sandwich.

In France, especially, the GA may be judged initially by his ability to withstand a formal meal commencing at noon and terminating at four o'clock in the afternoon. As dish succeeds dish and wine follows wine, his grip on the fundamentals or his trade tends to relax, so that many a good man has become confused between a "penal" and a "strategic" hazard, or been forced to hurry secretly back to find the missing element in his layout of 17 holes.

The *apéritifs* having done their work, there is, it is true, a stage shortly after the *écrevisses* (which a Muscadet helps to slip deliciously down) when the GA feels not only master of his own destiny, but also the sort of man the Ambassador would be glad to have at his right hand to deal with any ticklish diplomatic matter. The talents which the GA always suspected were lying down there doggo now appear on the surface. His French takes an idiomatic turn, he ranges widely through current affairs, art and archaeology to golf, conjuring bunkers out of the air with expansive gestures and merry references to the joys of playing out of them.

The reaction comes two courses later when the wedge of underdone steak looks up, blue and uninviting, from the cold plate. The Burgundy has the venerable tinge of a Persian carpet the GA remembers at home; it tastes like it, too. He is no longer inclined to ease the downward passage of the solids with wine. Indeed, it is becoming dangerous to do so.

The cheeses, strawberries, pastries, champagne, coffee and cognac follow inexorably. It is too late to follow any sort of rotation among the glasses even if he could focus on one long enough to grasp it. The smoke of dark, undesirable tobacco adds to discomfort; fresh air seems infinitely far away. So do the indigestion tablets which are locked away in his bag in somebody's car.

His hosts then lean back expectantly, and the senior inquisitor gives a crisp review of all relevant factors and invites an appreciation of the site, potential length, hectares to be sown, rate of sowing, seeds mixture, trees to be cut down, cost of water system, and date of opening the course for play.

The man whose soul comes through this ordeal unscathed has lived. His future is proportionately reduced, yet there is one precious moment in it, after the grass has grown and before play has begun, when the excess or absence of food, the lost sleep and the wet feet seem to have been worthwhile.

And there are other compensations. When I arrived at Dover with a table bought at the Flea Market in Paris, the Customs Officer eyed it suspiciously.

"Is it an antique?"

I explained that at the price paid, it must be a well-used reproduction. Nevertheless, it was just the thing my wife was looking for, so I was not much concerned.

"Are you sure it's not an antique?"

I could not be sure, but I didn't think so. He thumbed ominously through my passport, observing the large number of trips abroad. Then:

"Oh, you're a golf architect. Aren't you doing the alterations at Royal Liverpool? Won't the 18th be easier if you drive down the right-hand side of the fairway?"

I explained that if the pin was on the right of the green, it should be still more difficult from that side. The basic idea of the changes was to be able to present the hole in a difficult or a relatively simple form according to the occasion. I learned that he was a member at a nearby Wirral club, and that the secretary was well known to us both.

After further conversation he signed the car's clearance certificate and was asking me to put it under the windscreen-wiper when he changed his mind: "No, wait a minute, I'll put it there myself."

Next time, I shall make it diamonds.

The desire in all golfers to discuss the playing value of a hole, or even a single bunker, is the chief obstacle to mutual understanding. The golf architect has to start much farther back and take so many factors into account, including money, that life is too short to explain all the reasons for the ultimate form of each element in a layout. Fortunately, there is a remarkable goodwill towards a new course. Its members are anxious to find good points, golf correspondents are in the main kindly, and visiting professionals will always tactfully find one hole which they say is the best in the country. Nevertheless, the designer knows the potential flaws, and has to hope that controversy alone may one day stimulate interest where he knows he has been obliged to drop below his highest standards.

To change a single hole on a famous course is still more alarming. There is automatically a body of players against any change. They will never be convinced by simple changes of bunkering. Whatever is done must be more striking and attractive visually – if possible completely new – to avoid the golf architect's nightmare; changing back.

When my father redesigned Royal Birkdale in the early Thirties, he wanted to make a new 12th and drop the short 17th so that the last four holes would provide a climactic finish uninterrupted by a par-three. It was not until crowd control added its weight 30 years later to the arguments in favour of this arrangement that I was able with filial piety to realise his ambition. The new 12th has the good looks which should guarantee its persistence, but will it play right? It was possible to improve the 18th without the 17th. Even so, the 17th was a good hole . . . there will be regrets . . . perhaps a difficult short hole at this critical stage of the round . . . who knows?

I felt such doubts by the 15th tee at Düsseldorf the day after the second nine holes were opened. We had dammed a stream and formed two pools on either side of the approach. Now a doctor I knew stood poised with a No.7 about to play the green framed by willows and poplars in the valley below.

His ball flew high in the air and it seemed an age before it fell with disagreeable finality into the pool on the left. I looked round for cover and moved quietly towards a bush which might serve. He teed another ball. It rose as before, described roughly the same trajectory and disappeared within three yards of the first.

The bush was certainly not good enough and I wondered whether a frank dash for the sand-pit nearby might not be wiser.

But he had already teed a third ball and, still with his No.7 and commendable consistency, scored another bull's-eye in the same pool.

At this point he observed the golf architect. Hastening down from the tee, he stretched out his hand and said: "Herr Hawtree, dies ist ein wunderbarer Golfplatz!"

So there are occasional rewards. Robert Lynd said, "It is almost impossible to remember how tragic a place the world is when one is playing golf." The abstract game which the golf architect plays is not really very different.

Chapter 11

MATCHPLAY

Henry Longhurst

It is natural to recall earlier Open championships more vividly than those of the recent past, not so much, I like to think, because of approaching senility but because they were won by different individuals, whereas nowadays one has to sort out whether it was a Locke year or a Thomson year.

I find that the memory crystallises sometimes on the finish, sometimes on the scene in general, sometimes on the man. In 1935 it was the finish.

Many people have one chance-in-a-lifetime and miss it by suddenly becoming afraid to win. Alfred Perry had his at Muirfield and took it as though the thought of losing had never entered his head. He used to slash at the ball with joyous abandon, and I have a film of him driving off for his final round. Whenever I show it, there is a momentary silence, followed by "A-a-a-h!" and admiring laughter. In the end he needed two fives to win. At each of the two long finishing holes he disdainfully skirted the bunkers with his drive, slammed the ball to the heart of the green with a wooden club and knocked off a couple of fours as though in a summer-evening fourball.

His oration at the prize-giving was a model of its kind. "I'd rather play a round of golf than make a speech," was all he said.

He was succeeded by Alfred Padgham, whose huge hands enveloped the club as though it were a toy and who played with a serenity that I myself have not seen equalled. You didn't *worry* when you watched Padgham. The game, after all, was simple, especially the matter of rolling the ball into the hole, so why try to make it look difficult? He won every worthwhile tournament except one in 1936, including the Open at Hoylake, which he finished with a six-yard putt and no change of expression.

People often ask me what is the finest round of golf I have ever seen. I am not at a loss for an answer. It is "Cotton's last round at Carnoustie in 1937". What a day, and what a triumph that was! This time the Americans really *were* there – the whole victorious Ryder Cup team.

In spite of torrential rain Cotton went round this gigantic course in 71 to edge out poor Reginald Whitcombe, who had already been photographed as the winner, by two strokes. It was his finest hour.

That the great Whitcombe family should pass on without winning the championship seemed unthinkable but increasingly likely. I dare say, therefore, that when Reginald won at Sandwich in 1938 no win had ever given more general satisfaction. Such, certainly, was my own reaction, though for an added reason. When the last day began, such a gale blew up as had not been known in golfing history. By 9 am the vast eight-masted exhibition tent had sunk with all hands. Steel-shafted clubs were twisted grotesquely into figures of eight; pullovers had already reached the sea a mile away.

In the last round only seven players broke 80, and four and even five putts per green were 10 a penny. Padgham drove the 11th, 392 yards, and got a two – and took four wooden shots to reach the 14th in the opposite direction.

In these conditions the simple two-fisted style of the Whitcombes came into its own and Reginald, his feet anchored to the ground, finished with 75–78 for 295. And I, through sundry wagers with friends on the Stock Exchange regarding the winning score, finished with what it would take £1,000 worth of honest toil to earn, tax-free, today. It's an ill wind, indeed.

In the Thirties I played a great deal of golf myself, accumulating gradually a "score" of about 400 golf courses, so that it becomes increasingly difficult now to add a new one, but in all this varied and, I think, enviable experience I look back upon none with such nostalgic affection as the scene of the Halford Hewitt tournament, the Royal Cinque Ports links at Deal.

I realise now how incredibly fortunate I was. In the six years prior to the war the Old Carthusians won the tournament five times and were beaten in the semi-final in the other, so we saw the whole thing through, including the celebrations at the end, every time. On all these occasions it was my memorable lot to share a bedroom with Dale Bourn and play in the bottom foursome with J.S.F. Morrison.

Both were notable characters. Dale, I think it is fair to say, strayed from the fairway at times in life as well as in golf. He was rescued in the one instance by such charm of character that no one could be cross with him for long, and in the other by the fact that he always expected to be lucky, and was. Some of the strokes by which he won matches at the 21st hole – almost on the beach and tee-ed up on the only patch of grass in sight – left opponents gnashing their teeth and muttering that this really was too much.

Poor Dale! He was killed in a flying accident during the war. I often wonder what he would have made of the post-war world.

It would be idle to pretend that the partnership between Morrison and myself did not become something of a legend, though this was due almost entirely to the eccentricities of my partner, both on and off the course. In six years we were beaten only once – and that on the last hole when the main match was over – and I cannot help feeling that this was due partly to the amazement of our opponents at Morrison's methods and instruments.

He had been a tremendous athlete: cricket and football for Cambridge before the war and golf after it; full-back for the Corinthians and Sunderland and captain of the Corinthians on the great day when they beat Blackburn Rovers in the FA Cup.

His golf, however, was far from athletic. He had a set of seven or eight clubs sprouting from a torn canvas bag and bearing little or no relation to each other, mostly of hickory and some with handles as thick as cricket bats. He was, however, an extremely crafty golfer and, though he often made a bad shot, he never made a stupid one. As Lloyd Mangrum has said, "It isn't how. It's how many." If our opponents did not believe it, they could always look in tomorrow's paper.

I am often asked if the story of Morrison and the taxi is true. It is. One morning we were drawn to play at 7.25 am, when the Goodwins lightship was still flashing in the Channel. We won easily and by 9.20 were in the Chequers, a small incongruous pub away out by the 14th. Here Morrison held court until he not only had to summon a taxi to come and fetch us in time for the next round but also ordered it again for the afternoon. I have always felt it to be poetic justice that on the 14th I missed a putt to win; Morrison missed on the next, and with the taxi, unbeknown to our opponents, following slowly along in the field beside the course we were taken to the 18th green.

The pious founder, Halford W. Hewitt, was himself a Carthusian. He was also, being rather pompous by nature, the perfect butt. If he sat down to read a newspaper in our sitting-room, it was automatic on the part of the man nearest to him to light it. When he insisted on his evening game of bridge – he was very deaf – the nearest man conveyed the contents of his hand to the others. I dare say some of the most remarkable bids in the history of bridge were made in that sitting-room to get "Hal" out all square.

It all sounds a bit schoolboyish now but, like the undergraduate before the magistrate on the morning after, "I can only say, sir, that it appeared to be very funny at the time."

From the ridiculous to the sublime the link is yet another Carthusian stalwart of those days, John Beck, who was chosen to captain the 1938 Walker Cup team against the Americans at St Andrews. It was an honoured but unenviable task. Two years previously I had accompanied the team to Pine Valley and they had not scored a single point. (They had in fact halved three matches, but by the rather uncharitable practice of the day these were marked up as a nought to each side.)

Britain had never won the Walker Cup, and I came back firmly convinced that none of us would live to see the day when we did. The American team that came to St Andrews was substantially the same that had made such nonsense of us at Pine Valley.

Our own team did not look particularly impressive on paper, but by the time the match began they were in tremendous heart. This was due to three influences. One was Beck's firm but amiable personal leadership. The second was James Bruen and the third was Cotton. Bruen, a young Irishman of only 19, was remarkable for the loop in his swing, whereby the club at one moment would be pointing almost directly over the tee box before "righting itself" for the downswing. Seventy was rarely broken on the Old Course in those days but Bruen started flashing round in anything from 69 to 66 and played eight consecutive rounds, the worst four of which would have won any Open championship yet played at St Andrews. The rest of the team responded to this new standard. Where 73s would have done before, they started going round in 70.

On Cotton's arrival, Beck at once incorporated him to play with and encourage the team. Cotton was absolutely in his prime, and it was quite impossible to play with him in those days without playing better oneself. Furthermore, vast crowds followed him whenever he turned out and the Americans for once practised almost in obscurity. "Mirror, mirror, on the wall?" Could the answer really be "The British"?

In the event it was – but how near a thing and what palpitations were to be endured before that memorable final scene! The match was all square with three singles to come in. Charles Stowe won by 2 and 1, Cecil Ewing was known to be two up and Alex Kyle, known to be leading, was away out in the country.

But here now was Ewing all-square with two to play. He closed the Americans out with a four at the Road Hole and the whole world, it seemed, surged round him and his opponent, Ray Billows, on the last green. There was a great silence, but it was broken by a cheer from afar. Kyle was walking in and all was over.

The irrepressible Charlie Yates, of Atlanta, led the crowd in a rendering of *A Wee Doch-an-doris* from the steps of the Royal and Ancient, while inside an elderly member, pressing the bell, was heard to say, "Well, we've lived to see the day. *Steward!*"

18 AND 17

Charles Price

With his record in the PGA, "The Haig" was looked upon as almost unbeatable in matchplay. This reputation was bolstered considerably in 1926 when, with a hot putter, he trounced Bobby Jones in a 72-hole match in Florida by the lopsided margin of 12 and 11. Two years later, the year he finally relinquished his PGA crown, The Haig went to England with Bob Harlow to pick up the third of his four British Opens. One week before the championship, he was booked to play a 72-hole match against Big Archie Compston at Moor Park. It was the first of a series of matches Harlow had arranged for Hagen while they were there. Compston reeled off rounds of 67, 66 and 70 before walloping Hagen 18 and 17 for what should have been the most humiliating defeat ever handed one major professional by another. But not for The Haig. He laughed his way around the course, joking and waving at the spectators. After the match was over, he posed with Compston for photographers. Hagen wore an expression on his face that would have done him justice had he been the winner. Then he climbed into his Rolls-Royce and drove away with Harlow.

Fifteen minutes passed before The Haig and an exasperated Harlow said a word to one another. Realising that the entire exhibition schedule had now been smashed irreparably, Harlow sat steaming in silence. Finally The Haig spoke up. "You know something, Bob?" he said, lighting a cigarette.

"What?" said Harlow irritably.

The Haig leaned back and blew into the air a column of smoke that could have inflated a bicycle tyre. Then he said, "I can beat that sonofabitch the best day he ever had."

THE BIG, BIG TIME

Patrick Campbell

In 1949 the British Amateur Championship was played at Portmarnock, Eire – an interesting occasion in view of the fact that the British competitors had to submit to the rigours of passport examination and Customs inspection before being allowed to play in their own championship.

It was – making the situation slightly worse – won by an Irishman, Max Macready, from an American, Willie Turnesa, but what causes the event to linger in my memory is the fact that I got as far as the 15th hole in the fifth round – a 300 per cent improvement on all previous endeavours.

Having emigrated, like 92,000 other Irishmen, to England I was drawn to return home for this particular Amateur by the enormous advantage of being able to stay with my parents while it was in progress, and not in an hotel.

Hotels are murder during a championship week if you're not a member of the regular tournament mob. Unless you know – as the English, whose spiritual home is the Armed Forces, say – the drill, you're liable to find yourself shacked up with seven old ladies in a temperance guest-house 10 miles away from the course on which the championship is being played.

On all these occasions there is always one hotel in which the knowledgeable boys are gathered together, and if you're not in it it promotes an emotional climate in which you're already three down.

There are no means of assessing – say from the AA book – which this hotel is likely to be. Choose the four-star one and you find that all the boys are staying at half the price in a charming road-house immediately opposite the course. If the four-star hotel is the right one you can only get into it by booking a month ahead, before you've seen the draw. When you do see the draw, and find you've got Joe Carr in the first round, a reservation for five days at £5 per day, bed and breakfast, looks like being an unnecessary expense.

The night life of hotels can draw you out very fine, too. After dinner you can sit in the lounge on the outskirts of the knowledgeable boys listening to them talking about Amateurs they have taken part in in the past. There is no limit to the scope or the accuracy of their reminiscences. They can recount, shot by shot, the details of every round they've played over the last five years, with sidelights on the exceptional good fortune, in moments of crisis, enjoyed by other distinguished players who beat them at Deal, Troon, Hoylake and everywhere else. Attempts by the non-tournament man to introduce subjects of a more general nature, like the plays of Ionesco, Picasso's ceramics or the convoluted literary style of Henry James meet with no success.

The alternative is to go to bed and get a good night's sleep, to be alert and fresh for the morrow. But before retiring it's obviously a good idea to get out the putter, and knock a few balls up and down the carpet.

There's a design of stripes on the carpet which, by a happy coincidence, clearly demonstrates whether or not the clubhead is being taken back, and brought forward, square to the line of the tooth mug which has been placed on the floor in the opposite corner of the room. But, according to the stripes on the carpet, the clubhead is coming back *outside* the line, while the followthrough finishes several inches to the left of the tooth mug, and must, indeed, have been doing so for years. It's still, however, only 9.15. There's ample time to work on it –

By 10 pm you're getting only one in six into the tooth mug, against a previous average as high as three. Also, the carpet is much faster than the greens are likely to be. You achieve the conviction that you're practising a putting stroke which will not only push it six inches to the right of the hole every time, but also leave it at least two yards short. Throw the putter back into the bag and get into bed and try to forget all about the stripes. Try, indeed, not to think about golf at all –

Five minutes later you're up, in bare feet and pyjamas in front of the full-length mirror in the wardrobe, trying to see what it looks like if you really do pull the left hand *down* from the top of the swing, instead of shoving the right shoulder round. Suddenly, it feels right so you get the driver out of the bag and have a swish with it in front of the mirror and it demolishes an alabaster bowl concealing the light fitting in the ceiling. Clear it up and back into bed and try to think of some reasonable explanation for the chambermaid in the morning.

By midnight there's been another putting session – disastrous – and a spell of short chips into the wastepaper basket two of which, striking the door high up with an incredibly loud bang, provoked a thunderous and outraged knocking on the wall from the man next door. Back into bed – the feet are frozen – where you lie with the sheet up to the eyes wondering if the whole hotel has been roused and the manager, in his dressing-gown, will soon be in with a policeman, and they'll find you've smashed the alabaster bowl and knocked all the paint off the door and there's no explanation. None, except perhaps that you're playing in the Championship – or at it.

To sleep, perchance – except that it's an odds-on certainty – to dream. It's that very special nightmare, unhinging in its grinding frustration, of being on the 1st tee in the British Amateur Championship, except that the tee is enclosed by a small wooden shed and you're inside it and there's no room for your backswing and in any case the tee-shot, supposing you could hit it, has got to emerge through a tiny window high up near the roof –

Stark, staring awake and the time is five to five. Get up and have a bath? It might be so weakening that the driver will fly out of your hand and blind Willie Turnesa. Read? The more interesting passages in *Lady Chatterley's Lover* would have the impact of *Eric, Or Little by Little*.

Perhaps the greens are as fast as – much faster than – the carpet. Has anyone, in the Amateur, ever taken four putts on each of the first nine holes?

If the quick hooking starts will six new balls be enough? Has anyone, in the Amateur, ever had to *buy* a ball off his opponent as early as the 3rd hole? Is it allowed by the rules . . .?

The waiters are still laying the tables when you come down to breakfast, and the papers haven't arrived. To spread the meal out – it's only 7.30 am – you order grapefruit, porridge, a kipper, bacon and eggs, coffee, toast and marmalade. Each item goes to join the previous one in what feels like a hot croquet-ball, lodged at the base of the throat.

The chambermaid does want to know what happened to the alabaster light fitting.

The car, left outside all night because the hotel garage is full, won't start.

The contestant for the British Amateur title is ready to – and does – go down without a struggle to a 19-year-old medical student from Glasgow University, pulling his own trolley, 6 and 5.

For the 1949 Amateur, however, I not only had the comforting presence of my nearest and dearest around me after dark, to say nothing of free board and lodging, but also the benefit of the advice and counsel of Henry Longhurst, who was staying with us.

He was early in the field both with counsel and advice. Before going over to Portmarnock for the first round I had an hour loosening up at a course near my father's house, with Henry in attendance to see, even at this 11th hour, if something couldn't be done to put things right.

At the end of the first fusillade he said, through clenched teeth, "It's like watching a man scraping a knife against a pewter plate."

Put out – some of them had finished on the fairway – I asked him to be more precise about his discomfort.

"You're trying to hit them round corners," he said. "It's agony to watch it."

We conducted an interesting experiment. I stood up to the ball. Henry laid a club on the ground behind me, pointed in the direction which my stance suggested might be the eventual line of flight. When I came round to have a look I found to my surprise that I'd been aiming at a small shelter in the distance, perhaps 50 yards to the right of the true objective. "Swivel the whole gun round," said Coach, "and try firing one straight."

It seemed madness to tamper with the system now, and specially to try hitting one straight after years of hooking it back from the rough on the right. I tried it, however, just once. Aiming, it seemed to me, diagonally across the fairway to the left, I hit one straight down the middle, quail-high and all, perhaps a quarter of a mile.

"Right," said Coach. "We'll leave it at that. You've probably only got four more of those left."

It looked as though four would be enough. My section of the draw was infested with Americans, mostly from Winged Foot – a distinction which suggested that they were all probably well above Walker Cup standard. I'd drawn someone called Udo Reinach, a threatening set of syllables presenting a picture of a crew-cut, All-American tackle weighing 210 lb with a tee-shot like a naval gun. To remain with Udo for as many as 12 holes would surely see duty done.

I met him. He turned out to be Willie Turnesa's patron and protector who, as he said himself, had just come along for the ride. He was small and elderly and noticeably frail. In a ding-dong struggle, with no quarter given or asked, I beat him on the 17th by holing a long, uphill putt which went off some time before I was ready for it. If we'd completed the course both would have been round in the middle-80s.

Next day I met another American, also from Winged Foot. I've never been able to remember his name, but he was a friend of Udo's. Indeed, he'd known Udo for nearly 40 years, which put him in the late-60s. He confessed to me that he had no serious intentions about the Championship at all, having merely come along on the ride that Udo was on, and – owing to a latent heart condition – rather doubted his capacity to get round the whole of Portmarnock's 7,000 yards.

He very nearly had to. I beat him with a four on the 17th by putting a five-iron absolutely stiff after hitting my teeshot straight along the ground.

It was gratifying to see a line in one of the Dublin evening papers: "In the lower half of the draw Campbell, a local player, is steadily working his way through the American menace."

By the following evening I'd got through another round. I can't remember his name either, but I know he was a Dublin man who was about half my size and capable of playing, on the very top of his game, to a handicap in the region of nine. Coach summed up the situation at dinner that night.

"No one," he said, "since the inauguration of the Amateur has ever had it easier for the first three rounds. It's a pity, in a way, it's over now."

He was referring, graciously, to the fact that I was to meet Billy O'Sullivan in the morning, in the fourth round.

Billy, who was well known to me, had been Irish Amateur Champion so often that it didn't seem possible he hadn't turned pro. With a two-handed, blacksmith's grip he hit it farther off the tee than anyone in Ireland. A Killarney man himself, he'd brought two-thirds of that fiercely partisan area with him, to assist in the laying waste to the city of Dublin which would automatically follow his almost certain victory in the final on Saturday afternoon.

I was devoid of hope. My coach – creator with Valentine Castlerosse of the Killarney Golf Club – had transferred his loyalties without equivocation to the local man, even inviting me to share his pleasure in contemplation of the beating that Billy, with his fine, slashing Killarney swing, would hand out to the plodding, mechanical, American methods of Willie Turnesa. "We want him fresh," were my coach's last words of advice, "so don't keep him out there too long – not that you will."

By the 11th hole it looked as though Billy would be back in the clubhouse for a long and leisured lunch. He was four up and on a loose rein. I was aiming the gun right out over the head of mid-wicket and hauling it so far back around the corner that time after time it finished up in the sandhills on the left. We were unattended by an audience. Even the camp-followers from Killarney were drinking stout in the bar, preparing themselves for the rigours of the O'Sullivan-Turnesa final.

Abruptly – and I can't remember how – Billy came to pieces. I got two holes back, so that on the 14th tee he was two up with five to go, a margin still sufficiently large, it seemed to me, not to leave the result in doubt.

Then something extraordinary happened. The 14th is a long, narrow green sloping up into the sandhills, with several cavernous bunkers in front. You couldn't play short and if you were over you'd a vile, slippery chip all downhill on a green burnt brown and 10 miles an hour faster than any hotel carpet. On the left, however, pin-high, was a patch of short rough into which I'd hooked all three previous second shots, by accident. They had remained there, however, leaving a comparatively simple scuffle up to the hole.

It would, if nothing else, be interesting to see if I could put it into the rough on purpose. For the first time – not having dared to try the innovation before – I swivelled the gun, played the left of the green and it stayed there, a combination of almost unbelievable circumstances.

Billy, outside me as usual, played a beautiful iron shot which hit the middle of the green, ran up the slope and disappeared over the top edge. His chip back slid eight feet past. He missed the putt. I holed a shortish one for a four, to be only one down. Even in the white-hot glow of having played a hole with the loaf, and having seen Billy making the obvious mistake, I still regarded it merely as a postponement of the inevitable 3 and 2 defeat that was coming my way – particularly in view of the nature of the 15th.

It's a short hole – about 170 yards – from a raised tee on the edge of the beach to a green sunk in sandhills, with jungle country all round and a deep hollow on the left. A brisk breeze was blowing off the sea, straight across. A further assurance of disaster was provided by the presence of Laddie Lucas and I think – my eyesight was beginning to go – Gerald Micklem, an expert audience ready to enjoy to the full a high, looping hook which would not be seen again or, alternatively, a furtive, defensive socket on to the beach.

One – or both – of them remarked that they were glad to see I'd got so far, in view of the fact that rumour had it we'd been back in the clubhouse for quite some time. No disarmingly modest response occurred to me. An uncontrollable but still faint trembling had started in my legs, more or less guaranteeing a shank. I struck at it quickly with a three-iron. It travelled low and straight into the cross-wind, and finished six feet from the hole. Incredulous laughter, instantly and graciously muffled, broke from Messrs Lucas and Micklem. Billy, holding his too far up into the wind, finished on the right-hand edge. His putt was short. Playing for a certain half from six feet, I put mine into the hole, and we were all square. As we walked down to the 16th tee Billy, possibly echoing a thought put into his mind by Lucas and Micklem, made his first remark for some time. "I don't know how you do it," he said.

I couldn't have told him, even if he'd really wanted to know. I was too busy trying to think of a method, based upon past experience, which would put my tee-shot on the fairway, and at least 200 yards away. The 16th is a long par-five, and grouped around the distant green were something like 500 people, waiting for the close finishes. For reasons of personal dignity and self-respect I had no desire to intrude into their company, having already played four.

The knee-trembling was becoming more acute, very similar, in fact, to the time when as a child of 10 I was menaced by armed members of the

IRA. My only desire was that the match should be over, one way or the other. No trace of the killer instinct had established itself, although I'd won four holes in a row.

It felt like a fairly good one, though the follow-through was curtailed because long after I'd hit it I was still looking at the ground. It turned out to have been low and rather hooky, but on the hard ground it had gone quite a long way. Billy hit a rasper right down the middle.

Then, as we walked off the tee, we saw an extraordinary thing – a spectacle like an infantry regiment, charging towards us. It was the 500 people – probably 200 of them from Killarney – who'd been waiting round the green. Instinct seemed to have warned them that a Homeric struggle – I was thinking like a golf correspondent – was in progress, and they wanted to be in on the kill.

They engulfed us. I lost sight of Billy, over to the right. I became conscious of an excited steward, dragging a length of rope. "Jaysus –" he cried – "I never thought I'd be doin' this for you!" He put down the rope and I stepped over it. "Get back there!" he bawled at the crowd. "Back there now, an' give him room!"

The ball was lying just on the edge of the rough, but nicely cocked up. People were standing round it in a semi-circle, five deep, craning in death-like silence to see over one another's heads. Hundreds more, lining the fairway, made it look like a long, solid tunnel to the green. It had the curious effect of promoting confidence, so many people expecting to see it go straight.

I took a long, slow swing with a 3-wood, making it look right for the audience. There was a lovely whip off the shaft, but I never saw where it went. They were after it, almost before I'd hit it. All I saw was a mass of backs, running away from me. My caddie and I were left alone. He was a young and inexperienced lad, as staggered as I was that we'd got so far. "I never seen a t'ing," he said.

Billy and I were both short, left and right, though I only knew where he was by the crowd around him. Someone told me it was my shot, and asked me the score. I found I didn't know.

I'd a 50-yard chip, up to the hole. Again the crowd, pressing in, seemed to narrow down the possibilities of error. I left it two feet from the hole. Then the running-backs hid it from me again, forming a solid, brightly coloured wall around the green. I'd quite a job to push through them, to find that Billy was about four feet away. Both of us holed out putts. Before mine dropped the gallery were running for the next tee.

It was still my honour. The ball was looking dingy and scuffed after the hard, sandy fairways, but in a peculiar way I felt it was part of me, that it knew what we were trying to do. Nothing could have made me change it for a new one. We were both in this together, and what we were trying to do was to beat hell out of Billy O'Sullivan, for whom I'd suddenly conceived such a hatred that I could scarcely wait to bash one down the middle so far that he'd jump at his and please God leave himself with an unplayable lie in a bush.

We were both down the middle. As I walked slowly and shakily after the running-backs, now seemingly multiplied by four, I was accosted by a well-spoken stranger. "Are you all right?" he asked me. He appeared strangely concerned. "Yeah," I said. "Yes." He looked at me for a long moment. "You look," he said, "as if you're going to faint." I saw for the first time that it was my father. "I'm all right," I told him, and walked on.

We were both on in two. We both got our four. We walked in silence to the 18th tee – all-square and one to go.

It took a long time before the stewards were able to clear the course. It was round about lunch-time. People were pouring out of the clubhouse and the beer tents, running for positions of vantage. In a championship all-square and one to go will cause any true golf enthusiast even to put down his bottle of stout, and come out and have a look.

The 18th at Portmarnock is a nasty one. A long, high mound on the left means you've got to keep your tee-shot well out on the right, to get a view of the green, and even then there's a rise in front of it which stops you seeing more than the top half of the pin.

I stood up to the ball, still having the honour. All hatred of Billy O'Sullivan had subsided, having given way to a bone-cracking weariness in which whatever mental processes were still alive were focused upon the immediate warming and soothing after-effects of two large Irish whiskeys in one glass.

I was shifting the clubhead about, trying to get a grip with the left hand which would push the ball out to the right, away from the mound on the other side, when someone let out a roar that froze me solid. "Fore –" he bawled – "ya silly ole bitch!"

I looked up – and saw an elderly woman, her wits deranged by scores of shouted, contrary instructions, scurrying about in the middle of the fairway, like a rabbit fleeing from 2,000 dogs. A friend or relative fell upon her, and dragged her away to safety. I started all over again. A moment later, playing with the greatest care and concentration, I hooked my tee-shot straight into the base of the mound.

"Bad luck," said Billy. It seemed to me that his rugged features were irradiated by an expression of gentle, brotherly love. The swine hit a beauty, a mile long and out on the right, giving him an easy 6-iron to the green.

I was sloping after the running-backs again, trying to calculate the minutes that remained between me and the two large Irish, when I found myself confronted by H. Longhurst, my patron and coach, of whom I'd seen nothing during the heat of the day. "You're doing well," he said pleasantly. "Why not try winning, for a change?"

"Go," I told him, "and set them up inside. Plain water with mine." Knowledgeable man that he is, he walked away.

It wasn't lying too badly but, being under the mound, I couldn't see the green. I took out a five-iron and hit it high into the air. It felt fairly all right, but the gallery put me straight. They let out a great cry of, "Oooh –!" on a descending scale, indicating beyond doubt that we were up to the ears in the radishes, for the first time for six holes.

I'd no idea where it was and still hadn't when I reached the green, which was hemmed in by the largest crowd I'd ever seen. There was no trace of the ball or, indeed, of anyone who seemed to know where it might be found. I pushed through the people massed in front of me and then heard a disordered shouting away to the left. Someone over there was waving a small red flag on the end of a long pole. I was in a deep bunker so far off the line, and so little used, that it was full of scattered stones and weeds growing up through the sand.

I went in after it. It was lying all right, clear at least of the stones. It was only then that I remembered Billy, and the important part that he was playing in the proceedings. I asked someone what had happened to him. He didn't know. General conjecture and speculation broke out. Several people thought he'd put it stiff. Others believed he was out of bounds, in the garden of the clubhouse. In the middle of all this a man, carrying a ham sandwich and a cardboard glass of stout, came running over the hill, his face suffused with excitement. "He's up to his doodlers in the pot bunker!" he bawled. "Ye've got him cold!"

For the second time, in this last, vital hole, I was about to play a shot without being able to see the pin – a fair commentary, I had time to remark, upon the accuracy of my method under pressure. I climbed out to have a look and saw Billy, already standing in the deep pot bunker cut into the right-hand edge of the green. The pin was only a few yards away from him. He'd have to play a miraculous one to get his four. If I could scuffle mine out and take only two putts, we'd very shortly be starting off down the 1st again, drawing farther and farther away from the healing malt in the bar.

I climbed down into the bunker again. The only unforgivable thing would be to leave it there. Expelling every breath of air from my lungs that might build up unwanted pressure, I swung the clubhead slowly back and equally slowly forward. It nipped the ball rather sweetly. It disappeared over the brow of the hill.

When I pushed through the crowd and walked on to the green I knew at once which was mine. It was four feet from the hole, a not impossible, dead straight putt, slightly uphill. Billy was three or four yards past it. No one could have got any closer out of that pot bunker, with a burnt-up green.

He had a horrible curly one with a six-inch borrow all down the side of the hill. He missed it.

I can remember exactly how I holed mine. I gripped the putter so tightly that it was impossible to break the wrists, and shoved it straight in. So incalculable are the workings of the human mind that I knew, even under that nerve-crinkling pressure, that I couldn't miss.

I don't remember anything at all about the next half-hour. There must have been a great deal of pleasure in assuring people in the bar that I had, in fact, beaten Billy O'Sullivan. The opportunity must have arisen for the extra pleasure of telling them, in part, how. There must also have been the extreme physical joy of the corrosive malt, slowly seeping through the system shaky and dehydrated by tension, fear and the need to discipline muscles jumpy and wayward as jelly. It's all a blur, but I do remember the thing that suddenly gave it edge and shape. It was the reminder, by someone who'd just bought me another large one, that I had, within the hour, to go out and do it again.

I would like, at this point, to make the frank admission that I knew I hadn't won the Championship by getting through four rounds but, at the same time, that I had reached a state of euphoria in which it practically seemed that I had. That is, to well-deserved roars of applause, I'd got much further even than my own mother – a non-player – would ever have imagined and now, full of drink and glory, was more than ready to step off the bus. Except that I was still in the Championship, and was off at 2.15, facing the powerful, ruthless and determined Kenneth Thom.

I recall a private moment of agonising – you can say that again – reappraisal in the convenience section of the gentlemen's locker room. I had to go out again and, stiff, sore, blurred and exhausted, beat Ken Thom. Another one into the rough on the left of the 14th, chip up and hole the putt. Another wind-splitter to the short 15th, and hole that one too. Then the three long holes home and the feeling of evening coming on and tattered newspaper blowing across the course and the fairways shiny and slippery with the battering of countless feet and cars filled with careless merrymakers driving away down the road because the main excitement of the day is over – except that, to survive, I've still got to get a four at the 18th and I'm in behind the mound . . .

Another thought occurred to me in the cathedral silence of the convenience section of the gentlemen's locker room. With this next round the Championship proper was only about to begin. The first four rounds, which had brought me to my knees, were in fact only a routine clearing away of the dross – a removal of the cheerful, slap-happy elements who'd merely come along for the ride. From now on we were getting down to work, opening up a little on the tee-shots, really picking the spots, far out, where we could start drilling home those iron-shots, going for our threes. One more round today – and two more tomorrow – *two more tomorrow*! – followed by the 36-hole final – 36 HOLES AT THE END OF A WEEK! – after which one of us would step up to receive the trophy, remark that the course seemed to be in excellent condition and that the runner-up had played a really wonderful game – and then, with the whites of the eyes rolling up, keel over backwards and fall stone dead. Except, of course, that the real men who win championships don't have much time to hang around afterwards, dying or making idle remarks. They've got to look slippy and get to the airport, because there are only three day for practice before exactly the same thing begins all over again.

I concluded the agonizing reappraisal, stunned by the size of the suddenly revealed gap between the real men and the lucky mice, and went to have lunch. There was only half an hour left before Ken Thom helped himself to a victory, the ease of which would pleasurably surprise him, at this comparatively late stage.

As soon as I got into the tent I saw that he must have had lunch already. Or, perhaps, a prey – wholly unjustifiably – to tournament nerves, he'd decided to leave it out altogether. The wind had increased in severity. Every time it blew back the flap of the lunch tent I could see him in the distance on the practice ground. With a whiplash crack he was drilling iron shots into the teeth of the wind under the expert instruction of the late Fred Robson, although I can't imagine what either of them was worrying about. All they had to do, if they were anxious about being beaten, was to come into the tent and watch me trying to wash down a lobster salad with alternative draughts of Guinness and John Jameson, a menu chosen more or less at random.

There was nothing left in the horse. Indeed, so little competitive spirit remained that I remember nothing whatever of the fifth and final round, except for the incident at the second hole.

Ken won the first – I think with a shaky five which wasn't, however, threatened at any point. At the next, I was miles away in the long, tenacious grass on the left. A clump with an eight-iron failed to do it very much harm, apart from improving the lie. I put the next one on the green, and left it on the lip of the hole for a five.

Ken already had his four. He knocked my ball away. "Half," he said. As we walked to the next tee, having rejected the undesirable solution of charity, I decided he hadn't seen the abortive bash with the eight-iron, presumed I was on in two and might even be counting himself lucky that my long putt hadn't gone in for a birdie.

Some light shadow-boxing took place with my conscience which, however, was in no shape for a major contest. I was storing the incident away in my bottom drawer, with plenty of old clothes on top of it to keep it away from the light, when I found Coach once more by my side. "Well played," he said, with apparently genuine admiration. "A couple more of those and you'll beat him."

It proved a confusing spur. I was still only one down after four more holes, though in reality, of course, it was two. On the 5th tee I had a night –or day–mare. Suppose by some inconceivable chance I had another resurrection and holed a four-footer on the 18th, to win one-up, would it then be possible to walk over to Ken Thom and in the presence of 5,000 people tell him that he'd got his arithmetic all trollocked up on the second and in fact we were still all-square? And how would Ken Thom, a dark, thick-set and dour young man, take it? What he'd do would be to concede the match, on the grounds that it was his own fault, and I'd have to get down on my knees in the middle of the 18th green and beg him to reconsider his quixotic decision. He'd turn away from this pitiful snivelling and the gallery would start throwing ham sandwiches, shooting-sticks, umbrellas . . . .

The matter did not arise, nor did it ever look as if it would. Ken Thom won far out in the country, counting – probably having been tipped off by one of his supporters who'd seen the incident at the second – every one of the shower of sixes that turned out to be the best that I could do in the fifth round of the Amateur Championship, when all of us were opening the tap a bit and really starting to go for those threes.

At this late stage it seems improbable that I shall have another shot at the Amateur title.

You've got to qualify now before you're allowed in.

HISTORY IS MADE

Derek Lawrenson

The Americans refer to epic sporting moments in such terms as "The Game", or "The Drive", or "The Series". The definite article emphasises the Homeric contest that we have witnessed, something extraordinary enough to deserve its own unique niche. In this context, the 32nd Walker Cup fully deserves to be referred to as "The Match".

In one unforgettable afternoon, Great Britain and Ireland went from a certain win to a probable loss to a certain draw to the narrowest of victories, by 12 ½–11 ½.

The bewildering twist of plot left us breathless and wound up like a coil. How could they be so much better than the Americans? How could they undo all the good work? How did they manage to win? So many questions whispered through the spectacular Peachtree woodland. Our perception of the events unfolding before us changed as quickly as the mind of a Don Juan. No wonder, in its immediate aftermath, the United States Captain, Fred Ridley, described the momentous occasion as, "one of the greatest matches I have seen, heard or read about".

And at the end of it, the Americans, who had witnessed a rare lunar eclipse the previous day, found themselves suffering an eclipse of a still rarer nature. It was the first British and Irish Walker Cup victory on American soil in 67 years of trying. It left Peachtree with the sort of record that could give a place a complex.

It is unquestionably one of America's great courses and also one of the most exclusive, possessing not many more than 200 members. It is quite an achievement then to have produced three Walker Cup players. The only trouble is that every time Peachtree has a Walker Cup representative, America loses. It happened in 1938, again in 1971, and this time they put the tin lid on a bizarre coincidence, having both a player and being the venue for the day when the British and Irish registered only their third victory in 32 attempts.

And so our leading golfers at all levels continue to flatten the bastions of American golfing supremacy. "Isn't there a law agains all this silverware leaving the country?" the United States Golf Association official, Jim Morris, jokingly inquired. Four years ago, no British and Irish team had won a golf event in America. Now we are falling over ourselves with trophies.

The breakthrough victory by the Curtis Cup team in Kansas in 1986 was followed by the Ryder Cup win a year later. But the Walker Cup appeared the Holy Grail. Two years ago post-Sunningdale, notions of victory in this event would have been laughed out of court. But no world changes like the amateur one.

This team took no scarred memories from that event, bar that of the captain, Geoff Marks. And any loss of self-belief on his part had been erased by the Eisenhower Trophy victory last year. The esprit de corps was first-class. "There is a quiet confidence that we can do the job," said Peter McEvoy.

Ridley said: "When the bell rang you could see they had a serious look in their eyes." Two year ago, it was the look of a frightened rabbit. This time, fed on Perform nuts and raisin bars and Isostar drinks to combat the brutal humidity, Great Britain and Ireland really did perform.

The first indicator that things were to be different came in the foursomes match featuring McEvoy and the Irishman Eoghan O'Connell against Greg Lesher and Jay Sigel. Between them McEvoy and Sigel have played in a dozen Walker Cup matches but neither had known anything like it.

The Midland-Irish combination won 6 and 5, giving McEvoy his biggest win and handing Sigel his largest defeat in Walker Cup combat. As subsequent events were to prove, it was the start of a traumatic 48 hours for Sigel, America's most decorated amateur.

Ridley said: "I considered the pairing our second strongest, but they just ran into a buzz saw."

The news of this overwhelming victory had an inspirational effect elsewhere. The GB & I captain, Geoff Marks, said: "It was the sort of thing you look for. You hope for a big lead in one match by the turn. It gives everyone a boost if you can mentally put one point on the board.

McEvoy and O'Connell single-putted no fewer than eight of the first 11 holes, and this triumph was supported by a victory for Andrew Hare and Jim Milligan who defeated David Eger and Kevin Johnson by 2 and 1. The British duo had lived on their nerves. They were three up after four holes, but, by the time they entered the last four, the position was all-square.

Over these closing holes we saw another pointer for the events to follow. Far from crumbling altogether after losing their position of strength, Hare and Milligan came back to win the 15th and the 17th. "All week, the British and Irish players made the putts that mattered in a way that used to belong solely to the Americans," Ridley was to reflect later, echoing the words of all recent US team captains.

At the time though, British pessimism in Walker Cup matters was still a deeply-ingrained thing, and when the first hole of the first three singles after lunch all went America's way, the backlash looked to have begun. It did not get much further. McEvoy again symbolised the spirit. He played like a man possessed and he probably was after being left out of the team at Sunningdale. He was up against the Peachtree member Danny Yates and at two down after three holes, his shirt already soaked in sweat, he looked to be out of it. Yet McEvoy's concentration never wavered. He played some magnificent golf over the back nine and emerged a victor.

Russell Claydon bounced back from a foursomes defeat to win. Craig Cassells marked his first singles appearance with a victory. Milligan, meanwhile, lost 7 and 6. It is worth digesting that because it helps to place in perspective his performance a day later. But Milligan's misfortune was forgotten, buried amid a halfway score of 7½–4½ in favour of the visitors.

It was the biggest lead at that stage for 24 years and when GB & I won three and halved one of the following morning's foursomes, the confident filing of the copy had begun. Fleet Street's early editions resounded to the heady news that our boys were on the brink of a Walker Cup victory. They had so devastated their opponents that a rout appeared on the cards. The only reason the Americans had prevented a whitewash was because Robert Gamez and Doug Martin had birdied the last hole against McEvoy and O'Connell.

Elsewhere we had witnessed as complete a team performance as could be envisaged. An 80-minute storm merely delayed the victory thunder. Milligan and Hare won once more going through their now familiar routine of starting well, collapsing in the middle, and finishing strongly. Stephen Dodd and Garth McGimpsey won more conventionally, 2 and 1. Claydon and Craig Cassells triumphed 3 and 2.

It all meant that GB & I needed just 1½ points from the last eight singles, and when Ridley came in and said, "I like their chances right now," it looked the understatement to end them all. But that was before what Marks was to coin "the long afternoon".

How things can change in matchplay. Two hours into the singles, and the smiles had gone from the British and Irish faces. Mark's last words to his team had been along the lines of not looking over your shoulder to see if the fellow behind is getting the necessary point. Yet we looked over shoulders, looked everywhere, and we could not see anything. At one point, the Americans led in all eight matches. It was looking like a collapse of Devon Loch proportions, and perhaps the most spectacular in the history of team sports.

"For an hour I was listening on the radio and I don't think we won a single hole," Marks said. "I could not see anywhere where we were going to get the points." McEvoy, drained by the previous three games, was quickly a lost cause. Neil Roderick faded. Cassells was losing heavily. The Americans were ripping the heart out of their opponents with some stirring play.

And the biggest body blow was still elsewhere as Robert Gamez defeated Stephen Dodd. This was a match that had this observer stunned by its quality. Dodd played a catalogue of great shots. He chipped in at the 13th. He chipped stone dead for a birdie at the 16th. How he found the green from an impossible place on the 18th, only he will know.

His opponent was the American Gamez, their player of the week. He has the look of a Diego Maradona about him, a cocksure Latin who uses his hands as skilfully as the famous Argentinian footballer. But even a back nine of two under par coming up the last did not appear enough to deny the Welshman Dodd a precious half.

And then he holed from 30 feet on the final green, and the British stomachs hit the floor. "That was the real sickener," said Marks. "The cheer could be heard round the course, and the louder the Americans cheered, the more their putts seemed to drop."

Victory in all eight singles for the Americans was now a distinct possibility. From somewhere a courageous British team dragged itself from the depths of despair. Hare showed the way. He was two down with two to play but played wonderful shots into the heart of the last two greens and won both holes. At last a hopeful sign, a sign that the momentum was not on a one-way escalator headed in the direction of America.

Hare's half was followed quickly by one for O'Connell, who was the top British and Irish scorer of the week, with three points out of four. It will be surprising if this 21 year-old from Killarney, who attends Wake Forest University in North Carolina, does not enjoy a successful professional career.

He has that air of quiet arrogance possessed by all top sportsmen, who know they are good at what they are doing. His swing and temperament are equally sound. He was, for me, the player of the event.

On this afternoon he was up against another highly rated youngster, the 19-year-old left-handed American, Phil Mickelson. The visitors' joy at now inching within a half of the magic total was consumed by Mickelson holing a 12-foot putt at the last hole to secure his share of the spoils. All manner of American celebrations went on. He was immediately mobbed by his team-mates while O'Connell still had an 18-inch putt to ensure the stalemate.

Any reservations about American behaviour at this juncture however were quickly harboured. Mickelson had forgotten himself in the euphoria of holing that putt but he had enough presence of mind to walk up and pick up O'Connell's ball marker. Walker Cup tradition had been upheld.

So, it appeared, had US possession of the trophy. The importance of Mickelson's putt was that now there was only one match left on the course. The Americans had pulled within a point of what had earlier appeared an impossible target, and in this one game Sigel was two up with three to play against Milligan.

What odds would you have got on Milligan gaining a half at that point against Sigel, a veteran of seven Walker Cups, and the most revered name in world amateur golf? You could have named your own, but instead Milligan, a 26-year-old joiner, made a name for himself.

He holed from 12 feet to halve the 15th. He chipped stone dead at the 16th for a winning birdie. After fluffing a chip at the 17th, he then chipped in to win that one with a par. This time, a British player was mobbed by his team-mates.

It is at moments like these that a captain can influence events, and Marks stepped in. He was a member of the 1971 Walker Cup winning team, and the experience of that event no doubt had a hand to bear on his decision to interrupt Milligan's excited walk to the last tee of the last hole of the last game in the Walker Cup.

"I wanted Sigel to get to the tee first," Marks said. "I wanted Jim to compose himself and remember to think clearly and swing slowly. The shots that were to follow were clearly going to be the most important shots of his life and I must say how well he responded."

After two blows each, the chances of Milligan gaining the crucial half were still favourable. Both players had missed the green on the right. Then the Scot played an excellent pitch off a ball nestling dangerously in the Bermuda rough. It ran on 10 feet. There was still a slim chance for Sigel to show what he could do, the sort of opportunity in fact that became his trademark in the vintage years. But what followed now left a feeling of sadness, even if it did lead directly to a historic victory for GB & I.

Sigel quit on the pitch, just as any high handicapper might do. "It was a dumb shot," he admitted later. The 45-year-old veteran was playing his fourth match in two days, and he looked shattered by all that had gone before. The greatest of careers was drawing to an ignominious conclusion.

"Maybe he has been asked to play that role of anchor-man position once too often," Marks said. The Americans had fallen for the old British habit of picking a player on sentiment.

Sigel's chip had crawled onto the edge of the green, and when the putt that followed missed comfortably, Milligan had two putts from 10 feet to be forever remembered as the man who won the Walker Cup.

He rolled the first up to two inches and when Sigel shook his hand, Milligan was engulfed in a sea of Brits. How much Milligan and his nine colleagues wanted to win was now plainly evident. Claydon's last act as an amateur was to let out a victory roar that caused the green to shake. McEvoy's smile was that of a man a victor after four previous losing attempts. McGimpsey embraced his partner Dodd. And at the centre of it all was Milligan, who fully lived up to the legend of Scotland the Brave.

Great days in Peachtree, Atlanta. Now, whenever we think of the Walker Cup, we will always have Georgia on our minds.

A SLIGHT CASE OF IMAGINATION

Peter Alliss with Bob Ferrier

Jim Turnesa on the 17th tee was clearly nervous, fidgeting with his grip, but he got a good drive away. Wentworth's 17th is a dog-leg to the left, turning round the gardens of some houses and the left side is out of bounds. The right side makes it a long, long shot to the green. I decided to aim at the left-hand corner, hit the ball hard and let it drift back onto the fairway. I hit a real purler – but it did not fade back. It caught the corner, and there I was, out of bounds by a couple of feet. I made a four with my second ball, but he was down carefully in five and dormie. We were both now very tense, and it was Turnesa's turn to miss a drive. He hit an unbelievable slice, fully 60 yards into the trees down the right side. My drive was a good one, right where I wanted it. Hundreds of people swarmed around, in and out of the trees. One of them came over and said to me that he was in a shocking spot and could not possibly play it out of there. Then there was a great deal of crackling and crashing around in the trees, shouts of "Here it comes, here it comes," and the ball came reeling and staggering out into the fairway. Next he hit a wood shot some 40 yards short of the green. I let go with a good two-iron shot which finished almost pin-high and some 15 yards to the left of the stick. The shot had a little drag on it, caught the left-hand corner of the banked green and finished in a little, mossy hollow.

When I got there, I found that it was very close to the grandstand which had been built around the back of the green. This was the moment when, above all else, I needed some sound, mature advice. It did not come. Henry Cotton should have been there. He was not there. In fact he was on the other side of the green with his wife "Toots" and a group of journalists. I learned later that Henry was about to fight his way round to me – thousands were milling round the green – when someone said, "Oh, no, Henry, you simply cannot give blatant advice." Cotton it appears was going to suggest that I play the shot with a straight-faced club and run it up to the hole. The whole incident is almost stupid when I think back on it. The writers had a field day, describing how I had "frozen" on the situation. Nothing of the kind happened. As I walked round the ball, even as I stood by it, my mind was full of nothing but feet, rows and rows of feet – brogues, mocassins, sneakers, boots, shoes, spikes and rubbers, the shoes of the people perched on the front seats of the grandstand. In fact, my ball was within two club-lengths of the stands and in law, as it were, it could have been moved. The biggest pair of shoes belonged to Tony Duncan, Colonel Duncan, the former Walker Cup captain. Why I should notice that, I'll never know. The thought of Duncan, Duncan's feet and all those boots and shoes on the stands kept popping idiotically in and out of my mind. The ground between me and the hole was not as simple as it must have looked to many people. It was rather mossy and fluffy. The answer was to swing my wedge well back and slowly and carefully lob it well on to the green. Then of course I had the fear that if my backswing was a little too long, I might hit some of those damned shoes in the stand. I took a long steady swing at it, at the last moment forgot all about the ball and bumbled it a yard short of the green. I had to play again. This time I played a neat little run-up, just over a yard from the stick, played four. Turnesa was on and missed his putt for a five. Then from that short range, I missed. Half in six and for Alliss, a ridiculous, incredible, childish, delinquent six. I don't quite know how I lived through the next 15 minutes of my life. Next came Bernard Hunt, and it was his turn to walk alone in the wilderness, alone and solitary despite the thousands around that green. He was on the back of the green in three against Dave Douglas and needed the regulation two putts to win the match. Bernard three-putted and only halved and the entire Ryder Cup match was lost on the last green by Alliss and Hunt, the young ones.

Chapter 12

FROM HICKORY
TO GRAPHITE

James Balfour

Let us now turn to the changes that have taken place on the balls. Forty years ago, and indeed from time immemorial, the only kind of ball with which golf has been played was made of leather stuffed with feathers till it was as hard as a gutta-percha. In making it the leather was cut into three pieces, softened with alum and water, and sewed together by waxed thread, while a small hole was left for putting in the feathers, which was done with a strong stuffing-iron.

The hole in the leather, which did not affect the flight of the ball, but slightly interfered with its putting quality, was then sewed up, and the ball received three coats of paint. A man could make only four balls in a day. They were thus scarce and expensive, and were not round, but rather oblong. The only ball-maker at St Andrews was Allan Robertson. The trade was hereditary in his family, as both father and grandfather had likewise been ball-makers. He was assisted by Tom Morris and Lang Willie. They worked together in Allan's kitchen, and the balls were sold at the window at the back of his house, at the corner of the Links and Golf Place. Allan charged 1s. 8d. a ball, or £1 a dozen. Gourlay of Musselburgh charged 2s. for each of his. These balls did not last long, perhaps not more than one round. They opened at the seams, especially in wet weather. Indeed, whenever the seam of the ball was cut by the club, the ball burst, and became useless. This very frequently happened, insomuch that the caddies generally took out six or eight balls with them.

About the beginning of the year 1848 balls were first made of gutta-percha. I remember the commencement of them perfectly. My brother-in-law, Admiral Maitland Dougall, played a doubles match at Blackheath with the late Sir Ralph Anstruther and William Adam of Blair-Adam and another friend with gutta-percha balls on a very wet day. They afterwards dined together at Sir Charles Adam's at Greenwich Hospital, and Sir Ralph said after dinner: "A most curious thing – here is a golf ball of gutta-percha; Maitland and I have played with it all day in the rain, and it flies better at the end of the day than it did at the beginning." Maitland came to Edinburgh immediately after and told me of this. We at once wrote to London for some of these balls, and went to Musselburgh to try them. Gourlay the ball-maker had heard of them, and followed us round. He was astonished to see how they flew, and, being round, how they rolled straight to the hole on the putting green. He was alarmed for his craft, and having an order from Sir David Baird to send him some balls whenever he had a supply by him, he forwarded to him that evening six-dozen! Sir David accordingly was one of the last who adhered to the feather balls, and did not acknowledge the superiority of the others until his large supply was finished. At first they were made by hand by rolling them on a flat board; thus made, they were round and smooth. They were not painted, but used with their natural brown colour. When new, they did not fly well, but ducked in the air. To remedy this they were hammered with a heavy hammer, but this did not effect the object. They still ducked until they got some rough usage from the cleek or iron. This made cuts on their sides, which were not liked; but it made them fly. These cuts were easily removed by dipping them in hot water at night. I remember once playing with old Philp, the club-maker (who, by the way, was no contemptible player). I had a gutta ball, and he had a feather one. With the dislike which all the tradesmen then had for the former, he said, "Do you play with these putty balls?" "Yes," I answered. "But does not the cleek cut them?" "Oh yes," I said, "but if you give them a hot bath at night that puts them all right." "That's the mischief o't," he replied. Yet it was soon found out that this same hot bath, while it cured the wound, spoiled the ball. I remember an amusing proof of this. I and a friend on the day before the medal played with two guttas, and they worked beautifully, so that we resolved to play with them the next day for the medal. But as they had been a good deal hacked, we dipped them in hot water overnight, and removed these defects. When, however, we played off the tee next day before an assembled crowd, among whom were the ball and club-makers, both the balls whirred and ducked amid the chuckling and jeering and loud laughter of the onlookers; we had to put down feather balls next hole. The fact was, they required those indentations to make them fly. About this time it occurred to an ingenious saddler in South Street to hammer them all round with the thin or sharp end of the hammer. This experiment was completely successful, and the ball thus hammered come rapidly into use, and they were soon improved by being painted. But the ball-makers were still bitterly opposed to them, as they threatened to destroy their trade, and both Allan and Tom resolved that they would never play in a match where these balls were used. In an unlucky hour, however, Tom good-naturedly broke his pledge, and played with a gentleman as his partner who had gutta balls. When Allan discovered it he was much annoyed with Tom. Tom, when he saw this, gave up his employment under him, and opened a shop of his own, where he made both kinds of balls, and also clubs. Allan in a little time followed suit with the balls, as he discovered he could make a dozen guttas in a shorter time than he could make one feather ball, and the sale of them increased prodigiously. After that an iron mould was invented for making these balls, and on being taken from the mould, they were indented with the thin end of the hammer. But latterly the moulds have the indentations in them, so that the ball is now produced indented and ready for being painted. The balls are made everywhere now, but some are better than others, probably because the maker takes greater pains to use good gutta-percha.

THE HASKELL ARRIVES

Horace Hutchinson

In 1899 my brother-in-law, returning from a visit to America, came down to stay and to play golf with me at Ashdown Forest, and brought with him a dozen or two of a new kind of ball which, he said, had lately been invented in the United States and was the best ball in the world. The balls were called, as he told me, Haskells. We went out to play with them. He, as it happened, played very badly, and in a very short time he was perfectly ready to go into any court of law and take his oath that they were the worst balls in the world. I had formed my own opinion of them, much more in accord with the verdict with which he had first introduced them to me than with the condemnatory one which he passed on them after two days of being off his game; but I refrained from expressing my opinion too emphatically, with the result that when he went away he said that, as for the remnant of the balls, he was not going to be bothered "to take the beastly things away", so that I found myself the possessor of a couple of dozen or so of excellent Haskell balls – being as he had said, in the first instance, the best balls in the world – at a time when no one else in Great Britain had such a ball at all!

It is quite true that some months previously, at North Berwick, I had been given to try, by a professional who had just returned from the States, a ball which I now recognised to be the same, in some of its essentials, as these Haskells which my brother-in-law brought over. It was the same, except for one external but extremely important essential – its nicks were ridiculously too light and slight, not nearly enough indented. So I tried that ball and found it wanting – it would not fly at all. But what I did not realise at the time was the reason why it did not fly; or, if I did realise, as once could not fail to do, that the nicks were not emphatic enough, I had not a suspicion of the merit of its interior qualities. I had not appreciated that it was an amazingly good ball if only this slight matter of its exterior marking had been attended to. I had taken no more thought or notice of it.

Armed with these new weapons I prepared to go out to Biarritz, where the annual foursome match against Pau was just impending. My partner was to be Evy Martin Smith, and as soon as I arrived I told him that we must use these new balls for the match. He strongly objected, being a firm conservative, tried the balls, with every intention of disliking them, and disliked them accordingly. The fact is that I was, at this moment, just the last man in the world to appear on any scene as an advocate of a new ball. Only a year or two before I had taken an unfortunate interest in a patent substance called "Maponite", of which, in addition to a thousand and one other things for which gutta-percha and indiarubber are used, golf balls were to be made. And wherein exactly was the weak point of the stuff as a material for golf balls I never knew, for the trial balls that they made for us were excellent – I remember that I won an open tournament at Brancaster with them – but as soon as ever they began to turn them out in numbers they were useful for one end only – for the good of the club-makers – for they were hard stony things which broke up the wooden clubs as if one had used the clubs as stone hammers.

So I was not a good apostle of a new ball – rather discredited in fact – but I did induce Evy Smith to play with the ball finally, under deep protest, and we justified its use by winning. Meanwhile the balls were beginning to filter from America into England. It was difficult indeed to get people to appreciate their merits: the balls were not numerous, and were still hard to obtain. At Johnny Low's request I sent him one for trial. He was writing at the time in the *Athletic News*. He wrote a most amusing article about the ball – said that he had tried a stroke or two with it in his room, and found it so resilient that it went bounding about the room like a fives ball in a squash court and finally disappeared up the chimney and was never seen again.

In fine, he gave the ball his banning, "not because it was an expensive ball" – it is to be remembered that it was rather a shock to be asked to pay two and sixpence for a golf ball, whereas we had paid a shilling as the normal price – "but because it was a bad ball", meaning a ball "singularly ill-adapted for the purpose" of golf. So difficult is it for even a clever man and wise in the royal and ancient wisdom, as Johnny Low undoubtedly is, to keep an unprejudiced judgement about any new thing.

Expensive as the ball was in the beginning, it was soon found that it was far more economical than the solid "guttie", both because it lasted in playable condition far longer and also because it did not knock about the wooden club to anything like the same extent. But within a very short while there came such a demand for those balls, so greatly in excess of the supply, that there was a time when as much as a guinea apiece was paid for them, and numbers changed hands at ten shillings. That was round and about the time of the championships, both Open and Amateur being held that year at Hoylake, and both these championships were won with the Haskell balls.

I am calling these balls Haskells, because that is the name by which they were known and spoken of, after their American inventor, at this time. The reluctance of players to use them, and the gradual overcoming of that reluctance, had many comic incidents associated with it.

The Amateur Championship that year was full of wonders. It was won by Charles Hutchings, he being then a grandfather and 52 years of age. He knocked me out, among other better men, beating me at the last hole. And then he beat that brilliant and greatly to be regretted young golfer, Johnny Bramston. In the final he had to play Fry, and established a very big lead on him in the first round. He had about six holes in hand with only nine to play, and then Fry began to do conjuring tricks, holing putts from the edge of the green and so on. In the event Charles Hutchings just won by a single hole after one of the most remarkable final matches in the whole story of that championship. And it is to be noted that these two finalists, who proved themselves better able than most others to adapt themselves to the new touch of these livelier balls – for nearly all the competitors used the Haskells – were extremely good billiard players. Fry had won the Amateur Championship of billiards more than once, and Hutchings was quite capable of such atrocities as a three-figure break. I think the sensitive fingers of these billiard players helped them to get the touch of these livelier balls which were so "kittle" for the approach and putting.

After the Amateur came the Open, in which I did not take a hand, but I heard a great deal of the preliminary discussions about it. Of course, if the amateurs were difficult to convince about the merits of the new balls, the professionals, who had their vested interest in the old, and did not know how these were to be affected by the coming of the new, were harder still to convince. However, the balls were too good to be denied. Andrew Kirkaldy, a shrewd man, and one, besides, who had no interest in the sale of balls, solid or rubber cored, was one of the first and most enthusiastic converts. "The puggy," he declared, "is a great ba'." He called it "puggy", which is Scottish for monkey, because it jumped about so. "Ye canna' tak' 80 strokes to the roun' wi' a puggy – the puggy will na' gae roun' in 80 strokes."

BAFFIES, RUT-IRONS AND CLEEKS

James Balfour

The change in the clubs has not been so important as in the balls, but some have been discontinued that were formerly used, and others have been introduced. For example, the driving putter is never now played with. It was a club with a putter head, but with a flatter angle than a putter, a shaft about the length of a middle spoon, and, though stiff, had a spring in it. It was used to play out of bents and thick grass, but as these have now disappeared, so has the club. It was convenient, too, for playing against wind.

Another club that I fear is fast getting obsolete is the baffing spoon. As golfers know, to baff a ball is to touch the turf below the ball pretty firmly when it is struck, and the ball is thus raised into the air. The baffy is a very short spoon, about the length of a putter, but spooned twice the depth of an ordinary short spoon. It is used when near the hole, and when the ball has to be lifted over a hazard or uneven ground. There are few prettier strokes in the game. The ball is tossed high in the air, and hovers for a moment, as if to choose what blade of grass to alight on, then drops, and does not run above a foot or so. It is not only a pretty stroke, but a very effective one when well played. In the hands of Captain Dalgleish, Sir David Baird, Shihallion, or Sir Robert Hay, the baffy was a wonderful weapon. But now men have grown so fond of cleeks and irons in all shapes and sizes that it is despised. It is said that Allan Robertson introduced the use of the cleek when near the hole. If so, it is, I think, a pity that he did. It is not so pretty a stroke; it destroys the green, as some even intentionally cut the turf with it; and it is not more sure than the stroke with the baffy.

While these two clubs have gone out of fashion, two others have been introduced. One is the iron niblick, with which to play out of bunkers, or when in a hole or cart-rut. It is a heavy iron, with a short round head, and is admirably adapted for bunkers, as it takes much less sand than the ordinary heavy iron with which that stroke used to be played.

The other new club is the wooden niblick. It is long spoon, with a very short head, plated with brass on the bottom, from which it gets its other name of the brassey. It is used for playing a cupped or bad-lying ball, or a ball on a road. On a road the brass bottom saves the club from being destroyed by the hard surface, and with its short head many men can play a cupped ball as well as a ball from the tee with a play-club. No set would be complete without having both an iron niblick and a brassey.

TOOLS OF THE GAME

David Stirk

The early records of golf obviously mean that there were club-makers and ball-makers from the 15th century on, but as the number of golfers was small, and the eastern Scottish communities among whom the game was played had poor communications, there can have been few, if any, following the trade full-time for a living. Most golf clubs must have been made by enthusiastic local amateurs.

It was the taking up of golf by the King and his Court that gave rise to the trade of golf club-maker. The Royal Court demanded a higher standard of clubs – and was prepared to pay for them.

Until 1920 *all* golf clubs had wooden shafts, and the term "wooden golf club" implies a club with a wooden head as well. Those who made wooden clubs were commonly known as club-makers, and the earliest recorded one was a citizen of Perth whose main trade was that of a bower, or bow-maker. We do not know his name but we know that in 1502 James IV of Scotland purchased some "golf clubbes" from him. At that time bow-making was a common trade, and the fact that the clubs were ordered from a bow-maker rather than, say, one of the many carpenters or shipwrights suggests that he was chosen as a man who knew all about the elasticity and suppleness of various woods and so was in a better position to produce flexible, whippy clubs. But against this there are only two other references to bow-makers producing golf clubs. One was William Mayne, bow-maker, of Perth, from whom James IV of Scotland and I of England ordered clubs and whom he also appointed royal club-maker. The other was William Fergie (1856–1924), of Archers' Hall, Edinburgh, Bow-maker to the Queen's Bodyguard and golf club- and ball-maker.

Other craftsmen with a special knowledge of the elastic properties of different woods were those who made fishing rods, and there is clear evidence that some of them also made golf clubs, though the written evidence all refers to the late 19th and early 20th centuries.

In the 18th century we find many references to club-makers, a number of them doubling as ball-makers. The Dickson family of Leith, near Edinburgh, were among the most prominent, their best recorded member being John Dickson, club-maker. He died in 1787, but it is thought that earlier Dicksons were in the golf club-making trade. The first half of the century also records George and Henry Milne, club- and ball-makers, of St Andrews, and one David Dick of that town, but we know no more than that they plied the trade. A letter of 1735 refers to an Andrew Bailey then making clubs at Bruntsfield, Edinburgh, and later in the century a Thomas Comb also made clubs at Bruntsfield as well as running a local pub called the Foxtoun, which served at the Bruntsfield Clubhouse.

That there was a thriving Scottish trade in club- and ball-making during the 18th century is shown by bills of lading at the Port of Leith, which record that between 1743 and 1751 some 168 clubs and nearly 1,000 balls were exported from there to South Carolina and Virginia. A later (1765) bill of lading at the port of Glasgow records the despatch of 18 golf clubs and 144 balls to Maryland. Unfortunately there is no indication of who made these exports but they do show that the trades of club-maker and ball-maker were going concerns, and also prove conclusively that golf was being played in America some 130 years before its generally accepted starting time of 1880.

In 1770 Thomas Comb was followed at Bruntsfield by James McEwan, and Dickson was followed at Leith by Simon Cossar (1766–1811). McEwan and Cossar are significant, not only because theirs are the earliest authenticated wooden clubs still in existence, but also because they bring us into the 19th century, which saw the flowering of the club-maker's art.

The making of golf clubs during the first 70 years of the 19th century was largely in the hands of six families: the McEwans of Leith, and later of nearby Musselburgh; the Forgans of St Andrews; the Patricks of Leven, in Fife; the Morrises of St Andrews; the Parks of Musselburgh; and the Dunns of North Berwick. To these families must be added some individual club-makers: Simon Cossar, of Leith, who preceded all of them; Hugh Philp (1782–1856), who preceded the Forgans at St Andrews and became a founder member of the Forgan family business after his daughter married into that family; and John Jackson (1805–78), of Perth.

These were the recognised master craftsmen of the trade, who entirely hand-made their clubs with the help of apprentices. In their heyday they produced incomparable clubs which are now prized collectors' items. But by the end of the century only the Patricks and the Forgans were still active. The master craftsmen had been ousted by mass production, which had become necessary to meet the demands of an ever-growing number of golfers.

Until 1900 the head of a wooden club was fixed to the shaft by means of a long splice, a "scarffed" joint of the type long in use by shipwrights for repairing masts and spars. When clubmakers used it they called it a "scared" joint, and clubs made in this way are commonly called "scared head" clubs. The scared joint was held by glue and whipping, the latter usually of crude fisherman's twine. At the top of the shaft was the grip, which was of fine sheepskin and was thickened by having layers of cloth, known as "listings", beneath it. Before 1820 the shafts of clubs were made of ash, but at about that date hickory from the southern part of the United States was introduced because of its superior steely whip. The club was protected from the weather by prolonged rubbing down with "red keel", a substance whose composition is not now known and which was dropped from use after 1830, when varnish became available.

The clubs were several inches longer than modern ones, some 44–46 inches, and their feel was extremely whippy, with considerable torque. The heads were long (4–5 inches) and narrow (1½–2 inches). The face of the club was only an inch deep and was gracefully curved, being "turned in" at the toe, which made the face concave. Inserted into the leading edge of the club's sole, and held there by glue and three pegs was a strip of ram's-horn ½ inch wide and ⅛ inch thick, whose purpose was to protect the wood and prevent its being chipped. When the horn eventually became damaged it could be removed and replaced with a new piece. This feature must be of great antiquity because no wooden club without it has ever been found. Clubs of this general type continued to be made until 1880.

During the first half of the 19th century a "set" of golf clubs would be all wooden except for one iron. Wooden clubs – drivers or play clubs – were used for driving, and all shots through the green were effected with clubs such as long, middle and short spoons. These names referred to different lengths, but the clubs also had progressively increased loft. The putter was also of wood and was used for shots of up to 100 yards or even more. Essential for playing approach shots at this time was the "baffing spoon", a club of great character used particularly for lofted shots. It got its name from the fact that in use it "baffed" the ball, that is it struck the ground immediately behind it. As the club bounced off the ground it lifted the ball in the air. It was said to be a very pretty stroke in skilled hands but its length was difficult to control.

Another club much in use was the wooden niblick, much shorter in the head than other clubs and frequently equipped with a piece of brass on its sole to protect it from damage by stones. The wooden niblick was commonly used in any situation in which the longer-nosed clubs could not be made to "sole" behind the ball, for example where the ball was in a tight "cuppy" lie – in other words, lying in a slight small depression.

The solitary iron, which could easily burst a feather ball costing three times the price of the club itself, was used only for such desperate purposes as getting the ball out of bunkers, cart ruts or stony lies, situations in which a wooden head might disintegrate. When the new tough gutta-percha balls came into general use about 1850 iron clubs began to increase in numbers and wooden ones to decrease. This was not only because there was no danger of bursting the new balls. Lofted shots were found to be easier with iron clubs than with wooden ones, and the baffing spoon was relegated to the attic. Also, the hard new balls damaged the faces of wooden clubs, and clubs now cost more than balls.

In 1880 there came a change in the shape of club heads. They became much shorter (2–3½ inches) and wider (3–4 inches) but with deeper faces (1¼–1½ inches). But the most striking change was that the faces were now convex, bulging forward, so that they came to be called "bulgers". The new clubs were also shorter than earlier ones, with 40–42-inch shafts.

In 1900 a new wood for golf clubheads and a new way of fixing heads to shafts were introduced. Just as hickory from America had been found best for shafts, persimmon, a very hard wood, also American, was now found to be best for heads. Instead of fixing head to shaft by means of the long splice a hole was drilled in the head and the shaft's end inserted into it, in the same way that the shaft of an iron club was fitted into the head. The new clubs were called socket-headed clubs and the new method of fixing lent itself readily to machine production. American expertise came into play and by 1902 the US was exporting 100,000 golf clubs to Britain annually. The heads were rough-finished, and the British professional had merely to polish them up and stamp his name on them. The craftsmen club-makers were out of business.

The old club-makers were expert woodworkers but knew nothing of working metal. In the time of the feather ball few iron clubs were required and for those few the club-makers got blacksmiths to make the metal heads and themselves fitted shafts of the right length and spring into the sockets.

Generally a blacksmith would make an iron clubhead by taking a straight piece of iron of the right thickness and cutting it to the length of the desired clubface plus the length of the "hosel", or socket. He would then heat one end of this piece and hammer it so that the thickness was halved. This part he then hammered round the tapered end of a piece of iron called a mandrel, making a tapered socket. The two edges of the metal that joined to form the socket were completely fused together so that no join line could be seen. This left the socket still in line with the face as one straight piece, so it was reheated and, with the mandrel as a lever plus some further hammering, angled to the face by the right degree. A final procedure angled the face back, relative to the socket, to give it the right amount of loft. Such a blacksmith was an expert. If the line of fusion in a socket was visible he considered the head substandard and would probably sell it at the back door for a small sum to some keen player who would happily take it home and shaft it himself, thereby getting a cheap club.

When the club-maker received the metal clubhead he drilled a hole through the upper part of the hosel to take the fixing rivet, then selected a shaft which his experience told him was suitable for the weight of the head and the club's purpose. He tapered the end of the shaft to fit tightly into the hosel, further securing it with glue and the rivet. For still more security the blacksmith would have made a series of indentations round the top of the hosel, giving it a sawtooth appearance, to improve its grip on the shaft. This indenting was called "knopping", or "knurling", and as the iron clubs were heavy it was large and crude as was the hosel itself.

The faces of early 19th-century clubheads were smooth and usually concave because wooden heads had always been shaped like that. They were also often concave in the other axis, rather like a hollow-ground razor blade. Whereas iron clubheads of the early 19th century, despite being crude and heavy, were in general appearance like modern-day clubs, those of the 18th century presented a bizarre appearance, for the clubhead had no "toe", the end of the face being cut off vertically.

As the greater use of iron clubs quickly followed on the arrival, in 1848, of tough gutta-percha balls, and as golfers grew rapidly in number, blacksmiths skilled at making iron clubheads could make a living at it. Many smiths abandoned the other aspects of their trade and took up making clubheads full-time. At this stage the concave face was abandoned and the flat one was adopted.

An iron which had been available for some years and now became popular was the cleek, and from this the blacksmiths who specialised in making iron clubheads came to be known as "cleek-makers". The club-maker was the man who made up a club from the iron head, and it was he who sold it, taking the credit and giving little to the cleek-maker. But as cleek-makers became more important they began asserting themselves by putting their own marks on the heads they made, so that most iron heads now had the club-maker's name stamped on the back and the cleek-maker's mark in one corner. The marks were rather like the marks on pottery and porcelain, and they make interesting decorations on the iron clubs. Particular cleek-makers could be identified by such marks as pipes, anchors, crescent moons, crosses, diamonds, anvils, hearts, acorns, snakes, etc. Some famous early cleek-makers were: John Gray, in the Prestwick area; Carrick of Musselburgh; Wilson of St Andrews; Gourlay of Carnoustie; Condie of St Andrews; Anderson of Anstruther; Willie Park Junior of Musselburgh. By the end of the First World War nearly all of these craftsmen had ceased trading. Of the later cleek-makers Gibson of Kinghorn and Spalding (who had come from America and set up in London) continued well into the 1930s by entering the mass-production market.

Of the great variety of iron clubs eventually to be produced, all stemmed essentially from just three early forms: the rutter, the cleek and the lofter. The rutter, or rut-iron, evolved to meet the needs of early golfing, had a small head – not much bigger than a golf ball – and was usually heavy. It was for playing out of bunkers and, especially, cart ruts, a procedure for which the tiny head, which would fit into a narrow rut, made it invaluable. It was later to be modified into the niblick, which in turn was the forerunner of the pitching wedge and the sand wedge. The cleek was an iron with little loft and was used for long iron shots; it was the precursor of today's Nos 1, 2 and 3 irons. The lofter had more loft than the cleek and was deeper-faced; it was to lead to the mashie, which appeared in 1880, and the mashie-niblick. These clubs were the forerunners of all the irons now used to make approach shots – Nos 4–8. The "matched set" of irons did not appear until after the First World

War. By this time, as has already been noted, the cleek-makers and club-makers had been put out of business by the big mass-production factories which turned out complete clubs.

By the end of the First World War so many golf clubs were being made that the supply of good, properly seasoned hickory began to run out. But in the early 1920s, in the United States, a tubular steel golf shaft was developed. It was an excellent shaft, and within a few years it had taken over from hickory, which virtually disappeared from club-making after the early 1930s. Steel shafts were used in iron and wooden clubs, and the irons were further improved by 1930 with heads of rustless chrome steel. The steel shaft and persimmon head formed the typical golf club until after the Second World War, when supplies of seasoned persimmon began to run out. Laminate wood heads came into use and are still used today, though some persimmon is still available.

In recent years further technical developments have produced shafts of carbon fibre (graphite), aluminium and other man-made materials, and clubheads of glass fibre, aluminium and so on have also been devised. All of these materials are still rather on trial, but doubtless one day a definite "new club", the answer to every golfer's prayer, will emerge, at least temporarily, until it is replaced by yet another real or imaginary break-through.

• • • • • • •

As mentioned above, the early feather golf ball, or "featherie", cost some three times as much as a golf club. This was because it took so much skill and time to make, a good ball-maker being able to produce perhaps three in a day. Furthermore such balls were easily damaged, so a golfer needed three or four to play.

The ball had an outer casing of bull's hide which had to be hand-stitched inside-out, leaving unstitched only a slit some ¼ inch long. The casing next had to be turned "outside-in" through this tiny slit – no easy job – then stuffed with the boiled feathers of chickens or geese. The stuffing was done so tightly that more than an old-fashioned top-hatful of feathers was forced into the small ball – approximately the size of a modern golf ball – and in the later stages a long spike harnessed to the ballmaker's chest was used to exert maximum pressure. The slit was then closed with a single stitch and the ball was waterproofed with white lead paint.

Making such balls was a highly skilled trade requiring a long apprenticeship, and, as in early clubmaking, certain families became pre-eminent as ball-makers over several generations. Notable were the Dicksons of Leith, the Robertsons of St Andrews and the Gourlays of Musselburgh and Leith.

That the feather balls were good golf balls is shown by the fact that a drive of more than 300 yards with one is recorded. But they did not last long and they became soggy in wet conditions. And, as noted earlier, the prohibitive cost of the balls meant that only the wealthy could afford to play. Then, in 1848, the properties of gutta-percha became known.

Gutta-percha is a resin derived from a tree found in Malaya (now Malaysia). By judicious cutting of the tree's bark the resin can be made to exude from it. The resin sets and becomes hard, but it will readily soften again it immersed in hot water, when it can be shaped by hand or in a mould, then allowed to cool and harden in its new shape. It was soon realised that this material could be shaped into golf balls. The resulting balls were able to take a great deal of punishment, were impervious to wet and were much cheaper to make than the old feather balls. Suddenly golf was within the reach of the many. There was a dramatic growth in the number of golfers. Because the new balls – called "guttas" – could take so much punishment more iron play was possible. Indeed it was found that gutta-percha balls which had sustained some cuts and scars flew better than the smooth new ones, and it quickly became the practice of the makers to give them a textured surface. At first this was done by hand with the sharpened end of a tack hammer, but soon the textured pattern was embodied in the mould.

The situation had now changed. Balls were cheap and tough, excellent for iron play but liable to damage wooden clubfaces, which came increasingly to be made – or repaired – with animal horn or vulcanite inserts. The ball was now half the price of the club. Because of the nature of gutta-percha and the readiness with which it could be made into balls it was easy to devise mass-production methods which made them even cheaper. Toward the end of the century chemical additives made the gutta-percha balls fly better; they also became even tougher and more destructive of wooden clubfaces.

In 1900 the world of golf again became indebted to the United States, for in Akron, Ohio, there was invented an even better golf ball than the guttie, as the new composition gutta balls were called. It was made of rubber in the form of a narrow strip of great length wound tightly round a central core, the whole being then encased in a gutta-percha covering. The brainchild of Coburn Haskell, it was called a "Haskell", though others, such as John Gammeter, had more to do with its production. The new ball was as durable as the guttie but softer, so it did not damage clubfaces. And though a little more expensive than the guttie it was much easier to use, which more than outweighed the extra expense.

The Haskell method of making a golf ball, with minor improvements, is still the commonest method in use, though recently solid balls have appeared and are increasingly being used.

DRIVE IT 553 YARDS

Peter Dobereiner

On my home course we have a killer hole, about 460 yards and sharply dog-legged to the right around a stand of noble beech trees. The other day I was going through my regular routine in preparation to tackle the monster. This involves sucking in six deep breaths to load the system with oxygen, plus a mental wind-up based on yoga, self-hypnosis and a Zen exercise designed to persuade me that, sure, I can hit a power fade 20 yards around the corner. Just as I was about to unleash my double-hernia swing, a companion remarked, "Remember how you always used to whip one straight over those trees with your four-wood?"

It was a cruel reminder of advancing years. My game plan – to follow the drive with a blue-flamer fairway wood, then a middle-iron and hope to chip in for my par – was shattered. That evening I slumped into a chair, tucked a vitamin pill under my tongue and sought solace from back numbers of American golf magazines from around the world. Since I had already read the articles, I concentrated on the advertisements and gradually my spirits revived. Gad, what a fool I had been. Here, under my very nose, lay the answer to declining physical powers.

A pair of socks with a miracle sole, guaranteed to add 10 yards to my drive. Shoes promising another 10 yards, thanks to a similar miracle of technology and long-lasting tungsten spikes to boot. What's a few measly bucks? I'd give my entire fortune, which consists of a few measly bucks incidentally, for an extra 20 yards.

That dream proved to mere chicken feed. Now came the real stuff. A fancy grip promised to release the tremendous power in my legs, and drive the ball 300 yards or more. And only $6.95. Next comes a driver with an aerodynamic design to give me an extra 10 yards. If I get one of those and fit it with a graphite shaft (guaranteed 10 per cent more distance) and my new grip, that is 300 yards plus 10 plus 10 per cent. Wow, 341 yards!

For a mere $1.75 I can get a repair manual which will show me how to assemble this wonder club. Add my extra 20 yards for shoes and socks and I'm up to 361 yards. That is before I've even pulled on a glove. What latent power lies in gloves! I never dreamed that a glove could make me hit a ball 10 yards farther – but here they are, complete with guarantee. Now, 371 yards!

Frankly, I'm not overimpressed by the promises of swing trainers, practice nets, standing on a mat marked with Sam Snead's footprints, muscle-builders and fast improvement plans, "guaranteed to take fifteen strokes off your scores".

The same goes for range-finders which will save me five strokes a round, or a book of putting hints which will produce instant rhythm, tempo and overspin for $18.95 and save me another seven to 15 strokes a round. Right now I'm into power and I do not particularly want to take advantage of the promised 40 strokes which I could save every round by using all these aids, some of them not legal. I would make Jack Nicklaus look a fool, and I have no wish to do that. I just want to outdrive him.

Here is a device which looks like an ankle shackle from the chain-gang days. It will stop my swaying and enable me to hit the ball farther, harder and straighter, a bargain at $14.95, even if the extra distance is not actually specified. And what of this loaded wrist strap whose "miracle motion of weights develops real clubhead speed"? I'll take a chance and accept the offer to rush me one for only $4.95, although I'm worried about using it in conjunction with my wonder glove. Perhaps I could wear it on my other ankle to help release that tremendous power in my legs.

Between the two of them I should get an extra 10 yards at least. So far, all my calculations have been based on a regular golf ball and that has clearly been a mistake, for here we have an announcement headed: "Golf hustler's secret revealed." It goes on to make the confident assertion: "Here's what it *must* mean to you – 30 yards on every drive." Another brand also claims to outdistance all other balls by 30 yards, but adds, rather shamefacedly, that it is ever-so-slightly illegal. I'll have none of that malarky, but stick with my original choice at three for $5.

My guaranteed drive is now approaching a satisfactory 411 yards but there is more to come, for a ball-heater ("Plugs into any standard electric outlet") promises me a 20 per cent increase in distance boosting me to 493 yards.

I am disappointed in the golfer's belt, which makes no promises about extra distance but merely offers the assurance of keeping my stomach ventilated during wear. However, the marvels of science have not yet exhausted their beneficence, and one of the major sources of extra length is to be found in the unlikely shape of the tee peg. At a paltry $2 for 18, the Slant Tee's bellcrank action propels the ball and promises me 10 per cent more distance, giving me a guaranteed total of 542 yards.

But wait. The MighTee FlighTee not only will save me 75 cents but ensure me an extra 60 yards. And it is endorsed by Bob Toski, no less, giving me a grand total of 553 yards, every inch of it guaranteed by the advertisers. I must go with the MighTee FlighTee, especially as a later announcement adds: "Redesigned to conform with USGA regulations".

You may imagine you have detected a flaw in my dream. Armed with the full cornucopia of mail-order goodies, I will drive too far, flying every green – sometimes by 200 yards or more. I have thought of that and shall adjust my equipment on every tee, sometimes using a cold ball or discarding my ankle shackle, so that I reduce my potential to suit the length of the hole. But there is one gadget I will use faithfully on every tee. If I understand the illustration and description properly, it resembles a small handgun into which you load your tee peg. You then hold it against the surface of the ground and press a button which releases a pneumatic hammer to drive your peg into the earth. What a labour-saving device. The good ideas are always the simple ones.

OUT OF THE BAG

H.B. Farnie

The first thing that strikes the novice with wonder is the variety and number of clubs used by the more expert players in the game of golf. Unacquainted as the tyro necessarily must be with its mysteries, and having only a very vague idea how it is played, their number strikes him as being useless – at all events, unnecessary, and their variety as a result of whim. Nevertheless, they have each of them a shade of use different from that of the others; and this fact will show the novice inferentially to what a degree of nicety the game has been brought – how every possible mishap is countermet by a skilfully adapted tool; and, in a word, that at golf on the lengthened plain, as on the miniature "green" of the billiard table, a degree of perfection is attainable, astonishing to the uninitiated, and at once rebutting the ultra-philosophical view which sneers at the sport as childish and unmeaning.

A complete set of golfing clubs may be divided into four classes, contra-distinguished by technical names, viz:

> Drivers
> Spoons
> Irons, and
> Putters.

These kinds again, each embrace several clubs, having slight specific differences.

DRIVERS. Drivers, so called from being the clubs used to *drive*, *swipe*, or propel the ball a long distance, are distinguished by their long, tapering, and flexible shafts, their small raking heads, and the powerful *feel* they have when handled. There are two members of this class: the play club, and the grassed driver. The first is employed, as a rule, to play over safe ground where no hazards lie exposed to the stroke; as the play club, from the peculiarity of its make, does not *sky* the ball much, which would only have the effect of spending its velocity in the air while it shortened the actual distance accomplished. This, as the reader will at once perceive, is therefore the best club to drive those tremendous strokes which make the striker a hero of oral tradition amongst golfers for many a year after. The grassed driver is also used to effect distance when the ball happens to lie in one of three situations: when it is among soft grass; or on the downward slope of a hillock; or when a hazard looms dangerously in front of the stroke. The peculiarity of this club is, that in addition to sending the ball well away, it raises it considerably in the air. Were the play club used in any of these three predicaments we have enumerated, the ball would, in the first case, be propelled through the grass and instantly stopped; in the second, would not be elevated above the inequalities of the course; and in the last, would, in all probability, be comfortably lodged in the hazard ahead.

SPOONS. Spoons derive their very suggestive name from the great slope in the face of the clubhead, which gives them the power of skying the ball to almost any height, being the same property, only in a much greater degree, which is the characteristic of the grassed driver. They are most useful fellows, doing much of the sapper and miner work of the game, are four in number, and, as their names impart, are of various lengths, viz:

Long Spoon
Middle Spoon
Short Spoon, and
Baffing Spoon

which last is also the least of all.

The long and middle spoons are often pressed into doing duty for a grassed driver, from their ability to "loft" the ball; but besides this, from their tougher build, they are admirably fitted to jerk it out of a grassy rut – or a yielding whin – or, indeed, out of the thousand and one bad *lies* which the best-directed stroke will get into, and which would very likely shiver the more slender shaft of the grassed play club. The short spoon, besides assisting in the rougher work of its elder brethren, is used for those beautiful and difficult half-strokes on to the putting green over a hazard, where the ball lies sufficiently clear for the stroke. The Baffing Spoon, although the smallest in stature, is by no means the least in usefulness of this family. Why it is called by either this soubriquet, or by its other title of "the cutty", we leave speculative readers to determine; although its more common appellation "baffing" is most probably descriptive of the *thump* produced in making the stroke. It is employed only for skying a ball over a hazard on to the putting ground, when the stroke is too short for any of the other spoons. The Iron is employed by many players for effecting the same stroke, thus superseding the use of this spoon altogether.

Before quitting the subject of spoons, we shall notice an antiquated connection of the family, now seldom to be met with, unless as a supernumerary in the pack of an oldster. It is called a NIBLICK; has a tough yet effective driving shaft; and an exceedingly small head well-spooned back. Its use is, or rather *was*, to drive a ball out of a rut or cap large enough to admit the "diminished" head – and very effective strokes we have seen made with it. But it is exceedingly difficult to play with; and the precise *lie* it is intended for so seldom occurs, that even an experienced hand is rather nervous at using it, the chances being in favour of a total miss. Besides, either a spoon or an iron answers the same purpose well enough.

IRONS. Irons, so named from their heads being formed from that metal, are obviously intended to achieve the roughest of the golfing in trying ground. They are three in number – the bunker iron; the driving iron; and the cleek or click. The first of these clubs is especially at home in a bunker – in a thickset whin – amongst the stones of a road – or, in fact, in any scrape where a wooden-headed tool would be useless. Its iron head cleaves through every obstacle, and jerks the ball out of grief where every other club would fail. The driving-iron nearly resembles him of the bunker, in everything but weight; it is used amongst difficulties also, but only when the ball is intended to be, and admits of being, sent some distance. There are also finer uses to which this club is occasionally put. The cleek or click, deriving its name either from an old Scots word signifying "hook", or from the sharp clicking sound produced in making the stroke, is also an iron club, but lighter than either of the others. It is used chiefly for driving the ball out of rough ground when elevation is not so much an object, and when no impediments surround and obstruct the *lie* which would demand a heavier club. Sometimes again, it takes the sterner duties of the iron off its shoulders, and drives the ball out of a desperate hazard, when it happens to lie favourably for the stroke.

PUTTERS. Our last genus is that of putters, the most important clubs perhaps in the set. They are two in number: the green putter, and the driving putter. The first is used on the putting green, when the player is near enough to calculate with some certainty on the resistance of the grass, the length of the stroke, and the lie of the ground he intends his ball to pass over. Sometimes an iron-headed putter is used for the short game, instead of the more common kind; but it does not prove at all a desirable substitute. Driving putters are most frequently used in the place of short or baffing spoons, to drive the ball up to the putting green, when no hazard or awkward inequality in the ground intervenes to prevent the roll of the ball. They are also used occasionally in very boisterous weather to drive a ball in the wind's eye over the safe ground, and often answer this somewhat illegitimate use, even better than a play club.

We have now gone through the complete set of clubs, and have classed and distinguished them by their different uses. There are many players who carry particular clubs in duplicate, and others who have some fashioned with slight deviations from the usual make; but these peculiarities do not, of course, affect in any wise our classification.

Chapter 13

CLASSIC
INSTRUCTION

Henry Longhurst

I say without hesitation that this is just about the best, and certainly the most succinct, piece of golfing instruction that I have ever read. There is no lack of modesty in this assertion, since, as you will see, Thomson's contribution is everything and the writer's virtually nothing. My own part in the proceedings was to spend a couple of half-hours with him in the lounge of Rusack's Hotel at St Andrews and then set down what he said almost precisely as he said it. As seen, described, and played by Thomson, golf is indeed a simple game. It is the rest of us who make it so difficult!

All this began in a practice round before the recent Bowmaker tournament at Sunningdale. Though I had watched him many dozens of times, this was the first time that I had had the pleasure actually of playing with Peter Thomson. I had always found it difficult to describe his style to other people because it seemed so straightforward. There was nothing peculiar about it. It turned out not only that his ideas about the golf swing were as "simple" as his method but also, as I hope to prove, that he was equally good at communicating them.

I asked him, naturally, to case an eye over my own manifestly unsatisfactory efforts and he said at once, "Well, for a start you are set up all wrong."

This expression, "getting set up right", constitutes the absolute basis of Thomson's golf. "If you get set up right and look like a competent golfer, you won't go nearly so far wrong." Your set-up consists of how you stand, where you are aiming, your "triangle" (i.e. the two arms and shoulders), and where you put the ball in relation to your feet.

The nearer you are, before you start, to the position in which you will be when you hit the ball, the fewer adjustments you will have to make in the course of the shot. "Think how your body has to be when you strike the ball," he says, "and work back from there." Lest this sounds too obvious, take a look on the 1st tee on a Sunday morning and see how many people's starting position bears any relation to any position in which they could conceivably be at impact!

There is no reason why any of us, tall or short, fat or thin, should not get set up right. The stance, about which volumes have been written, is a piece of typical Thomsonian simplicity. Lay a club down on the ground, pointing to the hole, and put your toes against it. That is the end of that.

Now put the ball opposite your left foot with your left arm and the club in a straight line, as they will be, or should be, as you actually hit the ball. Your arm and the club will now be at right-angles to the imaginary club on the ground against which you have lined up your toes. If they are not, you have got the ball – *as almost everyone has* – too far back. (We are talking at the moment of wooden club shots.)

We now come to the critical point, the make-or-mar of the entire set-up. Your right arm is not long enough. It won't reach. How are you going to get it on to the club?

You do it instinctively as nature tells you, the easiest way. You reach *over* with the right hand, bringing the right shoulder forward in the process, and at the same time, probably without realising it, you bring the left hand back a bit to meet it. This is perfectly comfortable, but, to make it more so, you probably move forward a couple of inches at the last moment, thus, in effect, bringing the ball two inches back.

The whole set-up is now wrecked.

Let us retrace our steps. The right arm once again is not long enough. This time, keeping your right shoulder back and tilting your left shoulder up, you reach *under* with the right hand and attach it to the club. (This was accompanied in the *Sunday Times* by a picture of myself, taken on my lawn and bearing the caption, "I don't care what you say – I at least *look* like a golfer.")

I tried this experiment on many willing subjects and in every case, regardless of handicap, in this position they at once looked like a golfer. If it feels awkward at first, it only shows how wrong you were before. You can apply a simple test. When you have got "set up", keep your body still, lay the club flat across your chest and see where it is pointing. In the "easy" position you will find that it points yards to the left of the hole. If you are set up right, it will be pointing straight at the flag.

HOW FAR AWAY FROM THE BALL SHOULD YOU BE?

Thomson often uses the expression "measuring off". You will notice that he himself measures off quite deliberately before each shot. Stand relaxed, leaning slightly forward, with your knees slightly bent and the whole body *in balance*. Extend the left arm and the club in a straight line, not stiff as a ramrod, and you are now measured off. "Picture in mind your position at you strike the ball and make final adjustments from that." This applies to every club.

HOW DO YOU GRIP THE CLUB?

Again, delightfully simple. *Get set-up right and you won't notice!* Take it as you find it.

HOW HARD DO YOU HOLD ON TO THE CLUB?

"Often," says Thomson, "you can actually *see* the tension in a man's hand. You should start with a light touch, barely enough to lift it off the ground – so that it feels heavy. It is just like using an axe. You lift it with a light grip, enough to raise it, and it feels heavy. As you bring it down, your grip tightens without your thinking about it and reaches its tightest at the moment of impact.

"There is another likeness with golf. Using an axe, you do not *hit* with it; you *accelerate* it. That is exactly what you should do with a golf club."

HOW DO YOU START THE CLUB BACK?

"Well, you just *draw it straight back*. Never mind about what the books din into you about turns and pivots. Just draw it straight back as far as is comfortable and let nature take its course. Don't turn away; just draw it back – *but* – keep your weight squarely on both feet and make sure you don't sway back with it yourself."

Finally, what Thomson describes as the key axiom in the golf swing, namely, to be behind the ball when you strike it – not all of you, maybe, but certainly your head. "*A plumb line from your nose as you strike the ball should hit the ground several inches behind it*" – a sobering thought for us lurchers and swayers, to whom, as we heave forward, the ball so often appears to be moving rapidly backwards.

As a postscript I might add that, with the first shot in which Thomson was satisfied that he had got me satisfactorily "set-up", I ricked my back – probably using muscles which had not come into play for 30 years – to such an extent that we almost had to terminate the game there and then. This in no way shook my faith in his principles and I wish you the best of luck. You have been warned! (A few days after publication of the above, in July, I had a letter from a reader in Yorkshire. He had tried it on the lawn on a wet day, he said, and, having only slippers on, had fallen flat on his face. He had retired to the house, changed into spiked shoes, and tried again. "I then had to be helped back into the house. The doctor was summoned and he says that, given reasonable care, I should be able to play again in October.")

•   •   •   **•**   •   •   •

I described last week the emphasis placed by Peter Thomson – to whom congratulations on winning in the meanwhile the German Open Championship – on how important it is to get "set up" right before making a golf shot. The example taken was a wooden-club shot, but the same principle applies to all.

We are to imagine the position in which we shall be, or ought to be, when we hit the ball, and set ourselves up as nearly in that position as possible. It will involve, as always, the left arm and the club in a straight line, rather as though one were about to play a one-armed shot with the left arm.

The position of the ball with the driver was simple. It was opposite the left foot. Where is it to be with the other clubs? Again there are no complications. His answer is *"roughly an inch further back for each club"*.

This finds the ball mid-way between the feet with a five-iron and about off the right heel with a nine-iron. With the driver you hit the teed-up ball an ascending blow, the clubhead having already passed its lowest point. With the short irons you hit it a descending blow, taking a good-sized divot after the ball.

How far away do you stand? Again the same principles apply throughout. You "measure off", as before, with the left arm extended, and yourself poised and in balance, though naturally stooping a little more with the shorter clubs than you did with the driver.

Thomson also likes to have his feet progressively closer together as the shots become shorter. It all seems to fit into a very simple and intelligible pattern. As the shots become short enough to require judgement rather than power for their execution, he likes to open the stance slightly, drawing his left foot back a little.

For the short game his maxim, typically, is that one should always look for the *simplest* way. He describes the high wedge shot, which we so much admire when played by professionals, as, for most people, "a form of lunacy". The more you can picture a short approach as a kind of extended putt, he says, the better.

The ruin of most handicap players' short game comes from their efforts to hit the ball *up*. It is the golfer's job to hit it *forwards*, the lofted club's job to hit it *upwards*. It is an old professional trick, in trying to teach this to beginners, to put a lofted club into their hands and invite them to try to hit the ball along the ground into a bunker between them and the flag. They concentrate on hitting the ball forwards, whereupon it sails over the bunker.

Thomson is a supremely good bunker player. Perhaps his finest exhibition of this art was when he won the Open at Lytham, where they have innumerable bunkers, of which he encountered at least his share. I have always remembered his remark afterwards that he had "never seen such beautiful sand". He sincerely regards "splashing" the ball out of sand as the simplest shot in the whole game, if only because there is so much greater a margin for error than with a similar shot off grass.

"The chief factor is the club itself. There are some atrocious old sand-irons about that even Snead could not play with. You want one with a wide sole, with the back edge considerably lower than the front." He thinks little or nothing of most of the so-called "dual-purpose" clubs.

He reckons to stand well behind the ball and to "measure off" carefully to the exact point that he wishes to hit the sand. Instead of hitting the ball first and the turf afterwards, you hit the sand first and the ball afterwards. You can hit sand anything from two to six inches behind and it may well be sometimes that the clubface never actually touches the ball at all. So far as you are concerned at any rate, you are playing a shot at the sand rather than at the ball. His only golden rule is "swing very slowly".

Thomson is also – again in an unostentatious and "simple" way – a supremely good putter. I spent a long time drawing him out on the subject and from this I think three main points emerge. He does not think that the grip matters unduly – indeed he used the words "almost any grip will do" – but he has no doubt about his own method.

To initiate it, take a normal grip, then rotate your left hand to the left so that the back of it is at about 45 degrees to the ground; do likewise with your right hand to the right, and then stick your right thumb firmly on the shaft. He also reckons to stand with his eyes vertically over the ball. All this is common ground but there are many who might vastly improve by giving it a trial.

His second point interested me because I have so often referred to it as one of the main secrets of Locke's phenomenally successful putting and because it is something that we can all so easily do and, even when we mean to, so often don't. It is to carry out a sort of *drill*: in other words, to find a set of motions that suits our own particular eye and temperament and carry them out, without exception, every time we putt.

Locke's drill will be familiar to all who have seen him either in person or on the television: two practice strokes, a step up to the ball, one look at the hole and away it goes. Even with "this to tie for the Open" this drill never varies.

For his third point I quote Thomson's own words. "It must incorporate some sort of *determined tap*. What kills putting is the old so-called 'stroking' method. You don't stroke a putt like you stroke a cat. If you do, it is usually timid and damned lucky if it goes in the hole. The most natural way is to give it a tap, like a child instinctively does.

"None of the people who follow through like poor old . . . (and here he named four distinguished players who shall remain anonymous, two British and two Americans) . . . have ever really been any good on the greens." He named as the world's best putters Rosburg, Casper, Ford, Palmer and Venturi – all Americans who hit the ball with a firm tap rather than a smooth stroking movement. This, I need hardly add, is not to be confused with a quick jerk to jab!

Like Locke, Thomson thinks it essential to hold the club loosely with a very light, sensitive grip and likes to have the *feeling* that he is playing the same stroke every time, increasing the length more by lengthening the backswing than by hitting harder.

I believe all good putters, and the rest of us during our days "on", have this feeling, though whether we are any longer capable of a "very light sensitive grip" remains to be proved. I did not have the heart to ask him the $64,000 question "How, if at all, can you cure the 'jitters'?" After all, he was due next day to play in the Open Championship. Anyway, he would not have known. He is only 30 and has never had them!

THE MAN WHO CAN PUTT IS A MATCH FOR ANYONE

Willie Park

Thirty years ago I coined the aphorism which heads this page. It has stood the test of time, and it is as true today as when I first made it. The statement was always the subject of much controversy, but I proved it correct by my successes in the numerous stake matches I played; and the frequency with which you will hear the sentence today, uttered with all the ring of truism and conviction, is evidence that my assertion survives the controversy and has been proved right by experience.

THE CRAZE FOR LENGTH

Harry Vardon

The year 1902 was to prove an eventful one in the history of the game of golf. In this season a new type of ball was to make its appearance on the links. It is not too much to say that the advent of the Haskell, which was the name of this, the first rubber-cored ball, was to an enormous extent eventually to revolutionise the game. When the new ball was firmly established, golf slowly started to undergo such drastic changes that to those of us who were brought up with the guttie, it has never been the same since. This change was, as is only natural, comparatively slow. When the possibilities were realised, however, the old solid ball was doomed for ever. I personally shall always regret the passing of the guttie. In my own mind I am firmly convinced that with its passing, much of the real skill had gone for ever. Let me give my readers an instance of what I mean. With the guttie ball the game had to be thoroughly learned. No half-measures would do at that period if a player was to accomplish any success whatsoever.

Let us take the case of wooden-club play. In the days of the solid ball it was necessary for the drives to be properly struck if anything approaching a good round was to be recorded. By this I mean that a half-hit tee shot would not escape the hazards which had been placed to catch an indifferent stroke, as is so frequently the case with the modern ball. Consequently correct driving was more appreciated in those days than at the present period. I hold the opinion that the proper attitude towards the art of wooden-club play is not sufficiently appreciated by the modern golfer. I will go further and say that he does not fully realise what the art of driving really means. There can be little doubt in my mind that without accuracy a golfer is not entitled to consider himself a good wooden-club player. Accuracy is the keynote of successful golf. The accurate placing of the tee shot is the art of driving. Extremely long-hit balls which are badly off the fairway are nothing more or less than indifferent shots. It may at once be said that the rough grass off the fairway will prove to be sufficient punishment for this mistake. Further it may be pointed out that the rough, on a good many courses, is no better today than in the old days. This may be true. But the chief point which appears to be overlooked is the fact that the wonderful improvements in modern clubs and the more resilient ball have made recovery ever so much easier.

The advent of the rubber ball was instrumental in creating an entirely different method of striking the object. The solid ball required to be hit for carry, whereas it was quickly apparent that the Haskell lent itself to an enormous run. As this was the case golfers naturally started to hit this ball in the way they could get the maximum amount of distance which it was possible to obtain. This was the start of new methods being employed in the full shots. To gain the maximum amount of run it was deemed necessary to play for a hook. By this means the flight of the ball was lower and the carry considerably less. The run, however, by means of the overspin that had been imparted, was twice as much, and so actually longer distances were obtained. I hold the firm opinion that from this date the essential attitude towards accuracy was completely lost sight of. This was the start of the craze for length and still more length.

WHAT CAN YOUR BEST GOLF BE?

Tommy Armour

A discovery I've made as a contestant, observer, and student at innumerable professional and amateur golf championships is a simple fact that undoubtedly will improve your scoring. Here it is:

> It is not solely the capacity to make great shots that makes champions, but the essential quality of making very few bad shots.

Watch at the practice tee of any major tournament and you will see many players hit a very high percentage of perfect shots with every club in the bag. Then watch them as they play. They will make superb shots, but they will make too many bad ones.

Their bad shots may be because of faulty execution or the less pardonable reason of bad judgement. But regardless of the cause, they've exceeded the limit of allowable error. In major championship golf the margin of error is narrow. It's wide in the club competitions between higher handicap players, but there, as well as in expert competitions, you'll note that what distinguishes the winner is that he made fewer bad strokes than the rest.

The champion is the fellow who can make the fewest poor shots. What first vividly impressed me with that fact was an experience I had with Walter Hagen.

Walter and I were playing the final round of a North and South Open. I was leading the field when that fourth round started at Pinehurst. I played the first three holes of that round 4-4-3. Hagen had begun 6–6–5.

As we walked to the 4th tee, Hagen in his high drawl said to me: "I've missed all I can spare today; now I'm going to work."

He went to work – and on me.

He didn't miss any more shots that round.

He rubbed out my lead, finished with 68, and won the tournament.

That lesson cost me plenty, but although I fancied myself as a very keen scholar of golf, I hadn't known what I learned then. That was when I discovered the secret that the way to win was by making fewer bad shots.

Now let's go from the lesson to an application I made of it at Boca Raton. Among my pupils there is a prominent steel man. In lessons and in practice he hits many excellent shots. He's a good hitter but a bad player.

In a moment of high confidence in the grill room, he expressed his conviction that he could break 90. There were numerous differences of opinion. The outcome was as is customary when there are differences of opinion regarding sports events.

It was agreed that as I had risked a bold wager in support of my pupil, I could accompany him as counsellor during the round.

He hit a long, strong drive off the 1st tee, but in the rough, to the right.

He walked up to make his second shot and picked out a five-iron to go for the green.

"Put that back in the bag," I told him.

"I've got a chance to go for a birdie," he protested.

"You've got a bigger chance of missing the shot, then having another tough one to make before you get on," I explained. "Play an easy eight-iron shot out to the left to where you have another easy shot through the opening of the green. Then you may get yourself a one-putt par."

So that's the way he played the hole, and that's the way it showed on the card . . . par four.

To his and my amazement and delight – and profit – he went around in 79.

Hole after hole I'd had to argue with him and explain to him that there are two sound rules for low scoring that apply in 999 out of 1,000 cases.

These rules – or practical principles, are:

Play the shot you've got the greatest change of playing well, and
Play the shot that makes the next shot easy.

If it's mystified you to see fellows with worse swings than yours score better than you do, the mystery will be cleared if you'll note how, instinctively, or by deliberately using their heads, they've applied the two tactical principles I've just set before you.

When you get that lesson in your head, you will greatly improve your scoring. There are plenty of other lessons about making golf shots, but the main lesson about playing golf is the one I've just given you.

There are variations of this lesson in playing. The variations are determined by match and stroke play and by the player's proficiency. The expert can take more chances with less risk than can the average or high handicap golfer.

Some never learn to play the type of game that fits their capabilities. Countless times I've seen ordinary player try to play courses in ways that would require the shot-making techniques of the most highly gifted stars. Such players may know something about grip, stance and swing, but they don't know the first thing about playing golf.

That mistake isn't made by the champions. Walter Travis knew his weak points. He couldn't get much distance. And he also knew that he was superior in accuracy and in the short game. His winning tactics were to fit his game to the course he was playing.

Lawson Little was an excellent shot-maker before I ever saw him, but he wasn't winning as he should. About all I taught him was tactics. When he learned tactics, he won four American and British national amateur championships in two consecutive years, and later won the American National Open title and other events against fine professional fields.

Julius Boros was a very good shot-maker before he started winning major events. He wasn't winning because he didn't have a tactical plan of play that fitted his game. He was playing in a cautious way that fitted neither his ability nor his temperament.

I suggested to him that since he was one of the best I'd ever seen in playing out of traps, he could change from his plan of trying to steer shots and boldly let them fly. Then if a shot came to rest in a trap around a green he had nothing to worry about, as he could come out close enough to the cup to sink his putt.

He had been unnaturally cautious as a putter. When it was impressed upon him that he very, very rarely missed much to either side of the cup but often failed to get up to the hole with putts that were precisely on the line, he began putting with more confidence and by daring to get the ball to the hole, or even past, improved his putting.

Boros is a strong player who'd been trying to play with a tightening fear of being wild with his long shots. When he learned to swing freely rather than steer in making his long shots and to depend on the precision of his short game, he became a champion.

• • • • • • •

Every golfer scores better when he learns his capabilities.

This is the first time I've ever mentioned what I am certain is my greatest value to my pupils. I learn about them before I try to teach them. I determine, pretty closely, what is the best golf each individual can possibly play.

It is utterly illogical to expect a person with physical, temperamental, and manner-of-living limitations to become able to play par or sub-par championship golf. One might as well expect to become a great master of painting, sculpture, the violin or piano, become a scientific genius, or even to become rich, simply by taking lessons and practising.

I've taught some of the greatest golfers a few of the polishing details that have helped them get as near to perfection as is possible. That has been comparatively easy because they have an aptitude for learning, sound basic ability, and fine physical qualifications. But the utmost demands on my own capabilities as an instructor have been made by those who are shooting the courses in 85 or up into three figures, discovering what would be their best games and teaching them to perform consistently to the limit of their capacities.

Golf is a comparative game. That is the marvellous merit of golf's handicapping system.

Ellsworth Vines pointed out this attraction of golf when he told me that in tennis, when he was starring, there were less than a dozen who could give him an exciting and entertaining game, but in golf he could get a fine, close match with a dub or an expert because of the handicapping.

Certainly a game that permits many thousands all over the United States to play against champions, with the handicap making all contestants equal at the start, has a feature of enjoyment that makes it unique.

At Boca Raton, in the winter, and at northern courses in the spring, summer and fall, I play many rounds with players whose average scores range from 85 to 110, and we have very close games on the handicaps.

You might think I'd be bored playing with a real duffer, but I don't find that to be the case. In the first place he interests me by being so bad when he might well be so much better. He will hit some excellent shots, but they're hit by accident and I wonder how I might make such accidents become consistent.

The principal error in viewpoint of a majority of golfers is failure to understand that if they play to a uniform standard that is well within their capabilities, the handicapping system will take care of the rest. They'll probably take money from many proficient professionals and amateurs to whom the handicaps allow an extremely small margin of error.

But they all want to be stars when they just simply haven't got it in them. As the Bard might have said, 'Ambition is a grievous fault and grievously doth the duffer pay."

You see overvaulting ambition at its dirty work when the 95-shooter gets an 82 with 25 putts and 10 lucky bounces. He thinks he is an 82 performer, whereas he actually has a game of about 87 under best normal circumstances. If he has once shot an 82, he rarely realises that in scoring 87, considering his limitations, he's doing as well comparatively as the gifted player who goes around in 68.

The most difficult part of my responsibility as a teacher is to determine what is the best my pupil could consistently score. Then I can teach him to do that. If he shows unexpected promise after reaching that goal, we can advance together toward the next higher plateau of learning.

Heaven knows I want every pupil to become as good as is humanly possible, but the more realistic part of my work is to make reasonably certain that he never gets more than a few strokes worse than he should be.

The fact that at least 90 per cent of the millions of golfers score in the 90s – or approximately a stroke a hole over par – is highly significant. It is a plain indication of their inherent limitations. Few of them are reconciled to their limitations. Fortunately, practically all of them can learn to reduce many of the faults that are preventing them from getting as close to par as nature will allow them.

But they must be willing to learn.

There are at least six people who want to be taught golf to every one who wants to learn.

My task with those six is to make them understand primarily their attainable objective, the rational method of achieving their aim, and the relationship that must exist during a lesson.

The very best I can do for them – or for anybody else – is to get them started correctly on the most solid and lasting basis of improvement; a basis on which they establish the best game they ultimately can play.

FIRST UNDERSTAND WHAT YOU ARE TRYING TO DO

John Jacobs with Ken Bowden

"The only purpose of the golf swing is to move the club through the ball square to the target at maximum speed. How this is done is of no significance at all, so long as the method employed enables it to be done repetitively."

That is my number one credo. It is the basis on which I teach golf. It may sound elementary, but I am certain that the point it makes has been missed by most golfers. Ninety-five percent of the people who come to me for lessons don't really know what they are trying to do when they swing a golf club. Their prime concern is to get into certain "positions" during the swing. Therein, they believe, lies the elusive "secret" of golf. They have either never known or have long forgotten that the only reason such positions are necessary is *to get the club to swing correctly through the ball.*

There are four possible impact variations produced by the golf swing that, in concert, determine the behaviour of the ball. They are:

1   The direction in which the clubface looks.
2   The direction of the swing.
3   The angle of the club's approach to the ball.
4   The speed of the club.

Of these four, the alignment of the clubface at impact is the most vital. If it is not reasonably correct, it will cause errors in the other three areas. For example, the clubface being open – pointing right of target – invariable leads at impact to an out-to-in swing path through the ball. This in turn forces the club into too steep an angle of approach to the ball. The clubface *cannot* meet the ball either squarely or solidly. Conversely, a closed clubface at impact generally leads to an in-to-out swing path. That causes too shallow an angle of approach – the club reaches the bottom of its arc before it reaches the ball. Again, the clubface *cannot* meet the ball either solidly or square.

Do one thing right in the golf swing and it will lead to another right. Do one thing wrong and it will produce another wrong. In this sense, golf is a *reaction* game. Never forget that fact.

Most of what you read about curing slicing tells you to do things like "slide the hips as the first movement of the downswing", "stay inside", "tuck the right elbow in", "hit late", "hold back your shoulders", and so on, ad nauseam. Unless you cure the *basic* fault – your open clubface at impact – you'll never do those things. You *can't*, because your *natural reactions* oppose them. That is why the world is full of golfers who say "I know what to do but I can't do it." They can't do it because, whatever their conscious desires, their actual swing actions are *reactions* to basic major faults.

The thing we all react to most is the face of the club. You must realise – and never forget – that incorrect alignment of the clubface at impact on one shot affects the entire golf swing on the next. Any cure is not be found in swing "positions". It lies in developing a grip and swing that brings the clubface square to your swing line at impact. Do this and all your reactions will be correct ones. Everything suddenly – and miraculously – falls into place. Now, if you swing from out-to-in, the ball will go to the left. You will immediately, *subconsciously*, make a effort to hit more from inside the target line. Your *natural* adjustment to help you do that will be to pull your body around so that you can swing that way. And – bingo! – suddenly you are set up square instead of open. Now you can swing the club so that it can approach the ball at the right level to hit it solidly in the back. Your shots start straight and fly straight. You've got the "secret"! Fantastic! And not one word about "hit late", "slide your hips", "keep you head down"!

Technically, golf is a much simpler game than most people realise. Here's another way to look at it simply. If you are consistently mishitting and misdirecting the ball, it should cheer you to know that there are only two basic causes. Either:

1 *You have an open clubface at impact*, which makes you swing across the target line from outside to inside, which in turn makes the club descend too steeply into the ball and thus not meet it solidly – or
2 *You have a closed clubface at impact*, which makes you swing across the target line from inside to outside, which makes the clubhead descend too shallowly into the ball, thus either catching the ground behind it or hitting the ball "thin" at the start of the upswing.

The perfect impact occurs only when the clubhead at impact travels exactly along the target line and exactly faces the target. This is "square" – the only "square" in golf. This is your aim – the total objective of all you do with a golf club.

There's just one more point I must make. It is my number two credo as a teacher of golf. It is this: "The art of competing is to know your limitations and to try on every shot."

What this really means is that the technique of striking the ball – the thing I personally deal in most of the time – is no more than 50 per cent of the game. Temperament, intelligence, nerve, desire and many other mental qualities make up the other 50 per cent. So, when we are talking technique, you might like to keep in mind that we are not dealing with the whole game. Unfortunately, even if you can learn to hit it like Jack Nicklaus, you still have to learn to play like him.

• • • • • •

Learn – and never forget – golf's basic "geometry".
If what I said a moment ago makes sense, being able, *yourself*, to analyse errors in your clubface alignment and swing direction from the way your shots behave is obviously an absolute prerequisite to playing better golf.

Learning what I call the "geometry" of the game is a mental, not a practice-ground, process. It isn't difficult, but it involves sitting down and thinking for a few moments.

The behaviour of every shot you hit is caused by a specific inter-relationship of the clubface angle and the swing direction at impact. Here is how:

PULL – *ball flies on a straight line but to the left of your target.*
The club's head is travelling across your intended target line from outside to inside that line at impact. The clubface is square to the *line of your swing*, but not to your *target line*. These shots often feel solid even

though they fly in the wrong direction. The direction the clubface was looking and clubhead was moving "matched", thus obviating a glancing blow.

SLICE – *ball starts left of your target then bends to the right.*
The club is again travelling across the intended target line from out to in during impact, but this time the face is *open* – facing right – of your swing line. This creates a clockwise sidespin that bends the ball to the right as its forward impetus decreases. The more the clubface and swing path are in opposition, the more oblique the blow, the greater the sidespin and the bigger the slice. Also, the more your swing line is from outside your target line, the steeper will be the club's approach to the ball and the higher up – and thus more glancing – its contact on the ball.

PULLED HOOK – *ball starts left of your target, then bends farther to the left.*
Again, the club is travelling across your intended target line from out to in, but this time the face is *closed* to the line of swing. This combination of two faults in the same direction sends the ball disastrously to the left – the infamous "smothered hook".

PUSH – *ball flies straight but to the right of your target.*
Again, the clubhead is travelling across your intended target line at impact, but this time from in to out. Your clubface is square to your line of swing, but *not* to your target line. Obviously the ball flies where both the clubface and swing path direct it – to the right. As with the pull, this shot often feels solid, because the blow is not of the glancing variety.

HOOK – *ball starts right of your target, then bends to the left.*
The club is again travelling across your intended line from in to out, but this time the face is *closed*, facing left of the line of your swing. This creates counterclockwise sidespin that bends the ball left once its forward impetus decreases. Unless the clubhead's angle of approach is so low that it hits the ground before it gets to the ball, a hooked shot feels much more solidly struck than a slice. This is because the clubface, by moving parallel to the ground instead of sharply downward, contacts the back-centre of the ball, not its top as in a slice.

PUSHED SLICE – *ball starts right of your target then bends more to the right.*
Again, the club is travelling across your intended target line from in to out at impact, but this time the face is *open* to the line of your swing. These

two faults combining in the same direction send the ball devastatingly far right.

STRAIGHT SHOT – *Ball starts straight and flies straight along your target line.*
The clubface looks at the target and your swing line coincides with the target line at impact.

· · · ● · · ·

You are now able to analyse your own swing, and I hope you will at last appreciate what "analyse" really means in golfing terms. It doesn't mean standing in front of a mirror and trying to spot whether your left knee bends inwards or forwards, whether your left arm is straight or bent at the top, etc., etc. You can make a complete analysis of your swing while you shave, sit in a train, ride to the office, or lie in bed. *All you have to do is think about the way your golf ball reacts when you hit it.*

SOURCES AND ACKNOWLEDGEMENTS

1 ALMOST STRAIGHT DOWN THE MIDDLE
P. G. WODEHOUSE. 'The Magic Plus Fours' (*The Golf Omnibus*, Barrie & Jenkins)
MICHAEL PARKINSON. 'Golf Blight' (*In Celebration Of Golf*, Sunday Times)
ALISTAIR COOKE. 'The Lunatic Fringe' (*Golf Magazine*)
FRANK HANNIGAN. 'Golf Through TV Eyes' (*USGA Journal*)
STEPHEN LEACOCK. 'The Golfomaniac' (*Laugh with Leacock*, Dodd, Mead & Co)
PETER ANDREWS. 'Scenes from a Marriage: A Golfer's Lament' (*New York Times*)
MICHAEL WILLIAMS. 'A Lady of Quality' (*The Golfers*, Collins)
BOB SOMMERS. 'Dispensing Justice Without Venom' (*USGA Journal*)
PATRICK CAMPBELL. 'Le Style, C'est Le Scratch Homme' (*How To Become A Scratch Golfer*, Anthony Blond)
CHRIS PLUMRIDGE. 'Bwana Golf' (*Punch Book Of Golf*, Hutchinson)
NORMAN MAIR. 'Of Games and Golf' (*Golfer's Bedside Book*, Batsford)
MIKE BRITTEN. 'Playing The Nineteenth' (*The Golfers*, Collins)
BOB RODNEY. 'Doing A Danecki' (*Daily Mirror*)

2 CHAMPIONS OF A BYGONE AGE
CHARLES PRICE. 'The Haig and I' (*Golfer At Large*, Atheneum)
HERBERT WARREN WIND. 'Strength of Mind' (*Following Through*, Macmillan)
J. H. TAYLOR. 'Broadcast On the Death of Vardon' (*Golf, My Life's Work*, Jonathan Cape)
BERNARD DARWIN. 'The Triumvirate' (*Out of the Rough*, Chapman & Hall)
AL BARKOW. 'Lord Nelson After Pearl Harbour' (*Golf's Golden Grind*, Harcourt Brace)
PETER DOBEREINER. 'Cotton: The Immortal' (*The Observer*)

3 RECENT CHAMPIONS
PAT WARD-THOMAS. 'The Young Thomson' (*Masters Of Golf*, Heinemann, with the permission of
    Mrs Jean Ward-Thomas)
NICK SEITZ. 'Ben Hogan Today' (*Golf Digest*)
MICHAEL McDONNELL. 'Bobby Locke' (*Golf Illustrated*)
PETER DOBEREINER. 'Golden Bear of Golf Faces Up to the Fifties' (*The Observer*)
DONALD STEEL. 'Latin King' (*Golfer's Bedside Book*, Batsford)
NICK SEITZ. 'Last Look at Tony Lema' (*Golf Digest*)
JOHN UNDERWOOD. 'For Sam the Price is Always Right' (*Sports Illustrated*, this anthology is reprinted
    courtesy of *Sports Illustrated* from the 13.3.75 issue, copyright 1975 Time Inc., all rights reserved)
IAN WOOLDRIDGE. 'Like Some Demented Hamlet' (*Golf Illustrated*)
GARY PLAYER. 'The Old Transvaal' (*Grand Slam Golf*, Cassell)

4 LADIES SECTION
ENID WILSON. 'The Babe' (*Golfer's Bedside Book*, Batsford)
MICHAEL McDONNELL. 'You've Come a Long Way Baby' (*The World of Golf*, Kingswood)
PETER DOBEREINER. 'The Sound of Nancy' (*For The Love Of Golf*, Stanley Paul)
PETER RYDE. 'Catherine Lacoste, Championne du Monde' (*Golfer's Bedside Book*, Batsford)
HENRY LONGHURST. 'Never Play a Woman Level' (*Round In 68*, T. Werner Laurie UK)
STEPHEN POTTER. 'The Thin End' (*The Complete Golf Gamesmanship*, Heinemann)
O. B. KEELER. 'The Greatest?' (*The Golfer's Companion*, Macdonald)

5 GREAT COURSES

SAM McKINLAY. 'Golden Links on an Endless Chain' (*Golfer's Bedside Book*, Batsford)
ROBERT GREEN. 'Pine Valley' (*Golf World*)
RAYMOND JACOBS. 'Golf's Artful Dodger' (*Colgate Programme*)
CHRIS PLUMRIDGE. 'The Hole in the Road' (*Colgate Programme*)
R. C. ROBERTSON-GLASGOW. 'Golf at Rosemount' (*All In The Game*, Dobson)
HENRY LONGHURST. 'Pebble Beach' (*Round In 68*, T. Werner Laurie UK)
SARAH BALLARD. 'Golf and Glory' (*Sports Illustrated*, this anthology is reprinted courtesy of *Sports Illustrated* from the 13.7.87 issue, copyright 1987 Time Inc. all rights reserved)
BERNARD DARWIN. 'Carnoustie' (*The Golf Courses Of The British Isles*, Gerald Duckworth)
SIEGFRIED SASSOON. 'Amblehurst' (*Memoirs Of A Fox-Hunting Man*, Faber & Faber)
FURMAN BISHER. 'Jones, the Soul of it' (*The Masters: Augusta Revisited*, Oxmoor House)

6 CADDIES

MICHAEL McDONNELL. 'Man's Best Friend or Beast of Burden?' (*The World Of Golf*, Kingswood)
BILL ELLIOTT. 'They Also Serve Who Only Pace the Yardage' (*The Golfers*, Collins)
JOHN HOPKINS. 'Life With Lyle' (*Life With Lyle*, Heinemann)
G. GUNBY JORDAN WITH DON WADE. 'A Greater Honour Knows No Man' (*Caddies*, Green Island Press)
G. GUNBY JORDAN WITH DON WADE. 'If You've Seen One You've Seen Them All' (*Caddies*, Green Island Press)
PETER DOBEREINER. 'The Wit of the Caddie' (*Colgate Programme*)

7 GREAT CHAMPIONSHIPS

DAN JENKINS. 'The Doggedest Victim' (*The Dogged Victims Of Inexorable Fate*, Little, Brown and Company)
PETER THOMSON & DESMOND ZWAR. 'Let's Go For Broke' (*The Wonderful World Of Golf*, Pelham Books)
BERNARD DARWIN. 'That Small Colossus: Hogan at Carnoustie' (*Mostly Golf*, A. & C. Black)
SAM SNEAD WITH AL STUMP. 'Long Lags in the British Open' (*The Education Of A Golfer*, Cassell)
SEVERIANO BALLESTEROS WITH DUDLEY DOUST. 'My Colour Of Green' (*Seve: The Young Champion*, Hodder & Stoughton)
O. B. KEELER. 'Men Call it Fate' (*The Bobby Jones Story*, Foulsham)
DAN JENKINS. 'A Braw Brawl for Tom and Jack' (*Sports Illustrated*, this anthology is reprinted courtesy of *Sports Illustrated* copyright Time Inc., all rights reserved)
AL BARKOW. 'Nicklaus Goes For Broke' (*Golf Illustrated*, USA)
DAVE ANDERSON. 'Best Shot of My Life' (*New York Times*)
DEREK LAWRENSON. 'Brilliance had its Reward' (*Golf Monthly*)

8 ALL IN THE MIND

ROBERT TYRE JONES. 'Gamut of Emotions' (*The Golfer's Companion*, Macdonald)
SIR WALTER SIMPSON. 'Best for Idiots' (*Out of Copyright*)
MICHAEL MURPHY. 'Seamus MacDuff's Baffing Spoon' (*Golf In The Kingdom*, Latimer)
DEREK LAWRENSON, 'Time to Change his Tactics' (*Golf Monthly*)
LIZ KAHN, 'The Inner Conflict' (*Tony Jacklin: The Price Of Success*, Hamlyn)
PAT WARD-THOMAS, 'Time for a Change of Life' (*The Golfers*, Collins)
BOBBY LOCKE, 'Hiding Your Feelings' (*Bobby Locke On Golf*, Country Life)
GEORGE PLIMPTON, 'The Yips' (*The Bogeyman*, André Deutsch)

9 HAVE CLUBS WILL TRAVEL

MARK WILSON, 'Southern Hospitality' (*Golfer's Bedside Book*, Batsford)

RAYMOND JACOBS. How in the Name of Boeing...? (*Golfer's Bedside Book*, Batsford)
PAT WARD-THOMAS. 'Over the Wire is Out of Bounds' (*Not Only Golf*, Hodder & Stoughton, with the permission of Mrs Jean Ward-Thomas)
PETER DOBEREINER. 'Golf in Ireland' (*Golfer's Bedside Book*, Batsford)
TIM GLOVER. 'Nomad's Land' (*Volvo Tour Book 1989*, Home & Law)
CHRIS PLUMRIDGE. 'Is it True What They Say About Augusta?' (*Golf Illustrated*)

10 ARCHITECTURE
HENRY COTTON. 'The Competitive Urge' (*The Study Of The Golf Game*, Country Life/Hamlyn)
SIR GUY CAMPBELL. 'The British Linksland Courses' (*A History Of Golf In Great Britain*)
ROBERT TRENT JONES. 'What Makes it Great?' (Winthrop Laboratories)
JIMMY DEMARET. 'Outside of London' (*My Partner, Ben Hogan*, Peter Davies)
F. W. HAWTREE. 'Design For Living' (F. W. Hawtree)

11 MATCH-PLAY
HENRY LONGHURST. 'We Live to See the Day' (*Only On Sundays*, Cassell)
CHARLES PRICE. '18 and 17' (*The World Of Golf*, Cassell)
PATRICK CAMPBELL. 'The Big, Big Time' (*Patrick Campbell's Golfing Book*, Blond & Briggs)
DEREK LAWRENSON. 'History is Made' (*Golf Monthly*)
PETER ALLISS WITH BOB FERRIER. 'A Slight Case of Imagination' (*Alliss Through The Looking Glass*, Cassell)

12 FROM HICKORY TO GRAPHITE
JAMES BALFOUR. 'Improving the New Ball' (*Out of Copyright*)
HORACE HUTCHINSON. 'The Haskell Arrives' (*Out of Copyright*)
JAMES BALFOUR. 'Baffies, Rut-Irons and Cleeks' (*Out of Copyright*)
DAVID STIRK. 'Tools of the Game' (*Golf*, Phaidon)
PETER DOBEREINER. 'Drive it 553 Yards' (*For the Love of Golf*, Stanley Paul)
H. B. FARNIE. 'Out of the Bag' (*Out of Copyright*)

13 CLASSIC INSTRUCTION
HENRY LONGHURST. 'Peter Thomson Tells All' (*Only On Sundays*, Cassell/Sunday Times)
WILLIE PARK. 'The Man Who Can Putt is a Match for Anyone' (*Out of Copyright*)
HARRY VARDON. 'A Craze for Length' (*Out of Copyright*)
TOMMY ARMOUR. 'What Can Your Best Golf Be?' (*How to Play Your Best Golf All the Time*, Simon & Schuster)
JOHN JACOBS WITH KEN BOWDEN. 'First Understand What You Are Trying to Do' (*Practical Golf*, Stanley Paul)

The editors acknowledge with gratitude those who have given permission for the use of copyright material. Every effort has been made to trace all copyright holders and the editors apologise to anyone who has not been found or properly acknowledged. Subsequent editions will include any corrections or omissions notified to the editors.